Happiness and Tears, After Cavell

THE SUNY SERIES

HORIZONS OF CINEMA

MURRAY POMERANCE | EDITOR

RECENT TITLES

Luca Barattoni, *The Biopolitical Turn in World Cinema*

Ori Levin, *Celluloid Babel*

Roy Grundmann, *On Shoreless Sea*

Dominic Lash, *Haunting the World*

Gohar Siddiqui, *Déjà-Viewed*

Stanley Cavell, *Cavell on Film*

Saverio Giovacchini, *The Celluloid Atlantic*

John Caps, *Overhearing Film Music*

Hannah Holtzman, *Through a Nuclear Lens*

Benedict Morrison, *Eccentric Laughter*

Matthew Cipa, *Is Harpo Free?*

Daniel Varndell, *Torturous Etiquettes*

Seth Barry Watter, *The Human Figure on Film*

Jonah Corne and Monika Vrečar, *Yiddish Cinema*

Jason Jacobs, *Reluctant Sleuths, True Detectives*

Lucy J. Miller, *Distancing Representations in Transgender Film*

Tomoyuki Sasaki, *Cinema of Discontent*

Mary Ann McDonald Carolan, *Orienting Italy*

Matthew Rukgaber, *Nietzsche in Hollywood*

Jason Sperb, *The Hard Sell of Paradise*

A complete listing of books in this series can be found online at www.sunypress.edu.

Happiness and Tears, After Cavell

New Readings in Hollywood's Comedy of Remarriage and Melodrama of the Unknown Woman

Edited by

Paul Deb

SUNY PRESS

Cover credit: Leonardo DiCaprio and Kate Winslet in *Revolutionary Road* (Dreamworks, 2008). Courtesy Photofest, New York.

Published by State University of New York Press, Albany

EU GPSR Authorised Representative:
Logos Europe, 9 rue Nicolas Poussin, 17000, La Rochelle, France
contact@logoseurope.eu

For information, contact State University of New York Press, Albany, NY
www.sunypress.edu

Library of Congress Cataloging-in-Publication Data

Name: Deb, Paul, editor.
Title: Happiness and tears, after Cavell : New readings in Hollywood's comedy of remarriage and melodrama of the unknown woman / Paul Deb, editor.
Description: Albany : State University of New York Press, [2025]. | Includes bibliographical references and index.
Identifiers: ISBN 9798855804720 (hardcover : alk. paper) | ISBN 9798855804744 (ebook) | ISBN 9798855804737 (pbk. : alk. paper)
Further information is available at the Library of Congress.

For Stephen—who else.

These thoughts are my responses primarily directed to the two small but widely admired genres of film that I have mentioned, one of comedy and one of melodrama, which flourished half a century ago, when half of the population of America went to the movies each week, and moreover, to the same movies. A sequence of questions arises: Are remarriage comedies still made? What might it betoken if they are not? Are other strains of movies being made which suggest further evidence for the idea that film more generally bears an affinity with the morality of perfectionism? If there are, what is the good of them? Let's see where moving through these questions takes us.

—Stanley Cavell, "The Good of Film"

Contents

Illustrations

Abbreviations

CF   Cavell, Stanley, and Rothman, William. 2025. *Cavell on Film.* Second edition. State University of New York Press.

CHU   Cavell, Stanley. 1990. *Conditions Handsome and Unhandsome: The Constitution of Emersonian Perfectionism.* University of Chicago Press.

CR   Cavell, Stanley. 1979. *The Claim of Reason: Wittgenstein, Skepticism, Morality, and Tragedy.* Oxford University Press.

CT   Cavell, Stanley. 1996. *Contesting Tears: The Hollywood Melodrama of the Unknown Woman.* University of Chicago Press.

CW   Cavell, Stanley. 2004. *Cities of Words: Pedagogical Letters on a Register of the Moral Life.* Harvard University Press.

DK   Cavell, Stanley. 1987. *Disowning Knowledge in Six Plays of Shakespeare.* Cambridge University Press.

LDIK   Cavell, Stanley. 2010. *Little Did I Know: Excerpts from Memory.* Stanford University Press.

MWM Cavell, Stanley. 2002. *Must We Mean What We Say?: A Book of Essays.* Updated edition. Cambridge University Press.

NYUA Cavell, Stanley. 1989. *This New Yet Unapproachable America: Lectures After Emerson After Wittgenstein.* Living Batch Press.

PH   Cavell, Stanley. 1981. *Pursuits of Happiness: The Hollywood Comedy of Remarriage.* Harvard University Press.

PP   Cavell, Stanley. 1994. *A Pitch of Philosophy: Autobiographical Exercises.* Harvard University Press.

SW   Cavell, Stanley. 1972. *The Senses of Walden*. Viking Press.

WV   Cavell, Stanley. 1979. *The World Viewed: Reflections on the Ontology of Film*. Enlarged edition. Harvard University Press.

Acknowledgments

I must begin by thanking my contributors; not only for their fine contributions to this volume and their show of faith in agreeing to contribute, but also for their considerable patience in waiting for that faith to be rewarded. In particular I would like to thank the following, all of whom showed early enthusiasm for the project and gave helpful advice along the way: William Rothman; Murray Pomerance (the latter proving to be the astute series editor the former recommended him to be); David LaRocca; and Stephen Mulhall. To the last I owe a long-standing, unrepayable debt; and since that debt relates essentially to the letter and spirit of Cavell's work, this is a particularly apt occasion for me to provide an account or acknowledgment of it. For it relates not only to his help with the present volume, and not only to his having introduced me—over thirty years ago, when I was his student at the University of Essex (little did he know)—to Cavell's philosophy in the first place but also, crucially, to his own idiosyncratic inheritance of that philosophy (and so the work of certain other major philosophers), and hence to his deeply serious and intelligent, endlessly fruitful and surprising, inheritance of philosophy itself. For insofar as that inheritance is one I continue to wish for myself—in my own way, and as far as I am able—he has allowed me to find my own cares and concerns in philosophy, a way of going on with the subject that genuinely reflects me. And as if this wasn't reason enough to be extremely grateful to him, he has also, over the course of so many years, patiently provided me with helpful advice and encouragement, even when it seemed like I had left the serious study of philosophy behind. So, for first illuminating the path, and then helping me find my way back to it, this book is for him. I would also like to thank the Warden and Fellows of New College, Oxford, an institution with which it has been my privilege to be associated for the past three years (another thing for which I am indebted to Stephen Mulhall). The College's unstinting generosity, spirit of warm collegiality, and seriousness of intellectual purpose is humbling. Amongst its members, the friendship and kindness of the following must stand for the rest: Marco Grossi, Volker Halbach, Richard Mash, Stephen Anderson, Susan Bridge, Peter Boxall, William Poole, Gez Wells, and Hassan Hamed. I am also grateful for the friendship of others at Oxford, and beyond, during and before my work on this volume; each of the following has, in their own way, helped it see the light of day: Arnaud Petit and Eri Ichijo, Edward Howell, Andy Marshall, Oskari Kuusela, Matt Dean (as ever), and, especially, my dearly missed friend, Nick Pope. At SUNY Press, James Peltz and his team were a pleasure to work with and ensured that the publication process was a smooth and enjoyable one. Finally, I would like to thank my wife, Rashmi—the love of my life. Without her forbearance and support I would not have been able to take advantage of the opportunities for teaching and research recently afforded me. And to my wonderful children, Jasmine and Roshan, for those few occasions when, on my return, the provision of fresh, luxury cookies and doughnuts was insufficient compensation for my academic-related absence, I apologize (but am flattered).

An earlier version of chapter 5 was published under the same title in *Film-Philosophy* 25, no. 3 (2021): 251–71. Reprinted by permission of Edinburgh University Press.

I am grateful to the New College Ludwig Fund for the Humanities for its support in compiling the Index.

Introduction

Paul Deb

IT IS SOME TWENTY-FIVE YEARS since Stanley Cavell made the remarks that serve as the epigraph to this book. So, the two small but widely admired genres of film that he has mentioned, one of comedy and one of melodrama, now flourished three quarters of a century ago; and the idea of half of the population of America going to the movies each week, and moreover, to the same movies, now seems—since the advent of videos, DVDs, and most recently streaming—all the more old-fashioned, even quaint.

And yet, it is the motivating intuition of the present volume that the sequence of questions that arose for Cavell all those years ago are still worth stopping over today. Whether such comedies (and melodramas) are still made—and if not, what that might signifiy—and whether other strains of movies are being made which suggest further evidence for the idea that film more generally has an affinity with the morality of perfectionism—and if so, what their value is—will be our guiding thoughts as we move through the chapters that follow.

Cavell's own responses to these questions in "The Good of Film" (*CF*, 333–48) and elsewhere encompass a range of ideas. But in order to appreciate them, and at the same time to provide us with some initial orientation with respect to this collection's concerns, it will first be necessary to recall the main contours of his two genres of comedy and melodrama, and the associated understanding of morality to which he takes them to relate.

The Promise of a Marriage:
Comedy and Melodrama

It is in his *Pursuits of Happiness* (1981) and *Contesting Tears* (1996), respectively, that Cavell first claims that some of the most famous films from 1930s and 1940s Hollywood constitute two related, but previously undefined, genres in the history of American cinema. In the former, he provides readings of seven films that he takes as definitive of the genre he calls the "comedy of remarriage": *It Happened One Night* (Frank Capra, 1934); *The Awful Truth* (Leo McCarey, 1937); *Bringing Up Baby* (Howard Hawks, 1938); *His Girl Friday* (Howard Hawks, 1940); *The Philadelphia Story* (George Cukor, 1940); *The Lady Eve* (Preston Sturges, 1941); and *Adam's Rib* (George Cukor, 1949). And in the latter, he defines the genre that he names the "melodrama of the unknown woman" principally in terms of his readings of four films: *Stella Dallas* (King Vidor, 1937); *Now, Voyager* (Irving Rapper, 1942); *Gaslight* (George Cukor, 1944); and *Letter from an Unknown Woman* (Max Ophüls, 1948). Systematic connections within and between these two groups are not hard to discern, the films sharing as they do with one another certain directors (Howard Hawks, George Cukor) and stars (Katharine Hepburn, Barbara Stanwyck, Cary Grant, Ralph Bellamy); and, of course, the respective grouping together of these films is typically understood as a function of their falling under one or other of the more familiar Hollywood categories of "screwball comedy" and so-called "woman's films" ("tear-jerkers" or "weepies"). But for Cavell, the presence of such shared features or conventional groupings cannot account for the power, intelligence, and depth of the films (of their "bearing up [. . .] under the same critical pressure that one would bring to works in any of the other of the great arts" [*CW*, 11]), and are not the bases upon which he gathers them together. Indeed, his understanding of a genre of film is not of a form characterized by "features" at all, at least in the familiar sense of the word. Rather, he thinks of the members of a genre as sharing "the inheritance of certain conditions, procedures and subjects and goals of composition" (*PH*, 28).

What then, exactly, do the two genres inherit? Cavell claims both are bequeathed the preoccupations and discoveries of two segments of the history of theater: first, and most fundamentally, Shakespearean comedy and romance (centrally, *The Winter's Tale*); and second, the drama of Ibsen (particularly *A Doll's House*). The remarriage comedies emphasize the first, and distinguish themselves from their classical antecedents that show a young hero and heroine overcoming individual and social obstacles to pursue their happiness—figured as a reconciling, concluding marriage—by recasting the man and the woman as an older pair; and by a narrative driven not by getting the central couple together in the first place but rather by getting them *back* together, together *again*, by overcoming the fact or threat of divorce. Marriage here is thus fundamentally understood as remarriage, as finding legitimacy or ratification in nothing—not church, or state, or sex, or children—apart from the daily, mutual willingness for its own reaffirmation.

In contrast, the unknown woman melodramas emphasize the second part of the genres' inheritance by establishing the conditions or costs upon which the threat of divorce is overcome, by investigating relationships in which it fails to be—marriages the woman is no longer willing to reaffirm, and so cannot, generically speaking, be considered genuine marriages at all. That it is the woman, rather than the man, who decides the legitimacy or otherwise of the marriage reflects Cavell's view that in both genres the emphasis is on the heroine, since it is with the issue of "the creation of a new woman, or the new creation of a woman [. . .] a new creation of the human" (*PH*, 16) that they are most fundamentally concerned. For he takes it that in these films the woman has a sense of herself as somehow nonexistent or uncreated, as if she were haunting the world, and as in need of the man to create or recreate her. This need takes the form of the woman demanding from the man a certain kind of education, and it is on the condition that he can provide it—that a miracle of creation or change takes place—that the woman stakes her willingness to reaffirm their relationship. And while the presence of this condition suggests the woman's explicit scrutiny of the man's authority, insofar as the comedies' creation of the woman takes the form of her education by the man, they nonetheless suggest that even within their general atmosphere of equality, there is an undeniable privileging of the male (something Cavell detects in the lingering taint of villainy in even the best of their men that predicts or prepares for his understanding of the melodramas).

So, while in the comedies we are shown how a miracle of change may be brought about, and how a pair seeking divorce can instead find or create a true marriage between them, this privileging inevitably raises a question about the extent to which the happiness found in these marriages is compromised or contaminated. And insofar as the melodramas show us a pair in which the woman comes to realize that such a miracle cannot happen as long as she is with the man—that he is not the one to provide the education she needs, so in reality he cannot be her husband, that between them there is not and cannot ever be any real marriage—this privileging inevitably raises a question about whether it is the institution of marriage itself that is compromised, call it villainous or cursed.[1]

In relation to these central circumstances or concerns, Cavell goes on to suggest a constellation of associated features as their consequences or causes. While he admits it is natural, even irresistible, for him to speak of specific characteristics of a genre as its "features," he is at pains to distinguish his use of the term in the context of his unorthodox conception of a genre (what he labels "genre-as-medium") from its use in that conception's more conventional counterpart (what he labels "genre-as-cycle") (*CT*, 13). What is traditionally called a film genre is of course what we typically have in mind when, for example, we say of a movie that it is an action film, or a Western, or a thriller, or a musical, on the basis of its possessing (repeating, or recycling) the distinctive feature or features shared by other members of the relevant genre (say, a narrative emphasis on fighting, or a setting of the American frontier, or the eliciting of heightened feelings of suspense, or the interweaving of songs with the dialogue, and so on); as if a genre were an object characterized by properties. In contrast, since for Cavell a film's membership in a specific genre is a matter of its inheritance of certain conditions, he takes it that each member of a genre represents a study of those conditions, as bearing the responsibility of that inheritance in its own way, a point he makes by thinking of a genre's common inheritance—before, behind, beneath, or between its specifically Shakespearean and Ibsenian sources—as a story or myth; one that, in the case of remarriage comedy, he starts to (re)construct in the following way:

> A running quarrel is forcing apart a pair who recognize themselves as having known one another forever, that is from the beginning, not just in the past but in a period before there was a past, before history. This naturally

presents itself as their having shared childhood together, suggesting that they are brother and sister. They have discovered their sexuality together and find themselves required to enter this realm at roughly the same time that they are required to enter the social realm, as if the sexual and the social are to legitimize one another. This is the beginning of history, of an unending quarrel. The joining of the sexual and the social is called marriage. Something evidently internal to the task of marriage causes trouble in paradise—as if marriage, which was to be a ratification, is itself in need of ratification. So marriage has its disappointment—call this its impotence to domesticate sexuality without discouraging it, or its stupidity in the face of the riddle of intimacy, which repels where it attracts, or in the face of the puzzle of ecstasy, which is violent while it is tender, as if the leopard should lie down with the lamb. And the disappointment seeks revenge, a revenge, as it were, for having made one discover one's incompleteness, one's transience, one's homelessness. Upon separation the woman tries a regressive tack usually that of accepting as a husband a simpler, or mere, father-substitute, even one who brings along his own mother. This is psychologically an effort to put her desire, awakened by the original man, back to sleep . . . (*PH*, 31–32)

The comedies thus bear—as their emphasis on the creation of the woman by the man suggests—the inheritance of the book of Genesis's story of the Garden of Eden, with each member of the genre representing or recounting a particular interpretation or revision of it (something registered by the appearance of both Adam and Eve amongst the films' titles). On this picture of a genre, the idea of repeating or recycling features—understood as akin to the properties of an object—is replaced by an idea of features as the clauses or provisions of a story. There is, then, no such thing as *the* features of a genre that all its members have in common or repeat. Instead, like a medium in the visual arts or a "form" in music (*PH*, 28), Cavell takes it that each member will emphasize or discover different or further features of the genre's founding myth—sometimes as compensation for its apparent lack of a provision supplied by one or more of its companions—and so contribute to a new interpretation or retelling of that myth (quite as if the films are in argument with the genre and one another over their power to belong to it, and so define it). And insofar as that interpretation is open to further definition or development by new members bringing with them some new clause or clauses, it remains provisional, thereby allowing for the story to go on being told. In short, for Cavell, the group of features that constitute a given film's membership of a genre are as radically open-ended as the group of films that constitute that membership. (Such is the mysterious, prodigiously productive power of the mythological.)

In the case of the comedy of remarriage, these principal features include: the woman is never portrayed as, or shown to have, a mother; if the woman's father (or a figure for her father) is present, he is always on the side of her desire; the woman's body is emphasized in some way; the central pair's past is open, imagined as a shared place of happiness; time itself is conceived of as recurrent or repeating; and the drama opens in a city, and moves to the country, a place of perspective and resolution (a Shakespearean "green world," typically Connecticut). But for Cavell, the genre's most pervasive feature is the one for which its films are most famous—a mode of fierce and witty conversation between the woman and the man that in effect celebrates, by exploiting, the then-recent advent of film sound. For Cavell, this mode of conversation is the means by which the woman's transformative education is accomplished, making it the basis or fact of marriage, an idea he finds manifested in Milton's characterization of marriage (from his tract on divorce) as participation in a "meet and happy conversation" (a phrase that recalls the genre's founding Adamic myth)—meaning not only talking but a mode of association or form of life, an intimate union of verbal, social, and sexual inter-course. For these couples, "talking together is fully and plainly being together" (*PH*, 87–88).

While each member of the genre of remarriage contests, by contributing to, these features, Cavell thinks that the films compris-ing the melodrama of the unknown woman neither exhibit these features, nor in their absence, attempt to compensate for them with new features that might further define or redefine the genre. Rather, the melodramas systematically negate features of the comedies (a mechanism or process Cavell calls "derivation" [*CT*, 5]), forming a related but distinct—an adjacent—genre, and thereby recounting a different underlying story:

> A woman achieves existence (or fails to) or establishes her right to existence in the form of a metamorphosis (or fails to) apart from or beyond satisfaction by marriage (of a certain kind) and with the presence of her mother and of her children, where something in her language must be as traumatic in her case as the conversation of marriage is for her comedic sisters—perhaps it will be an aria of divorce, from husband, lover, mother, or child. (*CT*, 88)

The chief negation of the comedies by the melodramas is thus the negation of marriage itself: their women realizing that it cannot after all provide the route to the creation or re-creation they require, and so is no longer worthy of their willing reaffirmation. This negation or rejection of marriage entails the negation of many further features of remarriage comedy. For example, the woman is always shown in relation to (or in fateful separation from) her mother, and always in relation to a child; if the woman's father (or his proxy) is present, he is never on the side of her desire but on the side of the law, which he is prepared to call down if she goes against his wishes; the past of the central pair is presented as closed, a place of mystery and forbidden topics, in which time itself is cursed to be frozen; and rather than moving to a "green world," the action of the narration returns to and concludes in the place where it began. And if the comedies' most pervasive feature is their distinctive mode of conversation, we should expect to find in the melodramas the equally pervasive presence of its negation; and it is this that Cavell sees in the exchanges between their central pairs as everywhere undercut or defeated by a heavy, stifling irony. Rather than a "meet and happy conversation" holding the two together, each pair is involved in an estranging struggle of misunderstanding and miscommunication that leads to the woman's recognition of her isolation, an aspect of her unknownness that gives the genre its name.

As we have seen, despite these differing sets of features, the constant factor between the two genres is the creation of the woman; and it is this issue, and its accompanying emphasis on a specialized mode of educative conversation, that leads Cavell to see the films as bearing an affinity with a certain idea of morality, an understanding he presents most systematically in his *Cities of Words* (2004), where he provides readings of most of the principal comedies and melodramas in the light of what he calls moral or Emersonian perfectionism.

Introduced in *Conditions Handsome and Unhandsome* (1990), Cavell considers moral perfectionism an outlook or dimension of moral thinking—rather than a theory of morality, like deontology, teleology, or virtue ethics—that he takes to run throughout the history of Western culture, first in the work of Plato and Aristotle, but most decisively for him in the writings of Ralph Waldo Emerson. Perfectionism's founding myth or vision concerns "an idea of being true to oneself—or to the humanity in oneself, or of the soul as on a journey (upward or onward) that begins by finding oneself lost to the world" (*CHU*, 1) and requires, if one is to find oneself again, a refusal of the current state of one's society in the name of some further or future, more cultured or cultivated, state of society and the self. Perfectionism thus pictures the self and its society as inherently divided or doubled, split between what Emerson calls their "attained" and "unattained" states (*CHU*, 8–9), but nonetheless always at risk of occluding or repressing that division. For since each attained state constitutes a world within which the self's desires are manifested and might be satisfied, the standing danger to which perfectionism is sensitive is a form of spiritual crisis in which the self has become attached to, or fixated upon, the settled attractions of its attained state—often by a conformity to prevailing modes of thought and life—to the extent that its unattained self is effectively negated or eclipsed. In such a condition, the disorientated individual can either be confirmed in her conformity by the members of the society in which she finds herself, or instead be encouraged to seek its aversion by the interventions of another, who draws her to decline her attained state in favor of the unattained, but attainable, state that the other represents or exemplifies. In other words, this friend aims to educate her companion to reorient or re-create herself by resuscitating her individuality or autonomy—to enact Emerson's famous call for self-reliance.

This friendship, however, also contains a serious and self-defeating threat. Since the aim of the friend is to seduce the befriended into shifting the balance of her desires from the attractions of her attained to those of her unattained state, there is always the risk—insofar as that attainable state is embodied by the friend—that rather than perceiving the attractions of the friend as belonging to a next or further state of herself, she will instead attribute them solely to the person of the friend; that she will desire not her unattained self but the friend herself. By idolizing the friend in this way, the disorientated individual effectively replaces a fixation upon her attained state with a fixation upon the friend, merely substituting her conformity or reliance on the former with the same to the latter; thus, continuing to negate or eclipse her unattained self, and so the opportunity for genuine individuality that the friend represents.

It is I think not hard to see, even if it was somewhat surprising to Cavell himself, why he came to realize that the comedies and the melodramas participate in the ideas of moral perfectionism: that in effect their vision of the promise of marriage is an allegory or model of its particular form of edifying friendship (its constitutive conversation comprising "one soul's examination of another" [*CW*, 248]). For the women of the films share a recognizably perfectionist ambition to create or recreate themselves and their lives—to seek their unattained but attainable selves—by a process of education that they believe their men capable of providing. But it is the fate of the women of the melodramas to realize they cannot share their comedic sisters' good fortune—that these men are not, after all, the enabling Emersonian friends they supposed. Rather, they realize they have instead succumbed to a disabling idolatry (think, for example, of Stella's words to Stephen Dallas: "I wanted to be different ever since I met you. If I was around you long enough, I could be. Why, I could learn to talk like you and act like you") that they can only overcome by explicitly rejecting or transcending their partners and discovering the means for radical change, for transformation or metamorphosis—for a life genuinely their own—otherwise than in marriage.

Before turning to a brief examination of Cavell's own responses to the guiding questions of the present volume, it is worth recalling one final aspect of his understanding of remarriage comedy and unknown woman melodrama and their relationship to Emersonian perfectionism. For it may seem that perfectionism's concern with an individual's journey of self-knowledge and self-transformation is an essentially private matter, of no business or relevance to the wider society of which that individual is a part. But as perfectionism's founding myth emphasizes, this personal concern is inseparable from a political concern with the transformation of the culture in which that journey takes place. And for Cavell, the conjunction of these two matters is yet another shared feature of the comedies and melodramas. For he thinks that the bond of marriage between each of their principal pairs is not merely analogous to the bond between a democratic society and its citizens (since both are dependent, in the form of a covenant or contract, on the continuing consent or agreement of their members in order to legitimize the arrangements of their respective unions or institutions), but that such marriages in effect ratify that society as a setting in which its citizens are free to exercise those rights.

More specifically, Cavell takes it that the genres' shared central interest with the issue of the new creation of a woman is proof that this phase in the history of American cinema is bound up with a phase in the history of American feminism, of a development in the consciousness women hold of themselves in relation to the consciousness men hold of them; that a decade after American women won the right to vote in 1920, the films act as parables in which the struggle "for the reciprocity or equality of consciousness [. . .] for mutual freedom" (*PH*, 17) between the sexes continues to be played out. The comedies thus harbor a utopian vision of America as a place where both women and men have the liberty to pursue happiness, whereas in the darkened vision of the melodramas, their unknown women learn that the pursuit of happiness is very different from its achievement. The isolating unhappiness of their marriages stands as an emblem not of the success of America's democratic aspiration, but its failure. Finding that the price of their continuing consent to society is agonizingly high (requiring them to endure irony, suffer unknownness, and risk madness), these women in effect withdraw that consent through a melodramatic refusal of marriage that is also a refusal of society as it stands, imagining instead a further or future state of themselves and society that might more readily solicit their consent. The fact of women's unknownness thereby rebukes the present arrangements of society, and so represents an internal threat to, or measure of, the legitimacy of the social order as such. In this way, we might say that the comedies and the melodramas are in conversation, of the kind they dramatize, with what Cavell calls "the inner agenda" (*PH*, 17) of American culture, an aversive conversation that is—at its best—yet "meet and happy."

The Same and Different:
(Re)Generations of Genre

While it is from his remarks in the "The Good of Film" (written in 2000) that the present volume takes off, Cavell first broaches the question of whether remarriage comedies (at least) are still made at the very start of his account of them, in his introduction to *Pursuits of Happiness*. There he claims it is "not clear that the genre has yielded itself up completely" (*PH*, 26) and cites *An Unmarried Woman* (Paul Mazursky, 1978), *Starting Over* (Alan J. Pakula, 1979), and *Kramer vs. Kramer* (Robert Benton, 1979) as more recent American films that, in starting with divorce and including the prospect of remarriage, suggest the genre has not exhausted its possibilities or conventions; by which he means that its shared inheritance or myth has not reached a point where it can no longer generate or support new members or interpretations that emphasize or make explicit further features of it—has not yielded itself up in a state of absolute explicitness or "expressive saturation" (30). A natural question then arises: how does one know when it has?

With respect to the first two films, Cavell adds little to the thought that these more recent comedies share the ideas of divorce and remarriage with their precursors. And with respect to *Kramer vs. Kramer*, while he feels that certain features of the film mean that he cannot rule it out as a further development of the genre (one that includes the presence of children), certain others mean that he cannot rule it in either, with both views converging on the questions of whether the idea of remarriage is realized in the film's conclusion, and if so, of the changed nature of the relationship that is thereby reaffirmed.[2]

Cavell's ambivalence over whether the genre of remarriage is exhausted or saturated—whether its "myth has died, we have died to it" (*PH*, 33)—continues in his later work. On the one hand, he takes it that certain social, cultural, and artistic shifts in America count against the genre's survival: the fear of divorce and the threat of pregnancy have both changed, meaning marriage no longer has the same cultural role; men's sense of their own identity and authority is more insecure; the actors, directors, and writers who made the genre's definitive films are all gone; the products of Hollywood are now better understood in terms of something like genre-as-cycle rather than genre-as-medium;[3] and the role of film itself in America has dwindled (*CF*, 342; *CW*, 153–55; Cavell 2006, 300).

But on the other hand, as Cavell says in a lecture from 1999: "There are times when I am unsure whether [. . .] the genre of remarriage comedy has survived its flowering in the two decades after the introduction of sound. But along comes, quite unforeseen, a piece such as *Moonstruck* (1987) [. . .] which take[s] an essential register of remarriage comedy fully and securely into the late 1980s" (*CF*, 283). For Cavell, *Moonstruck* (Norman Jewison, 1987), presumably like *Kramer vs. Kramer* before it, sits alongside *Groundhog Day* (Harold Ramis, 1993), *The Untamed Heart* (Tony Bill, 1993), *Four Weddings and a Funeral* (Mike Newell, 1994), *O Brother, Where Art Thou?* (Coen brothers, 2000) and *Ocean's Eleven* (Steven Soderbergh, 2001) as one of the "many good films made that have remarriage elements in them" (*CW*, 153).[4] And in "The Good of Film," Cavell goes on to provide numerous other examples from 1980s and 1990s Hollywood—including *Tootsie* (Sydney Pollack, 1982), *Working Girl* (Mike Nichols, 1988), *Sleepless in Seattle* (Nora Ephron, 1993), *Clueless* (Amy Heckerling, 1995), *As Good as It Gets* (James L. Brooks, 1997), and *My Best Friend's Wedding* (P. J. Hogan, 1997) (the last two films being the respective subjects of Daniel Varndell's and Sandra Laugier's chapters in the present volume)—that by emphasizing one or more salient features of the genre, try to keep something like the "feel" or "surface" of remarriage (*CF*, 342; Butler 2001).[5]

Nonetheless, given the historical changes indicated above, Cavell felt that the genre was no longer what it was: it could not be said to inspire a continuous series of films, and those films it did inspire could not claim the cultural prominence of their predecessors as being amongst the principal and enduring successes of the Hollywood in which they were made (*CW*, 153–54; Cavell 2006, 300). For Cavell, these recent examples, rather than being "full-blown" remarriage comedies, were only "versions" or "fragments" of the genre that differed from their "classical" (*CW*, 154–55) instances in three main ways. The first concerned the leading men of the genre, or rather the absence of them. Despite Cavell's initial intuition that classical remarriage comedy came to an end when the small set of women who made it possible were no longer of an age to play its leads, he later came to think it was partly due to a lack of appropriate men—those secure enough to maintain a sense of their own identity without having it ratified by social role, and so able to risk entering into relationships with women in which their social standing is jeopardized (thereby acknowledging a general condition upon which perfectionism depends—that one's knowledge of oneself transcends that defined by one's society). So, while classical remarriage comedies featured men who conveyed a sense of age and experience, their more contemporary counterparts conveyed instead an air of innocence and youth (Cavell compares, for example, Spencer Tracy with John Cusack in *The Sure Thing* [Rob Reiner, 1985]) (*CW*, 154).

The second difference between early and late remarriage comedies further emphasizes this focus on youth, seeing it as a quality shared by both members of the principal pair. For Cavell, the men and women of the new films seemed on the whole too young to imagine the future as containing a habitable social world. Not because of some physical threat to that world—of war, say, or pandemic, or environmental catastrophe—but rather due to the pair losing any conviction in the possibility of a genuine change of institutions, marriage included (a prospect considered in Steven Affeldt's chapter here on *Palm Springs* [Max Barbakow, 2020]), that may transcend or transform what is depicted as the presently fixated and joyless conditions of human existence (*CF*, 343). Some comedy.

Lastly, Cavell took it that in recent versions of remarriage, the role of, or faith in, education had changed: unlike their classical instances, the new versions presented the woman as explicitly better educated than the man, who was taken to possess a form of knowledge independent of that afforded by her education, and to which she was attracted (*CW*, 155).

It would appear then that Cavell's settled answer to our guiding question of whether remarriage comedies are still made (at least at the time of his writing) was: Yes and no. If by "comedy of remarriage" we mean strictly that genre circumscribed by those films of Hollywood's Golden Age, of which Cavell gave an account of his experience in *Pursuits of Happiness*, then he thinks that it is gone. But if we take that label to refer not only to its early, classical form but also to its later, recent versions—films we might reasonably think of as remarriage comedy's recognizable descendants or heirs—then it appears that Cavell found ample evidence for something like the genre's continuation.

At the same time, however, one might wonder whether matters are quite so settled as this straightforward distinction between early and late forms of remarriage comedy would suggest. For as we have seen, Cavell's understanding of a genre is of an essentially open-ended medium, in which each film earns membership by providing a revision or interpretation of its respective founding myth or story. On this picture there is, in principle, always the possibility of some new film coming along, quite unforeseen, that provides a new clause or provision of that story thus demonstrating that despite the passage of time (the focus of William Day's chapter on *Before Midnight* [Richard Linklater, 2013]) and shifting historical contexts—say, the absence of certain stars, directors, or writers—the genre is still unsaturated or unexhausted, its myth having not yet died to us, or we to it (a thought perhaps motivating Cavell's remark that, "There is no way to know that the state of saturation, completeness of expression, has been reached" [*PH*, 30]). As Cavell himself says on the issue of locating current stars capable of continuing the genre, "one feels [. . .] if the culture needs them sufficiently, people will be found" (26). And his identification of two films starring George Clooney—*Ocean's Eleven* and *O Brother, Where Art Thou?*—that together define a subgenre of remarriage he labels "remarriage adventure" (*CW*, 155), and which in the latter (a film he associates with *It Happened One Night*), Cavell feels that Clooney "resembles, perhaps even plays (channels?) [Clark] Gable" (*CF*, 443) suggests he may well have found at least one contemporary leading man with the temperament and talent to project the maturity and experience of his generic predecessors.[6]

One might also wonder whether Cavell's ambivalence over, perhaps reluctance to acknowledge, the realization of the possibility to which his picture of a genre commits him—that of admitting new films as fully-fledged members of the genre of remarriage—is an expression of the depth of his attachment to the films which for him define it (as if a clinical issue was blocking a critical insight).[7] For as he declared in the often-quoted first words of the first book he published on film, *The World Viewed* (1971; Enlarged edition, 1979), "Memories of movies are strand over strand with memories of my life" (*WV*, xix), thus making that text a form of memoir in which Cavell attempts to account philosophically for, while simultaneously enacting, what he calls the break in his "natural relation to movies" (xix): the fact that the period of his life (of roughly a quarter of a century from 1936 to 1960) when going to the movies was a normal part of his week had now come to an end, and his writing on film had begun. Cavell's attachment to the films of Hollywood's Golden Age is thus strand over strand with the time of his life in which he, and those who accompanied him, saw them, a time for which he has an apparently inescapable nostalgia: "I realized that I was seeing fewer movies than ever before and wanting to see fewer, and at the same time memories of old movies, and of the friends I had seen them with, kept on asserting themselves" (xxii–xxiv). (It is perhaps an open question here whether this was a case of Cavell failing film or film failing him.) In the face of this sentiment, Cavell confesses his increasing difficulty in getting himself to go to new movies, of his failure to keep up faithfully with the latest releases; so making his experience of later American cinema increasingly limited or impoverished. As he puts it in *Pursuits of Happiness*, the study of specific films, of individual acts of criticism, "after all, comes down to a matter of personal attachment!" (*PH*, 130). It would appear new American films simply did not—could not—have a degree of personal significance for him equal to that of the films made in Hollywood between 1930 and 1950; those movies whose impact is "too massive [. . .] to speak politely of involvement. We involve the movies in us. They become further fragments of what happens to me [. . .]. Like childhood memories whose treasure no one else appreciates, whose content is nothing compared with their unspeakable importance for me" (*WV*, 154). Who would want to deny this of Cavell?

However one chooses to assess the validity and possible causes of Cavell's own response to the question of whether remarriage comedies are still being made, it is undeniable that a suggestive number of more recent American films continue to share some of the genre's characteristic themes and concerns, irrespective of whether one understands those films as belated fragments or versions of a genre that found its fullest expression in classical Hollywood, or as full-blown members of a genre to which Hollywood regularly returns, reviving or regenerating it for new audiences in ways that further define it (with all the aspects of identity and difference that suggests—a thought explored in William Rothman's discussion of the nature of a "remake," in his chapter on the latest version of *A Star is Born*

[Bradley Cooper, 2018]). But it is equally undeniable that, as Cavell emphasized, the historical circumstances in which these new films find themselves are very different from those of the genre's canonical instances. So, identifying more recent films that bear a relation to the genre may involve considering the ways its central concerns with regard to marriage—the nature of its equality, intimacy, education, and devotion; the threat to it of divorce; and the possibility of its producing children—are inflected by changes in those circumstances (Richard Eldridge's chapter further examines this idea with reference to *Mr. and Mrs. Smith* [Doug Liman, 2005] and *Ocean's Eleven*).

One such change, to which Cavell displays an early sensitivity, relates to the institution of marriage itself: of its increasingly not being conceived of as the specific relation between a man and woman due to the widespread social acceptance and legal recognition of same-sex marriage. While Cavell did not broach this topic in *Pursuits of Happiness* (its films evidently neither able to realize nor compensate for such a structure at their moment in American history), by the time of *Contesting Tears*, Cavell cites a later film, *Rich and Famous* (1981)—the last finished film by George Cukor, who had previously directed definitive examples of both genres—as proving the idea that the genre of remarriage may invite couples of the same sex; that the legitimacy of marriage found in conceiving of it as a willingness for remarriage replaces not only that legitimacy found in church, state, sex, or children, but also in gender (*CT*, 30) (a detailed discussion of *Rich and Famous* comprises Catherine Wheatley's chapter, and this emphasis on the bearing of same-sex relationships on remarriage continues in the chapters by Rex Butler on, amongst others, *I Love You, Man* [John Hamburg, 2009], and Robert Sinnerbrink on *Carol* [Todd Haynes, 2015]).[8]

Perhaps unsurprisingly, given the open-ended nature of the genre, Cavell's claim that the genders of the central couple are not a "generically fixed" requirement or feature of the comedies leads him to acknowledge the open-ended nature of the structure of that relationship, that "there is intuitively no reason why the pair should not be realized by two men or by an interracial pair, et cetera" (Cavell 2006, 300). And this reference to race raises the prospect of a further way in which the genre of remarriage may be inflected by changes in historical contexts: by shifts in the experience and cinematic representation of black Americans in the decades after the end of studio-era Hollywood, in the wake of the civil rights movement, and more recently, in the light of Black Lives Matter (Fiona Handyside takes race as one of her central concerns in her chapter on the role of women in the contemporary world of work in *On the Rocks* [Sofia Coppola, 2020]).[9]

For Cavell, then, this openness or responsiveness of the structure of remarriage to changing historical contexts (something suggested of course by his locating certain historical causes for its beginning, for the resurfacing of the original Shakespearean remarriage structure in 1930s America), raises the possibility that "as long as marriage continues to be problematized in movies, [. . .] the model or set of conditions of marriage as specified in remarriage comedy may be expected to persist, in forms that may be unheard of" (Cavell 2006, 300).

This persistence of the genre of remarriage, like the persistence of marriage itself (in whatever innovative new forms or shapes the two discover for each other), is something Cavell also takes to be true in relation to our next guiding question—whether there are other current strains of movies that tend to suggest film more generally bears an affinity with perfectionism: "There do seem to me a remarkable number of new films (within my limited experience) that concern a quest for transcendence, a step into an opposite or transformed mood, not so much by becoming another person, or taking a further step in attaining an unattained self, or becoming who you are, as by being recognized at the one you are by having, or giving, access to another world" (*CF*, 344). Here Cavell cites, amongst others, *Ghost Dog* (Jim Jarmusch, 1999), *The Matrix* (the Wachowskis, 1999), *Being John Malkovich* (Spike Jonze, 1999), and *American Beauty* (Sam Mendes, 1999) as recent examples of what he takes to be Hollywood's enduring taste—since at least its Golden Age, perhaps nowhere more colorfully than in *The Wizard of Oz* (Victor Fleming, 1939)—for contrasting the everyday world with that of the imaginary; something he also finds in the genre of horror (where the idea of the transformation of self and world may be ghastly or glorious) and the vast region of the Hollywood musical (in which the ordinary world is only a step away from an ecstatic harmony) (*CF*, 345–46). What may then strike us, in the face of this seemingly indefinite number of movies, spanning Hollywood's history and its genres, that bear on the good of perfectionism, is the thought that it is not simply (although perhaps especially) American film (something indicated by Cavell's reference in this context to the work of Éric Rohmer) but film as such, that has an affinity for this "transcendental moment" (346). It is quite as if this play of the two primordial possibilities of film, realism and fantasy, suggests that in the very act of projecting on a screen, a world, one is at the same time projecting, on the world, a possibility of perfectionism.

With the apparent existence of so much evidence for the idea that Hollywood continues to produce films that participate in the ideas of perfectionism, and particularly in ways recognizably related to those emphasized by the features of the genre of remarriage comedy, one might then wonder whether the same is true of its companion genre of the melodrama of the unknown woman. Although Cavell's remarks in "The Good of Film" begin by mentioning both genres, he subsequently concerns himself solely with the question of whether the comedies are still made. This focus is also true of his other writings on the matter: to my knowledge, he nowhere denies (but nowhere affirms) the possibility of a similar continuation of the melodramas. In one sense, of course, the sheer range of genres indicated by the many films with an affinity for perfectionism suggested above raises, in principle, the possibility of the making of new instances or fragments of the melodramas. If there are indeed new films that participate in the genre of remarriage, then, in principle, there is always the possibility that new films are being made that negate them in ways familiar from their melodramatic forebears (this possibility is explored in the chapters by Murray Pomerance on *Clouds of Sils Maria* [Olivier Assayas, 2014]; Robert Sinnerbrink on *Carol*; Stephen Mulhall on *Tenet* [Christopher Nolan, 2020]; and myself on *Revolutionary Road* [Sam Mendes, 2008]).

Whatever Cavell's reasons for this relative favoring of the comedies over the melodramas (he notes in the Introduction to *Contesting Tears* that the former "are individually more famous, or anyway more beloved" [*CT*, 4]) it is undoubtedly the case that the work on remarriage has been the more influential, extending its reach beyond academic circles to the writings of popular film critics who regularly refer to the genre. (A quick glance at recent film reviews finds remarriage comedy mentioned in relation to such varied Hollywood fare as *Babygirl* [Halina Reijn, 2024]; *Mother of the Bride* [Mark Waters, 2024]; *Twisters* [Lee Isaac Chung, 2024]; *The Union* [Julian Farino, 2024]; *Anora* [Sean Baker, 2024]; and *Venom: The Last Dance* [Kelly Marcel, 2024].) As Cavell himself recognized, writing in 2004:

> There has been a little flurry of interest in the book [*Cities of Words*] since two film reviewers have mentioned it in connection with the recently released film *Eternal Sunshine of the Spotless Mind*, written by Charlie Kaufman [. . .]. These reviewers describe *Eternal Sunshine* as following the contours I have traced for the genre of remarriage comedy. [. . .] The not infrequent references to it [*Pursuits of Happiness*] by critics responsible for regular columns have done something in my relation to that book that no other sources could do, namely, demonstrated the pertinence of this work of three decades ago to new films that can be spoken of as part of the present, perhaps even of the future, of filmmaking. (*LDIK*, 258–59)[10]

And it is not just film critics who have continued to keep Cavell's ideas in mind, for in a reflexive turn of events, those ideas have themselves now become a formative inheritance for new generations of filmmakers, with contemporary directors like Noah Baumbach (whose *While We're Young* [2014] is the subject of David LaRocca's chapter), Arnaud Desplechin, the Dardenne brothers, and Terrence Malick all finding inspiration in his work.[11]

Another two decades have now passed since Cavell remarked on the pertinence of his work on film genres. Against the background of the continuing critical and cinematic engagement with remarriage comedy and unknown woman melodrama, it is the aim of this book further to demonstrate their ongoing relevance. To show how the two genres have a bearing on new films that can be spoken of as part of the present, perhaps even of the future, of filmmaking—and thereby to suggest how their two founding stories can go on being told in new ways, after Cavell—is the burden of the sequel.

Postscript: Hope Against Hope

To echo the opening words of "Hope Against Hope" (*CHU*, 129–38), Cavell's 1985 convocation address that he placed as an appendix to the perfectionist political concerns of his three Carus lectures that constitute *Conditions Handsome and Unhandsome*, the completion of the present volume is a most happy occasion for me and I do not wish to mar it by speaking of unhappy things; but I will not belittle it by concluding my prefatory remarks without mentioning something that—given this collection's focus on recent examples of two genres of Hollywood film that are intimately related to the promise of American social and political life (to the "inner agenda" of American culture)—I take it as not just permissible but obligatory for me to acknowledge. Currently, many Americans (and not only Americans) harbor deep fear, if not despair, that the fundamental (perfectionist) idea of America that these two genres express—of America as a place where its citizens can pursue a dream of reciprocity and equality, of mutual happiness and freedom—may soon appear as old-fashioned, even quaint, as the idea of half of the population of America going to the same movies each week, with which I began my Introduction; and further, that the social and legal progress made with respect to the lives of women, of gays and lesbians, and Black people in America, of which I have spoken, may already sound—at a time when, for many, it appears powerful forces are seeking to roll back such progress—dangerously naive, at best.

Cavell's address was delivered at a time when the prospect of nuclear war was felt to be a real and urgent threat. In it, he claims that a certain Christian fundamentalist view of that prospect as the fulfillment of God's divine plan for mankind in preparation for the Second Coming—of "end-time" or "Armageddon theology" (a melodramatic picture of the victory of cosmic good over cosmic evil that President Reagan was regularly reported to have endorsed)—is an expression of despair. Cavell associates this despair with Emerson's thinking, for it was precisely in a climate or mood of despair (that Emerson called "silent melancholy," and that his disciple Thoreau called the "quiet desperation" of the lives led by the mass of men)—in the face of the existence of chattel slavery, of war with Mexico, and of America's war with itself—that "Emerson felt he wrote and which his writing was meant to withstand and disperse" (*CHU*, 130).

Cavell acknowledges that attempting to adopt an Emersonian cheerfulness and hopefulness in the face of the despair of nuclear annihilation can seem like simply expressing a childish ignorance of the real situation, an ignorance in keeping with the received view of Emerson as ignoring the (tragic) facts of life. But, on the contrary, for Cavell, it is Emerson's mood of cheer or joy—understood as the expression of his perfectionist participation in democracy in the face of the inevitable failures of it to comply with its own principles of justice—that exemplifies the latter's recognition or acknowledgment of life; and that for Emerson (and Cavell), casts despair not as a (tragic) recognition of life, but as a "fear of life, an avoidance of it"—one that "will ease the fulfillment of our worst fears" (*CHU*, 130) (as Cavell says elsewhere, since democracy depends upon a state of willingness to act for the common good, "despair is a political emotion, discouraging both participation and patience" [*CW*, 18]).

Here Cavell understands himself to be countering the widespread repression of Emerson's thinking in America. And since he takes Emerson as one of the founding thinkers of American culture, he takes that repression to present itself (in a recognizably perfectionist way) as a "refusal to listen to ourselves, to our own best thoughts" (*CHU*, 129). This refusal is found not least, for Cavell, in the denial, by both Emerson's supporters and detractors—in this instance Harold Bloom and John Updike, respectively—of the title of "philosophy" for that thinking; and in their reading of Emerson's famous call for self-reliance as a "doctrine of righteous selfishness" (134) continuous with authoritarian (specifically totalitarian) forms of government: "Totalitarian rule . . . offers a warped mirror in which we can recognize, distorted, Emerson's favorite concepts of genius and inspiration and whim; the totalitarian leader is a study in self-reliance gone amok, lawlessness enthroned in the place where law and debate and checks and balances should be" (136). It is quite as if, for Cavell, Emerson's founding thought of America—and so America itself—is always shadowed by, and always at risk of being eclipsed by (so throwing itself into darkness and despair) an intimate parody or perversion of its best self. How then can America learn to eclipse that eclipsing, to refuse the refusal to listen to itself? Cavell ends his address with the following words:

> When Emerson teaches that actions we take to define our lives, on which we stake the life and death of our families and our societies, should be taken in hope and on such claim to authority as only we alone, in our uncertainty, can bring to it, he is teaching what Kant called practical wisdom. It gives me hope—if small in our dangerous world, still concrete, clear, persistent, as large as my difficult sensibility can absorb. He tells me that those who have power over

us, who do not communicate to us their persistent hope of peace, are despairing of peace, and are placing what they call their hope in a favorable roll of scientific or magic dice. This is no more genuine hope than praying for such a favorable outcome is genuine prayer. They are caught by their power, by their images of themselves, by what they believe to be their public's expectations of them, our expectations. We must help to teach them otherwise, teach them hope, and first one another. (*CHU*, 138)

Such is Cavell's (American) faith as a teacher and a writer and a citizen. It is not optimism. But can it cheer us?

Oxford
January 2025

Notes

1. These concerns over the patriarchal nature of marriage lead to the vexed issue of the relation of Cavell's genres to feminism. This issue was originally raised by Tania Modleski in her scathing criticisms of Cavell's work on the melodramas, first in a letter to *Critical Enquiry* (1990) and then in her book, *Feminism without Women* (1991). She accused him of contributing to the very repression of women he identified as featured in them—by appropriating the voices of both the films' heroines and the feminist critics who had written on them, whom he failed to cite—thereby in effect perpetuating female unknownness. Cavell replied at length to Modleski's charges in the same journal issue (1990), and in the introduction and chapter 4 of *Contesting Tears*. He argued that, on the contrary, his readings of the films contested a certain condescension, even amongst feminist critics, that the melodramas he identified could not themselves possess the artistic and philosophical intelligence to counter the repression of women such critics took as obviously characteristic of the Hollywood of the period; and more specifically that their heroines, most notably Stella Dallas, were something other than the examples of female self-sacrifice the received interpretations took them to be. For a helpful discussion of these exchanges and the issue of gender in relation to Cavell's work on film, see chapter 5 of Wheatley (2019).

2. Admittedly, irrespective of whether the ending of the film contains that amount of happiness as such a remarriage may provide, one might argue

that *Kramer vs. Kramer* is obviously anything but a comedy. Instead, it might be better understood in relation to that as yet unnamed melodramatic genre which, in the same place, he predicts as the comedies' negating companion (*PH*, 30–31; *CT*, 83). And further, if one sides with Cavell in seeing the film's ending as presenting favorable conditions for the pair's remarriage (as negating the melodramas' negation of marriage) one might, more specifically, see it as related to that little subgenre of "remarriage melodrama," he takes to be defined by *Blonde Venus* (Josef von Sternberg, 1932), *Show Boat* (James Whale, 1936), and *Random Harvest* (Mervyn LeRoy, 1942) (*CT*, 14).

3. Cavell takes this shift to be exemplified by science fiction films, such as the *Star Wars* series. In a Hollywood recently dominated by CGI-laden superhero films, sequels, reboots, and increasingly elaborate cinematic crossovers, this idea may seem even more convincing.

4. For a discussion of remarriage in *Moonstruck*, see Day (2003).

5. I know of at least forty-two more recent American films (two are British-American co-productions) that Cavell mentions in the context of remarriage comedy, or moral perfectionism more generally. For those who like a list, I provide the following details of the films, and the places in which they are cited: *An Unmarried Woman* (Paul Mazursky, 1978) (*PH*, 26); *Kramer vs. Kramer* (Robert Benton, 1979) (*PH*, 26); *Starting Over* (Alan J. Pakula, 1979) (*PH*, 26); *Rich and Famous* (George Cukor, 1981) (*CT*, 30; *CF*, 170; Cavell 2006, 299); *Tootsie* (Sydney Pollack, 1982) (*CF*, 342); *The Sure Thing* (Rob Reiner, 1985) (*CW*, 153; *CF*, 342–43); *Crocodile Dundee* (Peter Faiman, 1986) (*CF*, 343); *Moonstruck* (Norman Jewison, 1987) (*CW*, 153; *CF*, 170–71, 283, 312–13, 315, 342); *Working Girl* (Mike Nichols, 1988) (*CW*, 343); *Say Anything* (Cameron Crowe, 1989) (*CW*, 153; *CF*, 343); *Joe Versus the Volcano* (John Patrick Shanley, 1990) (Butler 2001); *Groundhog Day* (Harold Ramis, 1993) (*CW*, 153; *CF*, 221–22, 342, 345); *Jurassic Park* (Steven Spielberg, 1993) (Butler 2001); *Sleepless in Seattle* (Nora Ephron, 1993) (*CF*, 342); *The Untamed Heart* (Tony Bill, 1993) (*CW*, 155; *CF*, 343); *Four Weddings and a Funeral* (Mike Newell, 1994) (*CW*, 153; *CF*, 343); *Clueless* (Amy Heckerling, 1995) (*CF*, 342); *Everyone Says I Love You* (Woody Allen, 1996) (*CF*, 343); *Twister* (Jan de Bont, 1996) (Butler 2001); *As Good as It Gets* (James L. Brooks, 1997) (*CF*, 342); *Grosse Point Blank* (George Armitage, 1997) (*CF*, 343); *Inventing the Abbotts* (Pat O'Connor, 1997) (*CF*, 343); *My Best Friend's Wedding* (P. J. Hogan, 1997) (*CF*, 343); *Ghost Dog* (Jim Jarmusch, 1999) (*CF*, 333, 344); *Cookie's Fortune* (Robert Altman, 1999) (*CF*, 343); *The Matrix* (the Wachowskis, 1999) (*CW*, 153; *CF*, 343, 345); *Being John Malkovich* (Spike Jonze, 1999) (*CF*, 345; *LDIK*, 258); *Fight Club* (David Fincher, 1999) (*CF*, 345); *Dogma* (Kevin Smith, 1999) (*CF*, 345); *American Beauty* (Sam Mendes, 1999) (*CF*, 345); *The Sixth Sense* (M. Night Shyamalan, 1999) (*CF*, 345); *The Cider House Rules* (Lars Sven Hallström, 1999) (*CF*, 345); *Flawless* (Joel Schumacher, 1999) (Cavell 2006,

300); *Waking the Dead* (Keith Gordon, 2000) (*CF*, 345); *O Brother, Where Art Thou?* (Coen brothers, 2000) (*CW*, 155, 305–6; *CF*, 435–52; Cavell and Desplechin 2008, 216); *Ocean's Eleven* (Steven Soderbergh, 2001) (*CW*, 155); *My First Mister* (Christine Lahti, 2001) (Cavell 2006, 300); *Daddy and Them* (Billy Bob Thornton, 2001) (Cavell 2006, 300); *About a Boy* (Paul Weitz and Chris Weitz, 2002) (Cavell 2006, 300); *Adaptation* (Spike Jonze, 2002) (*LDIK*, 258); *Eternal Sunshine of the Spotless Mind* (Michel Gondry, 2004) (*LDIK*, 258); and *Mr. and Mrs. Smith* (Doug Liman, 2005) (*CF*, 429–34; *LDIK*, 258).

6. *O Brother, Where Art Thou?* is the subject of the last major essay on film Cavell ever wrote (*CF*, 435–52).

7. Perhaps this is what Cavell senses when, in an interview, he reflects on his inclination to answer the question of whether the comedy of remarriage is any longer possible today: "There is clearly resistance here on my part; perhaps it is worth my asking what has caused it. I think it is worth asking" (Butler 2001).

8. For a book-length discussion of remarriage in relation to gay marriage in the context of recent American and British films, see Wallace (2020).

9. Like the issue of gender, Cavell's understanding of the relation of film to the issue of race has attracted significant critical debate, with some viewing his work here as another morally and politically fraught appropriation of the voice of oppressed members of American society. The focus of this debate doesn't relate specifically to Cavell's work on the genres of remarriage comedy and unknown women melodrama, but instead centers on his readings of two Fred Astaire dance routines from the musical *The Band Wagon* (Vincente Minnelli, 1953) contained in the essays "Something Out of the Ordinary" (*CF*, 223–40) and "Fred Astaire Asserts the Right to Praise" (*CF*, 397–428), respectively; and has its origin in an exchange between Robert Gooding-Williams (2006) and Cavell (2006). Once again, a helpful summary of this debate is provided by Wheatley (2019, chap. 7). As far as I am aware, the only attempts to explore the role of race in relation to Cavell's two genres are the essays by Jennifer Fay, "Hollywood's White Privacy: Stanley Cavell and James Baldwin" (2020), and William Rothman, "Viewing the World in Black and White" (2021); both of which focus on defining, classical examples of unknown woman melodrama.

10. I suspect that the two film reviewers to whom Cavell refers here are Scott (2004) and Edelstein (2004). For academic discussions of *Eternal Sunshine of the Spotless Mind* in relation to remarriage comedy, see Meyer (2008), Day (2011), and chapter 5 of Shaw (2019).

11. As LaRocca notes in chapter 8 of this volume, Baumbach talks of wanting to contribute to a tradition of films that begins with "the comedies of remarriage;" Desplechin not only explains that Cavell's writings on the two genres proved useful in the development of several of his films and coins his

own related hybrid subgenre of "disaster remarriage" (Cavell and Desplechin 2008, 212; Bauer 2010) but also makes matters even more explicit by having characters in his films recite passages from *Pursuits of Happiness* and *Little Did I Know* (see the discussion in Laugier [2021]); Luc Dardenne not only acknowledges the effect of reading *Cities of Words* on *La fille inconnue* (*The Unknown Girl*, 2016) but also gave a paper at a symposium on Cavell at the Sorbonne in 2011 (see the discussion in Rothman [2019a]); and the relations between Cavell's work more generally and that of Malick, his former student, are well documented (see, for example, Sinnerbrink [2019]; LaRocca [2020]; and Rothman [2019b]).

Works Cited

Bauer, Marko. 2010. " 'Films are Vulgar. And this Vulgarity, I Love it': An Interview with Arnaud Desplechin." *Senses of Cinema* 56 (October). https://www.sensesofcinema.com/2010/feature-articles/%E2%80%9Cfilms-are-vulgar-and-this-vulgarity-i-love-it%E2%80%9D-an-interview-with-arnaud-desplechin.

Butler, Rex. 2001. "An 'Exchange' with Stanley Cavell." *Senses of Cinema* 13 (April). https://www.sensesofcinema.com/2001/film-critics/cavell.

Cavell, Stanley. 1990. "Editorial Notes." *Critical Inquiry* 17 (1): 238–44.

Cavell, Stanley. 2006. "The Incessance and the Absence of the Political." In Norris, *The Claim to Community*.

Cavell, Stanley, and Arnaud Desplechin. 2008. "Pourquoi les films comptent-ils?" ["Why do movies matter?"] *Esprit* 8 (August–September): 208–19. https://doi.org/10.3917/espri.0808.0208.

Day, William. 2003. "*Moonstruck*, or How to Ruin Everything." In *Ordinary Language Criticism: Literary Thinking after Cavell after Wittgenstein*, edited by Kenneth Dauber and Walter Jost. Northwestern University Press.

Day, William. 2011. "I Don't Know, Just Wait: Remembering Remarriage in *Eternal Sunshine of the Spotless Mind*." In *The Philosophy of Charlie Kaufman*, edited by David LaRocca. University Press of Kentucky.

Edelstein, David. 2004. "Forget Me Not: The Genius of Charlie Kaufman's *Eternal Sunshine of the Spotless Mind*." *Slate*, March 18, 2004. https://slate.com/culture/2004/03/eternal-sunshine-is-unforgettable.html.

Fay, Jennifer. 2020. "Hollywood's White Privacy: Stanley Cavell and James Baldwin." Special issue, *Discourse: Journal for Theoretical Studies in Media and Culture* 42 (1–2): 100–106.

Gooding-Williams, Robert. 2006. "Aesthetics and Receptivity: Kant, Nietzsche, Cavell, and Astaire." In Norris, *The Claim to Community*.

Laugier, Sandra. 2021. "The Importance of Stanley Cavell for the Study of Film." In *Movies with Stanley Cavell in Mind*, edited by David LaRocca. Bloomsbury Academic.

LaRocca, David. 2020. "Thinking of Film: What Is Cavellian about Malick's Movies?" In *A Critical Companion to Terrence Malick*, edited by Joshua Sikora. Lexington Books.

Meyer, Michael, J. 2008. "Reflections on Comic Reconciliations: Ethics, Memory, and Anxious Happy Endings." *Journal of Aesthetics and Art Criticism* 66 (1): 77–87.

Modleski, Tania. 1990. "Editorial Notes." *Critical Inquiry* 17 (1): 237–38.

Modleski, Tania. 1991. *Feminism without Women: Culture and Criticism in a "Postfeminist" Age*. Routledge.

Norris, Andrew, ed. 2006. *The Claim to Community: Essays on Stanley Cavell and Political Philosophy*. Stanford University Press.

Rothman, William. 2019a. "A Film that is also a Handshake: Philosophy in the Films of the Dardenne Brothers." In *Tuitions and Intuitions: Essays at the Intersection of Film Criticism and Philosophy*. State University of New York Press.

Rothman, William. 2019b. "Precious Memories in Philosophy and Film: Stanley Cavell's *Little Did I Know* and Terrence Malick's *The Tree of Life*." In *Tuitions and Intuitions: Essays at the Intersection of Film Criticism and Philosophy*. State University of New York Press.

Rothman, William. 2021. "Viewing the World in Black and White." In *The Holiday in His Eye: Stanley Cavell's Vision of Film and Philosophy*. State University of New York Press.

Scott, A. O. 2004. "Charlie Kaufman's Critique of Pure Comedy." *The New York Times*, April 4, 2004. https://www.nytimes.com/2004/04/04/arts/film-charlie-kaufman-s-critique-of-pure-comedy.html.

Shaw, Dan. 2019. *Stanley Cavell and the Magic of Hollywood Films*. Edinburgh University Press.

Sinnerbrink, Robert. 2019. *Terrence Malick: Filmmaker and Philosopher*. Bloomsbury Academic.

Wallace, Lee. 2020. *Reattachment Theory: Queer Cinema of Remarriage*. Duke University Press.

Wheatley, Catherine. 2019. *Stanley Cavell and Film: Scepticism and Self-Reliance at the Cinema*. Bloomsbury Academic.

1

The Question of Sex

Thoughts on the Cavellian Couple Inspired by *Rich and Famous*

CATHERINE WHEATLEY

THIS CHAPTER RESPONDS TO a passage in Stanley Cavell's *Cities of Words*, first published in 2004, in which Cavell muses on the matter of whether it would be possible for a remarriage comedy to turn around a same sex–same couple. Here is the passage at hand:

> While the aggressive playfulness and instruction between the principal pair of remarriage comedy involves questions and exchanges of gender roles, the topic of gender, while explicitly not excluded, is not explicitly and systematically explored. [. . .] While same-sex marriages, or unions, have become common enough to force a consciousness, and elaboration, of the economic and legal consequences for partners and for children reared in such marriages, it is too

> early yet to know [. . .] what new shapes such marriages
> will discover for their investments in imaginativeness,
> exclusiveness, and equality. (*CW*, 16–17)

Cavell is taking up here a question he first raised approximately a decade earlier, in the opening chapter of *Contesting Tears* (1996). Considering the importance of gender to the films made in Hollywood in the 1930s and 1940s that Cavell brackets under the generic heading of the "comedy of remarriage," he states that it is a pair of equally essential laws of the genre that, speaking of the central romantic coupling, the man is required to claim the woman (that is, he must recognize his commitment to her), and the woman must both appreciate and contest the claim. Thus, a determining feature of the genre is its depiction of "what Hollywood at that time would have called the battle of the sexes" (*CT*, 29). In short, Cavell is claiming here it is definitive of the remarriage comedy that one half of the remarriage couple is female, the other male.

And yet, in the next paragraph, Cavell writes that what legitimizes marriage in these films is an exclusiveness and devotedness that is freely chosen, and that is not determined by external factors or institutions such as state, church, or children. In that case, Cavell states, the possibility raises itself that gender roles are not necessarily important to remarriage: indeed, he claims, this structure may well invite couples of the same sex. Of course, Hollywood was not producing such films during the period in question; the only film Cavell can think of that might thus serve as an example of a same-sex remarriage comedy is George Cukor's last finished film, *Rich and Famous* (1981).

A remake of Vincent Sherman's 1943 film *Old Acquaintance*, *Rich and Famous* follows the ups and downs of the friendship between Liz Hamilton (played by Jacqueline Bisset), and Merry Noel Blake (Candace Bergen), who, in Cavell's words, wind up "after years of comings and goings [. . .] at midnight in Connecticut with a kiss" (*CT*, 30). It is in many ways a strange example for Cavell to offer of a same-sex remarriage comedy, since it is not an explicitly queer text: Liz and Merry are never presented as any more than friends, both have explicitly sexual relationships with men, and that final kiss is extremely chaste, a kiss on the cheek only. But the aim of this chapter is not to answer directly Cavell's question of what light same-sex *marriage* might cast on the remarriage genre: this is work that has already been started by Lee Wallace in her ground-breaking book on "queer remarriage" (2020) and a cluster of related articles. Rather I want to look to *Rich and Famous*'s presentation of an enduring relationship between two women as an alternative case to heterosexual marriage, raising the question: if the remarriage comedy is about the education of the woman by the man within a marriage, what, if anything, changes when women are able to educate each another outside of one? In what follows, I want to think about what this seemingly casual mention of *Rich and Famous* might begin to tell us about the centrality of the couple, or the pair, to Cavell's philosophy, and the relative importance of romantic love, sexual desire, and platonic friendship to the pursuit of a moral education.

The Education of Women

Cavell coins the term the "Hollywood comedy of remarriage" in his book *Pursuits of Happiness* (1981), with reference to seven films produced during the period from 1934 to 1949: *It Happened One Night* (Frank Capra, 1934), *The Awful Truth* (Leo McCarey, 1937), *Bringing up Baby* (Howard Hawks, 1938), *His Girl Friday* (Howard Hawks, 1940), *The Philadelphia Story* (George Cukor, 1940), *The Lady Eve* (Preston Sturges, 1941), and *Adam's Rib* (George Cukor, 1949). In this group of films, the central couple—who seem to have known one another forever—are forced apart by an internal dispute. The goal of the narrative is then to get them "together *again, back* together" (*CW*, 10). The only way they can achieve this goal is through a running conversation, even perhaps an argument, about what happiness is and whether one can change, and what one is willing to accept. Conversation is for Cavell not merely the basis for marriage, but the very fact of marriage: without conversation, there is no marriage. Cavell finds further evidence of the importance of speech in what he describes in *Contesting Tears* as a "derivative" genre: "the Hollywood melodrama of the unknown woman" (*CT*, 5). Made during the same period of Hollywood's history, the films *Stella Dallas* (King Vidor, 1937), *Now, Voyager* (Irving Rapper, 1942), *Gaslight* (George Cukor, 1944), and *Letter from an Unknown Woman* (Max Ophüls, 1948) show us the negation of conversation, and therefore the negation of marriage. The couples in these films cannot find a shared language nor a shared worldview, and so their relationship is doomed to failure. Taken together the two genres demonstrate the grounding of linguistic meaning in subjective responsibility—that is, in the ongoing, daily attempt at communication in words and gestures that risk constantly being misunderstood or rejected. In this much, marriage can be understood not only as a romantic relationship, but a democratic one: a union between equals.

In each of these films, which were of course all produced during the Hays Code and at a period in American history when homosexuality was illegal, the central couple comprises a man and a woman. The genders of these couples matter to Cavell. He notes in the introduction to *Pursuits of Happiness* that the women who populate these films—Claudette Colbert, Irene Dunne, Katharine Hepburn, Rosalind Russell, Barbara Stanwyck—could only perhaps have existed at this moment, a moment when talking pictures were establishing themselves and women had established themselves as relatively autonomous outside the strictures of marriage (*PH*, 18). More than this, Cavell claims that both the remarriage comedies and the melodramas of the unknown woman turn around what Cavell calls variously "the creation of the woman" (16), "the creation of the new woman" (65), and "the woman's education" (171). In the comedies, the responsibility for this creation lies with the man. Cavell admits that this suggests "a privileging of the male" (*CT*, 5) even within the films' general atmosphere of equality, but adds that for the woman's part, she must choose—or better yet—authorize the correct man to educate her. (We might say the relationship is asymmetrical, but not unequal.) In the melodramas meanwhile, the woman's transformation must take place outside of marriage. Cavell writes: "It is as if the women of the melodramas are saying to their sisters in the comedies [. . .]: You may call yourselves lucky to have found a man with whom you can overcome the humiliation of marriage by marriage itself. For us, with our talents and tastes, there is no further or happy education to be found there; our integrity and metamorphosis happens elsewhere, in the abandoning of that shared wit and intelligence and exclusive appreciation" (6). So, in both genres a woman begins in an unhappy marriage and resolves to leave it. In the comedies, she participates in a conversation with her male counterpart, a conversation which reveals him as worthy to be her teacher, and the film ends in an atmosphere of festivity as the couples recommence their relationship. In the melodramas, the woman judges the man as unworthy and she ends the film alone. In his readings of at least two of the four films that make up the genre, Cavell understands this aloneness as a triumph, and yet it seems at best ambivalent. In these films, for a woman to be educated, she must be married (to the right man) or resigned to a solitary life (or worse yet, death).

Cavell hints, however, at an alternative to this double bind when he brings up *Rich and Famous*, a film that seems to traverse the genres of the remarriage comedy and the melodrama of the unknown woman. He mentions the film twice over the course of his writing: once in 1996, in the introduction to *Contesting Tears*, and again in a 1988 essay, "The Advent of Videos" (*CF*, 167–74). In both instances, he suggests that the film might allow us to think about the education of women outside of the heterosexual couple. In the first instance, Cavell argues that the film deliberately invokes the comedy of remarriage. In so doing, it shows "that the questions posed in the genre of the remarriage comedy—whether we know what the role of romance is in marriage, what the bond or meld is of devotion and intimacy that constitutes what we call marriage—remain in question" (170). Let's turn now, then, to that film.

Rich and Famous

Rich and Famous takes place over the course of twenty-two years, following the friendship between Liz and Merry, two women who meet as first-year students at Smith College in the 1950s. We are introduced to them in 1959, on the eve of Merry's elopement with a young man named Doug (David Selby), whom she met after he had taken Liz out on a date. We rejoin them in 1969, 1975, and 1981, at various turning points in their relationship.

It is easy enough to read *Rich and Famous* as a coded lesbian remarriage comedy, a reading that is lent further credence by Cukor's own notoriously open but unacknowledged homosexuality (see McGilligan 1997). The action begins in the girls' shared college bedroom, and with the rather on-the-nose non sequitur "What are you doing in the closet?" before a love triangle of sorts is set up: Doug, Merry's fiancé, had once taken Liz out on a date, and he is, according to Merry, far more Liz's type than her own. But Doug, for his part, apologizes to Liz for "stealing" her roommate from her, implying that Liz's interest is not in him, but in Merry. As the women bid a tearful goodbye on a train station platform, they pass a teddy bear back and forth between them, an emblem, perhaps of the shared childhood that Cavell sees as definitive of the couple in remarriage comedies. In the end it is Liz—who declares that next time the pair meet Merry will be a married woman, Liz an unmarried one—who is left holding the bear, alone on the station platform, as the train pulls out.

Cavell describes the central couple in remarriage comedies as having shared a childhood, discovered their sexuality together, and found themselves at around the same time required to enter the social realm. This joining of the social and the sexual, he calls marriage. But something in that marriage causes a rift: "call this its impotence to domesticate sexuality without discouraging it, or its stupidity in the face of the riddle of intimacy [. . .] or in the face of the puzzle of ecstasy" (*PH*, 30). And in the face of this disappointment one half of the couple—usually the woman—takes the regressive tactic of accepting as a partner a simpler, sexless person in an effort, Cavell claims, "to put her desire [. . .] back to sleep" (32). He also remarks that in both *Old Acquaintance* and *Rich and Famous*, the woman-writer—Kit (played by Bette Davis) and Liz, respectively—dresses in obviously "male-derived clothes," suggesting that she assumed the male role in the remarriage (*CF*, 170). Merry meanwhile wears pastels and prints, jewelry and elaborate hairstyles, as if parodying femininity. This is a somewhat throwaway remark of Cavell's, but an important one, and I will return to it. For now, we can say that Merry and Liz form the "original couple" of this remarriage comedy, having entered the sexual and social realm when they enrolled in college, where they shared a domestic space (their dorm room) and a substitute child (the bear). But Southern belle Merry, perhaps unable to conceive of a society in which she and Liz could live together unmarried, absconds with Doug, and thus the stage is set for a narrative of how this couple will eventually get back together.

Four features characteristic of the remarriage comedy define the shape of Merry and Liz's relationship over the next two decades. Firstly, it is premised on repetition and return, playing out as it does over a series of coming togethers over the years. Secondly, their interactions primarily take the form of bickering. This bickering is, Cavell argues, a sign of caring: the hallmark of a willingness "to bear up under an assault of words, to give as you get, where what is good must always, however strong, maintain its good spirits, a test of intellectual as well as spiritual stamina, of what you might call ear" (*PH*, 86). This leads me to the third feature, that their relationship is always given as equal: indeed, the first argument between the women takes place when Liz discovers that she is not the only one who aspires to literary success and that Merry, far from being a frivolous and unambitious housewife, harbors considerable talent. (This discovery—that the female half of the couple can match the male half—is a feature of both *Adam's Rib* and *The Awful Truth*.) And finally, that these arguments demand of each woman a willingness to reassess themselves and reconstitute themselves.

The Question of Sex

And what of the question of sex, a question that Liz raises with her much younger lover, Chris (Hart Bochner), in reference to sexual relations (although she might as well be thinking of the biological sex of the participants)? Both women engage in sexual encounters with men over the course of the film: Merry with Doug, Liz with three men that we see onscreen (a further two relationships are discussed and it is implied that there have been many more, although she tells Merry she has only had sex with three people). But sex in this film is intricately connected to the life of the mind. Having been seized by a fit of inspiration while in bed with Doug, Merry interrupts their lackluster lovemaking in order to engage in a feverish fit of novel-planning. Liz—suffering from both writer's block and a lack of libido—tells Doug that her therapist has assured her, "When I start writing again, I'll start loving." ("Actually he said fucking." She apologetically shrugs. "The man's a Freudian.") When Doug suggests that perhaps it's the other way around, Liz assures him that "Not writing is my problem." Later she will opine to Chris about the younger generation's "obsession with flesh." "We've got a whole generation who only want to talk with their bodies," she complains. "No one wants to talk anymore"; "What happened to the articulate guy?"

Liz herself is aware she has a tendency to take surrogate lovers, telling Chris that although she is aroused by object A, she makes loves to object B. But close attention to the film suggests some ambiguity around who exactly object A might be. In the first instance, Liz has sex with a stranger on a plane following a visit to Merry and Doug. The stranger is clearly object B; a straight reading of this scene might suggest that object A is Doug, with whom Liz has recently shared a tender chat. But the trip to the airport comes hot on the heels of a blazing argument with Merry that culminates in Liz storming off into the bathroom, in a scene that recalls a similar exit by Katharine Hepburn in *Adam's Rib*. In a later incident, which takes place following a gorgeously screwball comedy of entrances and exits, yet again reminiscent of Cukor's work with Hepburn in *Adam's Rib* and *The Philadelphia Story*, Merry will storm in and out of Liz's hotel room, offering a parting shot that Liz should sleep with Chris to ease some of her pent-up frustration. Immediately following Merry's departure, Liz angrily rips off her sweater, downs a double scotch, and heads out to the street, where she picks up an eighteen-year-old boy, who may or may not be a gigolo, for sex. Twice, then, a heated confrontation with Merry immediately precedes Liz having sex with a stranger. Viewed in this light, it seems clear who object A really is.

At the film's end, a final, dreadful confrontation between Liz and Merry leads to an apparently conclusive parting of ways. The argument takes place after Merry has learnt that Doug is to remarry, and that, while still married to Merry, he had proposed to Liz. (Who, we might ask, is Merry *really* jealous of here?) The latter, meanwhile, has just refused Chris's offer of marriage, suspecting that he has feelings for Merry's daughter Debbie. These two women, finally having severed themselves from their substitute marriages (to men), are then free to reconcile in Connecticut—the place that Cavell, after the literary historian Northrop Frye, refers to as "the green world": "a place from which the ordinary world is broken into, out of which beauty and isolation and strangeness intertwine to reveal a glimpse of community and the possibility of change" (*CF*, 344). It is here, at midnight, that Merry seeks Liz out. Having accepted Merry's suggestion that they should no longer argue, Liz renounces trying to write for men, and asks Merry to kiss her. And it is this kiss that Cavell cites as evidence for reading the film as a same-sex remarriage structure (*CT*, 30). In keeping with remarriage comedy convention, the film ends on a note of festivity, rather than festival: Merry has left the grand party she had organized to celebrate her triumphs (her getting back together with Doug and the literary prize win), in order to share a quiet moment with Liz, clinking glasses together and toasting their continuing friendship.

Performing Gender

Cavell's fullest consideration of homosexuality and its relationship to his philosophical concerns with skepticism and perfectionism comes in a chapter of *Contesting Tears* entitled "Postscript: To Whom It May Concern" (*CT*, 151–94). It follows a long psychoanalytical reading of *Now, Voyager*, and takes that film once more as its subject. Here, Cavell engages the work of Eve Kosofsky Sedgwick on homosexual panic, and most notably her reading of Henry James's novella "The Beast in the Jungle." Towards the end of the chapter, Cavell suggests a reading of *Now, Voyager* that takes Charlotte (Bette Davis) as a closeted lesbian of sorts, one who has refused marriage to a man because she wishes for "a passionate existence," (*CT*, 186) and whose mother has encouraged the match for precisely that reason; that Jerry, played by the soft-spoken European actor Paul Henreid, is for Charlotte "a feminine object" (*CT*, 186). Davis's arrogation of camp is a quality shared by Garbo and Dietrich, two actresses who frequently appear in masculine dress (for example, Dietrich's white tails and top hats in *Blonde Venus* [Josef von Sternberg, 1932] or Garbo's riding habit in *Queen Christina* [Rouben Mamoulian, 1933]). Turning to Freud's *Civilization and Its Discontents*, Cavell argues that the categories masculine/feminine can be mapped onto active/passive, and that each individual might oscillate between the two. What Dietrich and Garbo's cross-dressing implies is that they share the same desires as the men they are paired with in these films.

Returning to the remarriage comedies, Cavell now notes that "role reversal" does quite a lot of work in the films. The obvious image that springs to mind is Cary Grant dressed in a negligée and "suddenly going gay!" in *Bringing Up Baby*. But we might think, too, of the innocent, virginal figures of Henry Fonda in *The Lady Eve* and James Stewart in *The Philadelphia Story*. It is Cukor's *Adam's Rib* that best reveals the slipperiness of gender, though. Spencer Tracy may be man enough to show Katharine Hepburn the difference between a slap and a slug, but, Cavell tells us, he is also able to wear a hat to bed and produce tears on demand. Discussing the difference between a man and a woman, Tracy tells Hepburn, "there ain't any of us hasn't got our little tricks," suggesting that tears are a theatrical device, a performance that is traditionally distinctive of women, but which is not restricted to them. For Cavell, Tracy's tears invoke a structure in which men are taught not to cry, while women are, and makes a mockery of that structure. More than this, though, it announces Tracy as "something of an unknown woman himself." Tracy has his secrets, his privacy, which even Hepburn is on the outside of. Cavell writes:

> We should see the demonstration of his being trained not to cry means precisely that he has not gone on (many men seem to have) to learn the trick of becoming invulnerable [. . .] and that she might need the show of his flair for theatre, for the melodramatic, to be reminded of this fact—even she, even about him—the fact that expression is to be read, responded to, even when there is, on the surface so to speak, nothing to require responding to. (*CT*, 191)

If a reading of *Rich and Famous*—the reading I have offered above—takes it that Liz and Merry are in love with one another, that their relationship is the marriage at the center of *Rich and Famous's* remarriage plot, then Cavell's recourse to Freudian notions of gender and sexuality as—let's say—divorced from biological sex allows us to retain the importance of the male and the female in the remarriage comedies by understanding these terms as typings. Liz is forthright, she dresses in trousers and mannish garments, she is independent and unmarried and drinks scotch; the novels she writes are great literature. Merry is coquettish, and decorative, and is a mother and a homemaker and wife, and the novels she writes are bodice-rippers. Putting aside the reductive heteronormativity of these types, we can see how it becomes quite straightforward to transpose the "battle of the sexes" onto the years-long love-hate relationship that these two women share.

The problem with treating gender as performance, however, is that for Cavell, skepticism is a profoundly "male affair" (*PP*, 169), a matter recently taken up in writing by Ludger Viefhues-Bailey (2011) and Áine Mahon (2015), amongst others. Cavell perceives a threat to marriage in the Shakespearean dramas to which the film genres are both a return and revision, in the destructiveness of characters who lack an epistemological assurance of love and fidelity. In Othello's case, it is a doubt, expressed as jealousy, about Desdemona's faithlessness; in the case of *King Lear*, it is about whether he is loved; in Macbeth's case about the identity or nature of his wife; in *The Winter's Tale*, Leontes's doubt that his children are his (*CW*, 425). The problem of masculine doubt often poses itself, then, as a question of sex, most viscerally in Leontes's anxiety over the parentage of his children.

Viefhues-Bailey argues that the imbalance between men and woman and their relationship to problems of skeptical doubt have to do, too, with questions of desire and visibility. He cites Cavell's interpretation of *Othello*, in which he writes, "The violence in masculine knowing, explicitly associated with jealousy, seems to interpret the ambition of knowledge as that of exclusive possession, call it private property. Othello's problem, following my suggestion that his problem is over success, not failure, is that Desdemona's acceptance, or satisfaction, or reward, of his ambition strikes him as being possessed, as if he were the woman" (quoted in Viefhues-Bailey 2011, 455). Viefhues-Bailey surmises that not only does Othello want totally, unmediated access to Desdemona as the object of his desire, he is terrified of being known in return, since, according to the calculus of the skeptic's understanding of knowledge, being known involves being objectified (456). We are back to the thorny problem of masculine activity and female passivity, the subject and the object. Ultimately, though, Viefhues-Bailey concludes that Cavell's work on Hollywood film, when viewed in its entirety, offers a quite complex and fluid conception of gender relations and desire, most significantly through the way in which the woman (in the figure of the female star) is able to invite and direct the male gaze (one might think of Mae West instructing us to "Come up and see me," or of Irene Dunne performing her hokey vaudeville act for Cary Grant in *The Awful Truth*). Masculine and feminine agencies thus causally interact in these films, are mutually constructed through relationships between men and women, and are therefore able to be reconstructed. Against this, Mahon argues that Cavellian perfectionism is still heavily and problematically gendered (2015, 644). While she allows there are occasional moments "in which on-screen female empowerment is actualized," she nonetheless maintains that "Cavell's wives are consistently in thrall to husbands as trustworthy and credible educators; Cavell's scenes of instruction consistently employ a male figure in education of the female. And crucially, of course, it is consistently via subjective consent to Cavell's men that Cavell's women recover identity and voice" (645).

The World of Women

In *Cities of Words*, Cavell acknowledges that "marriage is a specialized moral relationship," and that what is perhaps of more interest to him is the "figure of the Friend" (*CW*, 27). Indeed, he tells us that marriage is *really* an allegory for friendship (15). This raises the question, why take a film about friendship, and read it as an allegory for marriage? Especially since, when we take *Rich and Famous* at face value, we can see that it radically troubles or disrupts debates around the relative agency of the genders by focusing, not only on a same sex pair, but on a pair for whom sexual desire, and the problems of objectivity and subjectivity that it throws up, is no longer at stake. Instead, *Rich and Famous* offers a vision of perfectionism, or mutual education, that takes place aside from the distractions of gender politics.

And indeed, the film has as much in common, perhaps, with the melodramas of the unknown woman. Here we have two women seeking an answer to the question of "whether her talent is for work or [. . .] the appreciation of work, whether romance is agreeable or marriage is refusable, how far idiosyncrasy is manageable" (*CT*, 198). They try out marriage, but while one man—Doug—is emasculated by his female partner's expression of her voice, through the writing, the other, Chris, refuses just as Stephen Dallas (John Boles) does to "read between the pitiful lines" of what Liz has to say, when she ostensibly sets him free to make a more appropriate match. Finally, the pair end up in Liz's house, in what we might understand as the "green world," but might equally understand as "the world of women," a space that is notably absent from the remarriage comedy, but which has a significant place in the melodramas of the unknown woman.[1] When Doug leaves Merry, she is philosophical, taking solace in the many consolations she enjoys: her career, her daughter, her friend. "Liz, you'll be my friend, won't you?" she asks, plaintively. Then, before Liz can answer, she rebuffs herself: "That's a stupid question. We'll always be old friends."

Friendship, unlike marriage, does not demand exclusivity or monogamy. It is not totalizing. And indeed, even more so than in marriage, it requires a daily renewal and recommitment. If the remarriage comedy is made possible in the 1930s with the ready availability of divorce, which analogizes the threat of dismissal, friendship takes the vulnerability of the couple further yet. Since friendship is non-exclusive, it also demands a greater acknowledgement and acceptance of the friend's privacy than marriage: an awareness that my friend will always be something else besides my friend, that our relationship is just one amongst a network of relations, part of a broader community.

It is not always easy to be so generous. Friendship is not immune to jealousy and doubt. In this sense the friend, as embodied by Liz and Merry, is different not only from the spouse but also from what Cavell calls, after Emerson, the "true man" or the "exemplar"—"the advanced figure who sets those who approach him on a path of education" (*CF*, 337). The exemplar is usually older, and essentially impersonal. Stephen Mulhall explains that although such a friend is always interested in his younger friend's state and fate, it is with a view to helping the younger friend to realize his own self-overcoming, not with a view to satisfying any of his own personal desires (in particular, not any romantic ones). Indeed, such an interest, according to Mulhall, "would in fact sabotage the perfectionist impulse, in so far as it would impose demands on the befriended one to conform to the friend's desires, and thereby substitute one form of conformity with society's sense of what is possible with another (the friend's sense of what is necessary, and in particular for him)" (2016, 35).

Who would want an impersonal, disinterested friend? Liz and Merry are bound together by loyalty and care and mutual respect. We see each of them show both pride and envy at the other's successes. They are competitive, and they are mutually supportive. Theirs is a complicated, ambivalent, enduring relationship. It is also one that exists beyond sexual desire. Indeed, at the film's end Liz effectively declares that she has spent her life looking for a man who could be her intellectual and physical equal; now she proposes a dual existence, where the needs of the flesh can be met by men, and the mind by Merry, "my oldest friend." Thus, Liz puts aside the question of sex in order to concentrate on a relationship of mutual education for women by women. "An examination of one soul by another" (*CF*, 339) need not involve the body. There are many types of love.

Conclusion

Merry's novels are old fashioned romances, of the sort that might once have been adapted by Hollywood into what was called "a woman's picture"—a film just like *Now, Voyager* or *Stella Dallas*. Bemoaning a certain formulaicness to these works, Liz asks Merry, "Why do they always have to end up alone, those women in those stories?" Cavell offers us one answer to this question: they end up alone by choice, because they have judged the world, and their partners, to be wanting, and they have chosen to strike out on their own in search of an education. But it doesn't *have* to look like this, does it? *Rich and Famous* presents us with an alternative model of mutual education, one in which the sexual and the social are not inherently bound up, but where the couple might yet be a model of democracy; in which women are able to occupy a role other than wife or spinster, but might be able to be alone, together. This is, of course, a projection of Cavell's own arguments: the two brief mentions of *Rich and Famous* are themselves uninterested in either the ethical potential of platonic friendship, or the mutual education of women. The films he is interested in broke no such possibility either: a consequence, no doubt, of the time and circumstances of their making. As we have seen, Cavell's understanding of gender relations is not without its problems. And yet, by holding on to what is good in his account of perfectionism and film, and pulling it forward into new contexts, we are able to open up new possibilities for understanding how we might live well in the world.

One such generative moment in Cavell's writing is his beautiful description of perfectionism, in which he tells us that the moral life is "a life whose texture is a weave of cares and commitments in which one is bound to become lost and to need the friendly and credible words of others in order to find one's way, in which at any time a choice may present itself [. . .] in pondering which you will have to decide whose view of you is most valuable to you" (*CW*, 16). This seems to me a fitting description of *Rich and Famous*'s denouement, in which Merry, having finally won a long-coveted book prize, walks away from a room of admirers to find Liz—the person whose view of her is most valuable to her. To paraphrase Áine Mahon, Liz and Merry are neither two happy halves of a remarriage couple, nor alienated and unknown women. Instead, their pairing offers a charming corrective to the Cavellian conception of the couple.[2]

Notes

1. He points to the convent-hospital in *Letter from An Unknown Woman*; the figure of the aunt in *Gaslight*; and most significantly to the relationship of mutual recognition that Stella Dallas shares with Mrs. Morrison (Barbara O'Neil), her husband's lover and ultimately the stepmother of her daughter.

2. With thanks to Paul Deb for his generous editorship, and to Michele Devereaux and Lee Wallace for their wise and inspiring insights during the writing of this chapter.

Works Cited

Mahon, Áine. 2015. "Marriage and Moral Perfectionism in Siri Hustvedt and Stanley Cavell." *Textual Practice* 29 (4): 631–51. https://doi.org/10.1080/0950236X.2014.963142.

McGilligan, Patrick. 1997. *George Cukor: A Double Life*. St. Martin's Griffin Press.

Mulhall, Stephen. 2016. "Film and Philosophy: Digital Cinema and Moral Perfectionism." Paper presented at "The Real of Reality" conference, ZKM Karlsruhe, Nov 6, 2016.

Viefhues-Bailey, Ludger. 2011. "Releasing the Feminine Voice: A Cavellian Epistemology for the Philosophy of Religion." *Modern Theology* 27 (3): 452–61. https://doi.org/10.1111/j.1468-0025.2011.01687.x.

Wallace, Lee. 2020. *Reattachment Theory: Queer Cinema of Remarriage*. Duke University Press.

2

Asking for More than
As Good as It Gets

Daniel Varndell

O, how bold one gets when one is sure of being loved.

—Sigmund Freud, Letter to Martha Bernays,
his fiancée (June 27, 1882)

∾

A COMMON FEATURE OF THE seven films comprising the canon of remarriage comedies is a childishness in the estranged couple that masks, but also gives expression to and seeks to recover, the loss of innocence arising from their disunion. By working through this same childishness (from which much of the comedy is derived), the separated couple learns to recover the means to forgive one another, thereby opening them up to the possibility of reunion (see *PH*, 60, 54, 261). A key obstacle, noted Stanley Cavell, is the failure of one (or both) of the marital partners to give up on some private, narcissistic fantasy which resists the compromise required of a life shared. Here is the "metaphysical problem," as Cavell put it, of whether one can "trace the progress from narcissism and incestuous privacy to objectivity and the acknowledgement of otherness as the path and goal of human happiness; and since this happiness is expressed as marriage, we understand it as the final condition for individual and for social happiness, namely the achieving of one's adult self and the creation of the social" (102). Similarly, Leslie Fiedler described marriage as the search for "a reconciliation with the divided self, a truce between heart and head, but also for a compromise with society, an acceptance of responsibility and drudgery and dullness . . . [and] an acceptance of the status of a father" (1970, 315). For the modern American male (in particular) there is a tendency, Fiedler concluded, to identify always with Jack rather than the Giant—to be perennially "one of the boys," a fatherless man, eternal son of mommy (315). In other words: a tendency to cling to the undivided incestuous fantasy and renounce the perceived risks that come with adult relationships.

Beyond the core films comprising the classic remarriage comedies, more contemporary examples have continued to wrestle with the same "metaphysical problem." Such films often don't feature a marriage (let alone remarriage), but do "retain," as Cavell himself put it, "something like a remarriage surface" (*CF*, 343). As the misanthropic writer in James L. Brooks's *As Good as It Gets* (1997), Jack Nicholson wields his character's antisocial behavior disorder as a stick to fend off anyone who might draw him from his narcissistic privacy. His smirking superciliousness (trademark Nicholson) wards off the possibility of romance or friendship, thereby securing that privacy, and critics of the film have tended to read the character as an ogreish monster whose sting must be drawn for him to be accepted into the society he both repels and rejects. However, this Cavellian reading reveals a man more painfully aware of his outward disgrace than has been assumed, an awareness Brooks's camera captures as a testament to his inner grace. Beneath the "antic disposition,"[1] I see a contemporary version of Cavell's man-child—traumatized by his own father and desperate to transcend his own self-imposed blockade to social acceptance. In line with the course charted in the remarriage comedies, he must find and put into words (the right words, spoken rightly) just how the relationships which have endured his vituperative tongue sustain his world, and how incalculably damaging their loss would be.

Walk Out: Nicholson's Man-Children

Brooks uses Nicholson to present this "Jack" type in two of his most successful romantic comedies, both of which draw on Nicholson's star image from the 1970s as a man-child shirking his responsibilities to become a father (to become, in fact, his father). At the end of Bob Rafelson's *Five Easy Pieces* (1970), Nicholson's Bobby Dupea walks out on his pregnant girlfriend (Karen Black) after failing to find the words to account for himself and the life he has lived during a one-sided conversation with his dying father (William Challee). In Michelangelo Antonioni's *The Passenger* (1975), Nicholson's David Locke walks out on his family when he trades lives with a dead stranger, only to prove he is unable to outrun himself and his habits. In Brooks's films, however, Nicholson transcends these limitations. But rather than successfully "outrunning himself," he becomes "who he already was," as Cavell put it in his essay "The Good of Film" (*CF*, 333–48). Here, the "soul's journey to itself" wends its way in a "zigzag of discontinuous steps following the lead of what Emerson calls my "unattained but attainable self," a path that "projects no unique point of arrival but only a willingness for change" (337). D. N. Rodowick argues that we are only capable of articulating this willingness after we have already embraced it (2013, 594). In other words, the thought of self-improvement already implies that resisting change (at least as long as the mood carries us) is no longer an option. But simple dissatisfaction with one's limited life is not enough.

In Brooks's *Terms of Endearment* (1983), Nicholson plays Garrett Breedlove, a former astronaut who spends his early retirement chasing women half his age and resisting relationship ties and familial responsibility. After finding love with Aurora (Shirley MacLaine)—a woman his own age—Garrett walks out on her for making him feel "obligated" to her and her family, breaking her heart. But when tragedy strikes, Garrett is there for Aurora, and in the final scene he literally takes her wayward grandson under his (distinctly paternal) wing. Nicholson's less playful, more cruel side is interrogated in *As Good as It Gets*, in which he plays Melvin Udall—a successful romance novelist with obsessive-compulsive disorder (OCD), who is so fearful of disorder and contamination by others that he spurns anyone who approaches him by uttering vile, bigoted, and often hateful remarks.

As with Garrett, childlike Melvin is eventually transformed by a mothering woman who demonstrates the value of social contact and whose patience, acceptance, and capacity to forgive opens him to change.

The blows to Melvin's life come gradually, then suddenly (to recall Hemmingway). The first disruption is the pollution of his home when his gay neighbor, Simon (Greg Kinnear), is hospitalized after a brutal assault, leaving Melvin to care for Verdell, Simon's Brussels Griffon, who has a penchant for reliving himself in the communal stairwell. Melvin is disgusted by the mutt, which he earlier in the film attempted to lure into an elevator before stuffing down the garbage chute. However, instead of feeling disburdened after Simon collects his beloved pup, Melvin realizes he misses Verdell. Worse, the dog's absence from the apartment exposes his loneliness. It is tempting to see Melvin's affection for Verdell as the small end of the wedge cleaving open his Grinch-like heart (two sizes too small), but for me it highlights what Cavell called "those necessities we cannot, being human, fail to know. Except that nothing is more human than to deny them" (quoted in Rodowick 2013, 592). The difficulty for Melvin is to figure out how he can stop denying what he needs (and knows he needs) to break out of his cloistered life.

The second disruption to Melvin's routines occurs when the only waitress who will suffer his abrasive personality to serve him breakfast leaves her job to care for her sickly son, Spencer (Jesse James). Carol (Helen Hunt) tolerates and even appears to enjoy Melvin's bitter banter, taking his peccadilloes in her stride. Without her protection, however, Melvin quickly gets himself barred from the restaurant—his only link to the outside world. To get Carol back, Melvin sets up and pays for Spencer to have private medical care, which she—a working-class single mom—cannot afford. To her delight, Spencer's asthma soon clears, but Carol is perturbed by the thought that Melvin's generosity carries an ulterior motive. When she confronts him, Melvin unconvincingly claims he paid so Carol would return to work to wait on him. To make it clear, she emphatically declares that she will not (not ever—never!) sleep with him. Along with caring for his neighbor's dog, here is another good deed that brings Melvin pain.

As with *Terms of Endearment*, Nicholson trades on his star image in *As Good as It Gets*, playing the playboy hiding his insecurities behind that famous wry grin and sarcastic riposte.[2] If we are "chained away," wrote Cavell, "incomprehensively, maddeningly, from the possibility of a happy world, it is inevitable that the human conceives itself as limited" (*PH*, 73). This is the point to which Nicholson's characters typically arrive—at a perception of himself as lacking. But in Brooks's films, Nicholson's characters are brought to a different point of self-awareness. He neither scampers from his responsibilities (as Bobby does in *Easy Pieces*), nor is he left in despair (as Jake Gittes is at the close of *Chinatown* [Roman Polanski, 1974]). Instead, he arrives at a new kind of thinking. This is perfectly articulated in the moment Melvin bursts from a disappointing meeting with his psychiatrist into a waiting room filled with anxious patients, at whom he loudly complains, "What if this is as good as it gets!?" The answer to this, Melvin realizes in the film, is "No, there must be more." Cavell conceived such moments not as those in which human limitation is limply registered and understood but in which our finitude, our mortality, is boldly seized as an opportunity to change. Rather than demonstrating a lack, such a thought suggests a desire for more.

Smirking: Melvin's Two Faces

Inconsiderate thinking is often the sign of a discordant inner state which craves numbness.

—Nietzsche, *Human, All Too Human*

Leading up to his assault, Simon (a successful artist) pays a street hustler (Skeet Ulrich) to model for him in his apartment. After mistakenly assuming he was being paid for sex, the hustler now sits confused about what he is to do for his money. "What I do is watch," Simon explains. "You ever watch somebody who doesn't know that you're watching them? An old woman sitting on a bus or kids going to school or somebody just waiting—and you see this flash come over them and you know immediately that it has nothing to do with anything external because that hasn't changed. And when you see it, they're just sort of realer and they're more alive. I mean, you look at someone long enough, you discover their humanity." As Simon explains his creative vision, the young hustler's eyes glisten as he is unexpectedly overcome with emotion, revealing to Simon the glimpse of humanity he has been looking for (and must now draw).[3]

In his analysis of the moment, Robert McRuer points out that it is with Simon's words still echoing in our ears that Brooks cuts from this scene to a ground level shot of Melvin scurrying along the street while avoiding cracks in the sidewalk, with scant regard for fellow pedestrians. "The focus on his legs," McRuer writes, "by reducing him to his body parts, more efficiently objectifies him and highlights his condition" (2003, 92). The implication, writes McRuer, is three-fold. First, that Melvin's humanity is not yet visible. Second, that it is his disability, rather than his bigotry, that codes his inhumanity. And third, that Melvin's transformation will come. "The audience," McRuer wryly notes, "will see even Melvin's humanity by the end of the film" (93). It is a transformation, he concludes, that moves from disability to picture-perfect able-bodied heteronormativity. Eliding Melvin's bigotry with his OCD is all the worse, McRuer damningly concludes, for the fact that obsessives typically agonize over how their behavior impacts on others (103n28).[4] But if we really look at him (as the film invites us to—following on as it does from Simon's speech about looking), Melvin's condition as well as his bigotry can be read another way (not to say oppositely).

"A person may be said to be *in wrong face*," wrote Erving Goffman, "when information is brought forth in some way about his social worth which cannot be integrated, even with effort, into the line that is being sustained for him." Moreover, a person can be described as being "out of face" when he is in contact with others without having ready "a line of the kind participants in such situations are expected to take." In both of these situations, a person is likely to feel ashamed and inferior, his "manner and bearing may falter, collapse, and crumble." By contrast, when a person senses that he is "in face" he "typically responds with feelings of confidence and assurance." We are said to have "poise" if we can conceal or cover up a moral failure, but flounder ("lose face") when a moral lapse is revealed (Goffman 1972, 8). Melvin's face registers agitation and discomposure as his obsessional behavior overrides any maintenance of poise. He unselfconsciously whirls and leaps about the street like a dervish to avoid stepping on the cracks in the sidewalk. He stutters in conversations and stumbles in unplanned social encounters. Somewhat ironically, Melvin conceals any shame arising from these obsessive behaviors by deliberately breaking social mores—ironic because these are the very actions (offensive, rude, etc.) that would ordinarily cause one to lose face.

There is a disjunct between the "line" Melvin sustains for himself and the one society expects him to take. This is present from the very first time we see Melvin. An elderly woman (Bibi Osterwald—one of a number of classical Hollywood actresses taking up minor roles in the film) emerges from her apartment to proclaim her happiness that it is tulip season. However, her smile quickly sours and her lips curl to form the words "Son of a bitch" as she spies Melvin in the communal hallway. She beats a hasty retreat to the sanctity of her apartment and slams the door shut. The way she mouths those words—words, we suspect, that ordinarily do not cross her lips—recalls the snarled responses of the furious wedding guests when Ben (Dustin Hoffman) crashes the nuptials at the end of *The Graduate* (Mike Nichols, 1967).[5] Lips curl and countenances collapse at the mere sight of a man like Melvin the Ogre. While an individual's "social face" can be his "most personal possession and the center of his security and pleasure," wrote Goffman, "it is only on loan to him from society; it will be withdrawn unless he conducts himself in a way that is worthy of it" (1972, 10). If social mores fail, the societal fabric itself will fray. Melvin is not just a man who breaks social mores; he is the kind of man who breaks them, an S.O.B.[6]

That Melvin is an S.O.B is confirmed when Simon chummily (if a little suspiciously) asks Melvin if he has seen his missing puppy. Melvin lashes out with homophobic and racist slurs before twisting the verbal knife by smarmily wishing Simon luck finding Verdell. "I love the little fella," he sarcastically says with a smirk, to which Simon—the neighborly smile now wiped from his kind face—coldly responds, "You don't love anything, Mr. Udall." Scenes like this dominate the first third of the movie. It seems counterintuitive to say that Melvin is in face when being cruel to others—that he draws confidence and assurance in himself, not to say sadistic pleasure, when lapsing with respect to his social role—but this seems to be the case. And when he loses face, the effect is registered in the appalled countenances of others. To stop here, however, is to miss a dimension to Nicholson's performance that seems self-reflexively to comment on the actor's own face and its capacity to withstand and even absorb social censure.

Nicholson's grin, his ex-wife Susan Anspach once observed, is "like Clark Gable's used to be—it comes from within" (quoted in Thompson 1998, 9). Inside that famous grin, however, Peter Thompson identified an "inner smirk."[7] Nicholson himself said of his famous grin that it enabled him "to say the most horrible things to people's faces and have a smile on mine and not have it disrupt the proceedings" (9). It is a "wonderful" grin, to appropriate Rosalind Russell's comment in *His Girl Friday* (Howard Hawks, 1940), "in a loathsome sort of way." Coming from any other actor, wrote Roger Ebert in his review of *As Good as It Gets*, Melvin's hurtful slurs would "bring the film to an appalled halt" (1997). For the characters in the diegetic world, however, Melvin's grin lacks the unimpeachable quality that protects the star from reproach. While Nicholson's face seems capable of suspending what Goffman described as the "approved attributes," Melvin's face establishes him as "his own jailer," safe in his cell (1972, 10).

But if we watch closely, Melvin's face suggests that he does care—cares in fact very deeply—what those he offends think of him. To return to the opening scene with Simon—accompanied by his black friend, Frank (Cuba Gooding Jr.)—Melvin's face is classic Nicholson, and the barb about "loving the little fella" is finished off with a smirking *coup de grâce* (see Figure 2.1).

However, when Simon responds that Melvin doesn't love any-thing, Brooks cuts back to Melvin, who briefly looks down, apparently momentarily deflated by Simon's caustic rebuke (see Figure 2.2).

Figure 2.1. Melvin (Jack Nicholson) "in face" in *As Good as It Gets* (James L. Brooks, 1997). Digital frame enlargement.

Figure 2.2. Melvin (Jack Nicholson) "out of face" in *As Good as It Gets* (James L. Brooks, 1997). Digital frame enlargement.

It could be said that that I am overreaching here, that what this depicts is Melvin privately relishing his vicious victory over Simon. But every other example of Melvin being rude, offensive, or hurtful contains this same brief look of self-defeat at the reaction of those he insults. In a later scene, Simon accuses Melvin of being a "horror of a human being," at which Melvin's face similarly sags. His eyes glaze. He deflates.

These moments don't just offer a glimpse of Melvin with his guard down—they suggest that Melvin's guard *is* his bigotry. While the offensive remark usually tips the hand of the inner bigot, revealing a smirk no longer covered by the veil of civility, here "the bigot" is the social mask. There are a couple of good reasons for bearing this in mind. First, when we go backstage of Melvin's abusive public performances, he shows a grace and cultivation at odds with his coarseness and vulgarity (inside his apartment, for example, we see walls adorned with large canvasses of black bodies and we hear music by black musicians, pointedly belying his apparent racism). Second, it suggests another way to read the presentation of Melvin's OCD, since it is in these little moments of deflation that he registers an understanding of his own dis-ease. What Melvin cannot bear is the smiling face of the other, the face that opens up to him and threatens to open him up. His barbs seek to deface that opening, but at the same time he cannot bear wiping those smiles. It is a tragic double bind. In this, Melvin seems no less terrified of the open invitation of the smiling face, than of the danger suggested by the cracks in the sidewalk: both threaten to swallow him up.

For me, this goes to the heart of Cavell's meaning in *The Claim of Reason* (1979), where he argued that, "in judging (saying something true or false) you have to be able or willing to judge a contraction of the face as a wince, to recognize a smile as forced, to find a slap on the forehead to express the overcoming of stupidity by insight, a fist to the heart to express the overcoming of stiff-neckedness by contrition, a tone of voice to be that of assertion" (*CR*, 35). It is not that Melvin delights in hurting others, nor that he fails to express his own pain at the effect of his compulsive barbs. Rather, he cannot express clearly (or legibly) to the other why he spontaneously sabotages every opportunity of opening up to them, just as the couples in comedies of remarriage cruelly tease one another instead of saying how they feel. Any truthful gesture that might inspire some sympathy of fellow feeling is hidden. It is not a question of how Melvin can become kind to others but of how he can allow his goodness to be seen by them.

Confessing: Opening Up

We must do violence to our thoughts.

—David Hume, *Treatise of Human Nature*

In one memorable scene, Melvin is accosted by a female fan (Julie Benz) of his fiction who earnestly gushes over his facility for writing what women think and feel (touching her fingertips to head and chest). Anxiously casting around for an escape route, Melvin gasps that "This is a nightmare," and wills the elevator to hurry. Undeterred, the admirer asks how he (a man) can write women so well, at which Melvin sneers, "I just think of a man, and take away reason and accountability." With hurt and confusion etched onto her young face, the fan quickly retreats as Melvin practically leaps into the now waiting elevator, clearly unsettled by the encounter. Contrast this with the moment Tracy (Katharine Hepburn) discovers Mike (James

Stewart) in the library in *The Philadelphia Story* (George Cukor, 1940). Her eyes still moist from reading his moving prose, Tracy, sighing, says, "You talk so big and tough and then you write like this. Which is which?" Both, he tries to answer—but she's got his number. "No, I believe you put the toughness on to save your skin. I know a little about that." Melvin certainly knows the value of a toughened skin, but unlike Mike he adds an additional prophylaxis: hurtful speech. To scorn his admirer, Melvin is willing to spurn his fiction—effectively making out that his novelistic truths are lies.

The problem with Carol is she doesn't appear to have read any of Melvin's books. What, then, does she see in him? Carol must be alert to, and capable of judging (to recall Cavell), the truth betrayed by Melvin's unintended gestures (gestures ordinarily tipped only to the film's audience). If Melvin's outer disgrace can be squared by intimations of some inner grace, observable by those with keen enough vision, then what remains to be seen is whether he can express that gracefulness directly, not just in dialogue written for characters in books Carol won't read. Something like this is at stake in *It Happened One Night* (Frank Capra, 1934), in which Peter (Clarke Gable) struggles to put together his perception and his imagination to connect the body and soul of the woman, Ellie (Claudette Colbert), with whom he has fallen in love. The gap is represented by a makeshift barrier keeping the pair—forced to bunk together while hitching a ride to New York—decent, in the colloquial sense of the term. Unable (because he is too gentlemanly) to transgress this barrier, Peter must imagine Ellie, such that "his capacity for imagination," wrote Cavell, "becomes his ability to imagine *her*," which he described as the film's "framing of the problem of other minds" (see *PH*, 109). In *As Good As It Gets*, it is Carol who must imagine the man that Melvin wishes he could become, but the danger of crossing the boundary is not imaginary. This is demonstrated by two scenes focusing on Carol and Simon.

In the philosophy of Emmanuel Levinas, an encounter with another who forces me from my privacy is experienced as "transcendental violence," on which Leonard Lawlor writes: "I am unable to stop what is coming and coming in," hence a modicum of violence exists in all social encounters, leaving me open to real bloodshed, to "real intrusion, real escape, and real violence" (2016, 102). This violence is literally expressed when the hustler modelling for Simon arranges for his pals to rob the artist, only for Simon to disturb them and suffer a grievous assault which leaves him badly injured and ashamed (for having been so naively open). After waking up in the hospital, his friend Frank holds up a mirror. After a lengthy silence, Simon chokes at his reflection: "Where'd I go?" The moment recalls Goffman, who quoted a patient struggling to come to terms with seeing his disfigured reflection for the first time, whom he regarded as a "stranger," a "little, pitiable, hideous figure, and a face that became, as I stared at it, painful and blushing with shame" (quoted in Goffman 1990, 19) (see Figure 2.3).

Simon is not alone in suffering from his openness to others. While Carol is not subject to physical violence or bloodshed, she is humiliated after returning home to have sex with a hot young date (Randall Batinkoff). Things don't go according to plan, however. As they passionately fumble on the sofa, the date finds a glob of her son's vomit. He leaves in disgust, claiming this is "too much 'reality' for a Friday night." Crushed, Carol later confesses to her mom (Shirley Knight) that without Spencer to worry about (his asthma having cleared up after Melvin's intervention), she fears she will remain alone, unloved, and unlovable. "Who needs these thoughts?" she despairs (see Figure 2.4).

For Melvin, the risk of transcendental violence—let alone real, actual bloodshed—is already much too great. Brooks contrasts his

Figure 2.3. Where'd I go? Simon (Greg Kinnear) in *As Good as It Gets* (James L. Brooks, 1997). Digital frame enlargement.

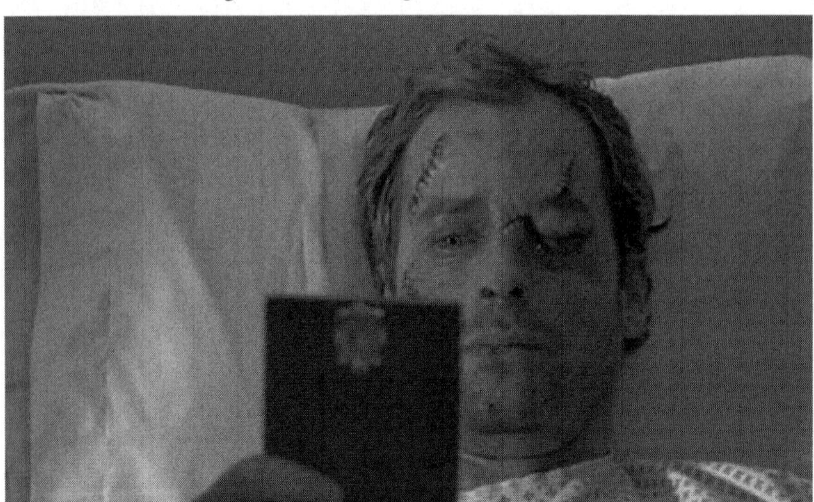

Figure 2.4. Lonely thoughts. Carol (Helen Hunt) in *As Good as It Gets* (James L. Brooks, 1997). Digital frame enlargement.

protective closedness with Simon and Carol's wounded openness. When Simon knocks on his door early on in the film, Melvin lashes out, warning him never to knock again. "Not even," he snaps, "if you hear the sound of a thud from my home and one week later, there's a smell coming from there that can only be a decaying body . . . even then, don't . . . come . . . knocking."[8] Don't bother me, even if I'm dead! The moment distinguishes Melvin from the other two as suffering what John Steiner calls a "psychic retreat," in which the ego is protected by maintaining one's "narcissistic pride." When patients in psychic retreat begin to recover, Steiner writes, they must emerge from their protective privacy and risk a corresponding "narcissistic humiliation." "Having felt hidden and protected, [the patient] now feels conspicuous and exposed to a gaze that makes him vulnerable to humiliation" (Steiner 2011, 25). This sense of growing self-consciousness links back to the first part of my argument, since a patient will often respond to feeling vulnerable by adopting a "superior position from which he could look down on others" (25), readable as a defensive, preemptive, strike. But recovery (whatever that means) requires seeing others and being seen by others. For Cavell, the release from what he called a "circle of vengeance" depends on "acknowledgement" (*PH*,

109), which often takes the form of telling one's story to another person (willing to hear it).

The moment of Cavellian "acknowledgement" in *As Good as It Gets* comes when the trio—each suffering their own pain, in their own unique way—take a trip to Baltimore, the film's equivalent of the journey into the green world.[9] Saddled with crippling medical bills, Simon must either go to Baltimore to beg money off the homophobic father who disowned him or face losing his home. Because Simon is still recovering, Frank presses Melvin into driving him, and Melvin convinces Carol to come along by reminding her of the generousness of his gift and her (nonsexual) obligation to him. It is on this trip that Melvin willingly risks exposing himself to transcendental violence. The trip to Baltimore increases, to paraphrase Goffman, not the chances taken by him but the chance that he will be obliged to take chances. He risks exposure to the "naked little spasms of the self" where one finds action and character (Goffman 1972, 269–70). Melvin could have said no to Frank, just as Simon and Carol could have said no to him. Likewise, Melvin doesn't need to invite Carol (who represents yet one more risky other to whom he might be fatally exposed). But all three say yes.

On the drive, Carol and Simon form an early alliance against Melvin's scathing tongue, and Simon soon opens up to Carol about his paternal estrangement. His father beat him as a child, he tells them, for sketching his mother in the nude, and later rejected him as a teen for coming out as gay (his father paid him to leave home). Sitting in the backseat, Melvin watches as Carol sympathizes with Simon, their bond cemented with a tender embrace. "You like sad stories?" he blurts. "Wanna hear mine?" Melvin tells them his reclusive father would hit him with a yardstick for making mistakes on the piano. We don't learn any more about Melvin's childhood, but from this brief insight his father seems to have been similarly obsessive, controlling, and punishing. It is tempting to read Melvin's piano playing against Bobby Dupea's in *Easy Pieces*, in which the piano also signifies unresolved paternal conflict. In this scene in *As Good as It Gets*, however, Melvin is outside of the quick bond that has formed between Simon and Carol. Brooks cuts to Melvin in closeup to show his empathy with Simon's sad story, but the impact of his own childhood trauma is not felt with the same weight. The scene ends with Melvin's defenses (and Carol's hackles), raised once more.

The scene reveals another facet of Melvin's emergence from psychic retreat. I have already explored how sensitivity to shame and humiliation and the fear of being looked down on drive him to humiliate, mock, and ridicule others. But Steiner also suggests that the risk of seeing and being seen carries the risk of envying and being envied. Envy draws us from our privacy by coveting something besides ourselves, as if alone we are not enough. More problematic is the neurotic thought that if I possess something good, others will envy me and wish to destroy what I have (or become). Envy impedes the urge to improve, and to be seen improving, and the acknowledgement from others this improvement brings (see Steiner 2011, 74). The link to perfectionism seems clear enough. Cavell wrote that "moral perfectionism" is the demand we place on ourselves to become "intelligible to one another," to move "not from coarseness to sophistication, or from commonness to prominence, but from loss to recovery, or [. . .] from despair to interest, or [. . .] from chatter to speech" (*CF*, 339–40). When Melvin finally finds the right words (as we will see), he speaks with good grace and perfect composure, standing in a light enabling first Simon, and then Carol, to see (that is, to recognize) him as the man he has hitherto only been able to write.

Smiling: Melvin's Acknowledgement

Indeed, when in doubt, play a smile.

—Erving Goffman, *Relations in Public: Microstudies of the Public Order*

The film's most Cavellian moment occurs when they arrive in Baltimore and Carol insists Melvin take her dancing. After speeding to a late-night suit retailer for a jacket to comply with the strict dress code (having first been turned away at the door—an early blow to his confidence), Melvin returns, somewhat flustered, to the restaurant. The floor manager offers to get Carol's attention, but Melvin declines, saying he'd prefer to watch her from across the room. He calms down and becomes engrossed in her smiling face. When she finally notices him, Melvin lights up, gives a big, warm smile back and waves. It is an unselfconscious smile, without a trace of mockery or scorn. But when they sit, Melvin struggles to make small talk. He is rude about Carol's dress, and she threatens to walk out unless he pays her a compliment, "Now . . . and mean it!" Melvin agitatedly orders food (orders for them both, hollering their choices across the room). Suddenly, he brightens. "I got a real great compliment for you," he beams, "and . . . it's true." Carol worries aloud that something "awful" is about to happen, but Melvin tells her not to be so pessimistic. He admits that when he was diagnosed with his "ailment" (as he calls it), he was prescribed pills. "I hate pills," he explains, "*hate*, I'm using the word 'hate' here, about *pills*—hate!" We cut to Carol looking confused. Melvin continues, telling her that the morning after she came to his apartment to make clear she would never sleep with him (the memory of which leaves Carol squirming with embarrassment), he started taking the hated pills. Melvin reclines in his chair, an air of triumph in his posture (as though the meaning of his "compliment" could not be clearer). Still bemused, however, Carol asks how this is a compliment for *her*, at which Melvin leans in and, with that same warm smile, says, "You make me want to be a better man." The camera zooms in on Carol who, after momentarily struggling for words, says, "That's probably the best compliment of my life."

The moment is soon soured, however, as Melvin struggles to sustain the small talk that follows. Burying his head in his hands, he complains it is too "exhausting" to speak this way, prompting Carol to sidle over to him and kiss him on the lips. Shocked, Melvin bumbles about her not owing him such affection, and she responds that the kiss wasn't payment—adding, "Now that your soft little underbelly is exposed, why did you bring me here?" Melvin falters ("Er . . . er . . . many reasons . . ."). "Tell me, even if you're scared," she softly says. "Scared!?" he exclaims, petrified. "It's okay," she soothes, "If you ask me, I'll say 'yes.'" Melvin stutters, then blurts, "One thought . . . if you had sex with Simon . . ." She recoils, then explodes. "Like I'm a . . . what?! And I owe you . . . what?!" Melvin quickly tries to salvage their date, but he's blown it. She storms out and the scene ends with Melvin staring dejectedly into space (another of his deflated expressions). But his look of defeat does not follow his usual mocking, scornful grin. We realize immediately what Carol has missed: that Melvin was not just soft, but really exposed; not a little scared, but terrified. The preceding warm smile, a true smile, was the smile of a man opening up.

We've seen Melvin smile like this before in the film. Shortly after taking responsibility for Simon's dog, he sat at his usual table in the restaurant, staring miserably at the dog tethered up outside. In response to Carol's shock that he has a dog, Melvin explains he was bullied into caring for it. "Aren't you worried someone might take it?" she asks, at which Melvin screws his face up and groans, "Well, not until now, for Christ's sake!" He quickly moves from his cherished table (from his privacy) to take up another one, closer to the door. Surprised he has moved from his coveted spot, Carol smiles to herself as she registers the break with one of Melvin's obsessive habits (which, earlier in the film, he'd protected with vile antisemitic remarks to a Jewish couple occupying "his" table). Distracted now as he watches some neighborhood kids pet the puppy outside, Melvin hears one of them gush, "I love his little face, it's so cute!" Brooks cuts right back to Melvin's little face, in close-up, unselfconsciously beaming (see Figure 2.5).

It is a moment that has not garnered much critical attention, yet, as with his smile at Carol on their date, the expression animates Melvin's face in a manner consistent with the demeanor of the man described by Emerson, quoted by Cavell, who, "by the moral quality radiating from his countenance [. . .] may abolish all considerations of magnitude, and in his manners equal the majesty of the world."

Figure 2.5. Melvin (Jack Nicholson) smiles in *As Good as It Gets* (James L. Brooks, 1997). Digital frame enlargement.

Such a man, Emerson wrote, carries "the holiday in his eye [. . .] if need be, calm, serious, and fit to stand the gaze of millions" (quoted in *PH*, 43).[10] It is a smile without a trace of a smirk or the stain of a sneer, the image of a man who knows, rather than hopes, there is more to life in love. If only he can find the right words to say what he knows to Carol (who, despite their calamitous dinner date, we know is ready to say yes) (see Figure 2.6).

After Melvin's blunder at the restaurant, we find him languishing at the bar drowning his sorrows, explaining his faux pas to a sympathetic barman. "I got nervous, I screwed up—said the wrong thing," he complains. Sighing, he points out that if he hadn't screwed up, he could be in bed "right now with a woman who, you make her laugh, you got a life." The correct answer to Carol's question, "Why did you bring me here?" was that watching her laugh makes him feel alive. (Likewise, the answer to her earlier question about why he paid for Spencer's healthcare wasn't, "So you would come back to work and wait on me," but something closer to, "So I could see and speak with you every day.") Like so many other characters played by Nicholson, however, Melvin simply cannot say "I love you" to the person he loves.[11] Unlike his previous characters, however, as Melvin he does find the right words.

Figure 2.6. The holiday in Melvin's (Jack Nicholson's) eye in *As Good as It Gets* (James L. Brooks, 1997). Digital frame enlargement.

On the drive back to NYC, the atmosphere in the car is arctic. No one speaks. Melvin attempts to repair the damage caused by his restaurant blunder by playing a mixtape labelled "For Emergency Use Only," which opens with Nat King Cole's rendition of "(I Love You) For Sentimental Reasons."[12] This tape, we presume, responds to the emergency of being unable to find (or to speak) the right words. If Melvin can't say it himself, at least Cole might sing it on his behalf. But Carol is too mad. She insists he turn the music off, ignoring his protest that this one "has meaning." Melvin is further crushed when, on their return to New York, Carol informs him she wants nothing more to do with him. Simon attempts to mediate, but she won't be mollified.

After convincing Simon, who is now homeless after refusing to beg money from his homophobic father, to live with him in his home, Simon tells Melvin that he loves him.[13] He marvels at the transformation in Melvin. But how to get Carol to see it, too? Simon convinces him to go to her. "The best thing you have going for you is your willingness to humiliate yourself!" Simon says. A modern hero, wrote Cavell, must be willing "to suffer a certain indignity, as if what stands in the way of change, psychologically speaking, is a false dignity." Such suffering elevates the social, he concluded, "as if the dignity of one part of society is the cause of the opposite part's indignity," which is "a sure sign of a disordered state of affairs" (*PH*, 8). Realizing he has nothing to lose and everything to gain, Melvin goes to Carol. Stopping at the door, he registers with astonishment that he had forgotten to lock it (too busy caring for Simon, just as he'd been too busy caring for Simon's pup to think about losing "his" table at the restaurant). Melvin realizes what Cavell described as the necessity to "act in order to make things happen"—say, to see the laughing face of the woman you love—"and to act from within the world, within your connection with others, forgoing the wish for a place outside from which to view and to direct your fate." There is no external authority from whom Melvin can secure such a connection in the world (just as the patient in psychoanalysis must ultimately reject the analyst's supposed authority and undertake to go on alone). "You cannot wait for the perfected community to be presented," Cavell concluded. "And yet, in matters of the heart, to make things happen, you must let them happen" (109). Melvin goes to Carol, but not to seize or win her, as in the sexist fantasy. He goes to expose himself to her judgement and offer himself as an object worthy of her notice. "Her worth is no longer in need of proof," wrote Cavell, "her treasure, which she more and more fears may have been lost, is merely hidden" (78). And Melvin (to paraphrase Cavell) knows this because he seeks it, and he will not be lost in the seeking (at least not this time).

Kissing: A Remarriage Surface

Walk in newness of life.

—*King James Bible*, Romans 6:4

As a teenager prone to some relatively mild but still fatiguing obsessional traits (compulsive hand washing, avoidance of paving cracks, extended procrastination, and so on), I admit on first viewing this film that I cheered Melvin all the way into Carol's arms and celebrated the apparent curative effects of their kiss—as when Jean Marais's beast kisses Josette Day's Belle at the end of Jean Cocteau's *La Belle et la Bête* (1946). But looking at the ending today, especially in light of reading Cavell, I find the conclusion more complex, more ambivalent. Having gone to her, Melvin and Carol reach an impasse at her apartment. She still cannot set aside his character flaws any more than he can really claim to be incapable of saying hurtful or bigoted things to defend his wounded ego. He proposes they take a walk to a local bakery which, despite the hour (it is *very* early in the morning), will soon open to sell fresh bread. As they walk, Melvin begins to hum the Nat King Cole tune he had to abort during the ride back from Baltimore. I still really want you to hear this, he says, and begins crooning: "And darling, I'm never lonely, whenever you're in sight . . ." Carol smiles, but her delight is short-lived as Melvin distractedly walks around a lamppost to avoid the cracks in the sidewalk. Whatever "this" is, she tells him, it is not going to work. Deflated, Melvin tells her she is the greatest woman alive, and only he sees her kindness. "This makes me feel better," he adds with a smile, "about myself." Then he (somewhat awkwardly) kisses her. Still not satisfied, he tells her he'd like another try, and, sure enough, the second time around—and with Hans Zimmer's score rising—the romantic moment appears sealed. It is the moment about which Roger Ebert complained: the film "creates memorable people," he moaned, "but is not quite willing to follow them down unconventional paths." Rather, "they're dragged toward the happy ending, screaming and kicking all the way" (1997). Likewise, for Mark D. Rubinfeld the film cynically uses the "key kiss and the happy ending to redeem its hateful hero, reaffirm its sacrificial heroine, and reverse the potential of its earlier ideological challenges" (2001, 198n10). A more progressive ending, Rubinfeld suggests, would have been what he calls "self-actualization through uncoupling," which would have challenged the "relevance and benevolence of the institution of marriage" itself, valorizing the woman's capacity to flourish independently from the man (113).[14]

But a closer look at the film's very final shot suggests that the maligned happy ending (a concession, nay capitulation, Rubinfeld says, to pressure from the studio), is more ambivalent or unstable than has been suggested. As they walk off arm in arm, we cut to Melvin and Carol's feet. But rather than step onto the highly patterned paving, Melvin's feet leave the shot, and as the camera pans upwards to pick the couple up, we clearly see he has stepped on to the larger slabs, enabling him to go on avoiding the cracks. Brooks does not track them with the camera as they walk down the street. They stop as the lights go on in the bakery—time for fresh rolls. Opening the door for Carol, however, Melvin must step aside to let one of the employees through. "Excuse us," he says, before looking down to realize he has inadvertently stepped on one of the cracks in the patterned pavement. Still framed in a static long shot, we see Melvin raise an eyebrow to himself before smiling again as he follows Carol into the bakery.

Now, this raised eyebrow connotes something of the final expression on Cary Grant's face at the end of *Bringing Up Baby* (Howard Hawks, 1938), an expression that bothered Cavell for being somewhat unreadable. The ambiguity of this final look, Cavell suggested, was the film's final lesson: here is a character still in doubt about his own right to happiness, of his right even to pursue it (*PH*, 131). And what right has Melvin to find happiness with Carol? This bigot, this man much older than she, who makes her feel so badly about herself (and is likely to do so again) . . . As in *Baby* (albeit with a gender reversal), Carol is in the position of David, who must justify remaining with the madcap heiress (Katharine Hepburn) despite her unruliness. For Cavell, the only satisfactory answer is that the problem compels us, the spectators of the film, either to accept their union "hypnotically," as it were, or to question it (to question, or at least to think about, the idea of marriage). In any case, the responsibility is David's/Carol's/ours, and we must embrace it (132). Such endings are more precarious in their balancing, as Katherina Glitre puts it, of "total anarchy and stable resolution" (2006, 62) that, *pace* the critics who read such ambivalence as evidence of the genre's conservatism,[15] emphasizes instead something more radical about (re)marriage: the recognition that the couple cannot ever "finish up" at this point. Rather, they "keep on playing, keep on reinventing themselves, and keep on learning to love each other" (Glitre 2006, 62–63). In that final moment, Melvin not only demonstrates grace as he pirouettes with Carol to enter the bakery, as he leads her to enter before him and steps aside to allow the worker to pass; with his smile he seems to announce "no contest," to confirm the work he must still do, must go on doing to sustain a viable image of himself in the eyes of this woman and the society to which he can now belong.

For me, Melvin's arched eyebrow (another quintessential expression of Nicholson's famous face) exemplifies Northrop Frye's observation that happy endings are not inevitable in romantic comedies because they are true but because they are desirable. And if such endings are brought about by manipulation, then it is because "something gets born at the end of comedy, and the watcher of birth is a member of a busy society" (Frye 1957, 170). This is what I take Cavell to have meant when he identified *As Good as It Gets* as a contemporary film with a remarriage surface, for Brooks's film literally ends with a couple of hurt people breaking bread with one another (the literal meaning of "companion"). By opening up, they risk being hurt again. But then again, perhaps they will survive, even thrive together. Some risks are worth taking.

Notes

1. After Hamlet, qtd. from Shakespeare, *Hamlet*, 1.5.172. Reference is to act, scene, and line.

2. Peter Thompson notes that Nicholson was too-easily identified in the popular press with the misogynistic heels he often played in the seventies, most notoriously in *Carnal Knowledge* (Mike Nichols, 1971) (Thompson

1998, 119–23). By contrast, Brooks celebrated Nicholson's performance in *Terms of Endearment* for not allowing his vanity to get in the way of playing a potentially unlikeable character. See James L. Brooks, interviewed by Kenneth Turan (Brooks and Turan 1984, 22).

3. For this viewer, a recent experience of watching Gus van Sant's *My Own Private Idaho* (1991) intensified the emotional reaction of the hustler to Simon's words in this scene.

4. As Paul Cefalu writes, "obsessives typically worry, even in the face of countervailing evidence, that they either have or will hurt those around them" (2009, 49). Unlike McRuer, Cefalu is among several critics who view the depiction of OCD in *As Good as It Gets* much more positively. See also Levine (2013) as well as Tripathi et al (2017).

5. Geoffrey Hughes points out that already by the early twentieth century, "son of a bitch" had been "dephlogisticated" in American linguistic usage and was by the late twentieth century practically a term of endearment, especially among men—but only when delivered in the correct way (for example, with a wink or a nudge). In both of these examples, however, the term is infused with venom, and restores to the epithet its older, more pejorative meaning (perhaps especially coming from the mouths of women, for whom "bitch" was historically "the most offensive appellation that can be given to an English woman") (Hughes 1991, 166–69).

6. "To *be* a given kind of person," wrote Goffman, "is not merely to possess the required attributes, but also to sustain the standards of conduct and appearance that one's social grouping attaches thereto." Social status, position, and place, he concluded, is "not a material thing, to be possessed and then displayed," but "a pattern of appropriate conduct, coherent, embellished, and well articulated" (1972, 81). See also his *Relations in Public* (1971, 97–99).

7. Paul McDonald writes that by exaggerating his grin as the Joker in *Batman* (1989), Tim Burton produced an "excessive display of Jack Nicholson-ness." (McDonald 1998, 198).

8. Nicholson reprises the withering and menacing sarcasm with which his character rebuked his wife (Shelley Duvall) for interrupting him while typing in *The Shining* (Stanley Kubrick, 1980).

9. The "Green World," wrote Northrop Frye, is where "life and love" triumph "over the wasteland" (1957, 182).

10. Cavell uses this quote as an epigraph to *Pursuits of Happiness* beneath an image of Cary Grant in *The Awful Truth* (Leo McCarey, 1937), whose character beams as his ex-wife (Irene Dunne) dances awkwardly with her partner.

11. When his pregnant girlfriend asks if he loves her in *Easy Pieces*, all Bobby can think to reply is, "What do you think?" When Aurora declares that she still loves Garrett in *Terms of Endearment*, he looks on awkwardly

and stammers for a bit, before admitting (with Nicholson's trademark toothy grin), "I don't know what else to say except my stock answer: 'I love you too, kid.'" (With this response, at least Garrett won't empty the sentiment by reducing it to a cliché.)

12. Written by Ivory "Deek" Watson and Willie "Pat" Best (1945).

13. It is difficult not to read this moment as echoing Cavell's statement that while marriage isn't necessarily incompatible with children, they nonetheless appear as intruders, such that parents are obliged to "make them welcome, to make room for them, to make them be at home, hence to transform one's idea of home" (*PH*, 59). In *As Good as It Gets*, Simon seems to have reclaimed the incestuous object of his mother—sublimated in the form of his new muse, Carol, whom he sketched nude while in Baltimore. He has also sublimated his bad father into a good one (the somewhat reformed Melvin). This reading only seems to reinforce Kyle Stevens's convincing and damning analysis of the representation of queer desire in the film, which he claims is not only excluded but used to legitimize heterosexual love on the basis of its exclusion (2009, 144). Like Stevens, I find this aspect of the film difficult to excuse.

14. Even the more generous readings of the ending struggle to wholly redeem it. Thomas E. Wartenberg regards Melvin and Carol as an example of what he calls an "unlikely couple"—subversive because their relationship is more uneven, more hesitant, more retreating, and even more incoherent than critics tend to acknowledge (1999, 233). In a similar vein, Jonathan Rosenbaum (a champion of Brooks's films), concludes that *As Good as It Gets* deflects criticism because it presents "profound, troubled, often contradictory" characters asking ethical questions about "performance, familial obligation, romance, and class" (2019).

15. As does Shumway, one of Cavell's most vociferous critics (1991).

Works Cited

Brooks, James L., and Kenneth Turan. 1984. "On His Own 'Terms.'" *Film Comment* 20 (2): 18–23.

Cefalu, Paul. 2009. "What's So Funny about Obsessive-Compulsive Disorder?" *PMLA/Publications of the Modern Language Association of America* 124 (1): 44–58. https://doi.org/10.1632/pmla.2009.124.1.44.

Ebert, Roger. 1997. "As Good as It Gets." *RogerEbert.com*, December 22, 1997. https://www.rogerebert.com/reviews/as-good-as-it-gets-1997.

Fiedler, Leslie A. 1970. *Love and Death in the American Novel*. Paladin.

Frye, Northrop. 1957. *Anatomy of Criticism: Four Essays*. Princeton University Press.

Glitre, Kathrina. 2006. *Hollywood Romantic Comedy: States of the Union, 1934–65*. Manchester: Manchester University Press.

Goffman, Erving. 1971. *Relations in Public: Microstudies of the Public Order*. Basic Books.

Goffman, Erving. 1972. *Interaction Ritual: Essays on Face-to-Face Behavior*. Allan Lane.

Goffman, Erving. 1972. 1990. *Stigma: Notes on the Management of Spoiled Identity*. Penguin Books.

Hughes, Geoffrey. 1991. *Swearing: A Social History of foul Language, Oaths and Profanity in English*. Blackwell.

Lawlor, Leonard. 2016. *From Violence to Speaking Out: Apocalypse and Expression in Foucault, Derrida and Deleuze*. Edinburgh University Press.

Levine, Ronnie. 2013. "As Good as It Gets." *Group* 37 (3): 251–53. https://doi.org/10.13186/group.37.3.0251.

McDonald, Paul. 1998. "Reconceptualising Stardom." In *Stars*, by Richard Dyer and Paul McDonald. New edition. British Film Institute.

McRuer, Robert. 2003. "As Good as It Gets: Queer Theory and Critical Disability." *GLQ: A Journal of Lesbian and Gay Studies* 9 (1–2): 79–105. https://doi.org/10.1215/10642684-9-1-2-79.

Rodowick, D. N. 2013. "The Value of Being Disagreeable." *Critical Inquiry* 39 (3): 592–613. https://doi.org/10.1086/670047.

Rosenbaum, Jonathan. 2019. "James L. Brooks." In *Cinematic Encounters 2: Portraits and Polemics*. University of Illinois Press.

Rubinfeld, Mark. 2001. *Bound to Bond: Gender, Genre, and the Hollywood Romantic Comedy*. Prager.

Shumway, David R. 1991. "Screwball Comedies: Constructing Romance, Mystifying Marriage." *Cinema Journal* 30 (4): 7–23. https://doi.org/10.2307/1224884.

Steiner, John. 2011. *Seeing and Being Seen: Emerging from a Psychic Retreat*. Routledge.

Stevens, Kyle. 2009. "What a Difference a Gay Makes: Marriage in the 1990s Romantic Comedy." In *Falling in Love Again: Romantic Comedy in Contemporary Cinema*, edited by Stacey Abbott and Deborah Jermyn. I. B. Tauris.

Thompson, Peter. 1998. *Jack Nicholson: The Life and Times of an Actor on the Edge*. Mainstream Publishing Projects.

Tripathi, Manjul et al. 2017. "Jack Nicholson: A Reel and Real-Life Contribution to Neurosciences." *World Neurosurgery* 101 (May): 718–21. https://doi.org/10.1016/j.wneu.2016.11.081.

Wartenberg, Thomas E. 1999. *Unlikely Couples: Movie Romance as Social Criticism*. Westview Press.

3

Contesting Marriage

My Best Friend's Wedding

SANDRA LAUGIER

*P*URSUITS OF *HAPPINESS* (1981), one of Stanley Cavell's earliest books, was published in French thirty years ago, in 1993, by *Cahiers du cinéma,* and has been recently reissued in paperback (Cavell and Laugier, 2017). Even before its publication, the book had already attained a cult status, gaining wide influence when it appeared. The subject of numerous reviews in the French press, it led to the multiplication of mentions of the remarriage comedy genre, recognized by critics and viewers alike in new films such as *Eyes Wide Shut* (Stanley Kubrick, 1999). It should be noted that the corpus of comedies analyzed in *Pursuits of Happiness* had been known and broadcast in France since the 1930s, while films like *Bringing Up Baby* (Howard Hawks, 1938), *The Philadelphia Story* (George Cukor, 1940), and *His Girl Friday* (Howard Hawks, 1940), are regularly shown in "Art et Essai" cinemas. Latin Quarter cinemas also often host so-called "Cavell Weeks," screening these remarriage comedies. Thus, the function of the Cavellian genre as a tool of moral and public education has been realized in the world, serving as a reading grid for subsequent films, giving viewers the pleasure of discovering for themselves new variations on the genre, whether in French auteur cinema (*De rouille et d'os* [*Rust and Bone*; Jacques Audiard, 2012] and *Les fantômes d'Ismaël* [*Ismael's Ghosts*; Arnaud Desplechin, 2017,]); brilliant recent Spanish films (like *Volvereis* [*The Other Way Around*]; Jonás Trueba, 2024); disaster films (*The Abyss* [James Cameron, 1989], *The Day After Tomorrow* [Roland Emmerich, 2004], and *War of the Worlds* [Steven Spielberg, 2005]); and, of course, in romantic comedies, a major genre that has taken over from remarriage comedies. The genre has also influenced TV series (*Dream On, How I Met Your Mother, The Affair*), even if the theme of remarriage is far less present here than in cinema—Cavell appears to have been right in identifying it as a feature of the cinematic medium itself. For Cavell, this pedagogical dimension of the genre is linked to the moral perfectionism expressed in the classic Hollywood corpus, extending beyond the seven films studied in *Pursuits of Happiness*. When he envisages the continuation of the remarriage genre, it is quite systematically along ethical lines. The comedies of remarriage determine what Cavell calls "the good of film": what cinema knows about goodness and what it can impart on us. The questions that remain, then, are: what values cinema can transmit today, and whether films can still perform this function.

In this chapter, I will first analyze the key characteristics of the remarriage genre that endow it with the power of interpretation, but also production. I will then explore how Cavell extends the genre to romantic comedies and films about young couples. Lastly, I will examine a romantic comedy that takes up the genre in an original way, staking its reception on the viewer's expectations of a remarriage comedy, and which thereby produces a powerful reflection on the ordinary, thus returning to the source of a remarriage comedy.

Genre, the Foundation of Popular Culture

How can we imagine continuing to grow after the end of childhood? Cavell's philosophy defines growth—once childhood and physical growth are over—as the capacity to change. This capacity is at work in Cavell's favored object of study, the apparently minor genre of remarriage comedies, which stage characters' mutual education and their transformation through separation and reunion: "In this light, philosophy becomes the education of grownups [. . .]. The anxiety in teaching, in serious communication, is that I myself require education. And for grownups, this is not natural growth, but *change*" (*CR*, 125). Cavell also gives this philosophical enterprise the outdated name "moral education," or "pedagogy," as in the subtitle of his *Cities of Words* (2004). For Cavell, whose childhood and youth were influenced by Hollywood movies, the culture in question is popular cinema. The educational value of popular culture is not merely anecdotal. Indeed, it seems to define what is meant by both "popular" and "culture" (in the sense of *Bildung*) in the term "popular culture." Within such a perspective, the vocation of popular culture is the moral education of a public, rather than the establishment and valorization of a socially targeted corpus. What Cavell claimed in the 1970s for mainstream Hollywood cinema has been transferred to other practices and bodies of work, such as television series, which have taken up cinema's role in educating adolescents and adults, if not replacing it (Laugier 2023; LaRocca and Laugier 2023).

Popular culture turns out to be a site for "the education of grownups," who, being exposed to it, revert to a form of education and cultivation of the self: subjective improvement (perfectionism); more precisely, a subjectivization that takes place through sharing and commenting on ordinary material woven into ordinary life. It is in this sense that Robert Warshow writes "we are all self-made men" and that cinema, for Warshow and Stanley Cavell, is at the heart of popular culture. As Warshow puts it, "Such a critique finds its best opportunity in the movies, which are the most highly developed and most engrossing of the popular arts, and which seem to have an almost unlimited power to absorb and transform the discordant elements of our fragmented culture" (2002, xxxviii). Erwin Panofsky sought to demonstrate that cinema adopted the popular genres of tragedy, romance, crime, adventure, and comedy "as soon as it was realized that they could be transfigured [. . .] by the exploitation of the unique and specific possibilities of the new *medium*" (quoted in *WV*, 30). The word "transfigure" here can be understood as the creation of another figure, another representation or expression ("dynamization of space" or "spatialization of time," the ability to show several events unfolding at the same time, "possibilities of the cinematographic *medium*" [quoted in Cavell 1971, 30]). The theme of cinema as an exploration of new aesthetic possibilities is central to the philosophy of film. But not to

Cavell's philosophy of film. For him, cinema is important because of its place in our lives, its exploration of genres, and its capacity to absorb and produce fragments of our experience.

One characteristic of cinema is its internal reference to genres, as a specific modality of examining its own expressive potentials. While other arts also use the notion of genre, often retrospectively to classify past productions or to distinguish themselves within a genre, for Cavell, cinema exists solely in its genres, which defines its popular nature. There is no essence of cinema or authorial mystique. In contrast to aristocratic distinction, popular culture proposes the paradigm of the self-made viewer who forms their taste through their favorite genres: action, romantic comedies, Westerns, science fiction, vulgar comedies for teens, vampire movies, etc.

For Cavell, the constitution of these genres, and their significance, rests on a specific property of film creation: its collective nature. "To understand a popular cinematographic work, it is necessary to find a system of reference that transcends individual wills and inspirations. This system of reference is the collectively constituted genre" (Bourdieu 2001, 44). Stephen Mulhall (2008) has highlighted what distinguishes Cavell's approach from other philosophers of cinema. The prevailing approach involves describing essential properties of the medium in order to prescribe its possibilities and potential genres. Cavell, on the other hand, suggests describing specific artistic successes or genres to elucidate the possibilities of the medium—just as for Wittgenstein there is no "essence of language" that would prescribe its norms and usages, nor a definition of our concepts that would determine their possible future application.

Cavellian genres are thus defined in relation to a particular body of actual works—for example, a group of comedies produced in the 1930s and 1940s within the structure of the large Hollywood studios of that era: "The expressive possibilities of cinema as an aesthetic medium are created by their realization. Thus, for Cavell, the potentialities of the medium—in particular its technical potentialities—are not even possibilities as such as long as they haven't been given meaning within a particular work" (Bourdieu 2001, 47). A genre in cinema or television is thus not merely a principle of classification applied after the fact or a normative system, but rather a creative force. As Cavell says, "[The genre strives] toward a state of absolute explicitness, of expressive saturation. At that point the genre would have nothing further to generate" (*PH*, 30) Thus, none of the traits defining a genre are necessary and sufficient conditions for belonging to that genre. The absence of a feature typical of a given genre (for example, the absence of a heroine's mother in most remarriage comedies) can always be offset by a "compensating circumstance" (*CT*, 5). However, membership in the remarriage comedy genre does seem to require that the heroine be a woman on a quest for perfection, with the film starting with a divorce or similar situation, and ending with her remarriage (or something akin to it). Yet this structure does not constitute a set of properties necessary and sufficient for a given work to belong to a genre, as the list of properties that define a genre is never definitive or complete.

The Creativity of the Genre

It is a genre's openness and creativity that allow for its productive capacity, including the development of new genres: for example, the perfectionist quest in the genre of melodrama; remarriage or its equivalent (reconciliation/conversation) in romantic comedies of the 1980s and 1990s; films of the aughts such as *Knocked Up* (Judd Apatow, 2007)—featuring a notable educational moment with Harold Ramis as the hero's father and several perfectionist conversations; and teen comedies such as *Superbad* (Greg Mottola, 2007). The productivity of genres also extends to television series, which have clearly inherited the conversational dynamics of couples in Hollywood comedies that form the grammar of their expressions, interactions, and emotions.

Hence, within a genre, there is an aspect of empowerment for subsequent generations of characters. In the seemingly banal comedy *The Holiday* (Nancy Meyers, 2007), the genre of remarriage plays a determining role. It allows the heroine in one of the storylines (Kate Winslet, whose character discovers a series of remarriage comedy films during a house exchange in California) to gain the strength to reject her former, toxic lover and develop new self-confidence. *The Holiday* is sprinkled with brief clips of films like *The Lady Eve* (Preston Sturges, 1941) and *His Girl Friday*, claiming not only the legacy of classic Hollywood cinema (underscored by the wonderful presence of Eli Wallach as a retired screenwriter) but also empowering Kate Winslet's character, who becomes the "leading lady" of her own life by the end. The genre of remarriage offers an aesthetic and moral framework for romantic comedies.

Ang Lee's *The Wedding Banquet* (1993), which has had an incredible success as an independent film, makes an explicit reference to the genre. Remarkably, it was not just the genre but Cavell's interpretation of it that served as a resource and a pitch for the movie. Ang Lee recalls conceiving the idea for the movie (a Taiwanese gay love story) early in his career and later discussing it with his collaborator, James Schamus. Their conversation, included in the DVD release of the film, is quite revealing:

> LEE: So I pitched to James. James thinks I will do a good job here. He likes the idea. But then he read the translated script, the way I wrote about gay lifestyle is about fifteen years out-of-date.

> SCHAMUS: It was fun with *Wedding Banquet* because the original script was actually a drama. It was kind of a tragedy. They find out their son's gay, and it's really depressing, and everybody yells at each other, then they go home. My big pitch back was, I was teaching a great book by the Harvard philosopher Stanley Cavell, on screwball comedy. It's about what he calls the "comedy of remarriage." In these great screwball comedies they're always about couples who have divorced or split up, and then come back together. I looked at the structure of *Wedding Banquet*, and we realized that this was a comedy of remarriage. These guys, in order to stay together, they have to—one of them has to get married. That forces them to break up, and then they *should* get back together again. So it was a classic screwball comedy; it just happened to be gay and Chinese.

The genre, thus, is not merely an old formula: it is a catalyst for creativity and updating. The story, initially "fifteen years out-of-date," was revitalized and made innovative by being framed within the genre. To quote Schamus again: "Let's jump from genre to genre and be filmmakers and see what we can make of these gifts" (Pride, 1999). For Cavell, a distinct characteristic of cinema is its exploration of its own specific expressive potentials, often more so than other arts, through referencing genres. A unique aspect of popular culture is its acceptance of genres, unlike highbrow art's disdain for them: audiences enjoy action films, romantic comedies, melodramas, Westerns, war films, etc. As Emmanuel Bourdieu says,

> The motor, or one of the motors, of the production of films is the existence of common genres, the renewal of which we work on together. [. . .] It is important, in the case of a "popular" art such as cinema, to take into account not only "noble" models or those with strong cultural legitimacy but also more common, if not vulgar, models. The work of the filmmaker is thus constantly crossed by explicit or implicit references to archetypal works and to the genres that they contribute to constitute, in a given time. (Bourdieu 2001, 41)

One of the key characteristics of Cavellian genres is their openness to change in how they are used. A genre, as Cavell sees it, is not a set of rigid rules defined once and for all, as imposed by an academy, but an open system that always leaves room for future variations or derivations of new hybrid genres. "It is part of the idea of a genre I am working with that both the specific relevant 'features' of the genre and the general candidacy of an individual film for membership in the genre are radically open-ended" (*CT*, 5). While Cavell does not explicitly mention Wittgenstein here, the Wittgensteinian notion of a concept is at work here. A genre is an open structure. There are no necessary and sufficient properties for a given work to fall under a genre. By encompassing the possibility of various changes and evolutions, the genres that are operative in film prove to be particularly productive tools of creation, fostering the invention of new structures. This leads to different iterations like the Asian-gay remarriage comedy (*Wedding Banquet*), the remarriage after the painful process of having a child together (*Knocked Up*), the friendship-reconciliation following a fallout, and so on.

In an ambitious essay, "The Good of Film" (first published in French and later included in *Cavell on Film* [333–48]), Cavell reminds us that his interest in perfectionism actually comes from the genre of remarriage: "A third origin of my interest in perfectionism, the one that encouraged me to think that there may be a set of ideas here worth communicating to others, was my recognition that the genre of Hollywood comedy I had begun studying in the mid-1970s, those I name, in *Pursuits of Happiness*, comedies of remarriage, were working out ideas in Emersonian perfectionism" (*CF*, 337). In its extended meditation on film's affinity with Emersonian perfectionism, "The Good of Film" considers a broad array of 1990s movies (including *As Good as It Gets* [James L. Brooks, 1997), *Groundhog Day* [Harold Ramis, 1993], *Four Weddings and a Funeral* [Mike Newell, 1994], *My Best Friend's Wedding* [P. J. Hogan, 1997], *Everyone Says I Love You* [Woody Allen, 1997], *Cookie's Fortune* [Robert Altman, 1999], *Say Anything* [Cameron Crowe, 1989], *Good Will Hunting* [Gus Van Sant, 1998], etc.), asking if the genre of remarriage is still alive. These films diverge from the remarriage comedies of the 1930s and 1940s in several distinct ways, as explored in the essay. Cavell notes that "the fear of divorce has changed, the threat of pregnancy has changed, the male and female stars and the directors and writers who put them in action are gone" (342). However, there is also another, distinct kind of difference: the characters are younger, and what is at stake for them is not divorce but the capacity of facing a future together and being together. Nonetheless, Cavell argues, these films produce a moral input similar to the remarriage comedies, even if they do not stage an actual remarriage: "There do seem to me a remarkable number of new films (within my limited experience) that concern a quest for transcendence, a step into an opposite or transformed mood, not so much by becoming another person, or taking a further step in attaining an unattained self, or becoming who you are, as by being recognized as the one you are by having, or giving, access to another world" (342). For Cavell, 1990s films do not have the intellectual and cultural power of the major films made between 1934 and 1949, the years of the remarriage comedies in question, "when half of the population of America went to the movies each week, and moreover to the same movies" (341). This actually expresses Cavell's neglect of some mainstream popular culture, which is reflected in his low artistic regard for television.

In "The Good of Film," Cavell's interest lies not in blockbusters—although they often employ the structure of remarriage![1]—but "medium-sized" movies (what I would call ordinary movies, except that, regrettably, they are the kind of films that have nearly disappeared today):

> Some recent films nevertheless try to keep something like a remarriage surface. [. . .] But even while the cultural role of film has for various reasons dwindled, and I myself am a member merely of various fragmented film publics, and do not keep up faithfully with American films, I can recall at once, in this regard, *Moonstruck* (with Nicholas Cage and Cher) (1987), *Tootsie* (with Dustin Hoffman and Jessica Lange) (1982), *Sleepless in Seattle* (with Tom Hanks and Meg Ryan) (1993), *Clueless* (with Alicia Silverstone) (1995), *Groundhog Day* (with Andie MacDowell and Bill Murray) (1993), [. . .] *My Best Friend's Wedding* (with Cameron Diaz and Julia Roberts) (1997), [. . .] each of which provides an interpretation of one or another feature of remarriage development; for example, each provides a closing sequence worth an ambitious essay on its own. (*CF*, 342–43)

In this somewhat random and open-ended list of romantic comedies, Cavell only mentions the stars (in alphabetical order) and not the directors, showing again how a genre can also be determined by actresses who signal the genre, here, in particular, Julia Roberts, Meg Ryan, and Cameron Diaz, apt followers of the amazing generation of actresses that made the genre of remarriage possible, Katharine Hepburn, Rosalind Russell, Irene Dunne. "The Good of Film" shows ambivalence, in fact, evoking *two* genres from the 1980s and 1990s: coming-of-age comedies and romantic comedies, both of which inherit the remarriage genre and in quite different ways.

Cavell notes, for example, that *The Sure Thing* (Rob Reiner, 1985) shares a remarkable number of features with *It Happened One Night* (Frank Capra, 1934) (*CF*, 343): a young man accompanies a young woman to her fiancé in another part of the country, a fiancé who is a sure thing, safe and risk free; the couple hitchhikes; in both movies they are picked up by a driver who turns out to be dangerous; the young man feeds the young woman junk food and teaches her how to drink beer. Recall how Clark Gable cooks for Ellie (Claudette Colbert) in *It Happened One Night*, gathers carrots for her, and teaches her how to dunk doughnuts. In *The Sure Thing*, the young woman's father indirectly comes to their aid in a difficult moment by having provided her with a credit card; in *It Happened One Night*, Ellie's father's money plays a crucial role. In both movies, the young man gives the woman a practical education, but receives a lesson.

A series of films in the 1980s starring a young John Cusack are clear references to the values of the classic remarriage comedies, although their characters are much younger. As Cavell writes in the original English draft of an article translated into French and published in *Le Monde de l'Education* in November 1998:

> Let us take in evidence just the fact that the couple in these films from the 1980s are at the cusp between adolescence and adulthood, distinctly younger than the original remarriage couples, whose somewhat older age signifies a number of things—that virginity is not at issue exactly,—but the reception of another into one's autonomy is at issue exactly; that children are not unthinkable and moreover must soon be decided upon one way or another; that each, especially the man, has taken his place in society, let us say, consented to it.

For Cavell, the difference between so-called early and late remarriage comedies lies in the inability or difficulty of the recent, younger couple to imagine the future, and the fact that they haven't found their place in life and society. The perfectionist tone, the idea of moral progress through conversation, is what still qualifies these films as part of the genre, even if they lack several other elements. John Cusack is the quintessential star of these films about younger couples that inherit the remarriage spirit. Cavell lists three movies of the coming-of-age genre that cast him: *The Sure Thing* (Rob Reiner, 1985) and *Say Anything* (Cameron Crowe, 1989) in the 1980s, and *Grosse Point Blank* (George Armitage, 1997) in the 1990s (which is more of a noir comedy, a genre Cusack also contributes to very regularly). Still, Cusack's characters' charm and self-reliance and care of the other, combined with a male vulnerability beautifully displayed in *Say Anything*, make him the best incarnation of the specific perfectionism of the late remarriage comedy, the "education of grownups."

Cusack then becomes typecast in romantic comedies of the aughts, notably the cult *High Fidelity* (Stephen Frears, 2000), actually a perfect comedy of remarriage, with more mature characters, and also *America's Sweethearts* (Joe Roth, 2001; with Julia Roberts),

Serendipity (Peter Chelsom, 2001; with Kate Beckinsale), and *Must Love Dogs* (Gary David Goldberg, 2005; with Diane Lane). Cusack's trajectory interests us for the continuity it displays from remarriage comedies to both coming-of-age comedies and romantic comedies. The two subgenres of the remarriage genre are hence akin (cousins, Wittgenstein would say).

Some much more recent comedies involving teenagers or young adults similarly capture the feel of remarriage: I have already mentioned *Knocked Up* and *Superbad*, but one could also add the recent *Mid90s* (Jonah Hill, 2018), *Licorice Pizza* (Paul Thomas Anderson, 2021), *The Challenge* (Klim Shipenko, 2023), and the wonderful TV series *Love* (Judd Apatow again, 2016) *Platonic* (Francesca Delbanco and Nicholas Stoller, 2023) and *Nobody Wants This* (Erin Foster, 2024). These works feature a twenty-first-century, young adult sub-genre of remarriage, where moral education becomes an adventure, and where a strong friendship may be built between the lead characters beyond (or without) a love story. They are better inheritors of the classic remarriage comedies than lazy rehearsals of the scheme of remarriage (such as *Ticket to Paradise* [Ol Parker, 2022], with Julia Roberts, the earlier star of the genre).

Another method of inheriting the classic genre of remarriage is by contesting it, making the audience's expectations of remarriage fail, thus exposing the power of the genre and new avenues for its creativity.

Subverting Remarriage: *My Best Friend's Wedding*

My Best Friend's Wedding (P. J. Hogan, 1997), starring Julia Roberts and Cameron Diaz, is deeply original, as it brings together the genre of the younger couples and the earlier remarriage comedy, respectively represented by Diaz and Roberts. The main character, Julianne/Jules (Roberts), is a mature, accomplished woman. However, the movie is absolutely not a typical (Meg Ryan-style) 1990s romantic comedy, where a woman in her thirties finds love, is threatened with losing it, and recovers it, usually at the ten-minute mark before the end of the movie, in a scene that involves some running. In romantic comedies, the loss/separation/death, which is the basic element of the remarriage genre happens midway, after companionship is found in conversation and seduction. It is overcome through a journey of self-discovery, of accepting one's limitations and finitude (usually on the part of both partners, but not together through conversation). In the 1980s and 1990s, the genre of romantic comedy explicitly inherits from the genre of remarriage, and the final reconciliation is essential to it, yet it follows a different narrative structure.

My Best Friend's Wedding is among the films mentioned by Cavell, at the time of their release, as having "the feel of remarriage comedy . . . films in which a certain kind of feast of fast talk, never far from the topic of the basis of marriage" (*CF*, 342). But it is not a romantic comedy; the heroine does not find love, but finds herself. *My Best Friend's Wedding* can be viewed as a powerful and moving contemporary inheritor of both the genres of remarriage and melodrama. It clearly inherits features from the comedies of remarriage (with an actual wedding taking place), but also elements of melodrama, with a strong yet vulnerable female lead character who faces a metaphorical death. Julianne is in her thirties, similar in age to lead characters in classic remarriage comedies, as well as in other notable examples like *Moonstruck* (Norman Jewison, 1987) or *When Harry Met Sally* (Rob Reiner, 1989). However, these latter films also rely on a powerful and unexpectedly attractive male character. In *My Best Friend's Wedding*, the love interest, Michael (Dermot Mulroney), is nice and handsome but somewhat bland, much less interesting than "the other woman" in the story, Kimmy (Cameron Diaz). The film's originality lies in its focus on the heroine, as well as her relationships with her rival, and her gay friend George (Rupert Everett). Yet its real strength, which makes it unique among the good films listed by Cavell in "The Good of Film," is its reflexivity. It is a film that encourages reflection on the remarriage genre itself, not only for scholars but also viewers, demonstrating how genre is as much a key to interpretation and understanding as it is a creative tool.

Reminiscent of *The Philadelphia Story*, *My Best Friend's Wedding* revolves around preparations for a wedding. In both films, the occasion is the wedding of the protagonist's ex-partner to someone who is initially viewed as unsuitable by both the lead character and the audience. The protagonists share a past and have, in a way, "grown up together" (*PH*, 103), and they have important conversations in the course of the film. The distinct quality of *My Best Friend's Wedding* is the way it subverts the genre of remarriage, initially using the remarriage paradigm as a normative and perceptual background. Julianne and Michael, who had a brief relationship when they were young, had promised to get back together if they were both unmarried by twenty-eight. As the deadline approaches, Julianne, still single, daydreams about this plan, only for Michael to announce, much to her chagrin, his marriage to a woman who "isn't his type at all," in two weeks' time, in Chicago. In a defining moment early on, Julianne, on her way to the airport with George, angrily declares her intention to reclaim Michael, asserting that he belongs to her and vehemently denying the possibility of his marriage to a naive young heiress.

This set up strongly suggests a remarriage, along the lines of *The Philadelphia Story*, in which C. K. Dexter Haven (Cary Grant) turns up for his ex-wife Tracy's (Katharine Hepburn) upcoming wedding to a wealthy man, only to set the stage for their ultimate remarriage. This becomes clear towards the end, when George (John Howard), the spurned rival, points out Haven's role in their breakup.

What complicates *The Philadelphia Story* (but also offers a conclusion, by jeopardizing the wedding) is the attraction Tracy feels for a third man, a journalist named Mike (James Stewart). Cavell highlights Mike's seductive qualities, implying an alternative ending where the heroine could have actually married him, a possibility briefly alluded to by the movie itself. And according to Cavell, it is the genre that dictates the ending—similarly, it is the genre only that allows us to understand the somewhat bizarre ending of *The Affair* (Sarah Treem and Hagai Levi, 2014–19; see Laugier 2023).

Consequently, when Julianne arrives in Chicago, educated viewers expect her to remarry her former lover and "best friend," a remarriage that is predicated on the failure of Michael's impending wedding to the preppy-rich-naive fiancée. Accordingly, Diaz's character initially appears as cartoonishly bourgeois and immature, akin to C. K. Dexter Haven's first rival. The film then cleverly plays on the viewer's expectations, set by the genre, for Julianne to remarry Michael, only to subvert these expectations, and the viewer's attachment towards the heroine, making them oblivious to the reality of the situation and the rival's qualities, despite Michael's (unconvincing) praise of his fiancée from the start of the film. Thus, the viewer not only follows Jules's journey of moral education, but also undergoes a moral education of their own.

To understand the film's educational logic, it is important to note the ways in which everything is set up for the remarriage. Jules is beautiful, slender, and redheaded, just like Katharine Hepburn in *The Philadelphia Story*, and even sports the same nickname (Red) on her pajamas at the beginning of the film. Jules and Michael behave as if they've "grown up together," to borrow a constant theme from remarriage comedies. There is evident lingering sexual tension between them, such as when Michael walks in on Jules in her underwear. Still, this tension is low, distant. And all of Jules's attempts to sabotage the wedding consistently backfire, leading to disaster and humiliation. For instance, after learning of Kimmy's poor singing ability, Jules tries to embarrass her with a karaoke challenge, while also hinting at her and Michael's shared past. In this pivotal scene, Kimmy turns the tables by fully embracing her off-key signing, winning over the audience and, above all, renewing Michael's admiration. The scene, showcasing Kimmy's sass and Jules's spite, highlights the chemistry and dynamic interplay between the two actresses, Diaz and Roberts, while also offering a profound reflection on what it means to sing or speak properly, a question addressed by Cavell in his earlier book *A Pitch of Philosophy* (1994). Ultimately, the film is about Jules's delusion, the conviction that her ex-lover still loves her and only needs a nudge to realize his lasting feelings.

The structure of humiliation is certainly present in the comedy of remarriage, but even more so in melodrama. A striking example is *Letter from an Unknown Woman* (Max Ophüls, 1948), in which the heroine is convinced she has a deep relationship with a man who doesn't even know or recognize her. *My Best Friend's Wedding* aligns with melodrama through the total failure of the remarriage attempt and the humiliation of the main character, while inheriting the perfectionism of both genres. The paradigm of remarriage thus becomes an opportunity for contemporary romantic comedies to put forward alternative moral proposals and to deepen the concept of moral perfectionism.

Perfectionism Old and New

The film's perfectionism is enacted through the journey of disillusionment and self-knowledge. Jules realizes her mistake; but the film also educates the cinephile viewer, who must mourn the loss of remarriage, greedily expected based on their perceived competence of the genre, thus showing the limits of the genre as something that constantly evolves. The film proposes a perhaps higher or different morality, not defined by conventional good and evil, and even challenges the meaning of these categories. For example, Jules at one point decides to send a deceitful email to create a rift between Michael and his fiancée—an action that is morally reprehensible and that casts her as an immoral character. In a memorable and public confrontation with Kimmy, in the restrooms of Chicago's Comiskey Park baseball stadium, Jules confesses to being guilty of trying to "steal" Michael from his fiancée:

KIMMY: You came here . . . pretending to be my friend, and I made you my maid of honor!

JULES: Who asked you to do that? You knew me what, eight minutes?

KIMMY: Michael trusted you, so I trusted you.

JULES: You wanted to keep me close. You didn't trust me for a second.

KIMMY: I was right!

JULES: Of course, you were right.

(From this point on, sensing a fight, a group of women accompanies the argument with hostile comments.)

KIMMY: You kissed him! At my parents' house!

WOMEN: That's cold.

KIMMY: On my wedding day!

WOMEN: Bitch. Tramp.

KIMMY: Shut up! Now I love this man, and there is no way . . . I'm going to give him up to some two-faced, big-haired food critic!

JULES: All right. Okay, all right! I kissed him.

WOMEN: Oh.

JULES: I tried to steal him.

WOMEN: Oh.

JULES: I lost. He doesn't love me. He loves you.

WOMEN: (Approval)

JULES: I haven't done much that I'm proud of the last three days. I'd like to take you to the church . . . so you can walk down that aisle . . . and marry the man of our dreams. Because he sure wants to marry you.

(Jules and Kimmy hug, as if they are now the "best friends," another irony of the movie and the movie's title)

Despite the very conventional aspects of this scene, it is quite commendable how Jules (in a remarkable performance by Roberts) acknowledges both her guilt and defeat. However, the highlight of the scene is the chorus of other women, providing successively indignant or approving normative comments in the background. The comments represent societal or conformist morality, complementing the description offered by the two rivals with a moral judgment, thus highlighting the different, higher, and perfectionist morality at play, as expressed by the characters and the actresses.

To further contextualize this key scene, which directly leads to the denouement and the church wedding scene, it is important to discuss the role of Jules's friend George. Before the wedding itself, Jules takes the plunge and makes a very awkward confession (another great acting performance of a radical failure of expression) to Michael, professing her love and kissing him. Kimmy stumbles upon them and flees, followed by Michael, with Jules in pursuit. The scene is comical, but also serious, as George imparts a lesson to Jules during a phone call while she is chasing after Michael. The dialogue, which disrupts George's poetry reading in New York, represents a magnificent and revealing moment of education, for both Jules and the viewer:

JULES: It is not going well!

GEORGE: Where are you?

JULES: I have stolen a bread van, and I'm chasing Michael down Michigan Avenue! I told him the truth! I said that I loved him, and I kissed him. This is what's happened!

GEORGE: Jules, a question. When you kissed Michael, did he kiss you back?

JULES: What do you mean? We were lip to lip!

GEORGE: Was there anything there leading you to believe this chase will end happily?

JULES: That's beside the point. We were interrupted.

GEORGE: Who interrupted you?

JULES: Kimmy! She ruined everything! And Michael started chasing her before he could answer me.

GEORGE: Michael's chasing Kimmy? You're chasing Michael? *Who's chasing you? Nobody.* Get it? There's your answer. Jules, you are not the one! Now, for God's sake, the wedding is at 6:00 p.m. You have a small, but distinct, window of opportunity to do the right thing.

This moment of moral perfectionism is made all the more powerful by the fact that it transpires over the phone, over a distance, effectively opening the heroine's eyes through the harshness of the words spoken and the tragic reality she must finally accept: she is not loved ("you are not the one"), and Michael's marriage to Kimmy is inevitable.

But is this what *My Best Friend's Wedding* is truly about? Acceptance of the conformity of marriage? Here again, the remarriage genre serves as a tool for its own subversion. The film's opening credits, along with the description of the wedding preparations, are laced with irony—sometimes amused, sometimes tender—towards the heterosexual mythology of marriage. This suggests a questioning of the centrality of, or even obsession with, marriage in Hollywood narratives. The Kimmy-Michael pairing is rather dull, even as both characters become more endearing over time. In *The Philadelphia Story*, a subversive effect is created by the remarriage, featuring a perfectionist moment of egalitarianism among the protagonists (Dexter, Tracy, Liz [Ruth Hussey], Mike); a similar dynamic is present in *It Happened One Night*. The question arises: how can a couple's relationship retain its subversive power? *My Best Friend's Wedding* succeeds in affirming paths other than remarriage in the pursuit of happiness, while also establishing a distinction between remarriage and heterosexual conjugality. Here, the character of George, who merits an analysis of his own, serves to divert the heterosexuality proper to the remarriage genre, even if Cavell often insisted that the structure was applicable to all couples (and as demonstrated by *The Wedding Banquet*). The scene where the openly gay George pretends to be Jules's boyfriend, ostensibly to incite Michael's jealousy, is particularly significant in P. J. Hogan's critique of the heteronormativity of marriage and its portrayal in cinema, especially at the time in the late twentieth century when gay marriage had not yet been legalized.

In this regard, the final, almost supplementary, scene of the film is striking. Cavell points out in "The Good of Film" that each recent instance of the remarriage comedy offers a final scene that deserves a commentary in itself (*CF*, 343).

Jules, who eventually accepts her fate, even helping to realize it, attends the wedding of Michael and Kimmy. Once the couple have left, she finds herself alone at a table, when George calls her on her bulky 1990s mobile phone:

GEORGE: Hey, gorgeous, having a good time?

JULES: Not particularly, but I did what I came to do.

GEORGE: What? You split them up?

JULES: No, I said good-bye.

GEORGE: Good girl. I'm proud of you. Be prouder still
if you were dancing.

JULES: I have big plans for dancing. Just give me thirty
to thirty-five years.

GEORGE: The misery . . . the exquisite tragedy. The
Susan Hayward of it all. I can picture you there sitting
alone at your table in your lavender gown.

JULES: Did I tell you my gown was lavender?

The reference to melodrama here explicitly intertwines the two Cavellian genres, asserting their legacy and creative potential. George, to the tune of Aretha Franklin's *A Little Prayer* (a song that recurs and plays an essential role in the movie), describes Jules's situation as if he is describing the image on the screen, simultaneously a mind reader, narrator, writer, and director:

GEORGE: Haven't touched your cake. Probably drumming
your fingernails on the white linen tablecloth . . . the way
you do when you're really feeling down. Perhaps looking
at those nails thinking: "I should've stopped . . . my evil
plotting to have that manicure, but it's too late now." Suddenly, a familiar song. And you're off your chair in one,
exquisite movement . . . wondering, searching, sniffing the
wind . . . like a dappled deer.

Then George appears in real life ("And then, suddenly, the crowds part . . . and there he is: sleek, stylish . . . radiant with charisma"). Of course, he is here for Jules and it makes sense to end the film with the solace of friendship. But the claim by George, and by the movie itself, is stronger, and so are the last images of Jules and George dancing—it is the claim of the fun of a relationship without marriage, a rebutting of the remarriage paradigm:

GEORGE: And he comes towards you . . . the moves of a jungle cat. Although you quite correctly sense that he is—like most devastatingly handsome single men of his age are—gay; you think, what the hell . . . life goes on. Maybe there won't be marriage, maybe there won't be sex, but by God! there will be dancing.

The ending has all the ingredients of melodrama, as George points out: the woman who prefers to face her fate alone, and so on. George's poignant words echo the end of *Now Voyager* (Irving Rapper, 1942), "Don't ask for the moon, we have the stars," transforming it into his own declaration: "There won't be marriage, there won't be sex, but by God! there will be dancing." However, through the grace of Roberts, who accepts the dance, even indulges in it, the film underscores the joyful acceptance of the ordinary, free from melodrama or tragedy—as well as from remarriage. Of course, contrary to some delusional heteronormative suggestions, there is no implication that these two characters will end up together. This affirmation of single, individual life follows a sort of death (here symbolized by shame and the loss of the loved one) and a rebirth through the acceptance of the ordinary.

Return to the Rough Ground

This acceptance (that life goes on) acknowledges the limits and necessities of human individual life, and hence, of the human body. This idea is explicitly represented in the film by Julianne's multiple falls (at home, when she calls Michael and receives the news of the upcoming wedding, during the rehearsal). In the ending scene, this vulnerability is transformed and redirected through dance. It is as if the film here accepts and acknowledges the model of single life—that of the unmarried woman, that of the gay man—as a positive affirmation, the "yes" typical of the remarriage comedies. The film's insight lies not in disqualifying the path of marriage as a pursuit of happiness (despite the apparent silliness of the protagonists at the wedding). The dance scene with Roberts and Everett, improvised and ordinary, yet perfectly expressive and fitting, also affirms, beyond the two genres from which the film is derived, the possibility of an alternative path, just as ordinary, for the pursuit of happiness.

What Cavell calls *photogenesis* is the film actor's (the star's) mysterious capacity, by bearing expression, to constitute the audience's experience. The experience of film thus becomes an experience in itself, constituting a part of our own existences.

This is something Cavell acknowledges in *The World Viewed*: "We involve the movies in us. They become further fragments of what happens to me, further cards in the shuffle of my memory, with no telling what place in the future" (1979b, 154). He continues in *Pursuits of Happiness*: "These films appear in their experience as memorable public events, constituent fragments of experiences, memories of an ordinary life" (*PH*, 46). Cinema helps us to see this ordinary truth, also elaborated by Wittgenstein: that only creatures endowed with language can express themselves through their bodies. Cinema is the privileged place for such exposure of the human form of life. The instances of harmony that cinema offers us, where an expression and a world align, exist through the expressiveness of the ordinary human body.

Consider Emerson's words in *The American Scholar*: "What would we really like to know the meaning of? Of the flour in the quart; of the milk in the pan; of the walk in the street; of the form and gait of the body" (Emerson [1837] 1982, 102). The intimate connection between film and philosophy is signaled here by the description of the ordinary that crystalizes into an evocation of the specific allure of the human—the ordinary of human existence defined by the gait of the body and its expressiveness.

I will end by insisting on *My Best Friend's Wedding*'s relationship to the burlesque, highlighting a transition between the adolescent world and the adult world of conformity, a rupture that is accomplished not as a rejection but as an acceptance and transfiguration of the failure and inadequacy inherent in the ordinary state of adolescence. Cavell opens this new line of reading film in "Slapstick without Sticks" (*CF*, 387–96), observing how film, especially remarriage comedies, shows "accidents of expression," often symbolized by actual "falls":

The most extended, or recurrent, image of the man's preparation for suffering indignity occurs in Preston Sturges' *The Lady Eve*, where the Henry Fonda character is knocked, or suffers a fall, to the floor, or to the ground, no fewer than six times, always in connection with the woman, played by

> Barbara Stanwyck. [. . .] It is clear that what has tripped
> him up, and continues throughout what we know of them,
> to trip him up, to knock him down—to, as the American
> expression goes, "floor" him—is the fact of the woman her-
> self, the force for him of her sexual presence. (*CF*, 390–91)

Such accidents/slips are meant to display human vulnerability, and
Jules's many falls in the movie are the revelation of her love and desire
for Michael (her disastrously failed declaration of love is echoed by
her physical fall), something she does not really acknowledge until
her friend's wedding. Cavell traces this vulnerability back to expression, to the expressive body: "Who, such as Austin, would so dwell
on excuses who did not surmise that the human necessity for action,
and of action for motion, is apt to become unbearable—its consequences, concomitants, upshots, effects, results, and so forth" (*PP*,
87). Excuses, with their permanent and obsessive acknowledgment of
human vulnerability, direct philosophy's attention to the fateful "fact
that human life is constrained to the life of the human body" (87). It
is worth remembering that this is—at least for Cavell—not just the
theme but essentially the ontology of film. Any human expression,
whether it's a failed attempt, like the passionate utterance, or something seemingly ridiculous, succeeds in performing and acknowledging
human vulnerability. As Wittgenstein says, "The human body is the
best image of the human soul" (part 2, §24). This vulnerability, though
it may manifest and be acted upon differently, is shared by both
women and men: "So we are reminded that there are worse things
than indignity, awkwardness, ridiculousness, and that there are good
things approachable perhaps only through indignity, awkwardness, and
ridiculousness, things such as expressiveness, the ability to speak one's
desire" (*CF*, 395). We can recall Cavell's thesis in *Pursuits of Happiness* that the remarriage comedies comically represent the essential
feature of skepticism—that the human condition is separation, that
one's "I" is irretrievably estranged from others and the world—and
dramatize the ability of the heroes and heroines of these films to
overcome this state of doubt and separation, to recover themselves.
The instrument of this reunion is precisely that which is threatened
by skepticism, namely conversation, of which the remarriage comedies
offer unparalleled examples: "Pervading each moment of the texture
and mood of remarriage comedy is the mode of conversation that

binds or sweeps together the principal pair. [. . .] Conversation is given a beautiful theory in John Milton's revolutionary tract to justify divorce, making the willingness for conversation (for 'a meet and happy conversation') the basis of marriage, even making conversation what I might call the fact of marriage" (*CT*, 5). Ordinary conversation is the instrument of recognition and forgiveness, but it also creates a space where a relationship of equality is forged, where education and acknowledgement of the other are established. *My Best Friend's Wedding* features several instances of conversation, but apart from a poignant exchange between Jules and a valet in a corridor at her lowest point, and a heartfelt final conversation with Michael at a Chicago train station, the only consistent conversation that takes place in the film is the one between her and George.

This conversational expressivity of the human body, prominent in *My Best Friend's Wedding* is particularly highlighted in cinema in scenes that are not focused on conversation, but rather on walking and dancing. A striking example is the scene where Fred Astaire sings "By Myself" (analyzed by Cavell in "Something out of the Ordinary" [*CF*, 223–40]). What is at work in this scene is the ordinary as represented not by speech but by walking. This relationship between the human, the ordinary, and walking (which one might be tempted to equate with thinking, although that is not the focus here) is constitutive of a whole philosophical process: in Emerson and Thoreau, Nietzsche and Heidegger; but also in Wittgenstein, who contrasts the slippery ice, where we think we are making better progress, and the ordinary, rough ground: "We want to walk: so we need *friction*. Back to the rough ground!" (Wittgenstein 1953, § 107).

In order to dance, we also need friction (and gravity). It seems to me here that this need for friction, and more generally the characteristics, possibilities, and (physical) limits of the human body, of the human form of life, are also remarkably asserted in the film scenes where we see, quite simply, ordinary people dancing. The last minutes of *My Best Friend's Wedding* are the best example. Much like in Astaire's scene, they establish a continuity between dancing and walking, suggesting that walking can, at any moment, be transformed into dance—just as the ordinary voice can at any moment be transformed into a song or a musical number. Most importantly, because dance can be seen an expression of the human form of life—equivalent and not derived from walking—and as an image of the ordinary.

In such scenes, it is crucial—and certainly part of the director's and the actors' intent—that all expression is in the dance (these scenes are almost silent, with music playing a central role). However, the key is that the dance appears ordinary, performed by nonprofessionals, by characters who dance for fun. A famous example of this is the scene in Quentin Tarantino's *Pulp Fiction* (1994; roughly contemporaneous with *My Best Friend's Wedding*), where John Travolta and Uma Thurman dance in a contest at a retro 1960s club. This scene plays homage to Travolta's filmography, just as in the case of Fred Astaire—the viewer knows that these actors can dance, and can dance extraordinarily well—but the subtlety of the scene lies in the degree of professionalism of the dancing. Travolta dances rather unprofessionally, Thurman even more so; the couple certainly dances quite well (the proof is that they win the contest), but above all they have fun, and this fun increases during the routine. The enjoyment and the truth of the scene lie precisely in this ordinary fun and the ordinariness of the characters.

In the context of remarriage comedies, these dance moments are perhaps most interesting, showcasing the genre's current vitality and creativity. *True Lies* (James Cameron, 1994), which stars Arnold Schwarzenegger and Jamie Lee Curtis, and, under the guise of a parody spy film, follows the structure of the remarriage, closes with a remarkable dance scene. Another example is *Something to Talk About* (a notable title in itself) (Lasse Hallstrom, 1995), starring Julia Roberts and Dennis Quaid, which follows a typical remarriage storyline: there is a separation of the couple at the beginning due to the infidelities of the philandering husband and a reconciliation at the end, after many casualties (including an attempted poisoning). Their unlikely reunion takes place at a dance party, beginning with a rather sour exchange about the future divorce. Music starts and he drags her into a dance, then asks for her forgiveness. Julia Roberts's performance is admirable. Her initial reluctance, gradually giving way to enjoyment, manages to represent, and even accomplish, the reconciliation operation. The dance, combining the eroticism and the fun inherent in the remarriage conversation, is often present in the remarriage comedies but here, because of its unremarkable character, it acquires an additional power.

Another particularly striking example can be found in the recent hit *Silver Linings Playbook* (David O. Russell, 2012). The protagonists, Pat (Bradley Cooper) and Tiffany (Jennifer Lawrence), haunted by difficult pasts and fragile psychological equilibrium, are not obvious candidates for the remarriage paradigm, but the film's belonging to the contemporary iteration of the genre is signaled by the young age of the two protagonists, their singular and intense conversations, their difficulty in being together, a radical breakup in the course of the film, and a memorable reconciliation in the final dance scene. As a part of a complex storyline, they enter a dance contest, aiming for an average score to save Pat's family's finances. The stakes are raised by the fact that Tiffany, who struggles with anxiety, is totally drunk by the time they take the stage, and that this amateur couple has to face professional competitors. The dance scene, which fits with all the requirements of the remarriage genre, including its amateurish charm, is a triumph when they achieve their desired score of 5 out of 10. The ecstatic celebration by the couple and their families (including the father, played by an amazing Robert De Niro) perplexes those around them, including the jury and the contest's actual winners. This singular moment of enjoyment of a certain mediocrity or averageness can only be understood in the context of the search for the ordinary inherent in these contemporary heirs to remarriage comedies, who are ready to give up perfection, and even quality.

These modern versions of remarriage comedies and their melo-dramatic cousins ultimately retain core aspects of the genre: the desire for moral progress, for knowledge of the other and of oneself, the refusal of conformism, the acceptance of vulnerability and even deviance, and the perfectionist aspirations that continue to structure narratives and unite audiences. They celebrate the accomplishment of the everyday, of being ordinary, embracing the physical and moral constraints that ground us in our earthy existence, signifying not just finitude and mediocrity but new forms of agency and hope. On the slapstick dimension of the comedies, Cavell says this, which turns out to be actually true of both early and recent (twisted) versions of the genre of remarriage:

> But if this pair finds, as they seem always to do, a finer way to establish communication than by poking and ridiculing and tripping each other, to find a commonality of spirit and flesh conveyed in a conversation of mutual wit and understanding and forgiveness and passion, and if there are those who continue to make works, such as these films, for

a public of friends and strangers, that help us imagine this possibility of human exchange, who knows what we may hope for? (*CF*, 396)

Note

1. This applies to most disaster films (*The Day after Tomorrow* [2004], *War of the Worlds* [2005]), as well as many adventure films. For example, *Indiana Jones and the Dial of Destiny* (James Mangold, 2023), the latest film of the *Indiana Jones* saga, features the hero's estranged wife, Marion Raven-wood, played by Karen Allen, the original actress in the first film, *Indiana Jones and the Raiders of the Lost Ark* (Steven Spielberg, 1981), who returns home in the last minutes of the movie; cf. the reunion of the aging heroes of *Jurassic Park* (Steven Spielberg, 1993) in the latest film of the saga, *Jurassic World: Dominion* (Colin Trevorrow, 2022).

Works Cited

Cavell, Stanley, and Sandra Laugier. 2017. *A la recherche du bonheur: Hollywood et la comédie du remariage*. J. Vrin.

Bourdieu, Emmanuel. 2001. "Stanley Cavell: pour une esthétique d'un art impur." ("Stanley Cavell: for an aesthetics of impure art.") In *Stanley Cavell: Cinema et Philosophie*, edited by Sandra Laugier and Marc Ceri-suelo. Presses de la Sorbonne Nouvelle.

Emerson, Ralph Waldo. (1837) 1982. "The American Scholar." In *Ralph Waldo Emerson: Selected Essays*. Penguin Classics.

LaRocca, David. and Laugier, Sandra, eds. 2023. *Television with Stanley Cavell in Mind*. University of Exeter Press.

Laugier, Sandra. 2023. *TV-Philosophy. How TV Series Change Our Thinking*. Translated by Daniela Ginsburg. University of Exeter Press.

Mulhall, Stephen. 2008. *On Film*. Second edition. Routledge.

Pride, Ray. 1999. "Interview: The Architect/Poet, James Schamus Takes a 'Ride with the Devil'—Part 2." *IndieWire*, December 3, 1999. https://www.indiewire.com/features/general/interview-the-architectpoet-james-schamus-takes-a-ride-with-the-devil-part-2-81929.

Warshow, Robert. 1962. 2002. *The Immediate Experience: Movies, Comics, Theatre, and Other Aspects of Popular Culture*. Harvard University Press.

Wittgenstein, Ludwig. 1953. *Philosophical Investigations*. Translated by G. E. M. Anscombe. Oxford University Press.

4

Imagining Life Together

Psychosexual Intimacy, Social Roles, and Contemporary Comedies of Remarriage

RICHARD ELDRIDGE

IT IS A DEEP ORGANIZING theme of *Pursuits of Happiness* that the seven films it analyzes, made between 1934 and 1949, somehow manage to show how the psychosexual and the social might, despite difficulties, nonetheless ratify one another. Private intimacy and the occupying of public social roles as husband and wife might be compatible with or even ultimately require one another. Achieving remarriage is shown to require both mysterious, witty intimacy that is incomprehensible to outsiders and the winning of social approval. The individuals that form the principal pairs themselves come to understand that their remarriage is necessary, so that they arrive at allegiance to a public institution as compellingly apt for them, and in turn their commitment and allegiance are approved by their external audiences (including us) even when the audiences do not fully understand or share in the intimacies of the pair. One measure of a

95

just society is then the extent to which it makes room for anyone to enter into relations of this kind and the extent to which its citizens at least stand in analogous conversational relations to each other. The films propose jointly, as Cavell puts it, "a criterion for the success or happiness of a society, namely that it is happy to the extent that it permits conversations of this character, or a moral equivalent of them, between its citizens" and a criterion for private happiness: "the pair is attractive, their wishes are human, their happiness would make us happy" (*PH*, 32).

In the contemporary world, however, such proposals are likely to seem to many to be fantastic, escapist, and irrelevant: the empty consolations of art in its appeal to fantasy and in its detachment from the serious business of life. What, then, in the world might have happened that at least constitutes a commonly enough perceived threat to the very possibility of sustained and sustainable intimacy, psychosexual and social, within the institution of marriage? And can that threat be answered, or at least addressed? Or are both remarriage *à la* Cavell and the movies that urge it as an ideal and a criterion of personal and civic happiness instead consigned to the dustbin of history and the realm of empty, irrelevant fantasy?

One way to approach these difficult questions is to note that Cavell's thinking about remarriage comedies is from the beginning thoroughly historical and critical: an engagement with evolving conditions of psychosexual and social life, not the specification of an abstract Platonic ideal. In general, Cavell holds that philosophy, including his own thinking and the thinking he finds in the films, "aims to disquiet the foundations of our lives" as they stand, "and this on the basis of no expert knowledge" of a kind that might be acquired by the specially intelligent through consulting a domain of fixed, abstract ideals (*PH*, 9). Instead, in philosophy and in life, one must begin from one's attractions and aversions as they first present themselves, often inchoately, and then "let the object or the work of your interest teach you how to consider it." Cavell calls this a piece of advice about how to think that is simultaneously theoretical and practical (10), thus emphasizing that philosophizing requires a turning of both thought and activity in relation to present conditions. Attentiveness to the present and to one's inextricably cognitive, emotional, erotic, attitudinal engagements with it is all. It is a matter of "checking one's experience," that is, "of consulting one's experience and of subjecting it to examination, and beyond these of momentarily *stopping*, turning yourself away from whatever your preoccupation and turning your experience away from its expected, habitual track, to find itself, its own track: coming to attention" (12).

This fact about Cavell's critical-philosophical practice is frequently missed by those who complain that Cavell has failed to offer an adequate definition, in the form of atemporal necessary and sufficient conditions, for the genre of the comedy of remarriage. Edwin Curley finds that Cavell's "conception of the genre of the comedy of remarriage is highly arbitrary, both in its inclusions and exclusions. [. . .] We have so little theorizing about the concept [of compensating features that link genre members], and so few examples of its use to guide us, that, in the absence of an official pronouncement by Cavell, we can hardly tell whether a film belongs to the genre or not." (1988–89, 581, 592). Noël Carroll objects both that Cavell's conception of genre is too weak in focusing only on a shared myth or plot, too broad in being open to counterexamples, and vague to the point of arbitrariness in failing to specify what counts as a compensation (Carroll 1982, 104–5). The underlying assumption driving the objections of both Curley and Carroll is that philosophy should provide clear, necessarily true statements of necessary and sufficient conditions that (more or less) inform clear identification in the absence of detailed critical readings.

While this is certainly a common enough demand in philosophy, it is at odds with Cavell's conception of philosophy—a conception that is also exemplified in the improvisatory work of the principal pairs of the comedies as they get to know themselves and each other through their interactions. For Cavell and for his principal pairs, arriving at critical self-understanding is instead centrally a matter of getting clearer about one's experience, about what is going on in it, from an initial point of obscurities of attraction and aversion. It is a core modernist trope of Cavell's writing that we suffer not from mistaken definitions, but from failures of attentiveness to our experiences, as if we were sleepwalking within the dominant ethical universal, so that we might and should awaken ourselves within and from where we are. The typical *sine qua nons* of philosophy, detachment and critical neutrality, are foreign to Cavell's spirit and enterprise. Curley concedes that "If the function of criticism is to alter permanently our perception of a work of art, to show that it can bear the weight of detailed analysis and discussion, that it illuminates our deepest human concerns, then

Cavell has written criticism of the highest order" (1988–89, 600). Despite the praise, however, there is an implicit sneer here that Cavell has written only criticism, not philosophy, and excellent criticism only if we accept further (unargued?) assumptions about the nature of criticism.

Cavell is clear that the account he gives of the genre of the comedy of remarriage as defined by myth and mutually compensating features is not intended either to substitute for or to foreclose critical reading (of the kind the principal pairs do of themselves and each other). "There is," he remarks, "nothing one is tempted to call *the* features of a genre which all its members have in common. First, nothing would count as a feature until an act of criticism defines it as such. (Otherwise it would always have been obvious that, for instance, the subject of remarriage was a feature, indeed a leading feature, of a genre)" [*PH*, 28].) Settling exactly which films are members of the genre and which are not is not the point. "Films other than the ones I give readings of belong to the genre of remarriage; six or seven of them are cited along the way" (2). These include *Together Again* (Charles Vidor, 1944), *Woman of the Year* (George Stevens, 1952), *Pat and Mike* (George Cukor, 1952), and one might add *That Uncertain Feeling* (Ernst Lubitsch, 1941), *The Palm Beach Story* (Preston Sturges, 1942), *My Favorite Wife* (Garson Kanin, 1940), *Love Crazy* (Jack Conway, 1941),[1] as well as the later *Kramer vs. Kramer* (Robert Benton, 1979), *An Unmarried Woman* (Paul Mazursky, 1978), *Starting Over* (Alan J. Pakula, 1979), and *Crazy Stupid Love* (Glenn Ficarra and John Requa, 2011). "But," Cavell adds, "I take the seven featured here to be definitive of the genre, the best of the genre, worthy successors of the great comedies of the Hollywood silent era" (2). What counts as a worthy successor is a matter of which films fully invite and sustain absorbed thought and interest, in particular in relation to the issue of the nature and value of a certain kind of marriage. Cavell takes the films he reads in *Pursuits of Happiness* (as well as, perhaps, his readings of them) to be "exercises in explicitness" about features that matter *to* the argument about remarriage and that "reflect upon one another, looping back and forth among the members" and "striving toward a state of absolute explicitness, of expressive saturation" (30). That state might be unattainable, since the social circumstances within which marriage exists as an institution change, so that more argument is called for, and since the material-aesthetic medium of film is syntactically and semantically dense[2] in a way that cuts against the kind of explicitness that is achievable in language. The pursuit of permanent clarity about marriage might be a fool's Platonic errand. Or marriage as an institution might simply wither away or take on a shape that is unrecognizable in relation to current conceptions. But as long as that does not happen, what really matters for membership in the genre for any particular film is whether or not an argument about marriage is being productively advanced in it, whether a particular film engages "the inner agenda of a culture" (17).

The important issue, then, is not absoluteness and tidiness about the borderlines of the genre of the comedy of remarriage but rather whether any contemporary film productively takes up the argument about the nature and value of a certain kind of marriage (and a certain kind of democratic society) that was pursued exemplarily in the seven films that are the subjects of *Pursuits of Happiness*. Whether it is possible for a film productively to take up this argument is not only a matter of the inventiveness of writers, producers, and directors but also a matter of whether there is an argument to be made and an audience for it. With respect to the nature and value of marriage of a certain kind, these are matters of social fact. Cavell answers "the question why it was only in 1934, and in America of all places that the Shakespearean structure [of romance comedy] surfaced again" in the form of the comedy of remarriage by noting that 1934 was "a date at which a phase of human history, namely, a phase of feminism, and requirements of a genre inheriting a remarriage structure from Shakespeare, and the nature of film's transformation of its human subjects . . . met together on the issue of the new creation of a woman" (*PH*, 19–20). Cavell cites the feminist theorist Alice S. Rossi's claim that "the generation that followed the activist generation of suffragists may have been consolidating feminist ideas into the private stuff of their lives and seeking new outlets for the expression of the values that prompted their mothers' public [suffragist] behavior," himself adding that there is "no 'may have been' about it" (17). Given the historical circumstances, women and men found themselves in a new form of "the struggle [. . .] for the reciprocity or equality of consciousness between a woman and a man, [. . .] a struggle for mutual freedom" (17, 18). When women have at last achieved publicly acknowledged, formally equal political citizenship in winning the right to vote, then the pressing issues are: where can the energies of the struggle for full equality and reciprocity, economic and domestic as well as formal and political, now go, and what are the modes and fates of undertaking to redeploy these energies? Even more broadly, the issue is how to achieve "a proposed marriage or balance between Western culture's two forces of authority: Hellenism [as] *spontaneity of consciousness* [and] Hebraism [as] *strictness of conscience*, so that American mankind can refind its objects, its dedication to a more perfect union, toward the perfect human community, its right to the pursuit of happiness" (158–59).[3] This issue will not be on the table in the same way in all times and places, and it is evidently not on the table between men and women in the United States in the same way after 1949 as it was earlier. Cavell is clear that the genre of the remarriage comedy can continue and its guiding myth of the mutual ratification of the psychosexual and the democratic-social can be productively revised *only* "if the issue is still living" (33).

So is this large issue all at once of recognitive reciprocity between women and men, of the balance of spontaneity and conscience, and of the mutual ratification of the psychosexual and the democratic social still living? If not, or not in exactly the same way, why not? What about American life and the lives and hopes of men and women changed? And do the changes leave room for anything like a contemporary version of the comedy of remarriage that addresses these issues?

Writing in 2005 on *Mr. and Mrs. Smith* (Doug Liman, 2005), Cavell remarks that "surely the genre cannot command the cultural prominence it once enjoyed" (*CF*, 433). He notes the perception, forwarded by the film, that "the world itself has become inhospitable to the imagination of marriage as continuously ratified in remarriage, no longer willing to entertain the possibility of joining duty and inclination. [. . .] More generally the film shows the present world's inhospitability to the comedy of remarriage in active negating of the significance of words and of work" (432), as though all deep psychosocial satisfactions have become somehow privatized and not somehow expressible and ratifiable in public life. As a possible reason for this unhappy condition, he adduces the thought "that, somehow paradoxically, given the increase of freedom among the young beginning in the Sixties, shrinking again in recent years, it is harder to imagine a somewhat older pair, especially a male of the pair, say a decade past college age, risking all for love" (433). We can fill in this somewhat cryptic thought by noting that part of the relevant freedom is the ability to enjoy sexual experience significantly unencumbered by worries about pregnancy, in light of the general availability of largely effective birth control. Second, especially among the college-educated classes but also in general, the median age of marriage has significantly increased over the past seven decades, from 20 to 22 for women and 22.4 to 26.1 for men between 1890 and 1960, to 28.1 for women and 30.4 for men at present (US Census Bureau, n.d.). Among the many causes of this development, we might point to increasing economic uncertainty as the United States lost its international manufacturing hegemony, increasing demands from the workplace for formal education that requires time and energy, and increasing life expectancy, so that child rearing comes to occupy a smaller percentage of one's adult years, as well as the more ready availability and acceptance of sex outside marriage. Whatever their underlying causes are, however, the rise in the median age of marriage and widely available birth control are surely both effects and causes of psychological changes in how people think about relationships. Instead of being something expected (and generally approved of) at a relatively early stage of life, marriage becomes from the beginning something of a compromise between more fully formed and mature adults who are each individually seeking satisfactions of which they have had some experience. Marriage is now commonly thought to be hard work, with its burdens of care imposed as costs (albeit, it is hoped, worthwhile ones) on those who enter into it, rather than a mysterious, continuously transformative experience, offering a promise of things not seen. The very idea of transformative experience comes to seem less than credible, as the demands of economic credentialization come to dominate adolescent development. In *The Upswing* (2020), their comprehensive survey of economics, politics, society, and culture from 1890 to the present, Robert Putnam and Shaylyn Romney Garrett uncover a general upsurge of what they call "expressive individualism," (164) beginning sometime in the early to mid-1960s. As a result of what they call "the Sixties Earthquake," (138) "beliefs, values, and norms" (304) centering around solidarity, mutual responsibility, and equality were displaced by ones centering around personal liberation and individual happiness.[4] Ideologically, many people come to take economic, instrumental rationality—the efficient satisfaction of preferences and desires one takes oneself to have—as the default or sole form of practical rationality, at the expense of conceptions of rationality that have to do with justice, mutual recognition, and mutual citizenship. Identification with any social role—familial, gendered, economic, religious, or political—comes to seem more provisional in comparison with the strength of more labile individual interest.

On the level of couple formation, for some considerable historical stretch of time—perhaps the late 1700s for some and developing and spreading until the mid-1960s—companionate love or what we, drawing on Aristotle, might call an erotic friendship of virtue, was a significant possibility and aspiration. In this relationship, as Andrea C. Westlund puts it, "companion lovers are united in the ongoing process of forging a shared practical perspective—a perspective on what's to be done and why, on what is worth caring about, on what is valuable or important or choiceworthy and what is not—in short, a perspective on how to live (and, in particular, on how to live together)" (2008, 560). But when expressive individualism and economic rationality come to the fore and relatively formed individuals already know what they want, then the very idea of committing oneself to the process of forging and developing a shared perspective comes to seem unintelligible. Trust and faith in participating in a process that will involve change begin to lapse.[5]

Even in 1934–49 in the worlds of the comedies of remarriage, the overcoming of individual, instrumental rationality in favor of discovery of and submission to the demands and possibilities of transfigurative reciprocity required the existence of a space apart from daily life—the Shakespearean green world identified in *Pursuits of Happiness* primarily as Connecticut, sometimes as on the road—where a pair might, through happenstance, find themselves and so find each other and their surprising, unacknowledged deeper needs for each other. In such spaces out of the ordinary, mutual improvisation could be called for and its value could be suddenly made manifest, as in the playacting for the detectives scene in *It Happened One Night* (Frank Capra, 1934). Nowadays, however, such spaces seem less available. Adults carry more of their formed identities with them into unusual spaces, and the result of a camera following a couple cast into a forest or onto a desert island is likely to read more like a piece of theatricalized reality TV than as an occasion for transfigurative intimacy.

Given all this—the freedom to find sexual experience elsewhere, the necessity of spending time and energy on technical preparation for the workplace, the rise in the median age of marriage, the development of expressive individualism, the increasing strength of individual instrumental rationality, and the disappearance of spaces for mutual improvisation—it is then unsurprising that Cavell concludes, again, that "the world itself has become inhospitable to the imagination of marriage as continuously ratified in remarriage," with *Mr. and Mrs. Smith* counting as much as "satire of remarriage" as a continuation of it (*CF*, 432).

> The satiric value of the pair's being in the business of assassination gives their work an air of fantastic anti-work, dedicating themselves to destructiveness, work that is necessarily uncelebrated, socially unacknowledgeable. The object of the satire is nicely ambiguous. Is this a further mimesis of modern marriage, whose true basis is necessarily a secret from society, so that while the family is thought to secure the bond of the social, the privacy of the marriage at its origin is . . . a standing threat to the way society is? Or is the satire directed at remarriage comedy's internal relation to utopian ideas, what Tracy Lord's fiancé George, at the denouement of *The Philadelphia Story*, contemptuously calls "you and your sophisticated ideas"? (433)

Yet, despite the worry about the inhospitability of the world to marriage as daily remarriage, Cavell's assessment of *Mr. and Mrs. Smith* is not entirely one-sided or bleak. It may be a mimesis—a continuation—of modern marriage and its possibilities of intimacy as well as a satire of utopian fantasy. "The film recurrently takes its bearing *from, or away from*, the classical remarriage comedies" (433; emphasis added):—it is unclear exactly which. And if, at least in part, it takes its bearings from them, then the film is somehow still exploring a living issue. Here an interesting point of comparison with *Mr. and Mrs. Smith* is *Ocean's Eleven* (Steven Soderbergh, 2001). Where *Mr. and Mrs. Smith* is more or less a comedy of remarriage crossed with a buddy flick (was *Lethal Weapon* [Richard Donner, 1986] a model for Mr. and Mrs. Smith's wisecracking?), *Ocean's Eleven* is a comedy of remarriage crossed with a heist flick. While the heist caper is in the foreground, it is also crucial to the plot and to the film's appeal that Danny Ocean (George Clooney) is arranging the heist in order to unmask the mercenariness of Terry Benedict (Andy Garcia) and to show his not-yet-ex-wife, Tess (Julia Roberts), that he, not Terry, is still the one with whom, for her, (re)marriage makes sense. He makes her laugh.

As in *Mr. and Mrs. Smith*, however, we are not shown any process of the mutual transformation of the couple through conversation. Danny from the beginning is fully committed to Tess and to recovering her, albeit that he hides this from his fellows—though Rusty (Brad Pitt) has his suspicions—and from us. The pair share relatively little screen time, and the crucial transformation in Tess's perception occurs not directly in conversation with Danny but instead through her watching a security camera capture, arranged by Danny, of Terry agreeing to an offer of $165 million in exchange for Tess. Danny's fitness to win Tess is established more by Terry's cold instrumentalism, contrasted with Danny's poise and charm (George Clooney at his most self-deprecatingly attractive, frequently in interaction with Rusty). All the action takes place in Las Vegas, in connection with the heist, away from the ordinary worlds of work and life (as in *Mr. and Mrs. Smith*, where assassination is no ordinary occupation) but not in the green world of Connecticut. Yet both films succeed in presenting the accomplishment of remarriage, despite their limits in displaying conversational action, and through their genre crossings both films find places (foreign assassination sites, Las Vegas) or modes of action (mutual assassination, the heist) apart from the ordinary within which this accomplishment is possible. Each of them at least encourages the thought, central to the comedy of remarriage, that "what this pair does together is less important than the fact that they do whatever it is together, that they know how to spend time together, even that they would rather waste time together than do anything else—except that no time they are together could be wasted" (*PH*, 88).

To this strain of guarded optimism, we can add the thought that the canonical comedies of remarriage still work for many audiences in soliciting their enjoyments, their identifications, and their thought. Echoes of these enjoyments, identifications, and lines of thought are to be found in their less canonical successors. At the same time, given the shape of the public world and its ideology of instrumentalist individualism, many will have trouble trusting their enjoyments and identifications as having any cognitive significance. As Nietzsche mordantly remarks in criticizing utilitarianism, when we focus only on the means to subjectively individual or broadly ameliorative social ends, then we become "unknown to ourselves, we knowers," (Nietzsche 2006, 3) in being suspicious of trust and transformation, and hence likely to will the shapes of our lives half-heartedly, as a kind of compromise. And of course promises of transformation can be hollow and coercive, especially so when they are associated with peremptory authorities and highly parameterized social roles. Sometimes art's own dramatic closures and happily-ever-afters continue, rightly, to call forth mistrust, given any realistic understanding of the demands and complexities of social, economic, political, and sexual life over time.

Beyond its costs, increasing individualism has also yielded the benefits of increasing fluidities both in gender identities and in possibilities of relationship as well as increasing approval of these fluidities. Nonheterosexual comedies of remarriage are at least a live possibility, even if nonheterosexual relationships and marriages also face the same pressures of economic and social circumstances as heterosexual ones. *The Kids Are All Right* (Lisa Cholodenko, 2010) is an interesting case, both complicated and enriched by the presence of children.

But can art, and art in the form of comedies of remarriage, also nonetheless sometimes make a difference?[6] Is trust in transformation within the world and in the powers of art to inform it still possible? Early in his career, in the fraught era of the Vietnam War and the civil rights movement, where chaos seemed everywhere, Cavell wrote that what we might hope for, from art and from life, is "not the re-assembly of community, but personal relationship unsponsored by that community; not the overcoming of our isolation, but the sharing of that isolation—not to save the world out of love, but to save love for the world, until it is responsive again" (*MWM*, 229). Full community may be too much to ask for, given relentless individualism and given the value and the sheer facts of difference. Political liberalism and competition have their points. Yet there remain the surprising transfigurations of attention that are afforded by art, by humor, by sports, by music, and by personal intimacies in daily life, among other things. To keep the significance of these intimacies alive and the dream of them relevant to how we live, there is little that is more pertinent than the canonical comedies of remarriage and their less canonical successors, together with thought and talk about them.[7]

Notes

1. Thompson (2020) mounts an extended argument on behalf of *Love Crazy* as well as noting *That Uncertain Feeling* and *The Palm Beach Story*.

2. I take these terms from Nelson Goodman's valuable account of visual depiction vs. verbal description in *The Languages of Art* (1976).

3. Cavell takes the terms "Hebraism" and "Hellenism," and the descriptions associated with them, from Matthew Arnold (1869), *Culture and Anarchy*, Smith, Elder and Co.

4. It should not go without saying, and Putnam and Romney Garrett take care to say it, that these developments involved significant improvements in the lives of women and racial minorities who had been significantly blocked from full entry into economic and political life.

5. Interestingly, two forms of practice in contemporary life where this kind of trust and faith still seem viable are participation in team sports and participation in musical performance. These can be important educative experiences. But they are also often experienced as offering forms of relationship and satisfaction that are disjoined from economic, political, and familial life.

6. Television comedies and dramas continue to explore characters and relationships, and they have the flexibility of open-endedness in doing so. The price of this flexibility, however, is frequently less achievement of dramatic closure. I am not aware of any television shows that are clearly and directly concerned with remarriage, even if restorations of broken or threatened relationships are common.

7. I am grateful to the philosophy department of Middle Tennessee State University and to the Southern Aesthetics Workshop for opportunities to present earlier versions of this work to each of them and for productive discussions on both occasions. Thanks in particular to Kelly Jolley and Eliza Little, my sharp and insightful commentators in the Workshop.

Works Cited

Carroll, Noël. 1982. "Review of *Pursuits of Happiness*." *The Journal of Aesthetics and Art Criticism* 41 (1): 103–6.

Curley, Edwin. 1988–89. "Cavell and the Comedy of Remarriage." *Philosophy Research Archives* 14:581–603. https://doi.org/10.5840/pra1988/19891425.

Goodman, Nelson. 1976. *The Languages of Art*. Second edition. Hackett Publishing Company.

Nietzsche, Friedrich. 2006. *Nietzsche: 'On the Genealogy of Morality' and Other Writings*. Edited by Keith Ansell-Pearson. Translated by Carol Diethe. Second edition. Cambridge University Press.

Putnam, Robert D., and Shaylyn Romney Garrett. 2020. *The Upswing: How America Came Together a Century Ago and How We Can Do It Again*. Simon & Schuster.

Thompson, Lucas. 2020. "Marriage as Madness: *Love Crazy* and the Hollywood Comedy of Remarriage." *Conversations: The Journal of Cavell Studies* 8:92–125. https://doi.org/10.18192/cjcs.vi8.5792.

United States Census Bureau. n.d. "Figure MS-2: Median Age at First Marriage, 1890 to Present." https://www.census.gov/content/dam/Census/library/visualizations/time-series/demo/families-and-households/ms-2.pdf/.

Westlund, Andrea C. 2008. "The Reunion of Marriage." *The Monist* 91 (3–4): 558–77. https://doi.org/10.5840/monist2008913/430.

5

"I Saw a Different Life. I Can't Stop Seeing It"

Perfectionist Visions in *Revolutionary Road*

PAUL DEB

FOR ANYONE ACQUAINTED WITH the work of Stanley Cavell, *Revolutionary Road* (Sam Mendes, 2008) provides much food for thought. Adapted from Richard Yates's now celebrated 1961 novel of the same name, its story of the unhappy marriage of Frank (Leonardo DiCaprio) and April Wheeler (Kate Winslet) in suburban Connecticut in the mid-1950s, is at once suggestive not only of Cavell's interest in the blessings and (more particularly) the costs of marriage, but also of his concern with the threat to individual and social life posed by conformity, and his commitment to the idea and promise of America. Most obviously, however, it is Cavell's understanding of these themes as finding expression in certain Hollywood films of the 1930s and 1940s definitive of his two related cinematic genres of remarriage comedy and unknown woman melodrama that is most pertinent here. The central issue faced by the female protagonists in these films is whether marriage as such can be accepted as an arena in which they might overcome conformity's repressive demands or should instead be rejected as a further occasion of that repression—a choice Cavell sees as the films' embodiment of a register of the moral life that he relates to perfectionism, and which he developed in his work reclaiming Emerson and Thoreau as the founders of a distinctively American tradition of thinking.

While Cavell doesn't discuss the relation of more recent Hollywood films to the genre of unknown woman melodrama, he does discuss their relation to the genre of remarriage comedy; identifying numerous movies which, although not "full-blown" instances of the genre, nonetheless retain its "feel" or "surface" (*CF*, 342). Such recent "versions" or "fragments" of remarriage contain interpretations of certain of its features, but at the same time differ in various ways from their "classical" antecedents (*CW*, 153–55). In this chapter, I assume this mode of inheritance is also true for unknown woman melodrama, and claim that *Revolutionary Road* is one such inheritor of the genre; so making April Wheeler (and so Kate Winslet) a recognizable cinematic descendent or sister of the women who populated its classical instances: Stella Dallas (Barbara Stanwyck), Charlotte Vale (Bette Davis), Paula Alquist Anton (Ingrid Bergman), and Lisa Berndle (Joan Fontaine).

My discussion is organized around two key features of the film. First, its insistent thematic and dramatic focus on conversation—from beginning to end it expresses an overriding concern with modes of talking, and so with the nature and possibilities of speech; and second, the social or political significance of the Wheelers' unhappiness—the relation of their personal crisis to the wider question of America. However, in order to give a sense of the initial plausibility of understanding *Revolutionary Road* as related to unknown woman melodrama, its fairly straightforward fulfilment of its generic obligations and perfectionist commitments can be quickly adduced. In the melodramas, the woman's rejection of marriage entails that she is always presented as a mother (April has two children, and, decisively, comes to expect a third); the movement of the action tends to end where it began (brutally, in the house on the road which gives to the film its name); and, primarily, the central pair's conversation is characterized by irony and estrangement, leading to the woman's recognition of her isolation and unknownness (the film is centered around Frank and April's constant series of violent arguments, which reflect and reinforce the latter's crippling loneliness). And since for Cavell, marriage is an allegory or model for perfectionist friendship, the woman's rejection of it is at the same time a rejection of marriage as a realm in which the spiritual rewards of such a friendship may be gained. For while the women of the melodramas share their comedic sisters' perfectionist ambition to create or recreate themselves—by declining the conformity of their current attained selves by seeking their future unattained but attainable selves—they come to realize that they cannot share the conviction that their male companions are, after all, the enabling Emersonian friends capable of providing the education necessary to help them fulfil that ambition. Rather, they find they have instead succumbed to a disabling idolatry which can only be overcome by explicitly rejecting or transcending their men, and so discovering the means for their transformation otherwise than in marriage.

We can thus understand April's profound sense of disappointment in her life—a life she could be more properly said to haunt rather than live (a condition Cavell finds diagnosed by Emerson and Thoreau a hundred years earlier, in their claim that the majority lead lives of "secret melancholy" or "quiet desperation")—as expressing her despairing perfectionist judgment at the current state of the world in contrast with the world as it could be. This leads her to demand or desire its transformation—to reject her present life in suburban Connecticut in favor of a vision of a future life in Paris. However, when this plan collapses—ostensibly due to April's pregnancy and Frank's promotion (examples of the many levels of irony of dialogue, plot, imagery, and camera motion which Cavell takes to be characteristic of the melodramas)—she comes to realize that the education she thought she needed from men ("the most valuable and wonderful thing[s] in the world"), and from Frank in particular ("a man with a fine mind," "the most interesting person [she's] ever met"), is one he is unfit to provide (that he is, after all, "just a boy who made me laugh at a party—once"). In other words, although Frank is capable of inspiring April's fantasy of Paris (when she finds a faded photograph of him in his army uniform standing in front of the Eiffel Tower, and recalls the conversation years before when he wistfully declared his ambition to return there with her), it appears he no longer believes in it (if he ever really did), and so feels incapable of enacting it. April's realization of Frank's inability or inadequacy to feed her perfectionist aspirations thus leads her to reject him and their marriage (in their increasingly antagonistic and isolating exchanges, and a perfunctory instance of infidelity); and, ultimately, it would seem, to stake her life on the possibility of attaining a future state of herself which she could genuinely call her own.

Negations of Conversation: Argument, Madness, Gossip

It would I think be fair to say that, rather than action, it is conversation—or more accurately, its argumentative negation—that carries the drama of *Revolutionary Road* (forgetting for a moment that talking is as much an action as, for example, smoking a cigarette or preparing breakfast). I also take it as obvious that the film is explicitly concerned (not least in its memorable image of the morning tide of men in drab suits and fedoras commuting into Grand Central Station) with working out the problematic of self-reliance and conformity, of hope and despair. I mean that this not only constitutes the apparent subject matter of the film but the explicit concern of the characters within it—the source of the sequence of wounding exchanges between April and Frank of which the film essentially consists. It is thus tempting to say that the film is nothing more (though nothing less) than a conversation about conformity and its aversion. Put otherwise, we might describe the film as being obsessed or haunted by this idea, in the way that April finds herself obsessed or haunted by a paralyzed perfectionist vision of that aversion—of her unattained self and its world—in the course of the film itself. As she confides to her neighbor, Shep (David Harbour), in the bar after Frank has left to drive Shep's drunken wife, Milly (Kathryn Hahn), home, "I saw a different life. I can't stop seeing it. Can't leave, can't stay. No damn use to anyone."

For Cavell, since a meet and happy conversation is the fact or basis of marriage, the failure or loss of genuine marriage can be characterized by the negation or loss of genuine conversation. In *Revolutionary Road,* this sense that conversation equates with marriage is perhaps most obvious when April implies that the extent of her desire for Frank is equivalent to the extent of her desire to talk to him. When Frank confesses his need for April to care about him, she explains: "Oh, I know you do. And I suppose I would if I loved you. But you see I don't think I do anymore. And I only just figured that out. And that's why I'd just as soon not do any talking right now." In fact it would seem that, for April, not talking to Frank is more important than whatever it is that he could find for them to talk about. It is not the specific subject matter of any particular conversation that is the problem, but the very fact of talking to him at all—as if, as Emerson put it, every word he says chagrins her. For example, when Frank attempts to initiate a conversation by asking April what she would like to talk about, she angrily refuses: "Would it be all right if we didn't talk about anything? Can't we just take each day as it comes, and do the best we can, and not feel we have to talk about everything all the time?" This sense of irritated negation is primarily figured between the couple as an apparently daily round of bitterly hostile argument. Indeed, April and Frank rarely do anything else; for them, arguing has become their way of being together, the distinctive (and destructive) mode of their shared form of life. But how did this argument start? How, or more precisely when, does *Revolutionary Road* begin?

The film opens with Frank's flashback to a cocktail party in New York's Greenwich Village, the bohemian setting for his first meeting with April some seven years before. The camera introduces us first to April who—as if immediately declaring her kinship with her melodramatic sisters—is shown standing holding a cigarette in an exaggerated pose reminiscent of Bette Davis (we learn immediately afterwards that April is studying to be an actress). Next, we witness the couple's instant rapport, the easy wit of Frank's initial seductive exchanges, and April's immediate interest in talking about matters of genuine self-expression or realization, rather than the more prosaic subject of earning a living. When Frank replies to her question about what he does by saying that he's a longshoreman, she presses him, "No, I mean really . . . I don't mean how you make money. I mean what are you interested in?" Can we hear in these opening words the start of a conversation on a perfectionist topic that will continue as long as they share a life together, before that conversation is violently negated? Or can we instead hear that conversation as already having been negated at its very start, not only in Frank's refusal to take the question seriously—in his humorous deflection, "Honey, if I had the answer to that one, I bet I'd bore us both to death in half an hour" (a boredom we see, in the end, to be more properly measured in years rather than hours)—but also in April's apparent earnestness?

For we might view April's conversation here as merely conforming to contemporary fashions, as simply an empty rehearsal of popular existentialist tropes drawn from post-war, Parisian café culture. If so, could we then accuse her of having an, as it were, inauthentic grasp of the authentic; of pretending to be someone other than she really is (a penchant suggested by her theatrical aspirations), and so, of acting in what Sartre would call "bad faith"? After all, the flashback ends by ironically cutting to a close-up of Frank's face as he sits watching the curtain fall at the end of April's disappointing performance in a disastrous amateur theatre production.[1] This scene raises the possibility that April's desire to be an actress was as much an affectation—as little a reflection of her true self—as her opening exchange and its ability truly to reflect that self; an example of the self-subverting trading of genuine conversation for its counterfeit that we will also see at work in the film's ending.

However long we choose to understand April and Frank to have been arguing about these matters (and so whether there was ever really a marriage between them, insofar as it lacked a genuine conversational basis), this argument undeniably reaches its climax during the concluding scene in their kitchen, in which April's maddened aria of divorce rises to the pitch of a shrill, ear-piercing scream. This moment of utter incommunicability and isolation, of conversation's absolute negation, is preceded by April warning Frank that, "If you come any closer, if you touch me or anything I think I'll scream." In transcribing these words, I am struck by the fact that, dependent on whether one chooses to place a comma before or after "I think," April's threat could be heard in one of two ways: as a hesitant attempt to protect her physical well-being, or a more confident defense of not just her body but her mind (anything she might think). The latter would be consistent with the need or desire for thinking she expresses shortly afterwards when, pursued by Frank, she finds herself in a dark wood on the hill opposite their house and shouts at him in exhausted exasperation, "Are you still talking? Isn't there any way to stop your talking? I need to think. Can't you see that?"[2]

April's worry that Frank might, after all, do her harm instead of good can be understood as a response to what Cavell identifies as the taint of villainy in the leading men of both genres, something that, amongst other things, expresses their ability to use language for their own negating purposes (*CT*, 5). Frank's villainy is shown by a certain quality of aggression in his character that presents a constant threat of physical and mental violence. The former variously finds expression in the repeated raising of a fist, the punching of the roof of a car, the slinging of a chair against a wall, and the scattering of perfume bottles from a dressing table. The latter is illustrated by Frank's gaslighting of April, as he talks to her in ways designed to make her question her own sanity (thus recalling the experiences of April's cinematic sister, Paula, in the film whose title gave rise to this term). Frank repeatedly accuses April of being "sick," of not being in her "right mind," and of doing something that "a normal woman, a normal sane mother" would not (namely, buying the items necessary to perform an abortion on herself); something he claims she is not "entirely rational about" and is thus symptomatic of her need to see a psychiatrist (for which he would pay, "obviously"). Throughout this, Frank never stops to consider any other possible explanation for what might drive a woman to such an action (his inability to read between such pitiful lines thereby confirms April's unknownness). And yet, in making such diagnoses, Frank endows himself with the authority to explain such behavior, casting himself in the role of a therapist whose apparently ignorant commitment to a form of incessant talking cure (and dubious definitions of insanity) seems in danger of causing, rather than alleviating, the condition he purports to treat (as April pleads, "All right, Frank. Could you just stop talking now, before you drive me crazy, please?"). In this method, Frank, perversely, and to his supposed patient's frustration, does most of the talking, even going so far as to put words into April's mouth: "Right? Isn't that what you're going to say?" She replies, "Apparently, I don't have to. You're saying it for me." Frank thus takes it to be within his powers both to read April's mind and speak with her voice—thereby perpetrating the very psychical violation that her scream was meant to warn him against.

The figure of the therapist is something which Cavell takes to be common to the comedies and the melodramas (most explicitly in the latter, via Charlotte's psychiatrist in *Now, Voyager* [Irving Rapper, 1943]) (*CW*, 239). Despite Frank's feeble and self-serving impersonation, in the film this figure actually takes the form of John Givings (Michael Shannon), the mentally disturbed son of Helen Givings (Kathy Bates), the local real estate agent from whom the Wheelers purchased their house. For Cavell, the therapist in remarriage is a comic, marginal figure, while in the melodramas he is a serious character capable of leading the action (239). Here we might say that he is both.[3] While John's two visits to the Wheeler home contain moments of scene-stealing and undeniably dark humor, they are also laced with a palpable sense of both the personal tragedy and defeat to which he has been subjected, and the keenness of his still undiminished powers for the perception and blunt expression of the truth (in an ironic inversion or questioning of the roles of therapist and patient, of the nature of sanity and insanity, that links him to the literary tradition of the wise fool). Indeed, such is the nature of John's insight that, after his first visit, Frank and April declare that, unlike their neighbors and colleagues, he is the only person with whom they can truly converse (thus confirming their shared marginality):

> APRIL: You know, he's the first person who seemed to know what we were talking about.

> FRANK: That's true. Maybe we are just as crazy as he is.

> APRIL: If being crazy means living life as if it matters then I don't care if we are completely insane. Do you?

> FRANK: No.

> APRIL: I love you so much.

But by the time of John's second visit, when the Wheelers reveal that they no longer plan to leave for Europe, this solidarity is exchanged for hostility and the threat of violence. His uncanny ability to divine that the real reason for that decision lies not with April ("too tough and adequate as hell") but in Frank's inadequacy—his failure to live up to her perfectionist ambitions (to "never have to find out what he's really made of")—leads the latter furiously to demand that John should "keep his fucking opinions in the fucking insane asylum where they belong!" Thus, Frank now identifies John as suffering from a variant of the same condition he diagnosed in April.

Nevertheless, we can understand Frank and April's initial positive or affirming conception of madness (in contrast with what we might call Frank's subsequent pathological or clinical one) as recalling the perfectionist thought of Emerson's disciple Thoreau, that we may be beside ourselves in a sane sense—able to recognize that our attained state is always next to, or neighboring, its unattained counterpart (*CHU*, 9). The perfectionist picture of the self as inherently split or doubled is itself dramatized in a further instance of conversation at work in the film: Frank's apparent monologue (an example of talking to oneself, which, in another context, could be taken as a clichéd sign of madness) in the scene when, staying late at the office (he works in the sales promotions department of a business machines firm), he uses his dictation machine to record and then play back to himself copy for a sales brochure for the new Knox 500 model and its claimed benefits for coordinating factory production: "Knowing what you've got, comma, knowing what you need, comma, knowing what you can do without, dash. That's inventory control." In listening to his own words in this way, hearing his voice as if it were that of another, we might understand Frank as thereby acknowledging himself as essentially divided or doubled; that rather than a monologue, he is engaged here in an internal dialogue or conversation between his attained and unattained selves, in which economic ideas are tropes for spiritual issues. The voice Frank hears emanating from the Dictaphone is thus that of his unattained self, calling him to take stock, or control, of the internal economy or inventory of his desires: of knowing what he's got, what he (really) needs, and what he doesn't (call them false desires or necessities, borne in conformity). But pivotally, this is a voice from which he literally immediately turns away, instead turning towards the approaching figure of Maureen Grube (Zoe Kazan), the young secretary with whom he is having an affair, taking advantage of her late, suggestive invitation; cynically calculating that the benefits of the settled attractions of his attained self exceed the costs of changing them.

Frank's cynicism in his professional expertise with words reflects his natural gift for talking. As April puts it, "Oh, Frank, you really are a wonderful talker! If black could be made into white by talking, you'd be the man for the job." She thus likens his verbal talents to an alchemic linguistic power to turn something into its opposite, to make something into what it is not—an ability that identifies him as a maker of appearances, as someone for whom the business of making false, rather than true, statements about reality would be an ideal occupation (what philosophy would call sophistry). He employs this talent in the pursuit of not only professional, but personal goals (attempting to persuade his wife that she is losing her mind, and conjuring "Visual Aids" departments[4] into existence out of thin air in order to spend the afternoon with his mistress). It seems that, despite his ironic protestations to the contrary, and as emphasized by his sudden promotion, Frank is well-suited to earning a living by means of his rhetorical effectiveness in representing or marketing matters without reference to, or indeed grasping, their true nature ("I don't even know what the Knox 500 does. . . . Do you?").

While Frank might be a particularly adept or self-aware exponent (a self-confessed "little wise guy with a big mouth") of this sophistical exploitation of language's inherent capacity to mispresent (as well as represent) reality, this air of falsity or insincerity also pervades the conversations of the characters that comprise the film's closing scenes, set a year after April's death, when he and the children have left Revolutionary Road and moved to New York City. In both Milly's disinterested recital of the Wheelers' story over drinks while entertaining the Braces (the young couple who are the new inhabitants of the Wheeler house), and Helen's disingenuous remarks to her husband Howard (Richard Easton)—where she snobbishly dismisses the Wheelers as having been unsuitable neighbors (too "whimsical" and "neurotic" for her taste), and willfully forgets the kindness they showed her by inviting John to their home (despite the threat of the very small-minded, moralizing condemnation that she now displays towards them)—we can hear a further negation of language's truth-disclosing side. For this perversion or debasement of genuine conversation into gossip or mere chatter (a major currency of conformity) forgoes the work of attempting to articulate the reality of the subject matter being talked about, and the talker's true relation to it, for the empty appearance of doing so. Milly and Helen's words are thereby divorced from the facts or truth that would give them any real weight or substance, allowing them and their speakers to float free of the tragic gravity or seriousness of the circumstances both women superficially seek to disseminate, and in which they are personally implicated.[5]

For their partners, however, it seems that participation in such a hollowed-out corruption of conversation is neither possible nor desirable, one which they can neither bear to speak nor to hear. As

Milly talks with the Braces, Shep can only remain silent, and afterwards he tearfully appeals to her not to speak anymore about the Wheelers. Similarly, when Howard turns off his hearing aid, he signals that he not only no longer wishes to hear what Helen has to say but also—since any genuine conversation obviously involves talking as well as listening—that he no longer has anything he wishes to say to her in return. Howard's deliberate deafness is thus a rejection of their marriage, a point of absolute conversational negation (call it a silent inversion of April's scream) that expresses the unhappy fact that the essential association of the conversational with the conjugal has been lost, and he no longer views Helen as a partner of any kind. Instead of the sound of her voice, he would prefer to hear only a thunderous sea of silence.

Dreams of America and of Paris: Politics, Snobbery, Exile

Given Cavell's claim that Emerson and Thoreau are amongst the founding fathers of American culture, it is perhaps hardly surprising to find that a film entitled *Revolutionary Road*—based on an American novel set in a place of the same name, and depicting a couple hoping to transform or convert, say revolutionize, their lives (a couple referred to as "the nice young revolutionaries on Wheeler Road," a reversal emphasizing that their very name suggests a capacity for such turning)—should stand in some relation to Emersonian moral perfectionism. At the same time, of course, the film's title also signals that the Wheelers' story stands in some relation to the work of the founding fathers of the United States itself; to their revolutionary ideals, and the recognition of the inalienable rights to "life, liberty and the pursuit of happiness" with which that nation declared its independence.

For Cavell, this conjunction of personal and political matters is yet another shared feature of the comedies and melodramas. He takes it that the bond of marriage between their principal pairs is not just analogous to the bond between a democratic society and its citizens, but that such marriages in effect ratify, or fail to ratify, that society as a setting in which its citizens are free to exercise those rights. They thus demonstrate, or fail to demonstrate, that America is—over a century and half after the Declaration of Independence—still a place in which happiness and liberty can be pursued (*PH*, 150–53). For the unknown women of the melodramas, the isolating unhappiness of their marriages stands as an emblem not of the success of America's democratic aspiration but its failure. In finding that the price of their continuing consent to society is agonizingly high (requiring them to endure irony, suffer unknownness, and court madness), such women in effect withdraw that consent through a melodramatic refusal of marriage that is also a refusal of society as it stands, instead imagining a further or future state of themselves and society that might more readily solicit it. April's experience of married life as a confining unhappiness, and her imagination of a happier future in the more cultured or cultivated surroundings of Paris is, then, not an essentially private concern, but a public one—a passionate indictment of America's inability to live up to its own founding principles; that it is, as it were, a nation still to be discovered or settled. Put otherwise, it is as if April embodies the idea that the revolutionary spirit of 1776 had, by the 1950s, reached something like a dead end on Revolutionary Road, thus providing the defining instance of the film's pervasive melodramatic ironies.

To see the fate of a marriage as epitomizing the fate of America in this way is to bestow upon a couple the sort of national importance usually reserved for royalty (*PH*, 147), and Frank and April are certainly regarded in superior or aristocratic terms by those around them. As Shep reveals, they are known by everyone as "*The* Wheelers," a "terrific couple" naturally endowed with certain special gifts or talents that their neighbors do not share (as symbolized by April's patrician beauty and capacity for glamor); as Helen tells April, "Well, you looked simply ravishing, and I just knew Frank did something terribly brilliant in town. You just seemed . . . special. Of course, you still are." Obviously, the danger of such adulation is that one comes to believe it oneself (as April admits to Shep in the bar, for years she thought that she and Frank would be "wonderful in the world"), thus leading one to cultivate a certain snobbery or condescension towards others.

For Cavell, this alienating disdain is the perpetual moral risk run by the principal pairs in the melodramas and the comedies, and so of those with perfectionist aspirations (*CW*, 189). He takes it that such aspirations are concentrated amongst those fortunate enough to find that social injustice or natural misfortune are not pressing or unpostponable issues—those who are possessed of sufficient means to preserve life and pursue happiness. He sees snobbery as the characteristic vice of those in a position of relative advantage within society, such as the middle classes (whose sudden expansion typified postwar American life, and whose members could afford—partly as a result of the low-cost loans offered by the GI Bill to veterans like Frank—the cars, houses, labor-saving domestic appliances, and televisions, that enabled their comparatively comfortable, suburban lives on the likes of Revolutionary Road) (*CHU*, xix). Like her later sophistical dismissal of the Wheelers themselves, Helen provides the clearest example of such snobbery. Driving the Wheelers to their first viewing of the house that will later become their home, she says, "Now of course, it isn't very desirable at this end. As you can see, Crawford Road is mostly these little cinder-blocky, pickup trucky places—plumbers, carpenters, little local people of that sort. But eventually, eventually, it leads up to Revolutionary Road, which is much nicer."[6] Frank's secret marking of this disdain by turning to April and lowering his sunglasses, and her stifled giggle in reply, suggests that they take themselves to be above or beyond such snobbery. But we might well wonder about the accuracy or sincerity of this sense. Not only do their neighbors regard the couple in elevated terms, but Frank and April themselves also succumb to this failing, taking pride in thinking of themselves as superior to both the residents of Revolutionary Road and the modest inhabitants of Crawford Road. Frank expresses this attitude when he declares that, "It's bad enough having to live out here among these damn people," and, more literally, in the shot where he leans smugly against the balustrade at Grand Central Station and looks down at his fellow commuters. Such hubris invites humbling, an opportunity for genuine self-knowledge; something that begins for April with her humiliation in her amateur dramatic debut, and which later causes her to admit that, "Our whole existence here is based on this great premise that we're somehow very special and superior to the whole thing, and you know what I've realized? We're not! We're just like everyone else . . . We were never special, or destined, or anything at all."

This form of humbling is, for Cavell, a prelude to the overcoming of snobbery which he takes to be vital to the middle classes' recognition of the extent to which they profit (knowingly or otherwise) from the disadvantaged lives of those whom they disdain. The degree of inequality present in their society (of which their material advantage is an indication) is thus something for which, insofar as they continue to consent to such an arrangement, they are responsible, and so are obliged to change (*CW*, 17). The failure to withdraw or refuse their consent to this inequality, by those who gain relative advantage from it, thereby reflects their having been complicit and compromised by it. This middle-class condescension thus masks guilt, and so the appropriate reaction by such individuals to this injustice is (as their humiliation suggests) not snobbery, but shame (68, 448). However, since any society will inevitably contain some degree of injustice—some partiality in its compliance with the principles of justice—the issue becomes how the relatively privileged might properly live with this continuing sense of compromise and shame (with the recognition, for example, that the inhabitants of Crawford Road are metaphorically and practically on the same road as oneself and one's apparently more esteemed neighbors) (*CHU*, xxiv). For Cavell, the inevitable failures of democracy are not to be understood as tempting (ultimately self-indulgent) occasions for excusal, cynicism, or despair but rather as vital calls for the change or transformation of oneself and one's society—a recognizably perfectionist ambition whose fulfilment depends on the forming of modes of character, education and friendship that invite oneself, and (by virtue of one's exemplarity or representativeness) others, to enter into an unattained, but attainable, state of self and society (56). In this way, perfectionism's seemingly self-interested and elitist concern with the development or growth of one's own soul, and the cultivation of a society reflective of that growth, is shown not only to be compatible with democracy but essential to its preservation, something it should honor so that the democratic hope might be kept alive in the face of disappointment with it (56).

Against this background, April's despairing response to the stifling injustice of her situation expresses her inability to keep that hope alive. It is not merely that her refusal of marriage stands as an enabling rebuke to her society's present arrangements which calls for or invites a vision of a future state of that society in which those arrangements are transformed. Rather, insofar as her refusal centers on a decision to move to Paris, it expresses April's conviction that America is no longer capable of such a transformation or revolution—that both she and it have lost faith with its democratic aspiration (as if the comedies' green world of Connecticut has now irreversibly darkened, requiring its displacement or relocation).[7] No longer finding herself either able or willing to withstand or conform to society's failures—to continue to suffer injustice as the necessary or worthwhile price of change—April judges that the cost of such toleration exceeds what she considers to be society's commitment to reform, and so whatever measure of justice it could presently be said to embody. Her averting withdrawal of consent is thus not made in the name of a future state of America but rather with the intuition that there is nothing America can do any longer to solicit it—an expression not of temporary separation but outright divorce. In other words, we might say that April comes to find the discrepancy or distance between the reality of America's attained state of imperfect justice and its promise of an attainable state more compliant with ideal justice (and so the distance of America from its founding idea of itself) to be so unbearable that she is undone by it. In her judgment, life on Revolutionary Road and in the nation on which that road exists, is now unlivable. America has become a place that April can no longer inhabit (not simply unsettled, but unsettleable), a place whose disappointing departure of actuality from possibility is one from which she feels she must now depart.

For Emerson, the idea that the inhabitants of America might find their true selves by travelling to one of the capitals of the old cultures of Europe is, as he puts it bluntly in "Self-Reliance," "a fool's paradise" ([1841] 2003, 198). For him, attempting to sustain oneself on a diet of what he saw as the withered and withering remains of European culture would be an essentially backward-looking idolatry, a betrayal of the opportunity for the creation of a distinctively American form of spiritual and cultural self-reliance, as promised by the Declaration of Independence some sixty years before. Indeed, from a perfectionist perspective, April's willingness for such self-imposed exile amounts to her interpreting the metaphysical distance between the attained and unattained states of herself and her society as a geographical one. But since perfectionism pictures these states as immanent to the self and its society—as indicative of their inherent division or doubling—the unattained is not so much separated by a measurable distance from the attained but rather haunts or shadows its every state (as the constancy of April's vision attests). A step into a further, attainable state of self and society is thus strictly immeasurable: it demands internal, rather than external, movement or migration, a traversing of spiritual, rather than physical, terrain. On this view, then, packing up one's family in Connecticut, and travelling three and a half thousand miles across the Atlantic in the hope of discovering one's next self appears as a dramatic false step, an almost comically profound misunderstanding of one's real openness to the future and one's genuine potentialities—a debased or perverted form of perfectionism's true vision.

And in any case, why should we imagine that things will be any better in Paris? On the contrary, there is good reason to suspect that the Wheelers' marriage would be just as unhappy in Europe as it is in America. After all, April's plan to move there was idolizingly intended to give Frank, not her, the opportunity for self-discovery. Instead, she would in effect continue to repress the question of her true identity by drowning in some anonymous secretarial pool of some nondescript, alphabet-soup-named European agency. It would seem, then, that it would only be a matter of time before April's unrelenting unhappiness followed her, and she was again made to face the stern and inescapable fact of her essentially divided or doubled nature; that, as Emerson puts it: "My giant goes with me wherever I go" ([1841] 2003, 198) (a thought echoed by one of Frank's colleagues, when he asks, "But, I mean, assuming there is a true vocation waiting for you. Wouldn't you be just as likely to discover it here as there?"). It is as if, in her desperation, April combats a hopeless pessimism with an equally hopeless optimism. Her dream of Paris is, in reality, nothing more than an attempt to recapture a past (surely romanticized) state of her relationship with Frank, a time when—lacking the burdens of work, money, and children—they were free to indulge in fashionable conversations about authenticity and self-becoming imported from the nicotine-stained existentialists of the Left Bank. In effect, rather than suggesting a turning away from her current state of self and society, April's adventurous fantasy of Paris could be understood as a turning towards it, a further symptom of her present fixated inability to imagine, and so to have, a future which manifests as a nostalgic fixation with the past (yet another of the false or fantastic excitements that suburban boredom craves).[8]

For Cavell, since the attainable world doesn't exist elsewhere, outside or beyond the borders of its presently attained state, but rather within it, perfectionism's distinctive moral calling is not for the repudiation or transcendence of one's world but for its reform or transfiguration (*CW*, 2). Rather than demanding a turn away from the familiar facts of one's existence, it requires a turn towards them—a rediscovery or reclaiming of one's ordinary or everyday life by discovering or claiming the possibilities for spiritual growth inherent within it. From this perspective, April's haunting vision of a different world becomes a vision of a world nowhere but here, of nothing but her present world transformed. Her calling is thus to reinhabit or reappropriate her life within the precincts of its suburban existence in ways that overcome or negate its undeniably repressive confinements and banalities; to come to see herself and the possibilities of her world in a new light, as if her present life were the womb containing the terms by which her future life could be delivered (*NYUA*, 46).

But is it really possible for April to discover the hitherto largely unacknowledged terms that would allow for such a transformation, to find hope in the apparently "hopeless emptiness" of 1950s suburban America, while continuing to live on Revolutionary Road (to show that, as Frank says, "It is possible that Parisians aren't the only ones who know how to lead interesting lives")? In closing, I think, despite everything, the film suggests a possible way in which such hope can be found; in which April's revolutionizing of her inhabitation of the world might, at the very least, be imagined. For while April's (and Frank's) unhappiness is pervasive, it's not absolute—once the couple decide to move to Paris, we are shown unprecedented visions of genuine happiness between them. Notably, these all feature figures who otherwise barely register in the rest of the film, and, indeed, are somewhat conspicuous by their absence—the Wheeler children (in the scenes of Frank's surprise birthday party; of bedtime; of playing on the lawn in the sunshine, leaping through the spray of a sprinkler while Frank and April embrace).[9] The question then becomes: Does the fact that this happiness is found in the expectation of leaving behind the life in which it is being experienced make it any less real? Does it necessarily make it any less possible as a potential way of living, together, at home, on Revolutionary Road? Perhaps it is April and Frank's failure to see that this is a possibility they have only to continue to realize, one they have only to keep willingly turning towards and embracing, that leads to the tragedy that is to come. But how can we know?

Conclusion: Contesting Tears

For April, then, it seems that whatever happiness there is to be had is (as indicated by her final fatal actions) essentially related to the fact of her being a mother. Exploring this thought must await another occasion, as must the exploration of others regarding the relation of certain features of the film to the genre of unknown woman melodrama.[10] Instead, I want to conclude by briefly considering the relevance of a key idea from Cavell's more general work on film: the distinctive nature of screen acting and its relation to cinematic stardom.[11] For on its release, a significant factor in the promotion of *Revolutionary Road* and its expectation by audiences was that it constituted the first time that Leonardo DiCaprio and Kate Winslet had been paired onscreen since their famous roles as Jack and Rose in James Cameron's record-breaking blockbuster *Titanic* (1997), the film which instantly transformed the two—albeit already successful—fledging young actors into fully fledged stars. At the time, this simple fact gave rise to an apparently irresistible urge by many to refer to *Revolutionary Road* as a sort of sequel to that earlier film, to see it as somehow representing audiences' much wished-for happy ending to Jack and Rose's romance (even if only briefly, as if the crossings of these stars are destined always to be star-crossed); in short, to picture it as a fantasy of what might have happened next to the young couple, had Jack not drowned in the icy black waters of the North Atlantic.

One way of accounting for this phenomenon—this inclination to see a death-defying continuity or constancy of identity underneath or behind the dramatic shifts of character and setting of the two films—is to understand it as an illustration or acknowledgment of what Cavell views as the natural ascendancy on film of the actor over the character she plays (unlike in theater where this relation is reversed), a priority determined by the photographic basis of the medium; the fact that the movie camera's automatic transcription or recording of reality depended (at least until the advent of digital technologies) on the physical presence of the actor placed before it. This mechanical emphasis on the physical reality of the screen actor, on her specific and total physiognomy (of face, figure, gait, mannerisms, temperament, etc.) as the particular individual she is, means that she relates to her role by subordinating it; accepting only those aspects of it which fit with her particular physical and temperamental endowment and leaving aside the rest—bringing the character to life by taking on or lending herself to the role, rather than (as with the stage actor) working herself into or yielding to it. And since the camera's recording of the actor both is and is not identical with its subject (the same insofar as they are indistinguishable in any specific respect and different insofar as an object in a photograph or film is not the object itself), Cavell sees the role of the camera as one of transformation or metamorphosis; a mysterious photogenesis of flesh and blood actors into something else—psychic shadows of themselves—that in certain exemplary and favorable instances, when projected on screen, results in stardom; a striking effect of the fateful, essentially unpredictable, alignment of the actor's individual physiognomy with the camera's gaze.[12]

Given this cinematic precedence of actor over character, it is thus hardly surprising to find that certain actors, particularly those who have attained the dizzying heights of stardom, should be readily identifiable across their successive incarnations of different characters in various films. But since that identification is at the same time an identification of precisely those aspects of the actor's individual physiognomy which she has in each case lent to the character in order to breathe life into it—that each part she plays is part of playing herself—then it should be equally unsurprising to find (at the very least) that one is tempted to identify any one of these particular incarnations with another, and so too the films within which those incarnations take place. In other words, whatever the film, part of what it means to see, for example, Kate Winslet and Leonardo DiCaprio onscreen is to see (amongst others) Rose and Jack, April and Frank; and so *Titanic* and *Revolutionary Road*.[13] In short, the intimate, inextricable relation between a screen actor and the character she gives birth to entails that the life and death of both is inexplicably entwined.

For anyone then who feels as I did in the course of studying *Revolutionary Road*, that the repeated witnessing of its harrowing conclusion is almost too high a price to pay for the knowledge gained from such study, it might be some comfort to end with the thought that, at the very same moment, it traces the path of a woman with a future, a star which shows no signs of fading.

Notes

1. Although the title of the play is not mentioned in the film, Yates's novel tells us that it's Robert E. Sherwood's *The Petrified Forest*, a story of a

young American woman (played by April) who dreams of escaping her banal existence by moving to France. In the film adaptation of the same name (Archie Mayo, 1936), she is played by Bette Davis.

2. The allusion to Dante is patent. This scene constitutes the first of the film's two glimpses of Cavell's green world, a place of perspective and reflection. The second, dappled with sunlight, is during Frank and April's walk with John Givings.

3. Thus, suggesting a possible difference here between the genre's early and later forms.

4. Named, presumably, because the assistance he takes Maureen to provide essentially concerns her physical appearance.

5. We can see this mode of essentially empty, moralizing gossip—in which the speakers have no real interest or stake in what is being said or its genuine relation to its putative subject matter—as symptomatic of the boredom from which suburbanites are often said to suffer. This is further registered in the film's recurrent interest in what people find interesting: in April's first expression of interest in Frank by asking him what really interests him, and in subsequently finding him the most interesting person she's ever met; in Frank's admission to John at their first meeting that there's nothing interesting about his job (a view obviously shared by his colleagues); in John's sarcastic remark about mathematics being interesting; in the supposedly interesting lives of Parisians; and, finally, during the chilling scene of the Wheelers' last breakfast, when Frank acknowledges April's suggestion that there is, after all, something interesting in what he does.

6. Crawford Road is not mentioned by name in Yates's novel. Here, we might like to fancy that the filmmakers are paying tribute to Joan Crawford, who played the heroine in *Mildred Pierce* (Michael Curtiz, 1945), a self-sacrificing, middle-class mother trapped in an unhappy marriage during the Great Depression. In Todd Haynes's 2011 television miniseries of the same name, Mildred Pierce was played by Kate Winslet.

7. In this regard, it is worth recalling that two of the four films Cavell takes as definitive of unknown woman melodrama—*Gaslight* (George Cukor, 1944) and *Letter from an Unknown Woman* (Max Ophüls, 1948)—have *fin de siècle* Europe as their setting, rather than America. At the same time, however, the America of *Now, Voyager* and *Stella Dallas* (King Vidor, 1937) is still a place where melodramatic transformation or revolution is possible. Whether April's disappointed refusal of America's darkened failure constitutes a difference between early and recent versions of the genre is then, perhaps, an open question.

8. This fact that rather than overcoming conformity April is still subject to it might be understood to constitute a central difference between *Revolutionary Road* and its classical antecedents. Indeed, more strongly, it

could perhaps be seen as reason enough not to consider her an example (of however different a later kind) of an unknown woman at all. But this would, in effect, not only amount to denying the significance of the generic features already discussed but, more importantly, to denying the depth and reality of the increasingly desperate and paralyzed perfectionist desire to which April attempts (in however distorted a way) to give expression. In this context, it is worth recalling the similarly pervasive condition of tragic, or hopeless, hope that affected April's melodramatic sister Lisa Berndle in *Letter from an Unknown Woman*; a woman, like April, whose unknownness follows her to the end.

9. Their son, Michael, is only mentioned by name twice, and we have to wait until the end credits to learn that their daughter is called Jennifer—as if she is already at risk of unknownness.

10. For example: the nature of April's self-sacrifice, and its relation to that of her cinematic sisters (whether April's sacrifice is suicidal appears to be a question that the film leaves open, but it is clear both to April and to us by that point that the issue of her self-realization does not turn on whether or not she has another child. As John asks mockingly: "Don't people have babies in Europe?"); and the role of the Wheeler house's picture window—through which April finally experiences a vanishingly brief, but total, moment of ecstatic freedom—as a figure for the movie screen (something that Cavell finds to be true of a similar, brilliantly lit, window at the end of *Stella Dallas*).

11. See especially chapter 4 of *WV*, and Mulhall's (2013) elaboration of these ideas.

12. This talk of transformation and metamorphosis suggests an analogy with perfectionism. If we think of the actor's successive incarnations of particular characters as analogous to the self's journey between a sequence of attained states—and so of the screen actor's cinematic soul as inherently split between its projected and as yet unprojected (flesh and blood) sides or personas—then each role constitutes not only the opportunity for the growth of their artistic or cinematic identity but also the risk of such growth being occluded; of the actor becoming so attached to or fixated with the settled satisfactions (financial or otherwise) provided by the inhabitation of a particular character (say by conforming to audience expectations by endlessly repeating it, allowing oneself to become idolizingly typecast) that she eclipses or negates her capacity to inhabit other characters which might better realize her unattained but attainable—unprojected but projectable—self. And we might further wonder whether this is merely an analogy. Given the extent to which screen acting is dependent on the person of the actor, and acting itself is taken to be a vocation, we could think of this artistic crisis as a deeply personal one. But just because something is personal does not mean that it

is private. Might we then understand the actor's attempts to relate to herself genuinely in this way (or her failure to do so) as presenting an enabling example or lesson from which others might learn? After all, the results of such attempts are projected on a screen big enough for all the world to see.

13. As if at April's and Frank's first meeting at the party in Greenwich Village the pair appear to recognize each other, as if having known one another forever—say, as having "grown up together" (*PH*, 103).

Works Cited

Emerson, Ralph Waldo. (1841) 2003. "Self-Reliance." In *Nature and Selected Essays*, edited by Larzer Ziff. Penguin Books.
Mulhall, Stephen. 2013. *On Film*. Third edition. Routledge.

6
____

I Love You, Man

The Bromance as Remarriage

REX BUTLER

THE WEDDING PARTY IS gathered on the lawn. The bride and groom, Zooey (Rashida Jones) and Peter (Paul Rudd), stand before the celebrant, with their bridesmaids and groomsmen to the side. The celebrant is about to start saying the words that will bring the couple together when a motorbike roars loudly into view, disturbing the hushed ceremony. It's Peter's new best friend, Sydney (Jason Segel), with whom he has recently fallen out, but who has been invited by Zooey because, in her words, "I saw you walking on the lawn [with your groomsmen] all sad, and I realized I couldn't let you get married without your best man." Sydney gets off his bike and, prompted by Zooey, walks up the aisle to join the couple, looking for all the world like a groom or even a bride about to get married. The two men now speak earnestly to each other while the ceremony is paused. "Sydney, I'm sorry for all of the stuff I said." "Peter, you called me out on a lot of my issues. I appreciate it. And for the record, I saw *Chocolat* [the film starring Johnny Depp and Juliette Binoche he had previously denied seeing]. Just delightful. It is, right?" At this point, the bridesmaids behind him murmur appreciatively. "I'm really glad you're here, Sydney," continues Peter. "Me too." "I can't even imagine getting married without you. I love you, man." The two men then exchange a series of increasingly bizarre endearments. "I love you, bud." "I love you, dude." "I love you, Bro Montana." "I love you, Holmes." "I love you, Broseph Goebbels." "I love you, muchacha." The celebrant interrupts, and the wedding continues with Sydney now in the role of best man. Peter looks Zooey in the eyes and tells her, "I so want to marry you." And Zooey replies, "You will." The vows are exchanged as the camera tilts up to a plane carrying a banner with the words "Congratulations! Peter & Zooey," Sydney's wedding gift to the couple, and the credits roll.

John Hamburg's *I Love You, Man* (2009) is an often discussed member of the recently declared genre of "bromance" or "male romance" films. It is mentioned, for example, in Claire Mortimer's survey *Romantic Comedy* (2010, 134–36). It is the subject of a chapter in Greg Singh's *Feeling Film: Affect and Authenticity in Popular Cinema* (2010, 122–41). And it is taken up in at least three of the essays in the Michael DeAngelis-edited *Reading the Bromance: Homosocial Relationships in Film and Television* (2014): Jenna Weinman's "Second Bananas and Gay Chicken: Bromancing the Rom-Com in the Fifties and Now," which relates it to such Hollywood sex comedies of the late 1950s and early 1960s as *Send Me No Flowers* (Norman Jewison, 1964); Hilary Radner's "Grumpy Old Men: 'Bros Before Hos,'" which points to the way that the recent wave of bromance films featuring young men can be seen to be drawing on such earlier films as the *Grumpy Old Men* series (Donald Petrie, 1993; Howard Deutch, 1995); and Ken Feil's "From *Batman* to *I Love You, Man*: Queer Taste, Vulgarity and the Bromance as Sensibility and Film Genre," which for its part relates contemporary bromance films to the famously camp 1960s TV series *Batman*. *I Love You, Man* is seen as typical of the bromance genre, which is defined broadly in the words of Heather Brook, who has written an important overview of the topic, as focusing on a "relationship between male characters, following a similar trajectory to the heterosexual relationship that is central to the romcom" (2015, 253).[1] But then, as any number of other commentators have pointed out, these films are also driven by a kind of repressed homosexuality, or at least homosociality. The tension or contradiction played out in them is that they are able to show us often explicit sexual or romantic interaction between the various male characters, but this is ultimately repressed or disregarded in light of an eventual relationship—which, importantly, this intervening male relationship is shown to be necessary for—with a woman. As Maria San Filippo puts it in *The B Word: Bisexuality in Contemporary Film and Television*: "The bromance recasts the American male as more heteroflexible, yet employs a strategy of containment designed to defuse any threat to herteromasculinity by presenting it as intended just for laughs" (2013, 196).

Perhaps the definitional example of the contemporary bromance film is *The Hangover* (Todd Phillips, 2009). Three old friends, schoolteacher Phil (Bradley Cooper), dentist Stu (Ed Helms), and occupation unidentified Doug (Justin Bartha), along with Alan (Zach Galifianakis), the eccentric brother of the bride, head off to Las Vegas for a bachelor party two days before Doug's wedding to Tracy (Sasha Barrese). Alan accidentally laces their celebratory rooftop drinks with the infamous date rape drug Rohypnol, and the rest of the evening is lost. Phil, Stu, and Alan wake up the next morning in a debris-strewn hotel room with a tiger in the bathroom and a small baby in a cupboard. The rest of the film features the three men trying to recall the events of the night before, their only way of discovering where Doug is and getting him back in time for the wedding. It involves a seemingly implausible series of events, including Stu getting married to an escort, Jade (Heather Graham), in one of Las Vegas's infamous marriage chapels (it is in fact Jade's baby in the cupboard in the hotel room), the three men sneaking a tiger from former heavyweight boxing champion Mike Tyson's gated compound (Tyson and an ominous-looking assistant at one point visit their hotel room and demand the tiger's return), and a Chinese gangster whose money they have accidentally taken from a blackjack table (he apparently holds Doug captive and offers him in return for the money). Throughout their adventures, Phil emerges as their natural leader, but at various points Stu deduces where Doug actually is—on top of the roof where they originally took the drug—and even the seemingly irredeemable Alan reveals himself to have the previously unknown ability to count cards, winning them the $80,000 they owe the gangster. They make it back in time for the wedding, changing into their tuxedoes on the way, and all four have either made or strengthened their friendships with the others, with a new respect for each other's talents. Stu even breaks up with his constantly critical fiancée Melissa (Rachael Harris) at the wedding reception, vowing to give his marriage with Jade a chance, and asks Alan to join him on the dance floor after Melissa has loudly shouted "Suck my dick" to him, an offer Alan refuses.[2]

Something like this can certainly be seen in *I Love You, Man*. The plot begins with Peter concerned that he has no close male friends, since he is unable to find a best man for his upcoming wedding with Zooey. Taking advice from his openly gay brother, he goes out on a date with a man in order to get to know him, being careful not to imply that it is romantic in nature. It inevitably goes wrong, with the other man taking an opportunity to try to kiss Peter. (Intriguingly, the man, shown throughout the film as still being annoyed at Peter's refusal, ends up as one of his groomsmen at the wedding.) It is at a house opening—Peter is a real estate agent—that Peter meets Sydney, and the two hit it off immediately. Sydney is fine with Peter's gauche and too-keen-to-please manner—Peter tries and fails repeatedly to speak in a cool and unaffected manner—and soon invites him back to his so-called man cave. (Sydney is unattached and appears only to have a series of exclusively sexual relationships with divorced women.) Once there, Sydney tells Peter where and how he masturbates, asks him why he is marrying Zooey, and shows him his collection of musical instruments and asks him whether he can play. The two are soon spending all of their time together making music, with Sydney passing on life lessons to Peter, although he himself appears outside of the usual social norms. Events come to a head when Sydney speaks inappropriately at Peter and Zooey's engagement dinner, where he reveals that Peter is concerned about Zooey's refusal to perform oral sex on him, and then at a rock concert when Peter and Sydney dance passionately and unselfconsciously with each other, ignoring Zooey, who is also there. Later, Peter asks Zooey, prompted by Sydney's earlier question to him, why they are getting married, and Zooey leaves their shared house and goes to live with some friends. Afterwards, Sydney produces a series of embarrassing billboards advertising Peter's services as a real estate agent, incidentally revealing just how intimately they have come to know each other (Peter is pictured in one in underwear thrusting his crotch towards the camera and in another suggestively blowing on an upturned finger like James Bond), and Peter decides to break off his relationship with Sydney. He then goes to the house where Zooey is staying to tell her that he still loves her, and she agrees to marry him again. It is Zooey, who has revealed herself throughout to be both sensible and sensitive, as opposed to her naive and susceptible fiancé, who invites Sydney to the wedding, telling Peter as she does so that she could tell that he was lonely without him. And after Sydney walks up the aisle and the two men make up their differences—almost something of a wedding itself with Zooey as the best man—the real ceremony between Peter and Zooey can begin.

Indeed, it is uncanny—and frequently observed—how often in these bromance films the breaking and then making up of men is a precursor to and necessary for not just the straight heterosexual relationship with the woman but the very possibility of marriage with them. In *The Hangover*, in order for the marriage to proceed, the various men involved in the bachelor party in Las Vegas have to locate the groom and make up their relationships with each other, which have become frayed both by their different lifestyles and their attempts to discover what happened the night before. Something like this is also seen in Judd Apatow's admittedly more misogynistic and less well put together *Knocked Up* (2007), in which, after an immature and unattractive slacker (Seth Rogen) gets a glamorous and self-assured TV presenter (Katherine Heigl) pregnant after a one-night stand, the film shows him slowly disengaging from and then reforming his relationships with his equally immature friends on the basis of his new status as father-to-be. And, on the rare occasion where there is a lack of resolution in the lead male character's relationships with other men, either by them ending or finding their proper place within a wider heterosexual field, this is shown as endangering, if not making impossible, not only marriage but any enduring relationship with a woman. This is the case with the equally tasteless *Humpday* (Lynn Shelton, 2009), in which two notionally straight men decide to make a gay porn film for an amateur film festival called Humpfest. One of them says about the endeavor, "I don't really understand why I want to do this." Both are unable to deal with the notional homosexual desire aroused in them as they begin to make the film and they retreat to their obviously unhappy heterosexual relationships, which are characterized by either a lack of sex or a fear of their partner's too-overt sexuality.

Of course, it is difficult to know how to take these bromances, with their seeming argument that some kind of necessary settling of sexual accounts is necessary before their male characters can enter into a successful relationship with a woman. The films are often misogynistic, deliberately outdated or stereotypical in their attitudes towards women—can we really laugh at Seth's disgust at women's menstrual blood in *Superbad* (Greg Mottola, 2007) or the racist and homophobic grandmother belittling her black maids and servants in *Wedding Crashers* (David Dobkin, 2005)? And, needless to say, even beyond these seemingly inadvertent lapses of taste or morality, there is the deliberate gross-out aspect of these films, where we can simply make no logical or narrative sense of what we are presented with and the films put forward no justification for it. The commonly cited examples here are the concluding shots of Katherine Heigl's character painfully giving birth to a crowning baby in *Knocked Up*, a scene that Apatow insisted remain in the film, and the long comic riff between Seth Rogen and Paul Rudd in *The 40 Year-Old Virgin* (Judd Apatow, 2005), in which each tells the other why they know they are gay, culminating in the line "You know why I know you're gay? Because your dick tastes like shit." But here again, in a kind of camp, conscious, deliberately ironic sense, these films also know that these scenes are gratuitous, make no sense, cannot be justified either ethically or aesthetically, and that is precisely the point.

Indeed, something like this difficulty of address—although it is hard to attribute to some authorial control or intent—can be seen altogether with the often-remarked ambiguity of male relationships in these films. Although the plot often resolves them in terms of a return to orthodox heterosexual relationships, and on a number of occasions an actual marriage to a woman, this is preceded by an interregnum period during which certain nonnormative desires and truths are revealed that are not so easily dismissed or put away in the closet, as it were. (And, in fact, it can even be the case that in the closing credit sequence of the film, after their apparent resolution, these desires are let out again, as in *Superbad*, *The Hangover*, and *The 40 Year-Old Virgin*.) This has been the subject of much of the commentary on these films and what they might be understood to be saying about society's treatment of homosexuality, and even the inextricable connection between homosexuality and heterosexuality. This was perhaps first observed by Lauren Bans, an early commentator on the genre, who in "The Upside of Bromance" (2010) wrote, "I do think Bromances are generally good for straight society, if only because they self-consciously carve a place for openly compassionate male-male friendship." It is also what Karen Boyle and Susan Berridge contend, if a little more skeptically, in "I Love You, Man: Gendered Narratives in Contemporary Hollywood Comedies": "In her influential work on male homosociality, Eve Kosofsky Sedgwick argues that homophobia is an essential component of male homosociality and men's power precisely because homosociality and homosexuality are, structurally, dangerously close to each other" (Boyle and Berridge 2014, 356). And, finally, this argument very much runs through such collections as DeAngelis's *Reading the Bromance* (2014), in which for example Peter Forster in "Rad Bromance (Or I Love You, Man, but We Won't Be Humping on Humpday)" speaks of the "shifting sands within the treacherous territory of homosociality, where same-sex intimacy cannot be reduced to sexual desire, but where the desire that might inflect this intimacy cannot be discounted or denied" (Forster 2014, 192).

All of this is undoubtedly part of the wider queering of contemporary culture, which we would want to say involves not merely an acknowledgement of nonheterosexual desire but at its most powerful implies that heterosexuality is a subset of or enabled by homosexual desire. In effect, we suggest, queer makes the argument that nonheterosexual desire precedes and makes possible heterosexual desire and is even something of its transcendental condition. This is the claim of Judith Butler, who proposes that we first give up our preoedipal attraction to our parents (including son for father and daughter for mother), and therefore our subsequent sex lives are marked by a kind of melancholy for what we have sacrificed, as though what we eventually choose—either hetero- or homosexual in nature, which is why "queer" is irreducible to either—is marked by a kind of loss or mourning for what is not chosen (Butler 1995).[3] This is also the argument—just to consider this in the context of film for a moment—put forward by Tania Modleski in "An Affair to Forget: Melancholia in Bromantic Comedy" (2014), drawing on Butler, in which she makes the point that those bromance films we have been looking at are unable definitively to resolve or bring to an end those romantic comedy interludes of "same" sex attraction, insofar as they are in some way the condition of possibility of romantic heterosexual attraction and all that it stands for. This is Modleski on *Superbad*: "The ending of *Superbad* perfectly illustrates my point that in these films the melancholic affair to forget is clearly *not* entirely forgotten and *not* foreclosed upon, as Butler maintains is the case with homosexual desires in a heteronormative society" (2014, 126–27).

We find a version of this also in Lee Wallace's recent *Reattachment Theory: Queer Cinema of Remarriage* (2020). In it she looks not at any "bromantic" picture, in which after a homosocial interlude the man eventually marries or gets together with a woman, but a series of films depicting gay marriage or its equivalent. Amongst the films Wallace treats in detail are *A Single Man* (Tom Ford, 2009), in which a gay man decides whether to enter a new relationship after losing his long-term partner; Lisa Cholodenko's trilogy *High Art* (1998), *Laurel Canyon* (2002), and *The Kids are Alright* (2011), which variously depict the beginning of a lesbian relationship, a young woman entering a three-way relationship with her boyfriend's mother and male partner, and a lesbian couple with children about to split up after one of them has an affair with their children's biological father; *Concussion* (Stacie Passon, 2013), in which one half of a long-standing lesbian couple decides to become a sex worker; and *Weekend* (Andrew Haigh, 2011), about two men meeting and becoming intimate the same weekend one of them is due to go and live overseas. Wallace then ends her book with a consideration of *45 Years* (Andrew Haigh, 2014), about a heterosexual couple celebrating their forty-fifth wedding anniversary, which concludes with a celebrated three-minute close-up of actress Charlotte Rampling's face lit by a revolving disco ball at the party, evidently deciding whether it has all been worth it.

In fact, the real subject of Wallace's book is the meaning of gay marriage after numerous countries—including Australia, where Wallace lives—have allowed legal marriage between same-sex couples. Wallace's polemical thrust—admittedly, as she acknowledges, against much gay polemic—is for the possibility, even suitability, of marriage as an expression of the love and commitment between gay couples. Therefore, the social and artistic expression of marriage between heterosexual couples offers a kind of exemplar and grounds for reflection for these couples. In effect, gay marriage is subject to many if not all of the same issues and concerns that heterosexual marriage is subject to. Wallace writes, in the chapter "Queer Skepticism and Gay Marriage": "Against the tide of the queer critique of marriage, I make a strong argument for the ongoing pertinence of the marriage plot—and the narrative sensibility it cultivates—as generative of the conditions through which we continue to experience ourselves as subjects of feeling and agents of change" (2020, 26). In order to bring out this idea that future gay marriage will be subject to the same pressures as straight marriage, the films Wallace speaks of depict gay relationships in crisis and couples splitting up, but then resolving the differences between them and getting back together again. This is not always the case—and perhaps the book is not as consistent and watertight in this regard as it would want to be—but it is nevertheless a consistent thread throughout the films she studies. In *A Single Man*, the single gay man in question has to decide whether to enter a new relationship or remain faithful to the memory of his old one. In Cholodenko's *Laurel Canyon*, the young man and woman have to decide whether to stay together after each has an affair (the young woman with the older woman and man, the young man with a fellow student), and in *The Kids are Alright* one half of the lesbian couple decides to return to her partner and children after an affair with their father. In *Concussion*, after engaging in sex work, the woman returns to her domestic life as one half of a couple with children. And in *45 Years*, the character Rampling plays is left deciding whether to stay with her husband after the body of the woman he was going to marry before her and who died while they were both crossing a mountain is discovered after many years and it is revealed that she was pregnant with their child. (And Cholodenko's *High Art* and Haigh's *Weekend*, although not involving established couples splitting up and getting back together again, nevertheless do involve people in same-sex relationships deciding whether or not to stay together.)

In thinking through how many of these couples break up and get back together again, Wallace turns to Stanley Cavell's *Pursuits of Happiness: The Hollywood Comedy of Remarriage* (1981), his now canonical study of the comedies of remarriage: a series of American screwball comedies from the 1930s and 1940s that feature a heterosexual couple breaking up, sometimes divorcing, and then deciding to get back together again. (As is also well-known, not all of the films in the cycle do exactly this but something like its equivalent is found in each of them.) Thus, for example, in the first film that Cavell treats, *The Lady Eve* (Preston Sturges, 1941), con woman Jean Harrington (Barbara Stanwyck) remarries Charles Pike (Henry Fonda) after first duping him and taking his money, but actually falls in love with him while doing so. In *It Happened One Night* (Frank Capra, 1934), heiress

Ellie Andrews (Claudette Colbert) runs away from her marriage with fortune hunter King Wesley (Jameson Thomas), once against her father's wishes, who wants her actually to divorce him, and once with his approval, when she wants instead to marry journalist Peter Warner (Clark Gable). In *The Philadelphia Story* (George Cukor, 1940), whose relation to *I Love You, Man* we will explore in a moment—no fewer than three men compete for the affections of Tracy Lord (Katharine Hepburn) as she is due to be married, but in the end she leaves her intended George Kittredge (John Howard), refuses the advances of Mike Connor (James Stewart), the besotted journalist who has come to cover the wedding, and decides to remarry her first husband, C. K. Dexter Haven (Cary Grant). And in the last of the films Cavell treats, *The Awful Truth* (Leo McCarey, 1937), Lucy Warriner (Irene Dunne) decides not to marry the naive but well-wishing country man Dan Lesson (Ralph Bellamy) and gets back together with her deceptive and jealous husband Jerry Warriner (Cary Grant) just before their divorce becomes official, despite the fact that he falsely accused her of an affair with her music teacher Armand Duvalle (Alexander Darcy).

Wallace wants to make the point that those contemporary films she studies—Ford's *A Single Man*, Cholodenko's trilogy, Passon's *Concussion*, and Haigh's *Weekend* and *45 Years*—even though they feature same-sex couples, in many ways, whether consciously or not, are indebted to the example of these Hollywood comedies of remarriage, just as perhaps in real life many of the concerns of heterosexual marriage carry over into gay marriage. But, against this or at the same time as it, Wallace will argue that heterosexual marriage has throughout its history been inseparable from something like gay marriage. And, perhaps even more speculatively, that this late series of films featuring gay marriage retrospectively contains the truth of those original heterosexual comedies of remarriage. Indeed—and here, of course, Wallace can sound like Butler or Modleski—not just gay marriage but *all* marriage is first of all queer. Or, to put this more precisely in terms of Wallace's argument and to explain her particular emphasis on the comedies of remarriage, we might say that all marriage is first of all *queer*, and then it can become either gay or straight. In other words, following Butler and Modleski, all marriage has something of that search for a lost object. While queer marriage acknowledges this, even when not finding it, straight marriage (and certain forms of gay marriage) can be seen to deny this loss altogether. Again, "queer" operates as something like the transcendental condition of *all* marriage, that which all straight marriages take the place of, whether between men and women, men and men or women and women. This is Wallace in the chapter "Reattachment Theory": "If, as Cavell argues, all marriage is remarriage after the social legitimation of divorce, then post-marriage equality all marriage can be considered gay marriage, at least for popular purposes" (2020, 138–39).[4]

Or let us start again. What exactly could Wallace mean by saying, with regard to *45 Years*, "Like those women before her [of the Cavellian comedies of remarriage], this wife is also responsible for securing her own romantic happiness, a task that sees her caught between the alternatives of marital tragedy and comedy, death and rebirth, genres and experiences previously understood as universal but, post-marriage equality, perhaps better understood as universally gay" (2020, 163)? Of course, as is well known—and Wallace reminds us of it several times in her book—Cavell makes the point that remarriage comes *before* marriage, that remarriage is as it were the prior condition of marriage. What he means by this is that the actual drama or comedy of remarriage—a married couple breaking up and then getting married again—merely reveals that, in any proper married relationship, the two parties involved are always testing the criteria for mutual satisfaction, in effect continually breaking up and getting back together again. That is to say, any shared understanding can take place only against the possibility of *misunderstanding* in Cavell's Wittgensteinian account of how human communication occurs as the overcoming of a prior doubt or skepticism. And, indeed—to look at all of this the other way around—any statement of disagreement is already itself an implicit agreement and necessarily implies a place from where this disagreement can be remarked on by both parties. Hence Cavell's conception of the arguments couples have in the throes of their breaking up as not only the prelude to their getting back together but already their getting back together. In other words, they are at least able to disagree with each other, and know that they are disagreeing with each other. The screwball banter between male and female—properly but progressively understood as equal partners—is at the same time their breaking up and getting back together again. Any attempt to restate the conventions that keep them together inevitably gets them wrong and opens up the grounds for further contestation. But the dispute itself, to the very extent it can be understood as a dispute, is already a form of mutual respect and understanding between the two parties.

However, Wallace's hypothesis regarding the priority of queer marriage—although she does not particularly do this herself—allows us to look again at a number of the films Cavell treats and see them in a different way. For it is undoubtedly true that, at least in a couple of them, their first marriage is gay or that, like those bromances we looked at earlier, it is a matter of a prior homosocial romance that must be dealt with before the heterosexual one can take place. The most obvious example is *The Philadelphia Story*, in which Connor is clearly taken by Dexter Haven, which gives him the confidence to make his pitch to Lord, while we suspect that Dexter Haven for his part is as much stimulated by his homosocial rivalry with Connor as any love he has for Lord in seeking to win her back.[5] We see something similar in *The Awful Truth*: Jerry Warriner does not realize that the man he accuses his wife of having an affair with, the music teacher Armand Duvalle, is gay, at least not until they end up locked in a bedroom together and it is possible that Armand makes a pass at him. Or, at least, it is this as much as his jealousy that might explain why a fight breaks out between them.[6] (And, of course, in both cases our reading of the films is influenced by the fact that we now know Grant was a queer man, closeted to a greater or lesser extent throughout his Hollywood career. Indeed, it is notable that Cavell in some way seems to be acknowledging this by titling his chapter on *The Awful Truth* "The Same and Different" [*PH*, 229–64], drawing on dialogue that Grant uses to describe himself in the film.)

In fact, it is only in the most recent example of the comedies of remarriage that Cavell treats in his book, *Adam's Rib* (George Cukor, 1949), featuring the now older Spencer Tracy and Katharine Hepburn, that there is no hint of a male rival for the woman with whom the main male character is in love—even if it was on previous occasions only her father—as though it is only with the absence of such a rival that the genre is no longer possible.

As a number of writers have pointed out, there is a so-called family resemblance between the comedies of romance and the contemporary bromance, which again—and this is something that Cavell in principle would not be opposed to—is not merely because the bromances inherit and vulgarize the back-in-the-day scandalous back-and-forth of the couples but because we can now look at those comedies through the lens of the bromances and see that they are not only about male-female relations but also about the relationships between men.

We might put this another way. A marriage is always a remarriage because it stands in for an ideal queer relationship. This is seen in those bromances where the queer relationship is so difficult for the protagonists to lay aside or other find a place for because it is so much better than not only any real-life male-female relationship but even any actual gay or male-male relationship depicted in the films. This is the subtle paradox or tension that is seen, for example, in *Reading the Bromance*: while in one way when its authors speak of queer relationships in the films it is obviously to refer to the actual relations we see between the men, in another way they are also gesturing towards something that any relationship falls short of, and certainly in the bromance films themselves, marked as they are by misogyny, homophobia, and the all-too-obvious conformity to social norms. "Queer" would be the standard we hold up not only against heterosexual relationships but against any actual homosexual ones we see in the films. And equally, even in Wallace's apparently more worldly and less utopian vision of queerness in *Reattachment Theory*, "queer" would be that still perfectible Cavellian relationship in which couples can actually work their way back to a reconciliation, in which misunderstanding is merely another form of understanding, as opposed to the actual failings and tentative reconciliations we see in the films Wallace discusses. There is, indeed, a Cavellian perfectionism at stake in marriage for Wallace, admittedly not yet perfect but always on the way. However, it is only queer marriage that aspires to this any longer, and again all other marriages, whether gay or straight, fall short of this ambition.[7]

Back to *I Love you, Man* for the last time. In fact—and this is true of all male bromances—the time the two men spend together can appear anything but utopian and queer: Sydney telling Peter how he masturbates, sharing pretend guitar solos at a Rush concert, the two exchanging sexist jokes and observations that would never be allowed in polite society. (Peter: "I literally met Zooey the day after we [he and his previous girlfriend] broke up." Sydney: "No laj in between the vag.") How could this be the standard that heterosexual and, indeed, all relationships are measured by? How could this be that transcendental relationship that precedes and makes possible any subsequent marriage? Precisely because it is not judged by conventional social standards, not only of heterosexuality but even of contemporary heteronormativity (nonsexist, nonmisogynistic, respectful of others). Butler is right: what we have here is something of the preoedipal, a residue of that time before our separation from others. It is what we see—against Cavell's democratic world of conversation as the continual testing of criteria, the necessity to overcome a prior skepticism—not in the witty and sophisticated exchange between man and woman that helps them get back together in the screwball comedies but in the jejune and inarticulate mumbles between men, in which there is no prior skepticism, no necessity at once to converse and speak about the rules of conversation. (By contrast to that moment in *It Happened One Night* when Ellie Andrews's father's detectives are about to enter the room in which she and Peter Warne are staying, and Peter changes tone to alert her and she must recognize it to join in, in the conversations between Peter and Sydney in *I Love You, Man* Peter is utterly unable to recognize the tone of the conversation, but there is nevertheless nothing that comes between them and no need for interpretation.) It is a premodern world, before the "properties of an object" are replaced by the "clause or provision of a story," to use Cavell's distinction (*PH*, 32).

In fact, to follow the lines of Wallace's argument—but also Butler's and Modleski's—there is a marriage before even that first marriage, a marriage whose loss or forgetting allows that first marriage as the attempt to recapture it. It is what enables marriage, what each marriage aspires to, and what means that each marriage fails in falling short of. It is what leads to the attempt to make up for this failure by marrying or remarrying again. Marriage is by definition perfectionist in that it attempts to do better, to make up for a prior loss. Indeed, it is something that exists only in its loss, that is visible only in retrospect, in a melancholy way, as it were. (As in *The Hangover*, where it is only after the marriage takes place that the men discover the homosocial joy that preceded it and exists only as what must be forgotten for the marriage to take place.) But it is also this first marriage that allows us to *remember* that something has been lost and to try to make up for it by getting married again. It is queer, in effect presexual, before its separation into any so-called normative sexuality: hetero, lesbian, gay. It is the plus at the end of LGBTQIA+: what exists only as what is left out, what cannot be named. It is what exists before we are separated from the other. It is a matter not of *I Love You, Man*, or even of *I Love You*, but simply of Love.

Notes

1. In fact, Brook is quoting from Mortimer (2010) here.

2. Throughout the film, the three main characters see each other in all kinds of revealing and vulnerable states (crying with each other, hugging each other, comforting each other). Famously, when the men are moving into their hotel room at the beginning of the film, Alan will say, "If we're sharing beds, I'm bunking with Phil" (the most obviously handsome of the four men). The next morning Phil and Stu will see Alan with no pants on, as his brother-in-law Doug earlier saw him wearing only a jockstrap when they were getting fitted for their wedding tuxedoes.

3. This essay is reprinted, along with a commentary by Adam Phillips and a reply by Butler, in Butler (1997).

4. See also Wallace (2022) and San Filippo (2013) on this connection between Cavell and gay marriage.

5. At the end of *The Philadelphia Story*, Dexter Haven, as he is waiting to walk down the aisle to marry Lord, gets Connor to be his best man, which can look as though—as in *I Love You, Man*—it is the two men who are getting married with Lord as the best man. We see something similar at the conclusion of *Wedding Crashers*, where it can appear that it is the two male characters, John and Jeremy, who are getting married at Jeremy and Gloria's wedding.

6. It is even possible that Warriner strikes out against Duvalle simply because he now realizes he is gay when he previously thought he was straight, with the thought that in so doing he is thereby striking out against himself. His manner throughout the film is thoroughly camp, and his unexpected interlude at the sports club in New York may well have been homosexual in nature, as the locker room banter earlier in the film suggests.

7. Admittedly, Wallace is not quite making the distinction between *gay* and *queer* we propose, but we would argue that one way of understanding Wallace's argument that all marriage is remarriage, and all marriage is gay (2020, 25, 138–39, 163), is to suggest that all marriage, including gay marriage, is an attempt to make up for that lost preoedipal attachment that precedes any actual sexual identification. All marriage is a remarriage and gay because marriage today is modern; but we might hypothesize that it is still driven by and stands in for a perfect, nonskeptical, premodern union that we would

call "queer." And do we not see something of this in those childlike figures atop the clock in *The Philadelphia Story*, spoken of by Cavell in *Pursuits of Happiness* (PH, 262)?

Works Cited

Bans, Lauren. 2010. "The Upside of Bromance." *Slate*. April 8, 2010. https://slate.com/human-interest/2010/04/the-upside-of-bromance.html.

Boyle, Karen, and Susan Berridge. 2014. "I Love You, Man: Gendered Narratives of Friendship in Contemporary Hollywood Comedies." *Feminist Media Studies* 14 (3): 353–68. https://doi.org/10.1080/14680777.2012.740494.

Brook, Heather. 2015. "Bros before Ho(mo)s: Hollywood Bromance and the Limits of Heterodoxy." *Men and Masculinities* 18 (2): 249–66. https://doi.org/10.1177/1097184X15584913.

Butler, Judith. 1995. "Melancholy Gender—Refused Identification." *Psychoanalytic Dialogues* 5 (2): 165–80. https://doi.org/10.1080/10481889509539059.

Butler, Judith. 1997. *The Psychic Life of Power: Theories in Subjection*. Stanford University Press.

DeAngelis, Michael, ed. 2014. *Reading the Bromance: Homosocial Relationships in Film and Television*. Wayne State University Press.

Feil, Ken. 2014. "From *Batman* to *I Love You, Man*: Queer Taste, Vulgarity, and the Bromance as Sensibility and Film Genre." In DeAngelis, *Reading the Bromance*.

Forster, Peter. 2014. "Rad Bromance (Or I Love You, Man, but We Won't Be Humping on Humpday)." In DeAngelis, *Reading the Bromance*.

Modleski, Tania. 2014. "An Affair to Forget: Melancholia in Bromantic Comedy." *Camera Obscura: Feminism, Culture, and Media Studies* 29 (2): 119–47. https://doi.org/10.1215/02705346-2704652.

Mortimer, Claire. 2010. *Romantic Comedy*. Routledge.

Radner, Hilary. 2014. "Grumpy Old Men: 'Bros Before Hos.'" In DeAngelis, *Reading the Bromance*.

San Filippo, Maria. 2013. "More than Buddies: *Wedding Crashers* and the Bromance as Cinema of (Re)Marriage Equality." In *Millennial Masculinity: Men in Contemporary American Cinema*, edited by Timothy Shary. Wayne State University Press.

San Filippo, Maria. 2013. *The B Word: Bisexuality in Contemporary Film and Television*. Indiana University Press.

Singh, Greg. 2014. "*I Love You, Man*: Mandate Movies, Bromantic Comedies and the 'Frat Pack.'" In *Feeling Film: Affect and Authenticity in Popular Cinema*. Routledge. https://doi.org/10.4324/9781315817453.

Wallace, Lee. 2020. *Reattachment Theory: Queer Cinema of Remarriage*. Duke University Press.

Wallace, Lee. 2022. "Stanley Cavell and the Queer Thought of Movies." *Screen* 63 (1): 115–22. https://doi.org/10.1093/screen/hjac010.

Weinman, Jenna. 2014. "Second Bananas and Gay Chicken: Bromancing the Rom-Com in the Fifties and Now." In DeAngelis, *Reading the Bromance*.

7

The Time of Their Lives

Before Midnight and the Conversation of Marriage

WILLIAM DAY

The Tricky Connection

IN THE OPENING SCENE OF Richard Linklater's *Before Midnight* (2013), Jesse (Ethan Hawk) is chaperoning his son Hank (Seamus Davey-Fitzpatrick) through a small Greek airport as the latter is about to board a plane back to the States.

JESSE: You feel confident about making the connection?

HANK: Yeah, I did this before.

JESSE: Yeah, but not with a tricky connection like this. Just remember that, when you land, you stay in your seat. Somebody from the airline's going to come get you and take you to the gate. . . .

In the final scene of the film, following their hard-to-watch marathon argument in the hotel room, Jesse, pretending to be a messenger through time from Céline's (Julie Delpy) eighty-two-year-old self to her present, forty-one-year-old self, reads aloud in the elder's letter to the younger the following: "I am sending you this young man. Yes, young—and he will be your escort. God knows, he has many problems and has struggled his whole life connecting and being present even with those he loves the most. And for that he is deeply sorry—but you are his only hope." These words, which function as an apology, look to be offering as well a thesis on the (or one) cause of their marathon argument. But is it sufficient? And is it a plausible explanation? Is making this connection so hard? It seemed comparatively easy, something natural, for the young Jesse and Céline in *Before Sunrise* (Richard Linklater, 1995). There, Jesse began his proposal to Céline, whom he'd just met—hoping to convince her to get off a train and join him for a night in Vienna—with the words, "I feel like we have some kind of connection." Céline responds, "Yeah, me too." What is it that has complicated their connection in *Before Midnight*, making it now tricky? And why is "Just sit and wait until somebody comes to get you" the best advice that can be offered, as it looks to be here—first as advice to Hank, then to Céline, and finally to Jesse?

The trick of making a connection, not with a new, possibly exciting stranger but, paradoxically, with someone with whom you share a long history of connections, is what distinguishes the genre Stanley Cavell identifies as the Hollywood comedy of remarriage from its related, broader, and more familiar genre of romantic comedies. An important piece of Cavell's understanding of a genre is that what undergirds distinctions among genres is our lives with others; we care about the movies that share a genre's guiding myth because they originate in an über-story that our lives together can seem to trace. With respect to remarriage comedies, their guiding myth as Cavell identifies it goes something like this:

> A running quarrel is forcing apart a pair who recognize themselves as having known one another forever, that is from the beginning, not just in the past but in a period before there was a past, before history. [. . .] Something evidently internal to the task of marriage causes trouble in paradise—as if marriage, which was to be a ratification,

is itself in need of ratification. So marriage has its disappointment—call this its impotence to domesticate sexuality without discouraging it, or its stupidity in the face of the riddle of intimacy, which repels where it attracts [. . .]. And the disappointment seeks revenge, a revenge, as it were, for having made one discover one's incompleteness, one's transience, one's homelessness. [. . .]

The pair is attractive, their wishes are human, their happiness would make us happy. So it seems that a criterion is being proposed for the success or happiness of a society, namely that it is happy to the extent that it provides conditions that permit conversations of this character, or a moral equivalent of them, between its citizens. Then the ending clarifies these themes *by deepening the mystery of the pair's connection.* (*PH*, 31–32; my emphasis)

I anticipate that this description helps to suggest the pertinence of the remarriage comedy myth to what's at stake for Jesse and Céline (and for us) in *Before Midnight.* Not least, our experience of the film relies on—as we'll consider shortly—our knowing this couple's knowing one another "from the beginning," the tale of knowing revealed in *Before Sunrise* and *Before Sunset* (Richard Linklater, 2004). Some features of *Before Midnight* are unusual for a remarriage comedy: Most consequentially, there are children, one of whom (Hank) figures decisively in the plot. We'll see how the movie incorporates this unusual feature to its advantage. But the central questions of the remarriage comedy genre strike me as undeniably the central questions we are left with to consider in *Before Midnight*: How are we to understand the running quarrel that threatens to force them apart? And what enables them to find a way (necessarily provisionally) back together, to remake their connection?

Nonetheless I may be alone, or at least the first, in placing *Before Midnight* among the genre of remarriage comedies, and so alongside such films as *The Awful Truth* (Leo McCarey, 1937) and *Adam's Rib* (George Cukor, 1949). Several commentators question whether *Before Midnight* should be identified as a comedy at all. James MacDowell suggests that the *Before* series "has become an ongoing romantic melodrama, climaxing (for now) in the bitterness and recrimination of [*Before*] *Midnight*" (2021, 49). Rob Stone and Dave Johnson agree that the *Before* films are "death-obsessed," becoming "more weighty" as they progress so that, taken together, they shouldn't be classified as fitting the task of comedy: "These are characters looking for a new genre" (2017). Dennis Lim identifies this "entirely different, and considerably trickier, genre than its predecessors" as "the marriage movie," noting Céline's allusion to *Journey to Italy* (Roberto Rossellini, 1954) (Lim 2017, 23, 26). (Céline, prompted by their surroundings during the long walk to their hotel, tells Jesse of a scene in a movie she saw as a teenager in which a couple visit the ruins of Pompeii and are shown the recently uncovered bodies, lying in place for centuries.) But to deny that *Before Midnight* is a type of comedy of romance because of the *Before* films' intertwined meditations on death is an odd, hasty deduction—as if the fragility of romance isn't haunted by mortality, as if the awareness expressed by, say, the speaker in Marvell's "To His Coy Mistress" is an outlier, or simply follows the logic of seduction, rather than serving as the foundation of romantic urgency.[1] Moreover, it isn't obvious what we're to make of *Before Midnight*'s internal reference to *Journey to Italy*. It can be read as a hint of a troubled night ahead for this couple. But it can also be read as giving notice of this film's distinction from that earlier film. In *Journey to Italy*, the couple's disenchantment with each other—and especially Alex's (George Sanders) habitual refusal to notice his wife Katherine (Ingrid Bergman)—is why their unfunny, unplayful, un-remarriage conversation is powerless to break the spell of disappointment for them, and consequently why a miracle (their journey's interruption by the procession for Saint Gennaro) must be invoked to reach the film's improbable, conciliatory ending.

By way of contrast, and to note the obvious: *Before Midnight*, like its *Before* trilogy predecessors, is fascinated by the extent to which the couple's conversation not only gives expression to their way of living together but *is* their way of living together. Even as Céline and Jesse, parents of young twin daughters, bemoan how long it has been since they last had uninterrupted talk-time—close to the start of their seventeen-minute, nearly uninterrupted scene walking to the hotel and the fateful night awaiting them there—we may be struck once more by the ease with which their conversation unfolds. As we join up with them on their walk, Jesse is telling Céline a story—a story, we gather, of his own invention. Céline interrupts because the story seems sad to her and because she had thought he was telling a different story about the man with an imaginary friend. Jesse mentions the name of that story and asks whether she likes that one. She says it's funny, and then she's reminded of another story he told her, about a letter he wrote to his forty-year-old self when he was twenty. This initial exchange from their walking scene is reminiscent of the give-and-take, the play of recollection and retelling, when a child is considering which story she wants you to read to her at bedtime. Are we asked to imagine that storytelling is an intimate part of Céline and Jesse's bedtime ritual, one kind of conversation preceding another kind of conversation, as they had hoped it would be here? Commentators who overlook *Before Midnight*'s roots in remarriage comedy, or who love the two previous *Before* films too well,[2] for the most part have little to say about this luxurious scene of conversation and what it reestablishes about the principal pair. It appears to be largely wiped away for them by the impact of the ensuing fight scene in the hotel room and by the assumption that the pair's fate is sealed. But I find in this scene and in the scenes that precede it the tools for us to understand both the quarrel that threatens their "meet and happy conversation"[3] and the provisional resolution in *Before Midnight*'s ending.

Placing Our Relation to *Before Midnight*

At the beginning of *The World Viewed*, Cavell explains the philosophical motive for his coming to write a set of "reflections on the ontology of film": First, he tells us, the book is a kind of metaphysical memoir of the circumstance of his having a life with movies, in particular his growing up at a time when going to the movies was a normal part of his week; and second, Cavell explains that his reflections are themselves meant to uncover his motive in writing about movies at all (*WV*, xix–xx). In finding myself drawn to the conversation in *Before Midnight* I am interested, in a parallel but film-specific way, in weighing the significance of the unusual metaphysical circumstance in which I and others encountered the film upon its release in 2013, as well as to discover why, in my experience, the film invites and rewards thoughts about the motives and confusions of marital conflict, and its dissolution—thoughts that might instruct an understanding of when humans find themselves at odds with one another generally, which is to say politically.

It's easy enough to describe what was unusual, if not unique in cinema,[4] about the circumstance of seeing *Before Midnight* when it premiered in 2013. To reiterate, *Before Midnight* is the third of three films that, over a span of eighteen years, follow an evolving relationship between Jesse and Céline. *Before Sunset* (the middle film) ended with Jesse in Céline's Paris apartment, about to miss his flight back to his wife and son in the US, not least because of his irrepressible joy, evident on his face as he watches Céline in the closing shot slow-dancing to Nina Simone, at having found her again after their initial and singular encounter in *Before Sunrise* nine years earlier. If you saw this second film, *Before Sunset*, roughly contemporaneous with its release in 2004, you entered a 2013 showing of *Before Midnight*—ideally in a movie theater, as I did; less ideally at home with family or friends—in a particular, shared relation to time. You shared with viewers sitting beside you the passage of nine years since you all first saw *Before Sunset*; you also shared with Jesse and Céline the passage of nine years since these characters were the age of the characters in *Before Sunset*; and you shared with Ethan Hawke and Julie Delpy the passage of nine years since these actors were the age of the actors in *Before Sunset*. The events we witness in this third film are not at some indifferent before- or after-time in relation to the events of the prior film, as is true of film sequels generally (think, for example, of the *Star Wars* franchise). Instead, they take place with those shared nine years having passed for the viewer, the characters, and the actors. The same is true, *eo ipso*, for those who saw *Before Sunrise* in 1995 and *Before Sunset* in 2004. But Jesse and Céline do not share a life for those nine years as they have—as we come to learn they have—in the subsequent nine years. Both passages of time and sets of conditions have their own storytelling interest. My focus here is on the later time and conditions; call these the preconditions of remarriage.

This not incidental feature of *Before Midnight* already places us, as we begin to watch, in a specific relation to Jesse and Céline, and to Ethan Hawke and Julie Delpy. Our relation to them goes beyond what we know about other characters (James Bond, Spider-Man) and other actors (or even these actors) from seeing them in other films. We know these embodied characters across the specific passage of time that we share with them, even as we missed sharing that time of their (imagined) lives with them. Our memory of them is necessarily, and I think deliberately, not unlike the memory we would have of a married couple we're fond of and with whom we had last spent some time nine years ago, and now meet up with again—struck, no doubt, by how they've aged in appearance, and interested to learn what the passage of time has meant for their relationship. As before, we overhear their private exchanges, but we also—new to this sequel in the series—hear them characterize their relationship in the presence of others. (These others, fairly clearly charmed in their own way by Céline and Jesse, whom they've met over a Greek summer and join for a celebratory dinner party, are fairly clearly stand-ins for us, for our interest in and delight in them.) Less evidently but no less significantly, we are placed in a particular relation to our experience of time itself. That's in part because the events in the film take place, as in Greek tragedy, over the course of a single day (though not in the minute-for-minute real time of *Before Sunset*). But in addition, and not unlike the experience of listening deeply to a passage of music, our experience of the time represented on the screen gains a kind of volume or presence from the shared passage of time (nine years since the events of *Before Sunset*, and eighteen years since the events of *Before Sunrise*), as well as from the anticipation of our (again) shared time that follows the movie's opening, stretching into the unknown, as well as the known, future.

Let that stand, for now, as a description of the metaphysical circumstance of viewing *Before Midnight* when it premiered. We'll see what role it plays in an experience of the film as we proceed.

Before Midnight and the Comedy of Remarriage

Return to the suggestion that *Before Midnight* is unique among the three *Before* films in bearing an internal relation to the Hollywood comedy of remarriage. If we put aside the minor detail that Jesse and Céline in *Before Midnight* are not officially married,[5] what grounds the suggestion is that, within the first six minutes of the film, we are reminded or discover (1) that they are now a long-established pair—long enough, at least, to find themselves caring for young school-age twins; (2) that we know their history before they were an established pair, so that these characters, like the heroes in Greek tragedies, step onstage with a story that is familiar to us—in this instance, an updated founding myth of young romantic love; and (3) that we find them in the southern Peloponnese, which is a fair stand-in for paradise—or what Cavell, following Northrup Frye, calls "the green world," a place removed from everyday society where scenes of reflection and renewal can take place (*PH*, 49, 105, 172, 182). (Jesse, at one point in their hotel room argument, speaks of their being in "the Garden of Eden.") That Jesse and Céline find themselves in at least a picture of Eden is evident when we see them arrive at the guest house of Patrick (Walter Lassally), the writer whose estate on the Mediterranean shore has been their vacation retreat for the past six weeks. As Richard Linklater has observed about this moment in the script, Jesse and Céline would gladly have signed up for this life nine years ago: They are together, the parents of two lovely twin daughters, with their own careers established if potentially in transition, summering in Greece, and surrounded by interesting people and conversation: "What's not to like?" (Linklater 2017).

As is characteristic of remarriage comedy, Jesse and Céline's conversation in *Before Midnight* often turns, in both comic and dark ways, to the subject of men and women—to their differences, to what each wants from the other, and to whether either understands the other's desire as well as (crucially) their own desire, which the other is to reveal to them. In *Before Sunrise*, when the subject of the difference between the sexes came up, the young Jesse and Céline decided after only a few moments' discussion that the topic depressed them, and they quickly dropped it. (Jesse: "It's like a skipping record, you know? Every couple's been having this conversation forever.") Eighteen years later in *Before Midnight*, evidence of its continuing fascination appears during the dinner party with Patrick and a handful of attractive young and old guests. At one point, Céline adopts the voice and manner of a female bimbo and admirer of Jesse, claiming (and proving) to all assembled that this is what the literate Jesse, "a closet macho," is drawn to.

CÉLINE (in her best bimbo voice): So you're a writer?

JESSE (playing along): Yeah. Yeah, sure.

CÉLINE: So you write like, books?

GROUP: (Laughing)

. . .

CÉLINE: You know, I read this book once, "Romeo and . . ."

JESSE: . . . Juliet." Right?

CÉLINE: Yeah! Wow, you know it!

JESSE: It's very good, yeah. It's a play actually. It's not a book. A play.

CÉLINE: Oh, I thought it was a book based on the movie.

JESSE: No—no, a play, yeah.

CÉLINE: Okay, it was a play. Wow. Well, actually I didn't read the whole thing because you know, sometimes I have to keep up and read those magazines to know exactly what's going on in all those people's lives.

JESSE: Well, that is important.

CÉLINE: Okay. Well, you're very, very smart and I bet [whispering] you have a gigantic penis.

JESSE (to the assembled dinner party): Why am I finding myself so attracted to this woman!

CÉLINE (as herself): Yes, he is!

Are we, who know the role played by thoughtful words in their mutual seduction years ago, surprised by this?[6] And if not completely surprised, how does that fact deepen our understanding of the forces at play in Jesse, and between Jesse and Céline, back at their initial conversation in the opening train scene of *Before Sunrise?* What in

Jesse's eyes is the common denominator between the young Céline of that film—Sorbonne-trained, reader of Bataille—and the middle-aged Céline's bimbo persona? (I offer an answer below.)

The dinner conversation circles back to various marks of the difference between masculine and feminine, the gist of which is to cast doubt on the possibility, and even the desirability, of a love affair that lasts until the lovers are parted by death. Not everyone present is skeptical, but it likely matters that the dinner party couples are a reflection of an entire life span of intimacy: There's the youthful couple (Achilleas [Yannis Papadopoulos] and Anna [Ariane Labed]), who mirror the principal pair in *Before Sunrise*; the married couple nine—or eighteen—years along (Jesse and Céline); the married couple somewhat further along (Stefanos [Panos Koronis] and Ariadne [Athina Rachel Tsangari]); and the aged pair who are living in the aftermath of a spouse's death (the host, Patrick, and his friend Natalia [Xenia Kalogeropoulou]). It is the youthful Anna who questions whether "this idea of 'love affair that lasts forever' is still relevant to us. I mean, we [she and Achilleas] know that we are going to break up eventually." Achilleas echoes, "Definitely." It seems right to interpret these pronouncements not as honest insight but as youthful bravado since, of course, Anna and Achilleas can't know this; no one can. (The human effort to forestall possibility and its possible disappointments is not new; this couple's up-to-date expression of romantic skepticism is simply one late version of it.)

Beyond the parallel to the earlier bravado of Céline and Jesse in *Before Sunrise*, who agree (before they don't) that as "rational adults" they will forego the wish to ever see each other again,[7] there is confirmation that Anna and Achilleas' relationship is a mirror of the youthful Céline and Jesse's in a small detail we learn in the dinner party scene. An important feature of the story of how Jesse and Céline found each other again (a story retold at the dinner party) is Jesse's first book, whose subject is the one-night affair we witness in *Before Sunrise*. As Jesse comes to discover, and as he says in *Before Sunset*, he wrote the book in order to find Céline. She is like Perdita in Shakespeare's *The Winter's Tale*, the young girl who was lost. The detail we learn at the dinner party about how the young Anna and Achilleas found each other is that they met at a cast party for a production of *The Winter's Tale* in which Anna played Perdita. (But unlike Céline, Anna won't be lost to Achilleas; they have Skype.)[8]

Jesse and Céline continue the conversation about the possibility of long love affairs as they walk to their hotel. Céline is taken aback to learn that Jesse's grandparents, recently departed, were married for seventy-four years. ("Fuck! . . . How is that even possible?") They do a quick calculation to discover they'll need another fifty-six years together to match that anniversary. Céline asks, "Will you be able to put up with me for another fifty-six more years? I need to know! Okay? 'Cause I don't know if I'm gonna be able to put up with you." What would such a love demand? At a minimum, and disregarding couples that just stay together grudgingly until one or the other dies, *Before Midnight* seems to declare that it demands self-knowledge. "*Gnothi seauton*," Patrick says, quoting the inscription over the portal of Apollo's temple at Delphi, in response to Jesse's asking how a self differs from an automated intelligence. Jesse later joins this philosophical project (the search for self-knowledge) to marriage, or at least to the best kind of Aristotelian friendship: He says to Céline, "If we're ever gonna truly know one another, I mean, I think we'd probably have to get to know ourselves better first." This sentiment is more than a faint echo (albeit a reversal) of a central plot point of the remarriage comedy—the joining and partial satisfaction of the search for oneself through a discovery that is born from being known by another (and vice versa). And yet Céline greets Jesse's heady insight with a visual and verbal shrug. Perhaps she recognizes the backwards, essentially macho, ordering of discovery as Jesse words it. (Do we know another through knowing ourselves [Jesse], or do we come to know ourselves through being known by another?) Perhaps she has a premonition—one also well-founded in ancient wisdom—that the pursuit of knowledge is incompatible with a continued life in Eden, or at least incompatible with a certain understanding of that life. A premonition that knowledge is nonetheless in the offing is given in an early scene when, driving back from the tiny airport in this Greek Eden, Jesse pilfers the half-eaten apple of his slumbering daughter Ella [Jennifer Prior] and takes a bite. Céline uses her phone to make a video of the incident, which they both narrate. Is the video evidence of evil—Céline: "You're gonna take food out of your child's mouth?"—or good—Jesse: "Ella, . . . I'm teaching you the value of sharing"? When are we to know?

What Goes Wrong in the Garden of Eden?

What troubles their Garden of Eden, and in particular their date night at the hotel in the southern Peloponnese, might be that, like the biblical Eden, this is not a garden of their own making but one that has been prepared for them, one they are just placed in, for the moment unaware of how they got here. (As Borges's Paracelsus all but says: What makes your garden an Eden is the recognition that Eden is where you've always been.)[9] How does one properly appreciate that one is in paradise? And why, as in the biblical Eden, must the adequacy of one's appreciation and love (whether of God or of someone else) be tested in ways one is ordained to fail? Céline, early in their late afternoon walk to the hotel, asks Jesse, "If we were meeting for the first time today on a train, would you find me attractive?" After Jesse offers a complicating answer ("I mean, what would my life situation be? I mean technically, wouldn't I be cheating on you?"), Céline gives him a failing grade: "I wanted you to say something romantic and you blew it." Later in their walk, Céline relates her distant memory of the scene from *Journey to Italy* set in the ruins of Pompeii, with bodies of couples buried in each others' arms. She mentions how, watching it as a teenager, "You romanticize the idea of dying with the person you love." Jesse asks, "Well, you wanna die with me?" Céline is quick to reply, "Maybe . . . our first night together then, a long time ago. But now, no. I'd like to live!" Jesse responds by repeating Céline's "You blew it," charmingly adding the French obscenity "Putain de merde!" (We're probably not surprised that this is the one French expression that Jesse, who lives in Paris, is shown to have learned and can beckon without thought.) They each play it for laughs, but their questions and answers, if not coming from somewhere dark, come from somewhere buried.

There are indeed complications in their present lives. A central one, distinguishing this film from its remarriage comedy predecessors, involves an abandoned child: Jesse wants to live closer to his teenage son Hank, who mostly resides with Jesse's ex-wife in Chicago, back in the States. Céline, frustrated over losing a political battle, wants to leave her job at an environmental nonprofit to go work for the French government. As here described, it's clear that the satisfaction of these disparate wishes points in different (geographical) directions. So one might be tempted, as some have been, to read their extended fight in the hotel room as a study of how each of them, familiar with each other's ways, tries to manipulate the other to move in his or her direction.[10] One might also think that this is why, during their walk, we hear Céline ask Jesse one of her "can't-win questions" as he calls it, and why after he turns the question to his favor she replies, "You're a very skilled manipulator." On the other hand, their so-called fight scene is evidently not about a fight they're looking to have; it begins as a tender and prolonged love scene. Moreover, for much of their fight, as Linklater observes, they're seated together on a couch or at a table—that is, not screaming, tossing things, etc. (Linklater 2017). Each may want the other to agree to something or to acknowledge something, but it's a mystery to each how these desires have led to this fight. (Jesse: "So this is how you now want to be spending this evening? I mean, this is what you wanna do tonight?" Céline: "Well, you started it.") Their conflict is not, at bottom, about career versus family, feminism versus macho privilege. It isn't, as in *Journey to Italy*, the result of long-simmering tensions or disenchantment, however much it picks up on and plays off of their (familiar to us) character differences. Just consider how *generic* their grievances are. (Jesse is messy; Céline is emotional; Jesse imagines himself the creative genius; Céline doesn't take care of herself.) Their conflict is better characterized as timeless, or untimely. It carries emotional weight with us because of the passage of time we share with them, because of what we know of them across that passage of time, and because of what they continue to confirm about what we know of them across that passage of time. Let me explain why.

There is a general sentiment shared among the *Before* films as well as with other of Linklater's films: A desire to be fully present to the moment, to "this time." (*This Time* is the fictional title of Jesse's first not-so-fictional book, the book that tells the story of their devouring time together in *Before Sunrise*.) Céline often expresses this idea negatively, as she does again in *Before Midnight*: "I've always had this feeling" she says, "no matter where I am in my life, that it's either a memory or a dream." For Jesse, that desire for every second of time to yield a full second of lived experience often succumbs to a general skepticism: "It's like, is this really my life?" he asks. "Like, is it happening right now?" "It is," Céline replies, with the expression of one conveying a terrible truth. The life they would have signed up for years ago is here and now. Jesse is no longer wanting "time to speed up" so he can just "wake up and be an adult." As he says with a disarming touch of doubt, "I kinda feel like that happened." The joke, of course, is that while there is no particular time when the rosy-fingered dawn of adulthood arrived, that particular transition is over, and middle-aged Jesse and Céline know this about themselves. Something, evidently, is standing in the way of their giving themselves over to this time of their lives together, not only in their fight scene but intermittently throughout their day in paradise. The problem, pointedly, is not a matter of their failing to notice things. They smell the tomatoes, they taste the Greek salad, they see the goats, they hear the barking dog, they marvel at the small chapel to Saint Odilia, the patron saint of eyesight. Nor are they guilty of what one might call a *false* or *blinkered* awareness, as if they're noticing the wrong aspects of things, or failing to notice or give proper attention to one another. Again, the hotel room scene is first of all (for longer than viewers tend to recollect and as commentators tend to gloss over) a tender love scene. Their careful attention to one another's spontaneous expressions is what captivates us in *Before Sunrise* and *Before Sunset*, and we recall that impression as we're recaptured by it in *Before Midnight*. Even their words of anger here match one another in quick-witted responsiveness. They are not the walking dead. (Here again, it's hard to miss how much Céline and Jesse differ, separately and together, from Katherine and Alex in *Journey to Italy*.)

If the myth underwriting remarriage comedies says that something intrudes on what, by all appearances, is an existence in paradise; if the way back requires the recognition that one is in paradise, which is to say, that the actual present cannot be improved upon; and if what stands in the way of that recognition for Jesse and Céline is not a matter of their failing to notice things, or one another; then what stands in the way? Why is their time in Eden out of joint?

"It's Time, but It's More Perception"

I want to hazard that the answer lies, as their remarks throughout the day suggest is true of each separately, in their perception of time, or their embodiment in time—in their lived relation to time. We have no good description—at least I have none—of all the myriad ways we humans inhabit time's "flow," experience or fail to experience its "passing," fill it so that it speeds up or not so that it stalls, and are occupied in anticipation of some time to come or with time's afterlife in memory. Nor are there adequate words for the myriad ways we try to arrest some whirl of thought and feeling that time has delineated, or the myriad ways we attempt in speech to arrest a friend's or stranger's whirl of thought and feeling, all for a connection. It seems that our best efforts at articulation occur in music, and in movies.

The idea that the obstacle standing between Jesse and Céline is a certain lived relation to or perception of time is, in fact, thematized in an early scene. Jesse, a novelist who writes from his experience, is describing for Patrick and Stefanos the peculiarities or "brain abnormalities" of the characters in his novel-in-progress. One character suffers a condition of "perpetual déjà vu": She feels of every experience that she has lived it in the recent past.[11] Her entire experience, in other words, is an experience of what has already happened. A second character suffers similarly but in the opposite direction: For him, every experience is colored by the transience of what he beholds. As Jesse says, it's "like he's seeing too far into the future." When Stefanos concludes that each of these characters is "lost in time," Jesse corrects him: "It's not time that they're lost in. . . . It's like perception. That's the deal."

These lines could stand as a corrective for the students of Linklater's films who link his concerns too closely with "the time thing." It's not time that he's interested in, but perception. That's his deal. In particular, the notion of time travel, despite some Linklater characters' allusion to it or claims for it, is never a centerpiece in his narratives; his narratives are concerned with only the constant and inevitable kind of time travel that we are doing literally all of the time. The personal and especially interpersonal issue in many of his films—The *Before* series, *Boyhood* (2014), *Waking Life* (2001), *Tape* (2001), *A Scanner Darkly* (2006), *Slacker* (1990), *Where'd You Go, Bernadette* (2019)—is the nature of our fragile, altering, conflicting perceptions in a world we ostensibly share. For readers of Wittgenstein, I note that Wittgenstein's late and recurring interest in the concept of aspect-seeing is a parallel fascination with the unanalyzable limits of our ostensibly shared world.[12]

In *Before Midnight*, Jesse and Céline each suffer their own periodic but persistent version of abnormal time perception, a condition not unfamiliar to those who find themselves midway in life's journey. (What is it about middle age that tends to alter a person's heretofore familiar relation to time? The fact is best captured, to my mind, by a phrase used by Frank Bascombe, the narrator of Richard Ford's novel *Independence Day*, who calls this time in his life "the Existence Period"—a time in which he is finding it curiously difficult to be present to whatever is present to him.) Jesse and Céline's joint manifestation of this condition might be described as their mutual mystification of one another brought on by their occupying different tracks of time, misconstruing the time of their lives.

For his part, Jesse, both in *Before Sunset* and here in *Before Midnight*, sees in the present a direct path to regret. In *Before Sunset*, he describes himself as feeling "like I'm designed to be slightly dissatisfied with everything." His thoughts repeatedly return to his and Céline's failed rendezvous six months after their first memorable night together, and how his unhappy marriage to another woman and years spent without Céline might have been averted. (At one point he all but cries out, "Oh God, why weren't you there in Vienna? . . . Oh God, why didn't we exchange phone numbers and stuff?") Now in *Before Midnight* he is reminded by the departure of Hank (the happy fruit of his failed marriage), and by each subsequent phone call from him, of how Jesse, in his own words, "just really fucked that up."[13] Like the female character in his novel-in-progress, Jesse, in these searing moments, experiences the present (the particular kind of present Augustine calls the present of things past) as something already—and painfully—experienced. ("Perpetual déjà vu" as a compulsive fixation.) Céline in *Before Sunset* seems to capture this state when she says, "Memory's a wonderful thing if you don't have to deal with the past." It's the self-imposed necessity to "deal" with the past, over and above reflecting on its trace in memory, that is Jesse's problem.

Céline's experience of the present as revealed in her exchanges with Jesse, on the other hand, is parked in the future, generating anxiety in her. This is in part because of her periodic conviction that Jesse means to coax her to move to Chicago and to a future that is conducive more to his needs than to hers. Her "secret fear" is that every man she's with wishes to turn her into "a submissive housewife." This she believes despite the evidence that, as Jesse points out to her and as every viewer of the *Before* series recognizes the truth of when he says it: "It would be easier to fit your head into a toaster than to turn you into anything submissive." But Céline expresses a more global panic drawn from her vision of the future. That future shows, for example, that the Greece they are vacationing in is on the brink of revolution, and that there is to be a worldwide environmental catastrophe. My point doesn't concern the accuracy of her vision of the future but the pervasiveness of it, in her thinking, in her occupations and preoccupations, and in her experience—from the drive after dropping off Hank at the airport to the final slamming of the hotel room door.

The Closing Scene and the
Shift in Perceiving One's Place in Time

So, regret and anxiety—a compulsion to experience the present as either repeating a dispiriting past or else supplanted by a vision that sees too far into the future—seem to fix Jesse and Céline's respective and contrasting relations to time.[14] There is nothing terribly unusual here; humans suffer innumerable misunderstandings of each other by missing, as we say, where the other is at (rendering time as a place). Nor are Céline's words at the climax of the scene in the hotel—"You know what's going on here? It's simple. I don't think I love you anymore"—out of the ordinary as an expression of the mutual incomprehensibility that underwrites the crisis in remarriage comedies. But those words also signal the underlying contradiction and longing, just beneath the hurt in the hearing of them, that makes the comedy of remarriage both more (though not fully) melodramatic and more sober, or thoughtful, than the generic romantic comedy. For what does it mean for Céline to say "I don't think I love you anymore"? Why the hesitation in the twisting of the knife? After Jesse surveys where he's at—with the camera, guided by Jesse's gaze, cutting from one tableau of the empty hotel room to the next in what Linklater calls, only half jokingly, the film's "Ozu sequence" (Linklater 2017)—we see, in the final shot of him sitting alone, his face slowly begin to register the sense conveyed in Céline's hesitation. As the subsequent scene of the film retrospectively reveals, he is here beginning to form, before our eyes, a new perception of time to replace the one he's been lost in, together with the nascent recognition of how he might alter Céline's perception of time as well. What he hears in Céline's "I don't *think* I love you anymore," beyond the explicit announcement, is an implicit wish, a yearning, for a way out of the confusion, a way back.[15]

What is nonetheless surprising in the face of Céline's declaration is how she and Jesse find this way back together, how they become aware that they are each, once more, happy to risk tending their Garden together. Their re-connection—no more provisional than we find in, say, *The Awful Truth* (where the insinuation of infidelity is also present)—begins with a shot of Céline at an outdoor café table, located on the same pier where earlier she sat with Jesse and watched the sunset. Now, with the approach of midnight, she is simply sitting. We don't know, with this close-up, what will happen next. (Can we describe her demeanor as that of someone waiting? And if so does she, like Hank, have an expectation that somebody will come to get her?) Soon, however, there is a cut to a medium distance shot and the camera approaches her, with Jesse soon stepping into the moving frame. He pretends at first to be an innocuous stranger, but in short order the younger Jesse, along with the present one, will be incorporated into his role. The make-believe that follows, I wish to stress, doesn't proceed by transporting the two of them out of their opposite, aberrant perceptions of time to some reawakened *awareness of the present*. Instead, Jesse begins to tell a story involving time travel. The screenwriters (Linklater, Hawke, Delpy) doubtless anticipate that viewers will hear in this Jesse recycling his memorable "time-machine riff"[16] from their first encounter on the train in *Before Sunrise*. But it would be a mistake to think that catching the allusion is enough, as if its meaning were obvious. Specifically, it would be a mistake to treat Jesse's story here, as some treat his efforts in the original, as an elaborate pickup line with its familiar, predetermined end. (Jesse explicitly denies that here.)

I want to highlight three aspects of Jesse's time-machine riff in *Before Midnight*.

(1) It begins with Jesse telling Céline, "I know something about tonight that you don't know . . . because I've actually already lived through this night. . . . I'm a time traveler." We could imagine these words being uttered by the character in Jesse's current book project who suffers from "perpetual déjà vu." But rather than describing a condition one suffers from or is subjected to, here the words indicate an attitude that becomes the source of an insight to be deployed. Perceiving in the present something beyond the present is not always odious—even for a champion of the present like director Richard Linklater. How you use that perception is key. ("Yeah, it's time but, it's more like perception.")

(2) Jesse next tells Céline, "I have a time machine up in my room. I've come to save you just like I said I would." Since we haven't heard Jesse tell Céline that he would be coming to save her, we're meant to wonder: Did we miss something? When did he tell her this? But he continues, "That guy you vaguely remember, the sweet romantic one who you met on a train? That is me." The implication we're to draw from this juxtaposition of assertions is that it was the sweet romantic guy on the train, the young Jesse, who vowed to save her. What the young Jesse tells Céline on the train in *Before Sunrise* is that, by adopting the time machine conceit and so spending the night with him wandering around Vienna, her future disenchantment with her future husband would dissolve thanks to the experience she was about to have with this particular representative of "all those guys you've met in your life." And now, unbeknownst to the younger Jesse but known to the present one, that husband whose re-enchantment he is accomplishing is himself.

What are we to make of the fact that so much of the force of this closing scene rests on our noticing that this moment not only recalls the earlier train scene from *Before Sunrise* but *answers* to it, completes it? That is, how do we register the weight of this moment in the film with its answer to another moment, a moment not only that these characters experienced eighteen years earlier, and that these actors created eighteen years ago, but that *we* (ideally) experienced eighteen years ago? What does that passage of time add to our understanding of Jesse's gesture? Well, what does it add to *his* understanding? And to Céline's? Wagner's *Die Meistersinger* stretches four and a half hours from the opening notes of its famous prelude to the return of the prelude's musical idea in the finale. A typical performance of Wagner's *Ring* cycle lasts fifteen hours spread over four nights, with leitmotifs from the first scene of *Das Rheingold* reappearing in the final scene of *Götterdämmerung*. But even that recycling is scarcely comparable to the reappearance after eighteen years of *Before Sunrise*'s time-machine riff and the fulfillment of its (and Jesse's) promise. If we notice the return and its answer to that earlier promise—as evidently Céline and Jesse do, judging by her initial response to it and Jesse's extended, alternately playful and desperate correction of her response—it should, at a minimum, reveal the paltriness of our skepticism about action at a distance.

(3) While the earlier time machine in *Before Sunrise* was invented to reveal the present to the future—that is, to show the future Céline that she was right not to have picked up with the losers she met in her youth—Jesse constructs the time machine in *Before Midnight* in order to reveal the future to the present. That is, he employs the eighty-two-year-old Céline to testify to the present Céline that both she and her daughters (and presumably whatever else her anxiety might have in view) will be fine, and that this night in the southern Peloponnese will furnish "the best sex of my life" and be memorable "to a new, ground-breaking level." Risking the vulnerability of any storyteller, Jesse answers to the requirement in remarriage comedies that the man show that he is able to make a fool of himself, subject to the woman's judgment. At first, Céline exploits this: "Okay, Jesse, can you stop this stupid game? We're not in one of your stories. Okay? Did you hear what I said to you back in the room? Did you hear me?" That Jesse's construction of the fictional time machine is a gesture of contriteness—over and above his having apologized, via the letter from the future, for his failure "connecting and being present even with those he loves the most"—is shown by his having created a time machine that answers to Céline's anxiety (one that travels to the future), not to his regret (one that would travel to the past, to make it right). But now it is Jesse's time to sit and wait. After forty seconds of silence, filled only with sideways glances, avoiding eye contact—a dark echo of the electric glances in the record listening booth in *Before Sunrise*—Céline finds or wills into being words expressive of her abandoning her prior perception of or location in time, and she responds to Jesse's gesture by offering a hint of sex (or more precisely, as we're about to consider, a hint of disrobing in Jesse's time machine).

What *Before Midnight* adds to the myth of remarriage comedies is the idea that, for the pair to reunite in the present, what's needed is not that they become present or attentive to each other in some meditative or New Agey or outdoorsy way but that they find a way to enter the other's time, that they discover a way to be in the same time together—whether that time is now, or eighteen years ago, or forty-one years from now. This requires not new technology or new discoveries about the space-time continuum (as appears to be the case in *Palm Springs* [Max Barbakow, 2020])[17] but the arrival of words born from knowledge—knowledge of one's heretofore blinkered perception no less than of the other's perception—and born, as always in remarriage comedies, from desire.

Further elaboration of this lesson will require a fuller explanation of why the words Céline finds to signal her new perception, and to claim her willingness to accept Jesse's gesture, are these: "Am I going to have to get naked to operate [the time machine]?" (These are the words that signal their departure from us, or ours from them: The camera responds to Céline's question by pulling away, slowly and discreetly, before eventually cutting to black.) The words invite us to wonder, first of all: What prompts Céline to imagine that she must travel in time? Even more strikingly: What makes her think, or how does she know, that she is in the driver's seat? We might have imagined that the question of who is active and who is passive was to be left open, much as it is at the conclusion of *Adam's Rib* (*PH*, 226–28). And yet some viewers of *Before Midnight*—burdened, perhaps, by theoretical or other commitments—decide that Jesse has won at the end, and that Céline's reverting to her bimbo voice is proof of this (see, for example, Cowley 2021). But even if one isn't convinced that the question of a winner has been swept off the table by the end of the closing scene, one still needs to remember who it was who told us, and knows how to prove, that Jesse "dreams of having a bimbo for a wife." The misplaced claim that Céline's voice and manner provide evidence of Jesse's victory overlooks the fact that this is *her* voice of conquest, the voice with which she demonstrates not only what it is that attracts Jesse (as it were, despite himself) but that she has the power to wield it at will—that she is in fact the home of what attracts him. In this respect, Céline is twin sister to Lucy and her powers of mimicry in *The Awful Truth*, the closest precursor to *Before Midnight* (*PH*, 251–53).[18]

As I imagine Céline's imagining, her sudden interest in time travel and in operating Jesse's time machine betokens a wish to meet her eighty-two-year-old self, to gain from her firsthand what knowledge and wisdom she can. That would be a perfectionist moment, an imagined literalization of Thoreau's remark: "With thinking we may be beside ourselves in a sane sense." Cavell comments on this passage from Thoreau's *Walden*: "It is the state, so far as I am able to estimate it, of . . . the absolute awareness of self without embarrassment—consciousness of self, and of the self's standing, beyond self-consciousness" (*SW*, 101). If Céline is able to adopt such a splitting of herself, to enjoy such a state, it will be because of her willingness to accept Jesse's suggestion—what the remarriage myth calls the man's education of the woman and of her desire—and to marry herself once more to his gift of literary imagination, of (bedtime) storytelling.

Addendum: A Public Moral

The political implications of this reading may seem insignificant. And I don't want, in any event, to contest the idea that the interpersonal has its limits when standing in for the political. But it seems right to say, at a minimum, that one source of conflict in both the interpersonal and political realms—*one* way that humans can speak past each other—occurs when the two parties express or unwittingly adopt two different perceptions of time. To give one example: Conflicts over how to treat or exploit the environment—say, concerning the reintroduction of wolves in the Western United States, which some see as returning to an earlier biodiversity and others see as introducing a new source of livestock predation—might be a symptom of two distinct fixations in time perception. Each imagines that the other's time-perception or -fixation—on this grazing season and its profits, or instead, on the future return of a pristine land of Eden—is not real, that it cannot or need not be adopted, and that only one's own guiding or tyrannizing relation to time is properly, really time.[19] How this difference in perception is to be overcome absent a founding myth, whether of romantic love or of some other mutuality, is not easy to generalize. It may be that the more powerful among us will mostly or usually win. But without an interest or a willingness to adopt a different view of time (like Jesse's interest, and then Céline's willingness), the more powerful may never come to see what winning will cost them. And they're not likely to offer to get naked to find out.[20]

Notes

1. Recall Ronny's meme-worthy pronouncement to Loretta outside in the cold from another post-1940s remarriage comedy, *Moonstruck* (Norman Jewison, 1987): "We are here to ruin ourselves, and to break our hearts, and

love the wrong people, and die. I mean the storybooks are bullshit!" (See my, "*Moonstruck*, or How to Ruin Everything," [2003].)

2. For a thoughtful consideration of what it means to love a film, see Maes and Schaubroeck's "Falling in Love with a Film (Series)" 2021, 157–73.

3. John Milton, *The Doctrine and Discipline of Divorce* (1644), chap. 2 (quoted in *PH*, 87, 146 and *CW*, 49, 53).

4. Richard Linklater acknowledges as precursors the *Up* documentary series (Paul Almond, 1964; Michael Apted, 1970, 1977, 1984, 1991, 1998, 2005, 2012, 2019) and François Truffaut's Antoine Doinel films.

5. In a memory sparked by their visiting the chapel to Saint Odilia, Céline speaks of telling the girls that their own wedding was "very low key." "So low key I don't even remember it," Jesse says. Then noting that they're in a church, he asks "Do you want to get married?" Céline answers off-handedly, "No." A bit earlier she had described their "wedding" as "Very Quaker." (The last time we saw them in a church, in *Before Sunrise*, Jesse described to Céline the Quaker wedding he once attended, which strikes her as "very beautiful.")

6. Jesse's susceptibility to the bimbo persona becomes a moment of contention later in the hotel room when Céline accuses Jesse of sleeping with a woman from one of his book tours, imitating her bimbo-ish praise of what she calls "The Grand Commander" passage from *Brothers Karamazov*.

7. Jesse: "Why do you think everybody thinks relationships are supposed to last forever anyway?"

8. Different reactions to or inflections of this subplot from *The Winter's Tale*—specifically, stories about finding the lost father of one's child—can be found in Cavell's readings of Éric Rohmer's *A Tale of Winter* (1992) and *The Marquise of O* (1976). See "Shakespeare and Rohmer: Two Tales of Winter" (*CW*, 421–43); and "The Conversation of Justice: Rawls and the Drama of Consent" (*CHU*, 101–26).

9. "'Where are we, then, if not in Paradise?' he asked. . . . 'Do you believe that the Fall is something other than not realizing that we are in Paradise?'" (Borges, 1998)

10. See Smith 2021, 6–23, especially 14–15; and Cowley 2021, 65–82, especially 76–79.

11. As Jesse notes, something like this is a recognized psychological condition, though he stumbles over the name for it (persistent psychogenic déjà vu).

12. See my, "Wanting to Say Something: Aspect-Blindness and Language," (2010).

13. Here is a place to ask about Hank, and more straightforwardly about the twin girls, Nina (Charlotte Prior) and Ella: Is their presence in the

film, so brief and seemingly peripheral, really a new feature of this remarriage comedy? Insofar as identifying these comedies rests on the quality of the conversation between the principal pair, does it matter that one of the things Jesse and Céline talk about is the (mostly absent) children? Although *Before Midnight* shares with *Kramer vs. Kramer* (Robert Benton, 1979) the plot element of a child of divorce figuring in a couple's conversation, Cavell's reasons for rejecting the latter as a comedy of remarriage—including that "we have no feeling for their lives before she left" (*PH*, 27)—don't apply to Jesse and Céline in *Before Midnight* any more than they apply to Lucy and Jerry, fighting over the custody of their dog, Mr. Smith, in *The Awful Truth*. Mr. Smith, who has more of a presence in *The Awful Truth* than do the children in *Before Midnight*, is however little more than a device for revealing certain truths and untruths about the couple's understanding of each other. Hank and the twin girls, on the other hand, while not the cause of Jesse and Céline's differing ways of finding themselves in time, are not incidental to their conversation or to those differing ways. One could argue that they are emblematic of those differences: Hank of Jesse's backward-gazing fixation, Nina and Ella of Céline's future-fantasizing anxiety. Hank's central role in their fight scene is, in any event, more than dependent on the fact that he is "their" child—that is, the child of their bad luck at not making the connection six months after their first evening together in *Before Sunrise*. That's a way of putting what I think of as *Before Midnight*'s innovation (the presence of children) as an extension of the features of the remarriage comedy genre. (My thanks to Paul Deb for offering a question and thoughts motivating what I've written here.)

14. Perhaps, as Paul Deb has suggested to me, the difference here is a gendered difference—the male backward-gazing, the woman forward-fearing. If so, is its basis related to the basis for the male-inflection of other-mind skepticism, our sense of our separation from others (cf. *CT*, 100–3)? As if something in the male condition that produces skepticism's particular passion of doubt also produces antipathy toward time, toward the fact that (as Nietzsche says) the Will cannot will backward.

15. MacDowell (2021)—whose reading of this film seems marked by his misremembering Céline's exit line as "I just don't love you anymore" (54)—finds fault with the camera's staying here with Jesse and even adopting his point of view as it surveys the empty room, rather than following Céline out the door to show us her emotional state "upon her momentous exit" (57). Putting aside the moral of MacDowell's reading of the film that his observation is meant to serve, I am suggesting that Céline's departing words show us exactly the complex emotional state she finds herself in, and that the camera waits here in the hotel room to learn—as is always its role

in the *Before* series—how the other hears those words and how and whether they will be moved to respond to them.

16. I refer here to (what I guess is) Sony Pictures Classics' characterization of Jesse's repeated improvisations on time travel: "While all three of the Jesse and Celine films are so vividly in the moment . . . the concept of time swirls through the entire decades-long enterprise. Past, future, aging, memory—there's even a time-machine riff that figures in at the first meeting in 1995 and the latest confrontation in the present" (*Before Midnight* press release, 2013).

17. For a reading of *Palm Springs* that places it alongside remarriage comedies, see Steven Affeldt's chapter in the present volume.

18. Consider in this regard the parallel scenes (ten minutes before the end of *The Awful Truth*; at the very end of *Before Sunset*) in which the woman reveals her special talent for a kind of song and dance, and the man—either in fact or for all practical purposes the sole member of her audience—displays a pleasure that is beyond all inhibition.

19. For another example, consider William MacAskill's pitch for longtermism. In his cheery abstraction that "There is remarkable overlap between the best ways we can promote the common good for people living right now and for our posterity" (2022a), he offers another way for wealthy individuals to forego thoughts of human suffering born of economic inequality right now, not far from their front door. See also MacAskill 2022b.

20. My thanks to Paul Deb for his insightful comments on an earlier draft, and to Steven Affeldt for ongoing conversations about film and other matters of mutual interest.

Works Cited

Before Midnight press release. Sony Picture Classics, 2013. https://perma.cc/ F3UG-U9TB.

Borges, Jorge Luis. 1998. "The Rose of Paracelsus." *New York Review of Books*, August 13, 1998. https://www.nybooks.com/articles/1998/08/13/ the-rose-of-paracelsus/.

Cowley, Christopher. 2021. "'Relational Vertigo' in *Before Midnight*." In Maes and Schaubroeck, *Before Sunrise, Before Sunset, Before Midnight*.

Day, William. 2003. "*Moonstruck*, or How to Ruin Everything." In *Ordinary Language Criticism: Literary Thinking after Cavell after Wittgenstein*, edited by Kenneth Dauber and Walter Jost. Northwestern University Press.

Day, William. 2010. "Wanting to Say Something: Aspect-Blindness and Language." In *Seeing Wittgenstein Anew*, edited by William Day and Victor J. Krebs. Cambridge University Press.

Ford, Richard. 1995. *Independence Day*. Vintage / Random House.

Johnson, Dave, and Rob Stone. 2017. "3x2: A Conversation." Special Edition Feature to *Before Sunrise*. In *The Before Trilogy: Three Films by Richard Linklater*.

Lim, Dennis. 2017. "Time Regained." Booklet accompanying *The Before Trilogy: Three Films by Richard Linklater*.

Linklater, Richard, dir. *The Before Trilogy: Three Films by Richard Linklater*. Criterion Collection, 2017. Blu-ray edition.

Linklater, Richard. 2017. "Audio Commentary on *Before Midnight*." In *The Before Trilogy: Three Films by Richard Linklater*.

MacAskill, William. 2022a "The Case for Longtermism." *New York Times*, August 8, 2022. https://www.nytimes.com/2022/08/05/opinion/the-case-for-longtermism.html/.

MacAskill, William. 2022b. *What We Owe the Future*. Basic Books.

MacDowell, James. 2021. "Comedy and Melodrama from *Sunrise* to *Midnight*: Genre and Gender in Richard Linklater's *Before* Series." In *After "Happily Ever After": Romantic Comedy in the Post-Romantic Age*, edited by Maria San Filippo. Wayne State University Press.

Maes, Hans, and Katrien Schaubroeck, eds. 2021. *Before Sunrise, Before Sunset, Before Midnight: A Philosophical Exploration*. Routledge.

Maes, Hans, and Katrien Schaubroeck. 2021. "Falling in Love with a Film (Series)." In Maes and Schaubroeck, *Before Sunrise, Before Sunset, Before Midnight*.

Smith, Michael. 2021. "The Poetry of Day-to-Day Life." In Maes and Schaubroeck, *Before Sunrise, Before Sunset, Before Midnight*.

8

Golden Years

Generational Contest, Terms of Talent, and Remarriage in Noah Baumbach's *While We're Young*

DAVID LAROCCA

CORNELIA: I wish we could just go back and meet each other all over again.

JOSH: . . . I think it's hard for me to have something great every day—and to acknowledge it.

—*While We're Young*

∼

STANLEY CAVELL OBSERVED that in movies of recent decades we find mainly remarriage "elements," "fragments," and "motifs," rather than full-blown Golden Age-style comedies, much less a major series of them (*CW*, 153–55).[1] Why is this? Because married couples may have become a diminished or disparaged cultural idiom

175

(Brooks 2020). As a consequence, married couples on film—learning from one another, educating one another, staying together—are less central to public interest and fascination. People are marrying later and later, less and less, or not at all. When a Gen Xer says of a couple of mid-twentysomethings, "They're children!," another middle-aged friend says, "But they're *married*," to a which a third friend in the same age cohort asks incredulously, "Why?" Instead of the comedy of remarriage—proposed and marvelously, inimitably presented by Cavell—we are more likely to encounter the more popular romantic comedy of casual dating that turns suddenly serious (a meet-cute, obstacles to romance, and some gesture toward union, still often a marriage—as if cinematic genre conventions are harder to change than societal ones). As with both Old and New comedies, the plot achieves fulfillment at the end, with marital consecration or its *au courant* correlates (will domestic cohabitation suffice?). Meanwhile, many contemporary films that start with married couples often end with the couple's mutual alienation, divorce, or both, so in these works, even if something is learned by the couple, we have shifted to a tragic or melodramatic mode.[2]

From early to late, writer-director Noah Baumbach's films have addressed marriage and its consequences: getting married in *Margot at the Wedding* (2007) and divorcing in *The Squid and the Whale* (2005). The ironically titled *Marriage Story* (2019) is, of course, about a wrenching divorce. The eponymous screen adaptation of Don DeLillo's satirical 1980s novel, *White Noise* (2022), stars Baumbach's own wife, Greta Gerwig as Babette, navigating a fourth marriage, one tested by experimental and illicit pharmaceuticals, an extramarital affair (hers), an airborne toxic event, an academic husband Jack's overwhelming existential dread, and his own fourth marriage. In *While We're Young* (2014), a married couple disquieted by their circumstances—showing flushes of forced satisfaction with one another alongside chagrin, doubt, and shame—live increasingly under the threat of infidelity and the specter of divorce as they navigate friends (new and old), peers, elders, and members of younger generations. In this film, befitting the comedy of remarriage proffered so astutely by Cavell, the couple examines and transforms its needs (individually and as a unit, and often conversationally) until the denouement reveals their ultimate reconciliation. *While We're Young* is, in effect, Baumbach's *Remarriage Story*. So, at least in this case, the Golden Age traits and structure recognizable in Cavell's exemplars appear intact—and more fully developed than merely as occasional elements, fragments, and motifs. The lines of dialogue set out in the epigraph offer a secret hint that Baumbach may have even read Cavell—but if not, Baumbach's ignorance would seem to be an independent ratification of the philosopher's trenchant and permanently pertinent sense of the importance of remarriage films.[3]

Not surprisingly, though, Baumbach is a noted fan of classic screwball comedies in and adjacent to Cavell's canon. "I really do love *Holiday*," he says, of George Cukor's 1938 film starring Cary Grant, but then quickly adds: "I really do love *The Awful Truth*," also starring Grant, made a year earlier with Leo McCarey, "which may be my favorite" (Robinson 2015). (The implications of *The Awful Truth*'s premiere status in Baumbach's private estimation will return in the final part of this chapter.) Baumbach is keen to add his admiration for the films of Ernst Lubitsch, such as *Trouble in Paradise* (1932), *Shop Around the Corner* (1940), and *To Be or Not to Be* (1942).[4] When promoting *While We're Young*, thinking of its place in relation to these films and their genres, he said:

> I wanted to make something in a tradition, like my version of an adult comedy. When I was growing up in the 1980s, and starting to become old enough to see movies about adults, like *Broadcast News* or *Working Girl* or *Tootsie*—there were movies that were made by the studios that were very funny and had broad aspects, but were really character-based. I wanted to do my version of that, so I felt I had certain responsibilities. The screwball comedy—the 1930s, 1940s comedy—is the predecessor to that. The comedies of remarriage. (Robinson 2015)

Baumbach's reverse chronology—starting with comedies he grew up on in the 1980s, then finding their counterparts in earlier generations—ends not just with a callout to the tradition of screwball comedies, but a phrase ("comedies of remarriage") that is distinctly Cavellian. If Baumbach doesn't know Cavell's work firsthand, he appears to have picked up the lingo from others and perhaps some of the analytical chops that attend it. Most importantly, given that Baumbach is a writer-director and not a film critic or philosopher, he knows how to translate his love of classical screwballs and remarriage comedies into his own style and era. For instance, in *Mistress Amer-*

ica (2015), cowritten with frequent collaborator Greta Gerwig (now spouse and mother of two of his children), they send the adventure out from Manhattan and into the green world, in 2015 still called Connecticut. When our couple in *While We're Young* is called away to Connecticut for the weekend by their friends-with-a-baby, they have to decline on account of a planned ayahuasca ceremony—but rest assured, they eventually get dropped off in the Land of Steady Habits, since, as the millennial Darby (Amanda Seyfried) says, "it has the best thrifting."[5] The pattern of presenting a green world—in opposition to Manhattan—persists in other Baumbach works, if not as Connecticut proper, then some fitting proxy: Sacramento in *Frances Ha* (2012) and the Hudson Valley in *The Meyerowitz Stories: New and Selected* (2017, also starring Ben Stiller). In Baumbach's blockbuster collaboration with Gerwig—*Barbie* (2023)—two (differently gendered) worlds are the leitmotif of the film.

The debts and propitious resonances between Baumbach and the Hollywood comedies he loves and admires continues in myriad valences. For instance, many reviewers note the presence of Adam Horovitz (Ad-Rock of Beastie Boys) and Peter Yarrow (of Peter, Paul, and Mary fame), and how face recognition functions to establish one's generational location and allegiances in *While We're Young*. But placing Peter Bogdanovich at the head of another of the movie's ceremonies (a career celebration of an esteemed documentarian, where he speaks as an emcee for filmmaking in the film's last act), reads as an even more subtle bit of stunt casting, that is, at least for other fans of screwball films. Bogdanovich's own *What's Up, Doc?* (1972) being an overt, studious, and inventive uptake of *Bringing Up Baby* (Howard Hawks, 1938; which Cavell wrote about in the aptly titled "Leopards in Connecticut").[6] In the same year his own film, *While We're Young*, was released, Baumbach was executive producer—along with longtime collaborator Wes Anderson—of what would be Bogdanovich's final feature film as a director, *She's Funny That Way* (2014), a screwball comedy that Bogdanovich cowrote with his ex-wife, Louise Stratten.[7]

Baumbach even uses Henrik Ibsen, a touchstone familiar to Cavell's approach to understanding marriage (and martial estrangement), as a point of departure for *While We're Young*—in lines from *The Master Builder* (1892) in which an older person, Solness, confides to Hilde how he is "disturbed by younger people." Her advice to him: "I think maybe you should open the door and let them in." The nervous temperament of our principal pair, a middle-aged married couple, suggests that openness is the trait—or practice—they are most in need of. Openness to others, yes, but also to one another, and strangely, most disconcertingly, to themselves. Damaged and despairing from miscarriages and professional mishaps, because of resentment and frustration with others, they may be closing-up, or closing-down, their lives too soon (much as Solness says of "younger people," "They upset me so much that I've sort of closed my doors here and locked myself in"). Time spent with younger people—millennials and babies alike, including a few boomers who may themselves exhibit infantile traits—provides occasion for an interrogation that, perhaps in ways that surprise even them, builds their confidence (individually and as a couple) and draws them closer together again.

In *While We're Young*, we also discover thematic resonances with the classical models familiar to screwball and remarriage comedy: generational contest (in this case mainly between boomers, born ca. 1946–64; Gen Xers, born ca. 1965–80; and millennials, born ca. 1981–96—and as it happens in our story, the men from these successive generations are all documentary filmmakers, thereby introducing a pronounced sense of reference and reflexivity native to metacinema [LaRocca 2021d] and metatelevision [LaRocca 2021d, 6, 27n22]); an exploration of the meaning of professional talent (and the ethics of exercising it, or struggling to achieve it, iteratively from the 1960s to the 2010s); questioning how a man's social role is framed by his work, and how coming to terms with his vocation is an aid to coming to terms with his marriage; and, ultimately, how remarriage is achieved. There are other traits too, ones that appear to have shifted from classical norms ("the films of our genre," Cavell writes, "are so emphatic in their avoidance of children" [*PH*, 58]), such as the way pregnancy, miscarriage, adoption, and/or the presence of small children inform the couple's imagination of themselves as individuals (for example, their personal worth, the purpose and thus meaning of life) and as a couple (for example, underwriting reasons why they should be together at all).

While both the man and the woman in *While We're Young* contend with "younger people" (are they themselves still young or is the film's title, if said by our principal pair, a mark of self-delusion?), the gender preoccupations seem familiar (traditional but also perhaps regressive). The woman dwells on having children, while the man remains mostly focused on the other issues noted above: the vanities of generational contest; professional status/achievement; masculine power as a function of creating art or receiving recognition for it; feminine responsiveness to/reception of such power; the shifting sands of what counts; evolving standards of what is cool, rude, sexy, etc. Baumbach's own obsessive interest in this network of issues receives another accomplished treatment in *The Meyerowitz Stories*, filled as it also is with three generations, and including another clenched and combustible performance by Ben Stiller. (Moreover, it is worth noting certain strains of resemblance between Baumbach, Stiller, and Cavell—aside from the obviousness of their Jewishness, however discretely modeled. For instance, when hearing Richard Rorty speak of Cavell as "a fleshy, ambitious, anxious, self-involved, self-doubting mortal," one may also find words for many Stiller characters, including Josh Srebnick [Rorty 1989, 38].)

In this chapter, as the above remarks should suggest, I both advance a case for Baumbach's knowing inheritance of the classical screwball comedies associated with Cavell's genre and show that despite the meaningful homage to forebears, Baumbach makes *While We're Young* decidedly pertinent to the contemporary moment—and not just for its many astute studies of generational mores (for instance, as captured in a visual montage of digital technologies set in counterpoint with analog items—artfully presented in *sonic* contrast with Vivaldi's concerto for violin and strings in D major). That is, Baumbach not only gathers, in Cavell's words placed at the top of our proceedings, remarriage "elements," "fragments," and "motifs," he also adroitly presents a novel and comprehensive upgrade to the genre, one that trades on the philosophical significance of the original canon, while also pushing forward to find the conditions of his own time—how they exemplify, interact with, and differ from earlier ages. Baumbach appreciates the way a marriage is the smallest institutional unit of a society, with the family being on another echelon; thus, he develops a micro-level interest in the behaviors of specific couples (in this film, three pairs of them), while also undertaking something like a macro-level ethnographic study at the scale of generations (again, at least three of them, but speculatively also of a fourth—with Gen X friends with an infant, and the couple's own late-arriving child). Mores, trends, articles of faith, cultural ephemera, the churn of technology, and all the rest become the context for examining where we have been, where we are, and where we are going. In these ways, Baumbach himself achieves something that echoes the insights of his characters: he learns from the famed and exalted masters of the form, of the genre, yet doesn't hesitate to represent the specificity of the time and place that informs his art.

Furthermore, given the conversation underway in this volume, it can be useful to think of Baumbach's work in relation to a handful of films that resonate usefully with *While We're Young*, not just as possible influences but also as more contemporary remarriage inter-texts, among them *Crimes and Misdemeanors* (Woody Allen, 1989), which also features a married, struggling documentary filmmaker; *As Good as It Gets* (James L. Brooks, 1997), in which a writer must learn how to speak agreeably with the woman he loves in order to win her over, that is, having so offended her, win her back; *What Women Want* (Nancy Meyers, 2000) in which the gender roles are swapped and the woman saves the man because she says *exactly* what is on her mind; and *Eternal Sunshine of the Spotless Mind* (Charlie Kaufman, 2004), in which the threatened expulsion of personal memories sets up a rethinking—and remembering—of the terms for relational reconciliation (see Day 2011). This small suite of films, all made by fellow writer-directors, can inform our appreciation of *While We're Young*. Along these lines, I hope to realize a conversation between eras—indeed, between generations of films and filmmakers—such that *While We're Young* becomes enriched as a work of art through fuller contact with Cavell's articulation of the famous, still-vital instances of his genre, and also indicates how Baumbach has evolved the form and content of the remarriage story in compelling, thought-provoking, satisfying, and ultimately revelatory ways.

Gentle and Ungentle Men

Noah Baumbach has expressed his affinity for screwball comedies in his remarks on the genre's classical instances, and he has also gone further, by creating films—as a writer and director—that place themselves overtly as the heirs and thus inheritors of a genre Stanley Cavell staked a significant portion of his philosophical career on: the Hollywood comedy of remarriage. Like the Dardennes brothers, Arnaud Desplechin, and other contemporaries, Baumbach has fathomed a way to keep the genre alive while also revitalizing it and making it new for further generations, many of whom (frankly, most of whom) may have never seen one of the Golden Age classics, or have no more than a vague sense of the existence of such cinematic luminaries as Cary Grant, Katharine Hepburn, Spencer Tracy, Irene Dunne, Henry Fonda, or Barbara Stanwyck. On another track of history, one that makes real-world circumstances refract the genre, Baumbach himself appears to be living something of a Hollywood screwball such that on the set of *Greenberg* (2010), starring his then-wife and mother of his first son, Jennifer Jason Leigh, he should find Greta Gerwig, darling of mumblecore cinema. In time the new duo would coauthor new instances of the genre (see again *Mistress America*, see also *Frances Ha*), unsettle screwball norms (since *Barbie* is a break-up movie), and coauthor two sons. Their having children together, of course, also deviates from the genre, but can speak to its contemporary updating in their hands.

Part of the updating exemplified in *While We're Young*—and the evolving suite of Baumbach, or Baumbach-plus-Gerwig films—is a persistent reflection upon and thus questioning of the inherited standards of value that shape our lives, and more often than not, torment us as part of that shaping. For instance, Louis Menand has suggested that generational designations are "silly," and perhaps worse. *While We're Young* can be taken as an illustration of this fact—where the silliness (befitting a screwball comedy) or even stupidity of the presumed temporal boundaries (many of them in Menand's account requiring a "leap of faith") is the basis for the conflict, and thus the comedy (Menand 2021).[8] (Consider the searing *Saturday Night Live* skit with Rachel Brosnahan, in which the boomers remain ascendant, self-satisfied, and overcompensated, while millennials writhe in penury, precarity, and general societal disenfranchisement—doubtless ascribed to the aforementioned boomers—and Gen Xers, just "sit on the sidelines and watch the world burn" [*SNL* 2019]. Herewith, another accomplished satire of this three-generation suite.)

Coupled with a new skepticism about the reality and functionality of generations as a heuristic and semiotic scheme, there is also a sense of dubiousness about the way we frame history, culture, ideas, and experiences in the neat packets known as decades. Thinking in terms of decades may function as a common form of truth. There is something mathematically clarifying, and thus emotionally satisfying, about the decade—as opposed to the shifting timelines and time spans of generations—with its routinized appearance and (seeming) renewal after ten years. And yet, we see plenty of cheating (for example, the 1990s started with the fall of the Berlin Wall in November 1989 ended on 9/11, and so on). The notion of a "decade" then functions as something of a cognitive packaging technique, a mnemonic, and indeed, may itself be understood as a shorthand metonym for a swirl of distinctive, if not always associated, socio-cultural-technical-economic-political phenomena.

In *While We're Young*, three generations of men—across twice as many decades—vie for our attention, sympathy, and judgment. They make their cases individually and at cross-purposes in the form of dialogue, debate, and, befitting a screwball denouement, shouting. Leslie Breitbart (the late Charles Grodin) embodies a 1960s direct-cinema documentary filmmaker who, in short, could make a living creating the kinds of films he wanted (and afford to buy a house in Manhattan). In Baumbach's staging, Breitbart is not only mentor to Gen Xer Josh Srebnick (Ben Stiller) but also his father-in-law—dad to Josh's wife, Cornelia Srebnick (Naomi Watts). In addition to Stiller's company-style role in several Baumbach films, viewers may recall how Stiller played the now iconic Michael Grates in the generation-defining *Reality Bites* (Ben Stiller, 1994).

If Michael—even in his try-hard earnestness—was grating then, what of his older incarnation or variant thereof in *While We're Young*? The existential pathos of mid-1990s angst and ennui finds itself squeezed between Breitbart's casual affluence and heady influence and the defiantly analog millennial hipster Jamie Massey's (Adam Driver) casual influence and seeming indifference to affluence. Josh, in effect, sees two distinct generational models (Breitbart's and Jamie's) that appear superior to his own generational sympathies—and, even more vexing, somehow complementary: as if Breitbart and Jamie are a better match, speaking across and over Josh's monkey-in-the-middle. Making things even harder for Josh, his attempts at critique are often complicated by his instinct to imitate. And as we think across generations, in a sort of cascade of time, from one to the other to the other, taking note of transient regeneration, we may also think of Mark Greif's observation that in the hipster we have found "the degeneration of our most visible recent subculture" (Greif 2016, 211). The question of the viability of the hipster—his ethos, his outlook, etc.—circa 2014 may be treated as a palpable and instructive subtheme of *While We're Young.*

For Breitbart (if the name is a callout to the conservative journalist Andrew Breitbart, who died two years prior, it is done in jest, ironically—as a counternaming), he and his generation (again, boomers for the sake of conversation) appear to live by the credo "the more the more"—meaning there is room for everyone to do their thing. (Josh's take when Cornelia shares the outlook? "That's because your dad has everything, then he gets more.") That such a *laissez-faire* approach may no longer be possible in a world of scarcity and precarity doesn't seem to occur to Leslie. He can be stuck in the 1960s and pay no price for failing to adapt; all of the further incarnations are not competition, just "more." Josh half-heartedly does come around, if momentarily: "He's right. There's enough to go around for everyone." Why bother getting upset? Josh tries to counsel himself, as if testing his faith in a foreign, borrowed sentiment. Meanwhile, by radical contrast, Jamie is loose, unfussy, and yet carries an edge of intensity (or maybe in Cornelia's word, "energy") that his elder, Josh, (now) lacks (maybe never had)—suggesting that it is possible for there to be a tradition that feeds the next generation, or from which it feeds. Jamie moves about the world with confidence, with unselfconscious bravado, even, and his self-possession rattles Josh—as do Leslie's quietly and calmly delivered, but searing assessments of his son-in-law's temperament ("My dad always said that about you: you don't collaborate well") and his work ("You just showed me a six-and-a-half-hour film that feels like it's seven hours too long").

Set chronologically and temperamentally between Leslie and Jamie, Josh is a bundle of overlapping anxieties and stress-induced panics: frustrated, resentful, solipsistic, revealing all three in registers of shame more than narcissism. Unlike the poise that lets Leslie and Jamie "do their thing," Josh is beset by a pathological habit of second-guessing. His character lives by asking questions, and suffers by not having clear or satisfying replies: How do we take up what is offered to us (as our socio-cultural-technical-economic-political inheritance)? What do we do when it is not on offer—that is, deferred, denied, or outdated? What does "getting in one's own way" look like—and can one liberate oneself from such (seemingly self-imposed) obstructions? Give up? Try harder? Do something else?

Beginning with a sketch of these three generations of men, I mean to set that sequencing and structure against the dominant mode of "equality"—or *pursuit* of equality—that we find in the classic run of Cavellian remarriage comedies. We haven't yet introduced a romance to seek equality for, in part, because Baumbach complicates things in productive ways. In early screwballs—both those that are part of Cavell's canon (*It Happened One Night* [Frank Capra, 1934], the earliest in the library, released just months before the Hays Code took full effect) and those that are not (*Easy Living* [Mitchell Leisen, 1937], screenplay by Preston Sturges)—parents, especially fathers, are featured in dominant, narratively significant roles. Cavell notes: "What our films show is that in the world of film if the woman's real father exists, he [. . .] actively supports the object of her true desire, that is, the man she is trying, and trying not, to leave" (*PH*, 56–57). Leslie does this for Cornelia, fulfilling his part in the genre (as Albert Brooks and John Lithgow do in *This is 40* [Judd Apatow, 2012]). Notably, as befits Cavell's account, all mothers of the eldest generation are absent in *While We're Young*. While motherhood—real and imagined—permeates the film (Darby says "I mother Jamie"; Cornelia lashes out at what she calls the "baby cult" among her female peers who have children), the mothers of our principal pair (and their friends) are physically absent. Cornelia's mother is mentioned only once, when her dad is admitting to his neglect of them both, and the death of Darby's mom from ovarian cancer becomes an autobiographical fact that Jamie steals for his own fabricated backstory (which Jamie relates while documenting, Kent, played by future director of *The Brutalist* [2024], Brady Corbet). Baumbach himself notes that for Josh and Cornelia, the twentysomethings are not just "younger selves," or "*other* selves": "They're surrogate children" (Robinson 2015).

Baumbach not only added an additional generation (drawing the number to three), he also makes the fate of yet another—a fourth—generation an issue (viz., the actual or possible children of the Gen Xers in this film: Marina [Maria Dizzia] and Fletcher [Adam Horovitz] have a baby, whom we see in the film's first frames; Josh and Cornelia debate how and whether to have one of their own—and the film concludes with them on their way to collect one, while a stranger's toddler sits across from them at the airport, marking the technological moment, absorbed by an iPhone, and what lies ahead for the new parents). Wherever these children fit—Gen Z, Gen Alpha, Gen C (the Covid generation)—is less important than the themes of descent, inheritance, and the way young people somehow suddenly become old. As Father John Misty sings the year after *While We're*

Young is released: "By this afternoon, I'll live in debt / By tomorrow, be replaced by children" (2015). It all happens so fast. Darby, our seer, court fool, and Greek chorus, shocks us with another wise truth from the mouths of babes: "You know, me and Jamie always wondered how are we going to get old. And the answer is: just like everyone else."

The Marriage and the Remarriage

The presence of four generations is complemented by various pairs and pairings within generations, and of course, the interaction of those people and pairs (hence the conflict between generations). Like a Woody Allen film—Allen being another major influence on Baumbach—we are given several couples to spend time with (alone and together) and the chance to see these couples interact, in our case, across generations. Josh and Cornelia socialize with friends in their age cohort, Marina and Fletcher, and also in a successive generation, with millennials such as Jamie and Darby. Just as Josh compares himself to Leslie and Jamie, so the group dynamics yield insights and confusions for the couples, but especially our principal pair, Josh and Cornelia—after all, we are following them through their encounters, we are learning with them (about other generations and other sensibilities), and trying to process the implications of all these tuitions.

If the multigenerational structure of *While We're Young* and the presence of parents and children (again, either real children or speculative children that become a point of tension in the marriage), we are nevertheless in Cavellian territory when the through line from first to last is whether Josh and Cornelia's marriage will survive these generational contests and the articulation of the terms of talent. In short, and in direct descent from Cavell's Hollywood exemplars of the 1930s and 1940s, the threat of divorce looms over their marriage. In this way, *While We're Young* tracks most closely with films such as *The Awful Truth* (Leo McCarey, 1937) and *Adam's Rib* (George Cukor, 1949), since those films begin and end with a married couple but have their running times devoted to the possibility of dissolving the union. (In *It Happened One Night*, for instance, the couple are strangers at the beginning; in *His Girl Friday* [Howard Hawks, 1940] the couple is already divorced—and thus remarries in the more conventional sense, to the same spouse as the first marriage.)

Cavell frames the possibility of a marriage's end as a function of obstacles internal to the principal pair as individuals and as a couple, not to outside forces such as parents, children, commerce, culture, or otherwise. And here again *While We're Young* offers an echo and an innovation: it sustains the screwball tradition and Cavellian genre traits while also using factors such as parents, children, generational contest, and vocational discernment in the context of real-world conditions as ways of reflecting the characters back upon themselves. Cornelia's thoughts about (desiring, creating, raising) children with Josh are seemingly more influenced by a traumatic few minutes at a Brooklyn playspace (with sing-along!) than anything he can say to enlighten her about the effects of successful procreation and its possible effects (negative or positive). Josh, likewise, receives more unvarnished commentary from Leslie and Jamie about his film work and aspirations as a filmmaker (including the ethics of the documentarian—more on this later) than he does from his wife. As Cavell says:

> I do not think we are being told that marriages as happy as the ones in these films promise to be are necessarily incompatible with children, that the forgoing of children is the necessary price of the romance of marriage. But we are at least being told that children, if they appear, must appear as intruders. Then one's obligation would be to make them welcome, to make room for them, to make them be at home, hence to transform one's idea of home, showing them that they are not responsible for their parents' happiness, nor for their parents' unhappiness. This strikes me as a very reasonable basis on which to work out a future. (*PH*, 59)

In studying the way(s) children interfere with the existing order of a couple (*any* couple), upsetting the balance of their lives, shuffling and transforming their priorities, Baumbach appears to be asking—from first frames to final ones—what the role of children is for marriage and its reaffirmation, indeed, whether in some, or all, cases the decision to have children is fundamentally a decision to remarry (in a Cavellian sense) one's partner. Indeed, the "threat of divorce" in the classical sequence of films seems to achieve its comedy (or aspire to it) precisely because kids aren't in the picture (*PH*, 2). Divorce with children on site tempts or taunts a shift to the melodramatic mode, such as we find in works by Judd Apatow, for instance, in *Funny People* (2009) and *This is 40* (2012). In these cases, the comedy alternates with the pathos, or it must give into it. In *This is 40*, while at a busy Starbucks but speaking in confidence with his friend, Barry (Robert Smigel), Pete (Paul Rudd) asks matter-of-factly: "This sounds terrible, but do you ever wonder what it would be like if, say, you were separated by something bigger, like death. Like her death?" Barry replies having shared similar thoughts about his own wife: "Absolutely. It has got to be peaceful. I mean, this is the mother of your children." And then they schematize remarriage in the conventional sense, though the thought remains laced with panic and the obvious illicitness of its topic. Wondering after his prospective, still-unknown second wife—whom he may never meet, nor marry—Barry says wistfully, "I hope she likes me better than this one." In *This is 40*, Debbie (Leslie Mann) and Pete reconcile . . . and have a third baby. In *Funny People* too, the couple with two kids, threatened with divorce—Laura (Leslie Mann, again) and Clarke (Eric Bana)—reconcile after her dalliance with interloper and long-lost love, George Simmons (Adam Sandler). The presence of children makes the fact or threat of divorce that much harder to sustain comedically; when kids stay in the picture, reconciliation appears the only way such films can conclude and still be called comedies.

Let's be sure to distance our comedy, *While We're Young*, from the cultural norms that prevailed in the classical period, namely, that the Gen X fathers are devoted ones (Fletcher says "I'm taking a leave of absence from the firm and am going to take care of Willow," their baby), whereas we have only inklings of Leslie's paternal presence with his child, or what Jamie's might be—though Leslie's boomer entitlement and professional preoccupation appears to have made him a less than devoted father: "Looking back at my career," he tells Cornelia when they are preparing for his tribute, "I wonder how did I accomplish so much. If I'm honest with myself, it sometimes took being a selfish prick at the expense of you and your mother. Of course, I don't say that. I say talent, work, luck." Jamie is still very much in the throes of his striving twenties, perhaps for this reason necessarily narcissistic. Still, we can see and hear something of a throwback to familiar worries before modern feminism, Women's Liberation, no-fault divorce, and the Pill, in Cornelia's ambivalence about having children (whether aside from or because of the pain of multiple miscarriages). And Darby's by-the-way comment to Cornelia about her kittens—Good Cop and Bad Cop—offers a searing surrogate for a sentiment, or nightmarish concern, one may hold about one's own children, real or prospective: "I hope they don't grown up to be assholes, because that can happen." Understandably, Cornelia is distracted by the cuteness of the cats, but we register the veiled panic. Cornelia, like women for centuries, for millennia, reasonably worries about "being *abandoned* to motherhood" (*PH*, 59; Cavell's knowing emphasis intact). In the first scene of the film, Cornelia and Josh look on with admiration at an infant, and try to tell it a nursery rhyme; when the baby cries, though, the adults panic, perhaps a bit too much. A solution needn't be found, since they are soon rescued, along with the baby, by the baby's real parents. Aside from being unable to soothe the baby, Cornelia and Josh find their confidence shaken by a lack of familiarity with nursery rhymes (while a music box version of David Bowie's "Golden Years" plays nondiegetically). In our heads, we can hear the familiar lyrics: "Don't let me hear you say life's taking you nowhere, Angel / Come get up / Look at that sky, life's begun / Nights are warm and the days are young."

While We're Young, as noted, is framed by babies, by the sudden appearance of children, but it also carries the theme into Cavellian territory when the notion of having a baby or being a baby shifts into the figurative. Consider Cavell's observation that sees the literal absence of children in the classical instances as creating the metaphorical conditions for the adults to regress, as if marriage required a degree of play in order to achieve its felt promise of happiness. The prospect of children forces an adult to become *homo economicus* (worrying after welfare along several registers: health, wealth, bodily pleasure, mental states, and similar fretting for anyone "abandoned to motherhood," or for that matter, fatherhood), whereas the lack of children stirs a perpetual possibility (even if endlessly deferred) of *homo ludens*—the playing human: "I mean, if we wanted to take off for Paris tomorrow, we could," says childless Cornelia with feigned plausibility. Josh tries to support her attempt at being fancy-free while encountering his own cascades of doubt: "Yeah, I mean I think it would be hard to find an affordable fare on such short notice, but yeah. . ."

The insistence of these films on the absence of children seems to me to say something more particular still. Almost without exception these films allow the principal pair to express the wish to be children again, or perhaps to be

children together. In part this is a wish to make room for
playfulness within the gravity of adulthood, in part it is a
wish to be cared for first, and unconditionally (e.g., without sexual demands, though doubtless not without sexual
favors). If it could be managed, it would turn the tables
on time, making marriage the arena and the discovery of
innocence. (*PH*, 60)

Josh especially seems fixated on the way Jamie and Darby provide
a quick way to "turn the tables on time." By studying Jamie and
Darby, and through some amount of imitation of them, Josh figures
paradise might be regained, if awkwardly, in a porkpie hat. (Cavell's
study of *The Lady Eve* provides a handy clinic on the way innocence
and experience express themselves through gender roles and attitudes
[see *PH*, 45–70].) As if it were a variation on Charles Dickens's *A
Christmas Carol*, time spent with Marina and Fletcher offers a glimpse
of the future (with a child, that is, as parents—"Oh, we've lost you to
the baby!" Cornelia says to the them, then to Josh, crestfallen: "We
have lost them to the baby"). Meanwhile, hanging out with Jamie and
Darby provides access to a childless past of play, experiment, sexiness,
and easygoing satisfaction with the present ("It's like their apartment
is full of everything we once threw out but it looks so good the way
they have it"). In what feels like a direct reference to *The Philadelphia
Story* (George Cukor, 1940), Darby laments: "I don't keep things yar."
And yet that dishevelment, that lack of order and care, is precisely
what makes her—and her unlofty loft lifestyle—so appealing to the
fawning, interloping, nostalgic Gen Xers.

But one's desires and the limits of one's personality may not
align. Here we are made to wonder whether something of the
quintessential Ben Stiller character—anxious, analytical, uptight,
pent-up, self-doubting, self-pitying, self-indulgent—isn't a comment
on the structural or dispositional impossibility of finding Eden again.
Whether Greg Focker in *Meet the Parents* (Jay Roach, 2000), Chas
in *The Royal Tenenbaums* (Wes Anderson, 2001), Reuben Feffer in
Along Came Polly (John Hamburg, 2004), Eddie in *The Heartbreak Kid*
(Bobby Farrelly and Peter Farrelly, 2007), Matthew in *The Meyerowitz
Stories*, Brad Sloan in *Brad's Status* (Mike White, 2017), and so on, for
this series of Stiller types (there are others—Zoolander, Greenberg,
Tugg Speedman from *Tropic Thunder* [Ben Stiller, 2008]), there is a

sense that it is always going to be a "rough year."[9] Baumbach makes his own distinctive contribution to the stellar Stiller lineup, since, he says, "For me, it was a luxury to write this thing for Ben. When I wrote *Greenberg*, I didn't necessarily know I was going to cast Ben. This time, I wrote it for him, and I was thinking about him. That was useful in the writing, and important because I think it informed the character and how I was going to tell the story" (Robinson 2015).

Consider how Josh's tumultuous emotional blowup at Jamie (and Leslie) at Lincoln Center seems to confirm patterns and outcomes familiar to Stiller's cast of characters. Even so, and this is where the Baumbach-Stiller connection rises to a new level of salience, the scenes that follow hint that Josh (perhaps especially with Cornelia) can gain a new perspective on years of self-imposed suffering, indeed something on the order of Ibsen's *The Master Builder*, which starts things off, recasting his opinion of Jamie (now famous): "No, you were right, he's not evil. He's just young." (A remark that gets Josh a passionate kiss from Cornelia—an effect we too may not have expected. Josh involuntarily chuckles with pleasure at how his outlook summoned his wife's heighted affection.) Josh was speaking to Cornelia about Jamie, but he might as well have been speaking of himself. Josh's clenched life—his worries, his fears, his variable, unpredictable moods—didn't make him evil either, just young. And so just as Jamie appears to be leaving the "cool-age demographic" and entering the "power-age demographic,"[10] Josh is marking a shift of his own and doing so with Cornelia by his side. Now the young one will be their baby.

Terms of Talent

Among the themes we have been tracking thus far, we should take note of how generational shifts—from (early/middle/late) adolescence to maturity—and the nature of marriage with and without children, also align intriguingly with notions of playfulness and seriousness. One of modernity's tricks has been, of course, the erosion of high/low hierarchies and qualitative distinctions, and postmodernity made this a calling card. ("Their taste is democratic. It's *The Goonies* and *Citizen Kane*. They don't distinguish between high and low, it's wonderful," Josh gushes to his fellow fortysomethings about his new twentysomething friends.) Should it not be surprising that Cavell, a philosopher who came of age at the cleave point between modernism and postmodernism found himself recurrently commenting on the nature of seriousness, perhaps especially as he endeavored to establish the intellectual credibility of film for philosophy, including the films and figure of Fred Astaire?[11] We can discern in Josh a similar struggle with the way seriousness haunts his art, or his attempt to make art—namely, documentary film, including his (again earnest, and is it also naïve?) sense of its meaning (Josh: "I'm trying to make movies to figure out the truth." Jamie, incredulous: "Really?"). Josh's contest with Leslie and Jamie illustrates how shifting trends, principles, and definitions complicate the inheritance of what might otherwise be thought of as a monolithic (and ossified) practice. "Things change. Different things matter now," Leslie says, as if to reassure his nervous son-in-law. Responding to Josh's complaint about what is taken to be Jamie's moral lapse in making a documentary ("But there are standards, there are . . . standards," Josh protests, policing old, maybe outdated boundaries), Leslie says dryly—in a definitive Charles Grodin delivery—"I don't know that it matters totally in this case." What matters, then, becomes part of the open-endedness of this three-tiered generational debate. Once there was high and low, insider and outsider, now everything is mixed together, flattened out, and anything can "count." When standards are quashed or removed (even standards that we acknowledge were arbitrary and fabricated), the effects can be dizzying, as they are for Josh, but not so much for Jamie.

Thus, as the once-innovative, field-defining work of Leslie (an avatar composite of Frederick Wiseman, Albert and David Maysles, and D. A. Pennebaker) becomes classical—entrenched, enshrined, celebrated by force of habit, and through integration into the wider culture—so Jamie skips over Josh's overdeliberative, completist, and paratactic style to begin the process of making documentary works for the social media age: instinctive, fragmentary, assertive. Not only is Jamie faster at making films than Josh, he's also tremendously at ease with himself while doing so; "You're not uncomfortable *at all*," Josh tells him. Sounding like Solness again, Josh barks at Jamie: "You kids have been told you can do anything. You can't." Jamie replies: "Nobody owns anything. If I hear a song I like, or a story, it's mine. It's mine to use. It's everybody's." Josh corrects him: "No it isn't! That's not sharing Jamie, that's . . . stealing." To which Jamie replies: "That's old man talk." Josh, for once, owns it: "I am an old man!"

Thus, what may have appeared to be Josh's emotional or dispositional fastidiousness—his endless worry, his mulling, his stocktaking, his pervasive discomfort—*also* extends to his moral sense, his understanding of documentary filmmaking as a genuinely epistemic enterprise (however dated that may make his ideas and commitments). Jamie's documentary tactics skip over the ethical parameters presumed (at least by Josh!) to range over the (their shared?) field. "Not all of the stuff in my movie happened exactly as I said it did. I played around with some of the timeline"—an echo of real-world controversy reaching back to *Nanook of the North* (Robert Flaherty, 1922) and extending to *Roger & Me* (Michael Moore, 1989), the former of which was evoked by Josh in the film's opening seminar (along with Jean-Luc Godard on the difference between fiction and nonfiction film). In *While We're Young*, there may be as many as three or four definitions of documentary on offer. Jamie's presumed violation of decorum—and the "standards" of the art—stirs Josh to action, to speech, to a public declamation of Jamie's moral lapses, in effect confirming Jamie's lack of seriousness. To which Leslie responds to Josh, in effect: lighten up, son.

Returning to the scene in which Josh screens his decade-in-the-making documentary for Leslie—and Leslie offers, among other notes, "Do you need the stuff about Turkish politics?"—we recall how Cornelia told Josh about Leslie's credo, "the more the more." It's as delightful and disarming a philosophy as it is brief and tautological. And yet, part of the joke in Baumbach's placement of the apothegm in this film is that Josh has trouble understanding it: on one occasion, he sees it as a way to be more generous, but on another, it seems an excuse to be greedier. In his approach to filmmaking, Josh takes the lesson literally (adding hour upon hour of running time, where massive themes open up further massive themes): "Well, I am trying to solve the problem that Eisenstein never solved: how to make a film that's both materialist and intellectual at the same time. It's about the distinctly American relationship between biography and history, theory and method, and how that relates to power and class in our country, particularly, the political, military, and economic elite. It's really about America." (He makes another attempt at a description of his film-of-epic-length-and-scope to a fatuous hedge fund manager about forty-five minutes later.) Josh also misunderstands what may be the spirit of Leslie's saying, namely, an allowance for varied methods that may, in fact, conflict with one's own habits as well as preciously held ethical convictions. Josh, in effect, is put upon by Jamie's amoralism (or worse, his "fraud," his "stealing," as Josh puts it) and—perhaps as a symptom of Josh's psychology—is compelled to call him out, to correct him, to find a way to punish him, here in a scene of public shaming that goes awry, in fact, that backfires—"You're hysterical, Josh," says Leslie. That scene ends with a particularly screwball flourish: Josh's sleeve accidentally catches fire, and Jamie douses him with water. ("The husband's exposure will require, as in the genre of remarriage it must, that he undergo a certain humiliation, a dunking of his dignity [. . .]" [*PH*, 197].) Who is publicly shamed now? Who is baptized in embarrassment by his own earnest attempt to negotiate the terms of art between two surrounding generations, the older and the younger?—"Joshy."

Let us not miss the chance to consider how "the more the more" may be an echo or an afterimage of the film's disciplined interest in the varieties and manifestations of generosity. *While We're Young* quietly becomes a film that ponders the possibility, presence, and limits of generosity in one's own life and in one's shared life with others. The notion of being generous (or its antithesis, ungenerous) appears explicitly in no fewer than five scenes, each with its own context to be explored: generosity as a spouse, as a professional artist, as a friend, indeed, as a general mindset or presiding orientation that one might adopt for oneself and in relation to other people. "I've been trained to hoard credit, these kids are so generous," Josh reflects early on. Later, when Darby asks why Josh let Jamie "use your scholar" (viz., Ira Mandelstam) for his film, Josh says: "I was trying out being generous." When Leslie finds himself assessing his son-in-law's films, and after a particularly grueling six-hour screening of one with Josh (albeit at Leslie's comfortable Gramercy Park apartment), he says that Josh's first film was "wonderful and entertaining," but the next one is "ungenerous": "It's like you took your ball and went home."

Perhaps most pointedly of all, however, is a scene in which Josh, high on ayahuasca, cuddles up unselfconsciously on Jamie's leg and, while prostrate, speaks with vulnerability and tenderness: "Thanks, Jamie. You're so kind. And so generous. I'm so proud and selfish. I want to be generous like you. I want to help you with your film. I'll come to Poughkeepsie and help you film the guy. I don't want credit or anything, just to help out." (Earlier, Josh rebuffed Leslie's offer to connect him to "finishing money," to which Leslie said: "Don't be proud." In this later scene, Josh is able to admit his pride—if only with the aid of hallucinogens. Josh appears to be borrowing yet another method from the elders of Leslie's generation—psychedelics from the sixties—in order to discover how to be vulnerable and accepting.) Given these iterative expressions on a shared theme, *While We're Young* encourages us to ask and answer what it means not just to be generous, but to be *genuinely* generous. After all, what Josh regards as Jamie's generosity proves to be largely a performance, an act meant to manipulate others for Jamie's own ambitions. Meanwhile, Josh's generosity may depend on the aid of dimethyltryptamine. Just as *The Awful Truth* and *The Lady Eve* play with duplicate identities (and *The Palm Beach Story* [Preston Sturges, 1942] with actual doubles, twins), here we have characters who "play" generous (Jamie) and who are "trying out being generous" (Josh).

Given the age differences (or the generational structure here emplaced by Baumbach, as in *The Meyerowitz Stories*), one may be tempted to conclude that Josh, despite his account of "trying out being generous," is motivated mainly by ugly feelings, such as revenge stemming from jealousy or anger upon learning that his wife, Cornelia, kissed Jamie—albeit with a touch of Shakespearean mistaken identity rounding out Baumbach's allusions. But such a reading, while proximate and plausible, seems to miss Josh's more prominent and elaborate—obsessive, compulsive—focus on moral probity (however self-indulgently or sophomorically expressed it might be). Josh, in other words, is sincere, while Jamie, and in a different register of the same, the elder Leslie, are cynical. No wonder Josh's pursuit of seriousness (serious art, serious topics, etc.) in a sincere mode is flummoxed by the all-powerful rebukes of irony, cynicism, or simply easygoing nonchalance he is surrounded by, including the bafflement of a witless hedge fund manager. Perhaps we can appreciate how working alone and having trouble collaborating with others are symptoms of Josh's pain—not personality glitches that ought to be overcome or that set him up for further humiliation.

The lead characters in the comedies of remarriage are faced, as Cavell puts it, with the "difficulty of overcoming moral cynicism"—especially trying "after the obligations and compromises of adulthood begin to obscure the promise and dreams of youth" (*CW*, 11). The deliberation over what one wants of oneself—and needs from one's partner—is decisive for the endurance or dissolution of a relationship. In *While We're Young*, as elsewhere in the now near century-old canon, we find characters who are susceptible to "a giving up on the aspiration to a life more coherent and admirable than seems affordable after the obligations and compromises of adulthood begin to obscure the dreams of youth and the rift between public demands and private desires comes to seem unbridgeable" (*CW*, 11). The kind of education we should wish ourselves prompted to undertake—in the seminar we have come to call *Cities of Words*—does not concern what we "ought to do, what it would be best or right" to do, but shifts our attention, as we see in the lives of the characters on film, "to the question of how they shall live their lives, what kind of persons they aspire to be" (11).

The invocation of moral cynicism implicitly calls us back to Cavell's thinking about moral perfectionism—an account of the moral life that permeates the nature of the relationships in *While We're Young*. Or, as an adjustment suited to the film's contemporary action, it may be that the identifiably perfectionist pursuits we see and hear are individual in nature (for instance, in the exemplary cases of Josh and Darby). Indeed, going further in our serious noticing of patterns of similarity and discord with the classical cases, why not also study the significance of an apparent lack of the genre's central and characteristic mode of witty conversation between Josh and Cornelia? After all, in the Cavell canon, incisive banter is also a form of flirting, and thus serves an expression of both erotic longing and a desire for companionship. Indeed, given the way they often talk to one another, Josh and Cornelia can come to seem like individuals set upon their own separate journeys who, from time to time, interact with one another—and in that interaction find themselves variously reinforced or thwarted by the company they keep. There is conversation, to be sure, and some of it may qualify as witty in the classical sense, but the operative mode or mood of talk in *While We're Young* appears to be—especially for our principal pair—one saturated with anxiety and despair. There are zingers, sure, and clever takes (and takedowns), lots of observational humor (across couples and friend groups, and of course generations), but the couple bonds primarily through a kind of middle-aged meditation on the world (and its confounding ways and puzzling people) that resolves itself into small essays on why things are the way they are and not some other way. Unlike speaking under the auspices and allowances of the Hays Code, Josh and Cornelia can speak more freely; despite their freedom, temperament and age cohort would seem to cause them to hold back. Though they may be said to muse together, they are not making love in language. Their shared reflections regularly turn inward, not quite or entirely self-absorbed but often veering close to hermetic, and they indulge counterfactuals as a form of melancholic comfort, as if wistful rumination and the articulation of regrets are their own forms of marital bonding.

Though we are trained by the classical instances of remarriage comedy to see the couple's project as joint, or joined—thereby reinforcing the stakes of marriage by the very structure of a union of two entities—our contemporary case highlights the extent to which moral perfectionism allows, or encourages, a greater familiarity with individuals who now and again talk with others, and are sometimes married to them. Compare how much we get to know Josh and Cornelia individually—apart from their lives as a married couple—with how little we know of the individual lives of Adam and Amanda Bonner in *Adam's Rib*.[12] Josh has many relationships in *While We're Young* besides his marital one. As a matter of screentime—that is, the broad extent to which those other relationships are featured at a remove from his conversations with Cornelia—we are encouraged to believe that Josh, in keeping with contemporary moral perfectionists, does not, perhaps cannot, rely solely on a spouse to give shape to his inner and outer experience. Josh's obsessive focus on Jamie and Leslie serves to illustrate this phenomenon: much of his time with his own wife is spent mulling how he (and she) feel about them. Is Josh's true romance, in fact, with Leslie and Jamie? Not homoerotically, but rather a matter of male development. Josh is fascinated (and frustrated) by the kinds of men Leslie and Jamie are—and is not sure whether he wants to be (more) like them or be (more) unlike them, if not quite being himself during that deliberation.

Jamie and Leslie share a casual certainty regarding their positions as men and as filmmakers. (Do their names rhyme to reinforce their similarities? Is the androgyny of their names meant to intimate the incomprehensibility or unfixedness of their status in Josh's life?) Their confidence, or self-regard, suggests they have succumbed to their own charms, and thus to the attractions of their present, attained states. In the face of Josh's incredulity, they are happy with themselves. For a nervous type of person, such mirthful contentment comes across as smugness, as good luck, even, and also as a personal afront to one's pain about not being as confident or clever or unconsumed by self-consciousness. By contrast with Jamie and Leslie, Josh's anxiety-ridden temperament suggests someone who does not feel (who never felt) the grip of such certainty, casual or otherwise. While Jamie and Leslie have forward momentum in their lives, especially their lives as artists (they are accomplishing things the world recognizes as legitimate, as praiseworthy), Josh appears comparatively stuck (unproductive, unheralded). And yet, Jamie and Leslie's complacency in the midst of momentum compromises their capacity to grow in ways we would recognize as perfectionist in nature. Josh, however, has a temperament fit for asking questions and thus—after Cavell's formulation of moral perfectionism—he is identifiable as a philosopher, someone who conducts philosophy's business in his associations with others (despite his qualms about them). As alluded to, Josh may also be seen as "stuck" between Jamie and Leslie chronologically as well as temperamentally. Even so, there is less reason to see *While We're Young* as offering us an evolutionary progression of states, lower then higher, younger then older—elevating incrementally from Jamie to Josh to Leslie—than to regard Jamie and Leslie as paired (and, as noted, entrenched in their own enviable places of charm and self-assuredness). Josh, meanwhile, is our seeker, our sufferer, trying to evolve despite the odds, the insults, his insecurity, and innumerable inner and outer incumbrances.

A signature strain of thinking about how moral perfectionism expresses itself in everyday life arrives in the Emersonian tandem of originality or imitation—an original relation contrasted with the secondhand. On this line of approach, there is evidence of Josh's abiding perfectionist—and thus philosophical—temperament, since he can be seen struggling to overcome (what I have called above) his instinct to imitate. The calm we find in Josh at the end of the film, sitting outside Lincoln Center with Cornelia, and at the airport one year later, suggests that something of his insistent comparison-making (with Jamie and Leslie, and we presume most everyone else) has been permanently broken. Some call this being an adult, or achieving maturity; we may see it as an advance without end—progress, no doubt, but an attribute one must continually attend to. The temptation to compare and imitate is persistent while our cool disinterest in those habits is not.

In the film's denouement, Josh appears increasingly capable of refusing the determining and destructive effects of other people's outsized influence on him, even as he comes to terms with the limitations of his own personal agency. We are privy, for instance, to his painful, porkpie-hat-wearing phase while idolizing Jamie, and we catch afterimages of his earlier expression of the same in relation to Leslie, in what appears to have been a conscious rejection of what must have been initially a deeply attractive influence. In the last scenes of the film, Josh finds his voice. He begins to hold people to task—and notably, also himself. He isn't flawless in his expression of his moral outrage and professional protest, nor immune from being at times ridiculous, or poised for humiliation, because of them, but something gets unstuck; there is a noticeably reduced amount of spinning in place. We watch him take steps, especially in late scenes with Cornelia, toward expressing judgments about others, about himself, in productive ways.

In a film entitled *While We're Young*, we may be approaching the insight that it is neither the older nor the younger friend who is adequate for one's education (in the Romantic sense, the building of one's character) as we find in the men of the melodramas—a further aspect of my suggestion of male leads here becoming feminized. Yet the feminization is also, less problematically, a way in which Baumbach can communicate with the classical remarriage comedies—update the genre, if you will, so that we can track where certain crises landed in the 1930s and 1940s and where they land now, in the 2010s and 2020s. In short, Baumbach is fulfilling a Cavellian take on the moral perfectionism of a willing pair in so far as Josh's feminization puts him in the place of the heroine, a feature of Old Comedy (*PH*, 1). The heroine, according to Cavell, "may hold the key to the successful conclusion of the plot, [. . .] may be disguised as a boy, and [. . .] may undergo something like a death and resurrection" (1).

Thus, neither older nor younger is truly an enabling friend at all. But if not Jamie and Leslie, younger and older, then who? Or is the question misleading, since for dramatic purposes (if not philosophical ones), the enabling friend may be destined to be a foil—perhaps suggesting that the perfectionist tendencies of the melodrama of the unknown man in the midst of a comedy of remarriage must be conducted agonistically, that is, as a struggle (*agon*) with his male models and" counterparts (again, with an echo of the gender swapping or androgyny in play)? As comedians are quick to admit, comedy doesn't often age well, and the so-called feminization of Josh's character may simply reinforce regressive notions of wives—as well as male artists—but such a complaint misses the gratifying sophistication of Baumbach's treatment of New Comedy in the 2010s. Like Josh, we are forced to skirt the line between being in on the joke (marveling at the caustic wit of the satire) and being humorless in denouncing it. On this kind of razor's edge, we are meant to join Josh from scene to scene (with Cornelia, with Darby, with Jamie, with Leslie, one after another, and so on), so that we can feel what it's like to *choose* a path—to decide to be gracious or offended, to speak up or remain quiet, to be meddlesome or to let things be as they are.[13]

Baumbach's earlier *Greenberg* is about not choosing paths, not making choices (or of having one's deferment be a choice): "I'm a carpenter, you know, for money, but now I'm really trying to do nothing for a while," Greenberg (Ben Stiller) tells Beth (Jennifer Jason Leigh, Baumbach's former wife).[14] She says: "That's brave at our age."[15] The interaction between culture critique and character-based "adult comedy" offered by *While We're Young*, we can now recognize as situated in the Obama years, amidst the rapid ascendence of social media, peak hipster, financial collapse, and the (always-ongoing?) crisis of male identity in maw of identity recalibrations. We arrive from the extended present: in the Trump era, the Covid aftermath, when extractivist social media and surveillance capitalism rule the day and AI is mounting a hostile takeover, as fractious nation-states destabilize the world order anew, and nuclear annihilation looms larger than its longer-term competitor, climate change. Amidst these many harrowing conditions, which mostly lay beyond one's immediate control, we wince and wonder how the private dreams of youth would find their agreeable expression in daily life—in one's principal relationship, in one's vocation, and with one's progeny. Then again, and for varied indecipherable reasons, the dreams of youth may *not* find expression in adulthood, but remain, instead, just that: figments that inform daily life by haunting it, or worse, preconceptions that actively trouble one's chances for happiness.

There is another, complementary way to read Cavell's sense of "a giving up on the aspiration to a life more coherent and admirable," in the way many contemporary remarriage comedies (*Moonstruck* [Norman Jewison, 1987], *Groundhog Day* [Harold Ramis, 1993], *Eternal*

Sunshine of the Spotless Mind [Michel Gondry, 2004]), present the creation of the human—of growing up, of the grown-up—as linked to ego death. There is a "giving up" or a "letting go" of the self (that one knew or held fast to) that is central to each plot, especially so that the principal pair may find each other again. The dreams of youth, let us say at last, are for the young; being an adult demands their erasure, or their lack of fit with reality. As adults, when we see things "clearly" (as Loretta [Cher] does in *Moonstruck*), we come to terms with what her beau, Ronny [Nicolas Cage], tells her, in his iconic Brooklyn patois:

> The past and the future is a joke to me now. I see that they're nothing. I see they ain't here. The only thing that's here is you and me. Love don't make things nice: it ruins everything, it breaks your heart, it makes things a mess. We aren't here to make things perfect. Snowflakes are perfect. The stars are perfect. Not us. Not us. We are here to ruin ourselves and, and to break our hearts and love the wrong people and, and die! I mean, the storybooks are bullshit.[16]

And one of those "storybooks" is "the self"—a library of fiction of our own making; in our saner moments, it should seem like a "joke." This suite of films—*Moonstruck, Groundhog Day, Eternal Sunshine of the Spotless Mind*—and their more recent kin (for example, *Another Round* [Thomas Vinterberg, 2020] and *Palm Springs* [Max Barbakow, 2020]) explore remarriage in terms of a love match (what gets in the way of it, who gets in the way), and *While We're Young* does this too, but it also offers a probing meditation of one's love for a vocation. As we live through the Great Resignation, we may finally see that our jobs "do not love us back," even as we pine for a calling (*vocare*), a daily, purposeful project amounting to something worthy of a life's worth of effort. Artificial Intelligence threatens to hasten the demise of careers (such as they are), of whole categories of human industry. Resignation twice over. In 2014, Josh is trying to find his way back to his wife, yes, but also to his love of documentary filmmaking—and how to practice the craft. This return under new conditions will require "a giving up on" what he once believed, what he once held dear.

As *While We're Young* concludes, and befitting a film transfixed by the shifting nature of professional art-making (technologically, socio-politically, personally) and its reception by others, we glean a stirring meditation on who gets to be celebrated as talented. Perhaps, for us, in the present era of fake news and alternative facts, of deepfakes and chatbots, this is a time that has already ended (however recent it may be or seem), one that has seen its debates about documentary objectivity, integrity, and truth consumed, commodified. "Now people have criticized me and some of my colleagues, saying that we were pretending to be objective when there is no objectivity," notes Leslie at the podium on the occasion of a tribute to his work—what he calls with macabre humor his "memorial." "Okay, we were trying to capture truth, but the truth of experience. . . . We *weren't* trying to be objective." Leslie sounds a lot like Jamie—both admitting a problem and dismissing it, in the process scrambling the categories and logic of the claims on offer. It is just the kind of two-step legerdemain that makes Josh, well, "hysterical." While he scolds Jamie for his dubious methodology, Leslie is speaking in crosscutting parallel: "We were trying to be open, and to learn from the people we were filming. We saw truth not through telling you what we thought but through a different ethical approach of filmmaking that allowed the world to reveal itself to us." Are the "we" and the "us" different here? Is a "different ethical approach" a euphemism for an unethical (or nonethical) approach? These Josh-like questions press on our (we viewers of *While We're Young*) sense of documentary ethics, yes, but also more broadly, how we regard the world of others, and our place in life among them.

Are we sincere or cynical? Trusting or paranoid? Selfish or generous? Comfortable or uncomfortable? "Success-oriented" or "process-oriented"? And so on. Maybe we, each and all, alternate between these tandems, or shift through them as moods on a spectrum. ("Why does it have to be one thing or another?" asks Leslie laconically.) Making sense of these shifts can put us in a state akin to Josh's attempted trial of Jamie at Leslie's fête. Helping us along, Baumbach writes in a metacinematic spirit conjuring the best of Preston Sturges, something that applies to the diegesis *and* to the film we are watching: "The movie works on so many levels, the happenstance of it, to be honest with you, is the least interesting part," says Leslie. And Cornelia, a child of the celebrated documentarian, adds her own zinger of an assessment of Jamie and his work: "I think he's an asshole, but the movie's pretty good." Josh, defeated at his failed case, narrates despondently: "I'm going to get no satisfaction here." Then he shifts from special pleading to the universal, laced with a hoped-for normativity: "This is not how the world works." The muted audience at the table ratifies for him, and for us, that this is *precisely* how the world works. The question, then, is how we will respond to such prevailing conditions. Is Josh's predicament (really) one of defeat, or is it something else more surprising? A liberation.

After Josh declares "I loved you" to Jamie, and Jamie replies in the present tense, "I really like you too," Baumbach recuperates his awareness of romantic comedy tropes invoked earlier by Darby ("This is the part where I say, 'I was a bet'"), so that Josh now plays the so-called woman's part ("he reminds me of my mother," Darby once said of him to Cornelia). With a lump in his throat, and voice quivering, Josh sees what had been hidden from him: "I was a bet." The insight helps him, and us, see why *While You're Young* is not a bromance but part of a subgenre where the male leads are feminized on their journey back to their wives. As in *What Women Want* and *I Love You, Man* (John Hamburg, 2009), women aren't the enemy—they are the path to marital redemption. Here Darby plays Josh's wingman, offering a sage reading of her own relationship with Jamie that in time allows Josh to claim it for himself. (Moreover, when Darby lunges at the "manfox," Josh, to kiss him, he recoils without a glimmer of desire for her.)

Being told by Jamie "I really like you too" is a painful moment for Josh, and also for Cornelia (because her love for him makes her sympathetic to his pain), but the realization, or revelation, underscores a further feature of Baumbach's approach to remarriage comedies: yes, his principal pair talk with one another, and explore the conditions for a marriage of equality, but they also—and quite conspicuously—learn from others. They have separate journeys (Josh with Jamie, Cornelia with Darby, Josh with Darby, Josh with Leslie, etc.) that help them back to one another as a married couple. At one point, still early in their relationship, Josh speaks to Jamie in a way that sounds like he is speaking to a lover, a way that, in another, traditional remarriage comedy, would be spoken across different sexes: "Before we met the only two feelings I had were wistful and disdainful. Being around you, I see what's possible again." Josh and Cornelia could be said to learn as much—or more—from their conversations with others (conversations that, like the best of the classic films of the genre, involve a lot of cross talk and talking over one another, a sign in some cases that people are not listening to one another, and in other cases, that they are so in sync that they already know or anticipate what the other is saying—in effect, that they are harmonizing, as in the opening scene when Marina and Fletcher pitch for what Cornelia would later call the "baby cult"). And importantly, even if those others are duplicitous in what they say, the lie isn't robust enough to conceal the truth it contains, or the lie acts as some kind of reagent that allows truths to appear. Whatever the trope, the results are evident: Josh and Cornelia find their way to discuss "what constitutes a union" (theirs) and in answering for themselves the question "When is marriage an honorable estate?" (*PH*, 53). They answer these queries by confessions of fears and failures, by admitting fatigue with habits that don't work or are actively harmful; they negotiate, cautiously at first, what it would mean to be different people—individually and as a couple.

By the film's end, Leslie has fulfilled his career-capping celebration at Lincoln Center. (The interior scenes were shot in the exhibition space at the Time Warner Center in Columbus Circle, with synthesizer music overlaid to evoke a 1980s movie; recall that Vangelis was played at the ayahuasca ceremony. Baumbach says the score "has an almost Michael Mann feel" [Robinson 2015].) Meanwhile, Jamie is seducing the Sundance crowd in Utah. And Josh and Cornelia are moving on, embarking on another path: Baumbach marks this journey with a compelling and fully articulated scene of remarriage outside Lincoln Center, and then a "one year later" postscript commonly denied to most screwball comedies of Cavell's vintage: the anticipated arrival of a child.

Different People

In *Pursuits of Happiness*, Cavell wrote that "it is not news for men to try, as Thoreau puts it, to walk in the direction of their dreams, to join the thoughts of day and night, of the public and the private, to pursue happiness. Nor is it news that this will require a revolution, of the social or of the individual constitution, or both" (*PH*, 65). He continues:

What is news is the acknowledgment that a woman might attempt this direction, even that a man and a woman might try it together and call that the conjugal. (It is roughly what Emerson did call that; but then, as you would expect, he did not expect to find it between real men and women.) For this we require a new creation of woman, call it a creation of the new woman; and what the problems of identification broached in these films seem to my mind to suggest is that this creation is a metaphysical enterprise, exacting a reconception of the world. How could it not? It is a new step in the creation of the human. The happiness in these comedies is honorable because they raise the right issues; they end in undermining and in madcap and in headaches because there is, as yet at least, no envisioned settlement for these issues. (65)

About the creation of men and women, of the human, we may wonder in good faith if Josh is made more central to the story than Cornelia, that is, whether we are nearer to the vicinity of New Comedy (rather than Old), which "stresses the young man's efforts to overcome obstacles posed by an older man" (1). Though Josh is at the "center" (in another sense)—situated as he is between Jamie and Leslie—we could spare a moment for Jamie having not one, but two *senex* figures to contend with. In all three cases (Jamie, Josh, Leslie, and perhaps also Fletcher, who says of taking a leave from work: "It's really just my ego at stake"), we can ask: what are the conditions that would underwrite the creation of a man who can be at peace with himself—and thus with his wife, and their child? Who can be a man worthy of their admiration? This man would resist the "positional suffering" (Bourdieu et al. 1999, 4) caused by (self-imposed) comparison, and eschew the mental chatter that whispers his personal value in material terms, that is, in measures his vanity (his ego) might easily comprehend (for example, job type, job status, income, peer esteem, the production of enduring work, and so on). Rather, he is a man of dignity, of poise, of composure aside from any of these worldly accounts. He is not necessarily without ego, but aware that his ego is just another story being told (and mostly to himself, by himself). Alas, such heights of mental, moral, and emotional maturity demand his attention on a daily basis, a continuous practice akin to spiritual exercises. "Taking steps," as Emerson would say, living incrementally. And for that steady pace, he may be rewarded with a possible glimpse of the present—the only reality there is or ever was (even memories of the past and aspirations for the future abide in it). "For the first time in my life," Josh tells Cornelia after the debacle at Leslie's tribute, "I stopped thinking of myself as a child imitating an adult." "You feel that way too?" Cornelia asks rhetorically, as if to affirm him and, even if it is feigned, find a common experience.

With Josh, we have the creation of a man, which is to say the proper maturation of a child. Throughout the film, we catch relatively briefer glimpses of Cornelia's maturation (the baby playspace, the hip-hop class, etc.), yet there is a sense that, at least when compared with Josh, she is already herself, already formed, already an adult woman. Cornelia, perhaps despite her own self-knowledge, is already created in Cavell's sense, so she is (unless she decides to leave the relationship, like Darby does hers) biding her time, waiting for Josh to be or to become a man. While she waits, while he matures, threats intercede—seductive, if confounding, millennial documentary filmmakers, for one; for another, the work of letting go of pregnancy (with its threat of further miscarriages) and of pursuing the existence of children by some other means, namely, by adoption.

Darby as seer, sage, court fool, and Greek chorus—with the smallest of the leading roles, she yet provides some of the film's most astute commentary on what is going on in the plot, and in reflexive terms, in the film we are watching. Her running bit—dismissible at first as cliché, as simplistic, but ultimately true—about people loving "before and after" stories (for example, as a way to structure a documentary film, or better, reality TV), becomes a leitmotif of this film, and of course, once we hear it pointed out to us, it is also clearly true of remarriage comedies generally. "Americans love before and after," she tells us. The arc is familiar: *before*, we were lost to ourselves, estranged from one another, on the brink of breaking up; *after*, we are found, connected, ready to move ahead together . . . and in this iteration from Baumbach, the "after" involves people becoming adults (together) so they may go on to have or claim a child of their own (together).

Baumbach's film, perhaps more than any of his other companion works about generational interaction, may add to the inherited distinction between New and Old comedies a novel *tertium quid*, "the comedy for couples" (of whatever sex or gender), which is to say, comedies of equality in which we are meant to take "a new step in the creation of the human" as such—and thus not as gendered (*PH*, 65). The asexual uptake may be a contribution to the current age and its comprehensive reimagining of gender and its relevance to sexuality and power as found in human intimacy. And so, whatever films (or television series) entertain the work of remarriage—of getting back together *again*—they will participate in the creation of the human as we know it, or might.

Thus, to reiterate in a mood of parting words, "what the problems of identification broached in these films seem to my mind to suggest is that this creation is a metaphysical enterprise, exacting a reconception of the world. How could it not?" (*PH*, 65). As a palpable illustration of such an enterprise, one that requires rethinking—and a bolt of metaphysical intersession, note the resemblances in this late scene with similar concluding scenes in *Adam's Rib* and *The Awful Truth*, among other indelible instances. That is, when two humans (in our cases, a man and a woman) take it upon themselves to marvel at sameness and difference, to wonder what it would mean to remain the same while also being different.

In *Adam's Rib*, Adam (Spencer Tracy) proclaims "*Vive la différence*," and when asked by his wife Amanda (Katharine Hepburn) to explain the implications of his celebration, he clarifies: "Hooray for that little difference"—a phrase alluding to sexual difference, to be sure, but also laden with a (necessary) Hays Code euphemism and a touch of genre-satisfying self-deprecation (see *PH*, 226). *The Awful Truth*, which we have noted may be Baumbach's "favorite film" (Robinson 2015) is *also* the instance Cavell says on certain screenings appears to be "the best, or the deepest of the comedies of remarriage (*PH*, 231).[17] To Cavell's ear, the sound of the film also makes it among the most philosophical, which is to say, it captures something distinctive about the comedy inherent to philosophy itself (*CW*, 377). For example, when Lucy Warriner (Irene Dunne) says "Things are just the same as they always were, only you're just the same, too, so I guess things will never be the same again," and Jerry Warriner (Cary Grant) replies: "Things are different, except in a different way. You're still the same, only I've been a fool. Well, I'm not now. So, as long as I'm different, don't you think things could be the same again? Only a little different." While Cavell hears in this exchange an echo of Plato's *Parmenides* (378). Baumbach sets out to write his own dialogue in a similar spirit:

> CORNELIA: I wish we could just go back and meet each other all over again.

> JOSH: I'd present myself differently. I think it's hard for me to have something great every day—and to acknowledge it.[18] I have something great every day. If we were different people, I'd ask you to renew our vows.

> CORNELIA: I think it's nice to renew vows.

> JOSH: Maybe we are different people.

These lines, delivered in the film's most moving scene, are followed by the reconciled couple's departure for Port-au-Prince to pick up their baby—and in that act, become parents—a kind of twenty-first-century epilogue to the classical screwball (since we never see those couples have kids, if they do). As Leslie says about having children: "You'll never regret it." As Fletcher says in counterpoint: "You know, before you have a kid, everyone tells you, 'It's the best thing you'll ever do.' As soon as you bring that baby back from the hospital, the same people say, 'Don't worry, it gets better.' It's like, what the fuck was that all about before?" To which the elder, Leslie, offers a perspective for general consideration: "Why does it have to be one thing or another? . . . Things change. Different things matter now." With Josh and Cornelia together again, things will be the same again, only a little different. The audience is left to estimate how much difference the presence of children makes in the life of a couple.

Notes

The pleasures of setting newer instances in relation to older ones have been reinforced and multiplied for me by, for example, teaching "Love and Conversation in Film" in the Cinema Department at Binghamton University (where the class was visited by special guest, William Day); coteaching

"Screwball Comedies" with Paul Cronin in the Art History Department at the School of Visual Arts; talking with Grégoire Halbout at La Pensée du Cinéma: En hommage à Stanley Cavell conference at the Université Paris 1 Panthéon Sorbonne, and subsequently having the chance to read his book in manuscript form, later published as *Hollywood Screwball Comedy 1934–45: Sex, Love, and Democratic Ideals*. Then there are the numerous scholars who have shaped and refined my approach to this subject, for example, in recent books such as *The Thought of Stanley Cavell and Cinema, Inheriting Stanley Cavell, Movies with Stanley Cavell in Mind, Music with Stanley Cavell in Mind*, a commemorative issue of *Conversations* (No. 7), and quite saliently, conversations and collaborations with Sandra Laugier, including *Television with Stanley Cavell in Mind*.

1. See also the opening portion of a chapter in which I discuss Baumbach in the context of Cavell and remarriage comedy (LaRocca 2021c, 274–318).

2. *Another Round* (Thomas Vinterberg, 2020) and the limited series *Wanderlust* (Luke Snellin and Lucy Tcherniak, 2018, created by Nick Payne) are worth pondering when questioning the status or degree of the comedic in remarriage stories, for instance, the extent to which comedy must define or dominate remarriage proceedings. While both of these examples are remarriage stories, their comedy is punctuated by intense periods of dramatic intensity; for this reason, remarriage comedies (especially in the screwball tradition) might be profitably compared with remarriage dramas, and even with other variations to be delineated, among them remarriage tragedies (when a couple reunites after a calamity or fraught separation). Another Naomi Watts film comes to mind—*The Impossible* (J. A. Bayona, 2012)—as does *The Wave* (Roar Uthaug, 2015), remarriage thrillers, remarriage adventures, and so on.

3. "The not infrequent references to [*Pursuits of Happiness*] by critics responsible for regular columns have done something in my relation to that book that no other sources could do, namely, demonstrated the pertinence of this work of three decades ago to new films that can be spoken of as part of the present, perhaps even of the future of filmmaking" (*LDIK*, 259).

4. For more on Ernst Lubitsch in the context of Cavell's study of Hollywood screwball comedies, see MacDonald (2020).

5. Aside from the varied role alcohol and narcotics (such as cocaine and heroin) play in film—ranging from the dire to the whimsical, scary to sexy—something can be said about the role psychedelics play in relationship comedies of the twenty-first century, for instance, how some drugs lower inhibitions that make for comedic moments. Marijuana is prevalent in the work produced by Judd Apatow (and other "stoner" comedies), and endows the erotic stakes of *Laurel Canyon* (Lisa Cholodenko, 2002). And as *The Anniversary Party* (Jennifer Jason Leigh and Alan Cumming, 2001) has ecstasy, *While We're Young* has ayahuasca. In these cases, such drugs provide conditions for scenes of vulnerability, recognition, confrontation, transformation, and revelation.

Perhaps these cognitive flights via hallucinogens can be understood as surrogates for literal flights—to the country, to the green world, to Connecticut. Or more desperately, to self-annihilation. Rather than overdose, a character gets a microdose—just enough to open the doors of perception, to catch a glimpse of what is possible beyond the present predicament.

6. Baumbach and Bogdanovich's relationship goes back many years, though, as the latter writer-director also appears in Baumbach's *Mr. Jealousy* (1997) and the now director-disowned *Highball* (1997).

7. See also Kenigsberg (2022).

8. See also Duffy (2021).

9. A phrase spoken by Chas Tenenbaum (Ben Stiller) at the end of *The Royal Tenenbaums*.

10. From the screenplay (121–22), though not in the film.

11. For more on Cavell's warm welcome of Fred Astaire into the realm of serious philosophical study, see "Fred Astaire Asserts the Right to Praise" (Cavell 2005, 61–82). See LaRocca (2021b) and (2021e). See also Evans (2012).

12. See LaRocca (2020b).

13. The preceding seven paragraphs were directly inspired by insightful prompts from Paul Deb. I am grateful to have such a perceptive and generous interlocuter for exploring the Cavellian resonances of moral perfectionism and genre traits as they find expression in this Baumbach film.

14. In something of a real-life remarriage story from Ben Stiller and wife, Christine Taylor, we glean from the headlines that after wedding in 2000, the couple separated in 2017, and then, defying trends for Hollywood marriages—but not screwball plotlines—they reconciled in 2022. Stiller said the marital reconstitution was "unexpected, and one of the things that came out of the pandemic" (Brisco 2022).

15. Leigh's work with collaborator Alan Cumming, *The Anniversary Party* (2001), should be introduced for its angle of approach, as it begins *after* a recent reconciliation. Where most remarriage stories, as we know them in a Cavellian context, end with the reunion of the principal pair, this film starts with what comes next.

16. See Day (2003).

17. See also Wheatley (2021).

18. In the screenplay, there is an added verb (*be*): "I think it's hard for me to have something be great every day and to acknowledge it."

Works Cited

Bourdieu, Pierre, et al. 1999. *The Weight of the World: Social Suffering in Contemporary Society*. Translated by Priscilla Parkhurst Ferguson et al. Stanford University Press. First published in French, 1993.

Brisco, Elise. 2022. "Ben Stiller and Christine Taylor are back together, rekindled relationship." *USA Today*, February 24, 2022. https://eu.usatoday.com/story/entertainment/celebrities/2022/02/24/ben-stiller-christine-taylor-reunite-relationship-after-separation/6921668001/.

Brooks, David. 2020. "The Nuclear Family Was a Mistake." *Atlantic*, March 2020. https://www.theatlantic.com/magazine/archive/2020/03/the-nuclear-family-was-a-mistake/605536/.

Cavell, Stanley. 2005. *Philosophy the Day After Tomorrow*. Belknap Press.

Day, William. 2003. "*Moonstruck*, or How to Ruin Everything." In *Ordinary Language Criticism: Literary Thinking after Cavell after Wittgenstein*, edited by Kenneth Dauber and Walter Jost. Northwestern University Press.

Day, William. 2011. "I Don't Know, Just Wait: Remembering Remarriage in *Eternal Sunshine of the Spotless Mind*." In *The Philosophy of Charlie Kaufman*, edited by David LaRocca. The University Press of Kentucky.

Duffy, Bobby. 2021. *The Generation Myth: Why When You're Born Matters Less Than You Think*. Basic Books.

Evans, K. L. 2012. "How Job Begat Larry: The Present Situation in *A Serious Man*." In *The Coen Brothers and Philosophy*, edited by Mark T. Conard. The University Press of Kentucky.

Father John Misty. 2015. "Bored in the USA." On *I Love You, Honeybear*. Sub Pop.

Greif, Mark. 2016. "What Was the Hipster?" In *Against Everything: Essays*. Vintage Books.

Kenigsberg, Ben. 2022. "Peter Bogdanovich Had a Vision for This Film. Now It's Finally Being Seen." *New York Times*, March 25, 2022. https://www.nytimes.com/2022/03/25/movies/peter-bogdanovich-squirrels-to-the-nuts.html/.

LaRocca, David, ed. 2020a. *The Thought of Stanley Cavell and Cinema: Turning Anew to the Ontology of Film a Half-Century after "The World Viewed."* Bloomsbury Academic.

LaRocca, David. 2020b. "On the Aesthetics of Amateur Filmmaking in Narrative Cinema: Negotiating Home Movies after *Adam's Rib*." In LaRocca, *The Thought of Stanley Cavell and Cinema*.

LaRocca, David, ed. 2020c. *Inheriting Stanley Cavell: Memories, Dreams, Reflections*. Bloomsbury Academic.

LaRocca, David, ed. 2021a. *Movies with Stanley Cavell in Mind*. Bloomsbury Academic.

LaRocca, David. 2021b. "Introduction: The Seriousness of Film Sustained." In LaRocca, *Movies with Stanley Cavell in Mind*.

LaRocca, David. 2021c. "Contemplating the Sounds of Contemplative Cinema: Stanley Cavell and Kelly Reichardt." In LaRocca, *Movies with Stanley Cavell in Mind*.

LaRocca, David, ed. 2021d. *Metacinema: The Form and Content of Filmic Reference and Reflexivity*. Oxford University Press.

LaRocca, David. 2021e "Literary Reflexiveness and Philosophical Self-Reflection in Cavell's Memoir." Paper presented at the "Stanley Cavell: A Retrospective" conference, Vita-Salute San Raffaele University of Milan, September 24, 2021.

MacDonald, Scott. 2020. "My Troubled Relationship with Stanley Cavell: In Pursuit of a Truly Cinematic Conversation." In LaRocca, *The Thought of Stanley Cavell and Cinema*.

Menand, Louis. 2021. "It's Time to Stop Talking about 'Generations.'" *New Yorker*, October 11, 2021. https://www.newyorker.com/magazine/2021/10/18/its-time-to-stop-talking-about-generations/.

Robinson, Tasha. 2015. "Noah Baumbach on *While We're Young*'s Screwball Spirit and Universal Regrets." *Dissolve*, March 27, 2015. https://thedissolve.com/features/interview/973-noah-baumbach-on-while-were-youngs-screwball-spiri/.

Rorty, Richard. 1989. "The Philosophy of the Oddball." Review of *In Quest of the Ordinary: Lines of Skepticism and Romanticism*, by Stanley Cavell. *New Republic* 200, no. 25 (June 19, 1989): 38–41.

SNL (*Saturday Night Live*). 2019. "Millennial Millions." *Saturday Night Live*, January 19, 2019. https://www.nbc.com/saturday-night-live/video/millennial-millions/3867395/.

Wheatley, Catherine. 2021. "Passionate Utterances: Cavell, Film, and the Female Voice." In LaRocca, *Movies with Stanley Cavell in Mind*.

9

Staging Unknown Women

MURRAY POMERANCE

In a film, unlike a painting or sculpture or piece of theater, we are given (captivated by) a forever fixed, captured, image of a human being in this precise environment, in these precise attitudes and relations, remaining silent or saying precisely these words precisely this way.

—Stanley Cavell, *Cities of Words*

Preamble

STANLEY CAVELL MAKES A sort of promise in *Contesting Tears* (1996), that somewhere near the "comedy of remarriage" (as he calls it) there "must exist" "a genre of film, in particular some form of melodrama, adjacent to, or derived from, that of remarriage comedy, in which the themes and structure of the comedy are modified or negated in such a way as to reveal systematically the threats (of misunderstanding, of violence) that in each of the remarriage comedies

Figure 9.1. Valentine (Kristen Stewart) and Maria (Juliette Binoche) observing the Maloja Snake in *Clouds of Sils Maria* (Olivier Assayas, 2014). Digital frame enlargement.

dog its happiness" (*CT*, 83). The centrality here of marriage as figure or background is made clear in a discussion he opens elsewhere of *Gaslight* (George Cukor, 1944): "The main contradiction of the comedies [of remarriage] by the melodramas [of the unknown woman] is that the woman seeks her unattained but attainable self otherwise than in marriage" (*CW*, 108). It is expressly in the figure of the "unknown woman," as Cavell calls her, that this "negation" of comedic structure is expressed. In approaching her and her condition, we of course creep through the territory of the known, implying if not openly averring that to be known is one of the possibilities in life, in this case one of the lost or as yet unattained possibilities.

Yet surely we all know that it is not one of the possibilities in life to be known. No one is ever known—what shall we say, really?, truly? It is as unknowns that all of us make the journey forward to an unknown country from which no traveler returns. On the other hand, the idea that a woman—particularly a woman—might be unknown is in its way a special idea, invoking source (Source) and origin (Origin), and pointing to a certain definitive and irresolute veil beyond which we do not explore. Beyond this veil is the "History" of which we hear and read, but which we never remember. If because we cannot say where we came from we are all unknowns, the woman who bore us not only bears the identity of an unknown person but embodies the Unknown in all its fullness. When he invokes the "unknown woman," Cavell is more than deeply aware of this.

Unknown Clouds

I want to seek this unknown creature in *Clouds of Sils Maria*, a stunning 2014 film by Olivier Assayas (who, before he was known as a filmmaker, of this and other vital films,[1] had established himself as a film critic for *Cahiers du cinéma*), all the while recognizing that in this work we meet not one but three stunning unknown women who at once know themselves and do not know themselves; who know one another yet in only the most limiting of ways; and who dance on the cusp of unknownness in peculiar, to me especially fascinating, ways. As the *spiel* of this film is very elaborate and complex,[2] I think it would be impossible for me to do the thing justice in a small endeavor like this one, if ever in an endeavor outside of it anyone can do justice to any film. Suffice it to summarize that in Switzerland a very grand and famous playwright has suddenly died. Maria Enders (Juliette Binoche), who twenty years ago inaugurated his most famous play, *Maloja Snake*, on the stage and has since moved over to the international screen, has been importuned to play in it once again as a kind of tribute (now an obituary). This celebrated actor is not alone—seemingly ever—but lives in the company of her twentysomething assistant, Valentine (Kristen Stewart), who flips like a tennis ball at Wimbledon between two stalwart cellphones to arrange all the details of the actor's life. Will Valentine be Maria's valentine? *Maloja Snake* involves two female characters, one roughly twenty years the other's senior and attracted both emotionally and physically to the young woman; their love affair breaks, very painfully for the senior partner. Maria made her name as the girl in *Maloja Snake* but is asked now to play the older character. What had been her role will be taken up by the third protagonist, Jo-Ann Ellis (Chloë Grace Moretz), a fabulously popular film star roughly Valentine's age. In the middle of all this is Valentine, one of her distinctive challenges being to help Maria learn her lines and develop a characterization while lurking with her in a remote cabin in the Swiss mountains (accompanied by the playwright's ghost) and running scenes—she, of course, playing the younger part that was once Maria's.

For Assayas, it is important that his audience struggle with the difficulties experienced by a woman in middle age trying to comprehend the conditions of a woman much younger, and also the difficulties experienced by the young in trying to understand the generation that came before. The unknownness offered by time and temporal separation is compounded here by another unknownness, involving the relation between performer and role and the relation between rehearsal and performance. We must try to think through some of the technical problems faced by the characters (Maria and Valentine), and therefore faced by the actors (Juliette and Kristen) playing them:

(1) Youth-Fresh (Valentine) and Youth-Remembered (Maria) face obstructions to knowing and knownness, that have to do with enduring life. Maria can remember what it was to be someone like Valentine (like, but indecipherably like) whereas Valentine cannot imagine what it will be like to be someone like Maria (like, but indecipherably like), a woman of that maturity, the woman she will become in two decades; nor can she imagine the "Valentine" Maria was two decades earlier—eager perhaps, frightened, and emerging into the world—someone possibly like (like, but indecipherably like) her present self. And could changes to self, as time passes, bear no influence from changes in cultural pattern or historical regard? That is, can it be supposed that when she was about twenty, Maria could possibly have been exactly as Valentine is now, a girl in her late twenties plain and simple, a type always and always recurring? Or, given that she was about twenty-five about twenty-five years ago, should it be supposed that she was then experiencing herself in the context of a different history and that the difference (as she might estimate it now) matters? Even in this single problem there is so much unknownness, so much indecipherability. Neither Maria nor Valentine would have reasonable cause to find it alarming or especially inexplicable—although of course it is unfathomable. We all go through life not troubling to be concerned about anyone else's real biography, not that such a thing could be made accessible at any rate. Broadly speaking this is the problem of skepticism, "whether I know with certainty of the existence of the external world and of myself and others in it" (*DK*, 3), access to someone else's biography being an aid to "knowing of others with certainty."

(2) Moreover, of the three women in the film, two are unknowns in the special sense that inside the diegesis they are actors, whereas the third is not. When I refer to challenges facing Maria, I mean *Maria the person who works as an actor*; but I cannot avoid meaning, too, Binoche the person who is at work as an actor playing a person who works as an actor, Binoche who "is"—only "is"—Maria. Or does the phrase *only "is"* mean anything valuable—after all, outside

this story there is no Maria Enders, and therefore Juliette Binoche working here is as fully and irremediably Maria Enders as it is possible to be: hence the issue of casting. Moretz is also a person who is an actor, playing a person who is an actor in the film. But Valentine, as far as we can see, because the job of assistant seems so pervasive and unbounded, is only Valentine, and at the same time only Stewart, and we must wonder whether Valentine's not being an actor might lead us to surmise, even for a half breath watching her, that she is not really an actor, either. Stewart is, of course, a consummate actor, this film being one of the venues by which she began to make that fact apparent in the world, and one of her real triumphs here is conveying so solidly a person who is not an actor; not an actor while she acts as an assistant, not an actor while she pretends to be an actor rehearsing lines. An underlying question, then: given the secrets of the acting trade, the camaraderie, the shared experience markedly not shared by lay audiences, the privacy out of which performance is hatched, do nonactors meeting actors actually know them? Can a person like Valentine ever know a person like Maria? Or else, might a layperson know an actor in just the same way that she meets others who are lay nonactors, or in the same way that actors come to know other actors, knowing being knowing, knowledge being knowledge, and are these two ways of knowing and being unknown the same? Indeterminate, all of this.

As to actors as unknowns to other actors: there is a very brusque moment late in the film when Maria takes Jo-Ann aside and offers a gentle suggestion about how a scene might be played. She speaks "from experience," which is always a certain presumption of knowledge. Jo-Ann bluntly rebuffs her, as though to say, yet not actually saying, "Look, I'm as professional as you are, and I can take care of myself onstage." Letting the content of the speech fly by, what we might note is the casualness of Jo-Ann's brusqueness—that this young performer, who does not have a long relationship with Maria, can feel it entirely acceptable to be curt this way in such a circumstance; and that Maria, who may think she knows the young performer because she was once a young performer, can recognize Jo-Ann as a wholly different person, representative of a new breed of stars who are unawed by tradition; recognize that the brusqueness is not exactly out of place, does not exactly betoken hostility, just (blithe) independence. Even more than independence: it betokens, Maria can know, and Jo-Ann can know with her, a certain professional shorthand actor-to-actor; since when they are hard at work rehearsing or performing actors have time and space to share with each other only very clear shorthand signals about the business at hand: *Maybe you move here and lean back, I'll come up very close.*

When they talk to each other, Maria and Jo-Ann have an awareness, perhaps on both sides courting the unknown. On talk and awareness, on the unknownness that comes with saying or not saying or knowing how to say or not knowing how to say, Cavell notes of Austin and Wittgenstein's procedures presenting themselves "as *returning us* to the ordinary, a place we have never been": "It seems that the more I might find their instances trivial, the more puzzled I could become that I had not realized, or could not retain the realization of, their discoveries—such as, in Wittgenstein, what it is we go on in calling something a chair, or saying that someone is expecting someone, or is walking, or why I sometimes imagine a difficulty over pointing to the color of an object (as opposed to pointing to the object)"[3] (*CF,* 225). In cinema, while we have visible gestural cues available to us, we very frequently interpret characters' knowledge, alignment, position, and method by virtue of what they say, which means, of course, what they know how to say and what we know how to hear them saying. The word made flesh.

Simpler, perhaps, to say (to suggest) that while it is undeniable that Maria and Jo-Ann converse in English nevertheless they employ two different Englishes, the separations between which are for each of them indecipherable and for both of which "the tempo and progression of spoken intelligibility are inexorable" (*WV,* 149). Cavell cavils at linguistic indecipherability, pointing to the "pain of first-generation immigrants to America whose accented language belongs neither to the old nor—without comedy or tragedy—to the new world" (*CW,* 412).

3) Although Assayas' film gives only sketches of *Maloja Snake,* we can easily presume that the onstage relationship between the younger and older female characters, Sigrid and Helena, reflects (albeit indecipherably) the offstage relationship between Valentine and Maria, who are rehearsing it. The "falling in love" onstage is very like the falling in love simulated at rehearsal in the cabin, and perhaps not only simulated. In this emotional connection, or this emotional wrap-up, Valentine's fearful tentativeness is something

Maria recognizes and understands, but Maria's growing passion for her (either real, or imagined by the actor and put on, we shall never know) is something from which Valentine is closed off. We can read this dance of feeling by interpreting Maria as a method actor, one who brings herself into a condition where she can live the character in real time; in such a case, in order to work up Helena she requires the help of an attractive younger Sigrid. In this respect—given that the opportunity to reprise *Maloja Snake* came up long after she engaged the young woman—Valentine is a perfect assistant. But Valentine may be in a much worse position for knowing this than Maria is. For Valentine, who is not as accustomed to actors working up roles or to rehearsals, to fully know the feeling her radiations stimulate in Maria would be a commitment this young woman doesn't apparently want to make, even in the "stagey" hypothetical condition we call rehearsal. Rehearsals lead to something. Erving Goffman notes how the practice in a rehearsal "allows for more or less full anticipation of what will be done in the live circumstances" (1974, 60), and thus, of course, implies live circumstances point-blank.

4) We mustn't forget that the difficulty of taking steps *as a professional piety* to enter into a dramatic role—steps to go through a gateway—is customary for the much experienced Maria but hardly so for Valentine, who is employed to, as it were, polish the gate, make arrangements for rendezvous there, but not to cross through. Stewart's Valentine's not being an actor must be read by us again and again as elemental to her. Stanislavsky describes an important pedagogical moment in acting class:

> "Calm yourself," said [the Director], looking her straight in the eye "and let us do a little play. This is the plot. . . . The curtain goes up, and you are sitting on the stage. You are alone. You sit and sit and sit. . . . At last the curtain comes down again. That is the whole play. Nothing simpler could be imagined, could it?"
>
> Maria did not answer, so he took her by the arm and without a word led her onto the stage . . . Not knowing where to look, or what to do, she began to change, to sit first one way and then another, to take awkward positions. . . .
>
> [The director says, "You were not simply sitting."]

"What ought we to have done?

Instead of giving his answer in words he rose quickly, walked up to the stage in a business-like way, and sat down heavily in an armchair to rest, as if he were at home. He neither did nor tried to do anything, yet his simple sitting posture was striking. We watched him, and wanted to know what was going on inside of him. He smiled. So did we. He looked thoughtful, and we were eager to know what was passing through his mind. He looked at something and we felt we must see what it was that had attracted his attention. . . .

"You see," the Director said calmly, addressing Grisha, "the external immobility of a person sitting on the stage does not imply passiveness. You may sit without a motion and at the same time be in full action." (1948, 31–34)

As they read their lines on a sunny day, light streaming into the cabin, with sometimes wearying repetition (in French, *rehearsal)*, it is possible to detect the way Maria's deportment, vocalization, openness, stance, and even apparent sense of self are all modified as the scene develops—not just Assayas' scene in this film but the scene in *Maloja Snake* that they are working on and that Assayas has made the subject of his scene. A scene about a scene, containing a scene. Valentine is tiptoeing at the edge of the strange lake of characterization and at the same time tiptoeing toward the, for her, strange homoerotic world of the character she's been assigned to read. Her tiptoeing is both encouraged and somehow abetted by the warming energies of Maria.

As for Maria, she must learn to inhabit a woman of her own age who can fall in love with someone like this assistant. Two interesting questions emerge. Is Maria's feeling, to the extent that in her acting she has her own feeling—yet who else's feeling could she have?—a genuine attraction for this girl? And is she acting out of the wellspring of that attraction? And is Valentine perhaps feeling attraction for Maria, but either unable to know that attraction, identify it, own it; or, knowing it, unable to proceed forward, since such proceeding, she thinks, could imply an inescapable commitment of self? We can all be flirted with by people who find us attractive, and recognize the flirting, while at the same time sensing something inescapable on the horizon (especially if the flirting is the substance of a rehearsal). Let us argue that both women can sense the tincture of touch nearby—but how to touch, or be touched by, an unknown? Cavell discerns "two dimensions or directions of all film, no more to be kept from touching or pervading one another than are fantasy and reality, or myth and ritual, or language and the world" (*CF*, 208). Two dimensions or directions; two women; two unknowns.

5) Valentine's fear of Maria's heightening warmth and proximity—summarized as Maria's *unknownness* to her—however real or imaginary it is for Valentine herself, is surely a part of the personality of the girl Maria is trying to grasp falling in love with, grasp because in the scene from the play being rehearsed, Maria's Helena is trying to grasp falling in love with Valentine's partly realized—or very fully realized!—Sigrid. At the moment she must be—that is, *be*—Helena as Valentine plays out Sigrid; and serious as she is in her working technique, if not in her sensibility to the moment, Maria is going beyond trying. What is desperately *unknown* in this endeavor is the borderline between one's personal self and one's working self, Maria personally striving and Maria in character striving as Helena; Valentine personally hesitant and Valentine, as much as she can achieve this, hesitant in character as Sigrid. In *Maloja Snake* the eroticism is palpable. Valentine is repeatedly confused (Stewart shows), by her uncertainty as to how much of Maria's warmth is coming from the script, that is, from Helena, and how much is coming from Maria. This is a boundary problem, since Helena exists only when the play-work is on the table while Maria exists always. Valentine will be bound to know and relate to Maria the person (her employer) once the rehearsal is done (yet, of course, only within working hours, such as they might be, in a strange business like movie-making). Helena and Sigrid know each other, to whatever depths, only while the "play" and the play are on. But, here in rehearsal in a cabin, as they are not on a stage before an audience, when exactly, Valentine has to wonder with considerably more than casual curiosity, is the play "on" as a "play" and when are they taking a coffee break? Ironically (if you like) in the play the two women work together in an office and they presumably do take coffee breaks; that is, Helena adores Sigrid even when they are not at their desks, and Maria Enders is working to catch all the angles of Helena.

To put this problem of unknownness more operationally: Cavell notes the requirement in romance for conversation: "sacred bonds may be dissolved when the meet and cheerful conversation for which they were entered into falls into a melancholy and intractable silence" (*CF*, 158–59). Is the exchange of scenic dialogue in the rehearsal a conversation at all? Or is the only real conversation they will manage? How can one speak at all, given that one is confronted by an unknown woman, a point of origin and source of who-knows-what? Unable to speak, may the two of them be using the script as an aid-to-the-tongue? The *aide memoire* is a cicerone for a voyage, after all, whilst the aid-to-the-tongue is a supporting arm for the footsteps of the present.

6) Back to the confrontational tête-à-tête between Jo-Ann and Maria, call it the "mother-daughter" scene. When eventually we see these two at work we can be dismayed by the realization that the younger one does not work in the same way the older one does, has adopted her own method, seems both more temperamental and more casually connected to what she does, and certainly does not inhabit her roles with a drive toward *being*: the old story of the Method actor (Maria) and the technical actor (Jo-Ann) being thrown together in a scene. Bluntly, two acting styles and theories of performance are at loggerheads, each theory in its depths an *unknown* to the other. We may presume that when *Maloja Snake* finds its way to the stage this time around, the onstage "love" between the two characters will be entirely concocted from skilled but superficial gestures on one side whilst on the other being felt and struggled with in torment. Audiences will have reason to *know* the characters' unknownness to each other in terms of their final (scripted) incompatibility, but of course the actors, however they work, must always be, or not appear not to be, wholly compatible—or properly incompatible—onstage. In the rehearsal tiff, the elder yields graciously to the younger: "You don't want my guidance; well, fine, you're not a child anymore." Onstage as off, Maria is a perpetual learner. she never stops working to inhabit her role. Seeing Jo-Ann's skillful gesturing technique, the almost balletic competence displayed in her slightest move, Maria must understand the exquisite superficiality in terms of Valentine, too, since like Jo-Ann and the stage role Jo-Ann is playing, Valentine keeps to herself, does not meet many people, does not learn the world by rubbing up against it, has her method. She is compounded of etiquettes. And etiquette is antithetical to orgasm—Cavell calls it "conversation" (a turning together).

Free and Nude

Two exposures now with closer focus.

First, to play out that professional/personal boundary, if boundary it is: Maria is taking Valentine hiking in the hills (the supramundane hills, one's face free under the sky, all the world yawning out green and purposeful and fresh and ready). As they climb they speak lines that are indeterminate for us: at once clearly from the play, because Valentine has the script in hand, yet also clearly about their actual presence with one another and the riddle of their closeness. They find a hillside above the Silsersee and perch together with the town of Maloja far in the distance, watching, as it were, the wind. In a television documentary they watched this, too, side by side, and this same spot was the camera's perch. Coming its way from around a curve far in the distance and reaching forward, forward, forward, forward until it passed like a cortège was a long silver-grey cloud mass shaped like a snake. This is the "Maloja snake" in fact, but we can appreciate how, since just beneath is the village of Sils Maria, it is also, effectively, the morphing title of the film. There was no break in the extensive massing of cloud, perhaps as though it stood—and stands—for some ultimate boundary that has no depth and no terminus and no light. It is a wonder of nature, and happens due to some particular weather formations. Or, it is now only a phantom skirting over the imaginations of these two women who are in the middle of their long hike through the drama, as it were in the middle of the pathway of their lives. Later in the film—I do not believe it gives away the central turn or thrill of the piece to mention this—Valentine vanishes, a vanishing valentine, dissipates in the hills, on a wintry day, while Maria's back is turned and the snake arrives. We will never come even close to finding out if she was swallowed by that snake. Or even if in coming here to be with Maria she was a cloud already.

Maria and Valentine on the hillside, at any rate, with wonder and astonishment, with awe, with mutual excitement, catching their breath together. A moment of supreme bonding. But also a moment set in a wide open space, so very contradictory to the smallish cabin where, over and over, they read through the scenes, touched each other with their voices. Oh, the voice that can touch, the supreme voice. In 1528, eulogizing him, Erasmus said of Albrecht Dürer that he could paint anything, "even things one cannot paint [. . .] almost even the voice itself" (quoted in Robison and Schröder [2013, 134]).

Under the sky, these women can have presence open-ended, airy, momentary: independent of their formal names, the names of their characters, their employer-employee relationship, their scripted "relationship" in rehearsal, their incidental personal feeling one for the other, even—we can have this feeling because of the splendid landscape—independent of their work for Olivier Assayas in this film and of this film altogether—if what is in film can exist outside of the film in which it is: Cavell: "It is my fate to exist and while I exist to be in one place rather than any other" (1979, 213). They can be, Maria and Valentine, as spirits on a hill, *unknowns* to us, *unknowns* to each other, and *unknowable*.

A second moment:

In this mountainous area there are some very tiny lakes—all quite splendid—and Maria and Valentine have found one to swim in. Off with the clothes, but for Valentine not off with the white panties and black bra—is this self-protection? The water is a chilling refreshment, plenty of screams to follow conversation about Valentine traveling to meet a boy she has met and likes, a boy Maria is curious to learn about (for reasons we must surmise). Though the scene dissolves on their splashing, can we sense that Valentine really *goes into the water* with Maria, gets involved, beyond shrieking at the refreshment, in a way that would raise her spirits above the elementary and the dutiful? As the play has it quite explicitly, the professional relationship and the personal relationship are not the same. What kind of relationship does Valentine think they are having when they are not pretending to be Sigrid and Helena and when there is no "work" Maria needs her to do? Is she with Maria to have a good time? Or is Valentine not quite grasping the complexities of Maria's way of working? Maria of course does understand how the work could involve pleasure. There never has been a boundary between work and pleasure for her. Perhaps she is clearer than Valentine is about the place of pleasure in the labor of the world, but only perhaps, since Valentine is so guarded, careful, and withholding about who she is and about the tinctures of pleasure she tastes.

How would a girl like Valentine ever become a grown woman like Maria? Because as a grown version of Valentine (she has "grown" from playing Sigrid into playing Helena) Maria is clearly not someone who guards and protects herself against the world, yet in order to see Valentine as an earlier self she is obliged to accept that long ago, once, she was. Since Maria is protected in a more elaborate way, by the labor (however equivocal) of her assistant, she can afford now to discard all memory of the fearful agony of youth.

Known

When one touches another living person, the nervous responses emerge from within, and the touch is a way to come into what we often like to call knowledge. When the touch is sexual as well as intimate, the knowledge may seem to be fuller. Yet, too, when touch proceeds outward from another with whom one can feel some distinct similarity it may seem a canny, a hunter's touch. Our Valentine is not to be touched—a Rodin in the Hôtel Biron—only admired (and yearned for) from without. She is an unknown woman because she proudly claims unknownness for herself as both an existential and a conditional state; because she turns away from attempts to know her; because she wills it that she will not be known, is not to be known, cannot be known. In holding herself back from knowledge, from being known, in keeping outside of contact, she does not experience life. She is Henry James's John Marcher. She is Galatea. And one of the truths Maria must face is that she has fallen in love with this pristine statue (a statue disguised as youth). Another truth is that in the play, Maria's Helena has fallen in love the same way, with the same alabaster. Her desires are all doomed to rebound back upon her. When long ago she played Sigrid, was she already a Method actor, and did she achieve Sigrid by turning herself into alabaster? How did that alabaster, over the years, come alive? What was—what is—Pygmalion's magic? Dürer could paint anything, "sun rays, thunder, electric storms, lightning, and banks of fog . . . all the feelings" (quoted in Robison and Schröder [2013, 134]).

Jo-Ann, too, has that porcelain rigidity, the same reserve as Valentine, and in this way can lead us to read Valentine and herself as designed by Assayas for pointing to generational distance. This is not an unfamiliar theme with him (see as well *L'heure d'été* [*Summer Hours,* 2008] and *Irma Vep* [1996]). However, Jo-Ann shows a close bonding with a boyfriend (Johnny Flynn) when she meets Maria and Valentine for coffee. She may be able to acknowledge—this film doesn't give her opportunity to—that withdrawal behind an impenetrable surface is but a professional working stance for her; and meeting a costar in preparation to do a play is but a working moment. To put this obversely is perhaps more revealing. Prone altogether in life to dividing herself into apartments, including separating off her professional self from her personal one, Jo-Ann has found in acting, at least acting her way, the perfect occupation. Removal from others, at least certain others, can be rationalized as professional method. Onstage "embraces" in place of embraces, then, with silence and darkness backstage. She is famous, to boot. And Valentine is a nobody. Between these two young ones there is no hunger to break the self-containment. "The world will not support me," each must think, "and so my faithlessness is reasonable." As for Jo-Ann, "I have become skillful at being unknown, and suspect, watching others, that perhaps it is better not to be known: yet to be unknown I must be wary. Guilty in my wariness, I feel myself to be a little artificial." Hence a declaration of performative style as excuse: excuse because an excuse is needed, at least by the one who makes excuses, who is hiding behind excuses, unknown.

The unknown woman who would not be known—because to be known is to be possessed, marked, corrupted—does not hide herself in the fire that purifies; she hides herself to stay away from that fire. We can imagine that in the passion of love this one will give off a perfect pretense of being fully known, all the while in retreat.

Maria's unknownness has grown more complex and more troubling:

(A) First, to herself and to any of us watching who have come to see ourselves through her, she both recognizes and does not recognize the person she once was, as re-presented to her now by both Valentine and Jo-Ann. This is a double problem, affecting both Maria the actor and Helena as Maria intends to play her. Even recognizing herself, Maria comes short of knowing. She must play the role of a woman who has grown past her youth but is faced with a version of it again, precisely as is happening in fact, because Maria is plenty conscious of her age. Helena's response to Sigrid is scripted, and so the words are given on both sides, but the inflection, the musicality and muscularity, the emotion required to conjure up the expressions, is not. Further, can Maria find a way to remember now what it was like twenty years ago to be infatuated with an attractive, powerful older woman, when her own free present desire is clouding her ability to remember how intimidated she may have been? Playing Helena now is so very challenging it may eclipse her memory of how challenging it was twenty years ago to play Sigrid: in short, if the actor is always facing an uphill climb, the present climb is now and always quite different from any other. If she is going to model a performance on the world as she presently knows it, Maria today must somehow, here and now, become her younger self to fulfill that knowing—become or remember having been that self—and the earlier self must join in with her present experience, just so that she may grasp the character she is talking to in the play. Or better: she must show herself trying to connect but visibly failing, the true fate of middle age facing the young. To really be Helena is to only reach for Sigrid, and Valentine is a good teacher. If her youth is utterly lost to her (just in the way that Valentine seems utterly lost in her own way) her past persists in being unknown and, being unknown, persists in being both inaccessible and without cogency. A person like Maria can be an unknown woman to herself, must somehow find a way to be that in order to do the performance.

(B) However, if Maria today can sense and even think about the schism or gulf between what she can bring back of her youthful feeling—or what she can imagine of it—and what a view of Valentine would suggest youthful feeling is today, if she can see how she was once like Valentine but also how she was once not at all like this Valentine, then in Valentine she finds or recognizes a self that is only, as she can know it, a "self," the image of a person who reminds her of her youth but only in some ineffable way. Valentine today is an unknown woman to her (an unknown woman working at her side, knowing all her phone numbers), perhaps even to her young self. It is largely the incompatibility between her image of Valentine and Valentine's conceivable image of herself that makes for the tension between them; that leads to what looks like Valentine's shyness, demureness, hesitation, withdrawal, doubt, finally evacuation. Why in the play it would be the younger person to abandon the relationship and not the older raises a still more profound issue that of course leaks into this film about working toward the play: Valentine leaves because . . . ? She has more places to go? Unknown is not only her person but also her trajectory. Maria has been only a waystation.

(C) Maria has more faith than Valentine does, more sureness keeping a footing in the slippery ether that is the world. Valentine's fear of falling is not different in kind from Maria's, but Maria has had twenty years of living it through. It has become part of her nature to exercise the necessary cautions while at the same time leaning out to take the necessary risks. Valentine has not discovered risk yet as something sometimes necessary. For her it is always the alluring, teasing, borderline-threatening green lake. She cannot imagine the riches that could open to her were she to give up her hesitation and commit to Maria, even briefly in the middle of a line reading. Or else, something sharper and even more intriguing: as Sigrid she is entirely, unreservedly committing herself to Maria, committing this self that is all she has, in pure generosity. Yet if Valentine is altogether Sigrid when they rehearse, who is she when the rehearsal stops? Maria must try with every line of the script and every line she utters outside of the script to make a commitment to this young woman, to touch her, and be constantly, interminably discovering herself not accepted. But a Method actor cannot count on another Method actor as scene partner. And at any rate, the refusal to accept will be, on Sigrid's part, exactly the call of the play.

(D) In seeing two Sigrids, Valentine now, and herself when the play was first put on, Maria is experiencing another kind of unknownness, something cold, even mathematical, and unyielding. This is the queer sensation of displacement, loss, and alien confrontation that one has as a young teacher when for the first time, after years and years of sitting in other people's classrooms, one stands before a group of students who represent one's earlier student self, forced now to play the opposite role. The stage play, its demands, its need for rehearsal—all this merely works in the film to stand in for and highlight this independent condition that comes with aging. One is repeating a conversation from a long time back, but then one was on the other side of the table. Suddenly now, speaking out of a natural and feeling self, one discovers a teacher of old—who was unknown at the time even if looked up to as Olympian. (And does one see what that teacher could have desired?) Maria can see now how she did not know the Helena she was playing to as Sigrid, can muster sympathy for Valentine—to a point: Valentine remains *unknown*; as a woman and a person she is a stranger.

(E) As "unknown women," then, both Maria and Valentine come to face the same horrible challenge, which is the presence—not only generally but now—of what we call *Time*. That each of us lives and continues to be, but continues in such a way that we reach a station in life where our own past has dropped beyond the pale. I remember distinctly a very small seminar at State University of Buffalo in the very late 1960s when Norman O. Brown came over from Rochester to give us a little talk. We were no more than ten souls around the table. He was the very definition of charming with his suntan and silvering hair. But when he was asked questions about *Love's Body* (his new book)—indeed some very penetrating questions, because we were all "in love" and very eager to speak with him—he kept answering, "Well . . . the author of the book believed that . . ." Never did he use the word "I." At the time I thought it was a kind of respect, an etiquette, even very admirable, to shrink the ego to nothingness. And it may have been that. But I can see today that it was also something else: that NOB, as he was affectionately called, was continually growing, moving forward, space-traveling, if you will, and that while he could recognize the self who had written the book in his hand, in truth he did not know him. Valentine is certainly aware she may be seeing the vagueness of her future under the clouds of Sils Maria. Can one clarify a vision of who one will be while striving to clarify a sense of who one is? As to Maria, about this riddle of unknownness, what can she do?

Cavell

There is yet another, very elemental sense of unknownness at play in the film and at play in our everyday lives. People come out of nowhere and approach us; . . . introduce themselves; . . . take us by the hand; . . . and we converse and "get to know" them, and they us, and we become associated. Thus, the early scene on the TGV high-speed train, with Maria and her assistant in a reserved cabin and the assistant texting on two phones at once. These two have already met. They have already said hello. But before two people meet, they are for each other figures from nowhere. What is the biography, the geographical memory, the rosary of crucial feeling in coming to know? What was each thinking about, worrying over, hoping for just before they came into each other's sight? One can come into a working relationship with someone without plumbing any of those depths. For all their businesslike smoothness and conversational efficiency, Maria and Valentine are fundamentally strangers. At least one of them would like that state of affairs to change. Or perhaps they both want change but want it differently, toward a different end, with a different feeling. Nor can we guess that for each woman, "stranger" means the same.

While of *Letter from an Unknown Woman* (Max Ophüls, 1948) Cavell writes, "The failure here is of a woman's unknownness to prove her existence to a man, to become created by a man" (*CT*, 107), I think it true of *Clouds of Sils Maria* that the importance of the man in the fraught equation of unknownness is of far less importance than the importance of the other woman. There are two men, principally, who engender our action, the dead playwright, Melchior, who is utterly unknown because he is no longer around for us to meet (we must know him only by virtue of his dramatic text); and the young director, Klaus Diesterweg (Lars Eidinger), who desperately wants to do the restaging and desperately wants Maria Enders in his cast. If the presentation of *Maloja Snake* is a spring for the action of this film, then these two men are the ones who will "re-create" the unknown woman, indeed unknown women, make them *known*, at least in a dramatic rendition. Klaus will make the unknown women characters known to his audience. He wants to bring Helena alive onstage again, to give her a new *knownness*, and if there is success here—the film leaves this up in the air—her transformation will be at the hands of a man, roughly speaking. I say roughly speaking because no matter what a director says or does, the performance will be the actor's and whatever it will be that Maria does onstage we shall not be seeing Klaus puppeteering or approving it.

Notably, while a film could have been made showing the actor and her assistant working hard under the tutelage of a director to develop a presence for a play (something of what happens, say, in *Vanya on 42nd Street* [Louis Malle, 1994]), that is not the film we have here. Diesterweg is introduced principally to establish the logic of the new production and thus rationalize Maria's challenge in this role. Not only do we not get to know him but we do not miss getting to know him. The signal "failure" here, to come back to Cavell, is of women's unknownness to prove their existence to one another, for each to be created by a woman, this "failure" running in both temporal directions. The girl cannot prove her existence to the woman; the woman cannot prove her existence to the girl. Jo-Ann makes it patently clear she has no intention of proving anything: she is a cipher necessary to motor the plot, and the script will take care of her business. Valentine cannot be created by Maria, notwithstanding their privacy and proximity. She cannot become Maria's Valentine. Maria cannot be created by Valentine. Shakespeare writes, "One man in his time plays many parts" (*As You Like It*, 2.7), an actor's credo, to be sure, but here we have a case of unknowns in their time playing many unknowns.

By the phrase "prove existence" Cavell surely means, and I echo that meaning, show every pertinent aspect of one's present experience in such a way that, if it cannot be completely understood it can at least be accepted as a gift. To prove, as in, *to give*. Shivering and laughing in the water, in her panties and bra, Valentine is declining to give herself to Maria, to be a gift. Back and forth in rehearsal, cajoling, urging, beckoning her younger partner, Maria is stopping short of being a gift for this Valentine who does not make a gift of herself. It may be that while both women know they are failing to come across, one is more experienced with the coming over, the metaphor, and therefore more responsible. Not that responsibility helps.

Postscriptum

I remember sitting with Talcott Parsons in his office in 1969 and asking what language is, and he replied that he thought it was a flexibility within a rigidity. Experience is language—not merely a compact of messages conveyed through speech but language directly, in its melding of formation with emotion. We can imagine Maria Enders wondering what this thing *Maloja Snake* is, after all, that she can have played it at a very young, impressionable age; made a glorious hit; built a career. All this in the role of a callow girl who takes on an older lover in a game of chance, but then aborts the affair, causing Helena to suicide. And now she can play Helena, confronting another Sigrid, earnest, eager, energetic, furiously (and unavoidably) selfish. Having been once and now being again, she can find herself onstage in the same rigid structure holding the flexible acts of two impassioned souls. What is this thing, that in the film is only represented by Melchior's play, that holds us all, that remains itself and subdivides its form into the same roles always to be replayed but always replayed differently? Maria and Valentine can sense themselves each imbricated with a role, caught into its meshes, but they cannot believe they are to be known this way, that they are already the full selves they can be here and now, in a metamorphosing frame that continually reallocates roles to different players and in a world where being fully a self is being, still, unknown. For all her greenness, that we can see her tasting with every shifting flicker of her tongue, Valentine is shockingly aware that "Youth's a stuff will not endure" (*Twelfth Night* 2.3), yet it is all she has. And Maria knows, with another shock, how every moment will bring Valentine forward in time, drag her away from this sculpted paragon who is so much to be adored now. Now but only now. Only in this breath. And she knows too, this older one, that she does not really know—can never really know—who she was before, that none of us have access to anything much beyond the breath of the moment in all its pungency. Maria's agony is that since she can perceive in Valentine qualities that Valentine does not claim, it would be impossible for her to become known to the girl, that is, to say, "Here is what I see you are, and why I love you." That would be indecipherable. Valentine perhaps has less trouble imagining that Maria would understand her if she made herself fully known, but she has not yet grown into the confidence to be known. She feels herself as unknowably small, insufficient, empty of what this grand movie star would certainly desire.

Still the curtain goes up on *Maloja Snake*. And twenty years after it comes down it will undoubtedly go up again. Always the curtain goes up again with the ingenue become an icon, and a newborn icon evermore unknown.

Notes

1. Notably, *Irma Vep* (1996), *Late August, Early September* (1998), *Demon Lover* (2002), *L'heure d'été* (2008), and *Carlos* (2010).

2. A very full descriptive analysis is provided by Logan (2018), who has also been most helpful to me here.

3. I pursue some thoughts about this language solution—this dissolving—in the Introduction, "A Map of Many Colors," in my *Color It True: Impressions of Cinema* (2022).

Works Cited

Goffman, Erving. 1974. *Frame Analysis: An Essay on the Organization of Experience*. Harvard University Press.

Logan, Elliott. 2018. "Kristen Stewart in *Clouds of Sils Maria*." In *Close-Up: Great Cinematic Performances Volume 1: America*, edited by Murray Pomerance and Kyle Stevens. Edinburgh University Press.

Pomerance, Murray. 2002. *Color It True: Impressions of Cinema*. Bloomsbury Academic.

Robison, Andrew, and Klaus Albrecht Schröder, eds. 2013. *Albrecht Dürer: Master Drawings, Watercolors, and Prints from the Albertina*. Washington, DC: National Gallery of Art.

Stanislavski, Constantin. 1948. *An Actor Prepares*. Translated by Elizabeth Reynolds Hapgood. Theatre Arts Books.

10

Moral Imperfectionism and Ethical Melodrama

The Case of *Carol*

ROBERT SINNERBRINK

CAVELL'S EXPLORATION OF (Emersonian) moral perfectionism, as enacted in the remarriage comedy and melodrama of the unknown woman, is his most recognized contribution to film-ethics.[1] With its emphasis on open-ended, individual and social self-transformation, it offers a creative and critical response to cultural and moral skepticism. Cavell emphasizes the successful pursuit of moral perfectionism as marking the ethical contribution of these films. The other side of this story, however, especially for the melodramas, involves the thwarting, breakdown, or impossibility of realizing this ethical path, thanks to the normative context within which characters may find themselves. We can examine some of the tensions in Cavell's moral perfectionism—namely, framing moral perfectionism via its social and democratic conditions, thereby making explicit the relation between ethics and politics—by way of a contemporary "melodrama of the unknown woman" that is also a lesbian romantic drama: *Carol* (Todd Haynes, 2015). Haynes's adaptation of Patricia Highsmith's novel explores not only the life-transforming experience of falling in love but also the challenges of same-sex love in a world where it remains suppressed and stigmatized. The film features many elements that we can identify with Cavell's moral perfectionism, notably the quest for the characters to transform themselves, to choose how they want to live, what kind of people they aspire to be, as a romantic couple struggling to articulate their love within the conservative constraints of 1950s New York society. As a melodramatic romance with a queer perspective, it offers a way of exploring what we might call "moral imperfectionism:" the difficulties involved in pursuing a moral perfectionist path of self-transformation within a socially constrained, morally prejudicial, imperfect social world.

Film and Moral Perfectionism

In elaborating cinematic responses to skepticism, in particular moral skepticism understood as a skepticism concerning the possibility of knowing others, Cavell focuses on the remarriage comedy and the melodrama of the unknown woman from the ethical perspective of moral perfectionism (*PH*; *CT*; *CW*). We can define the latter as a post-foundational, nonteleological conception of ethics that foregrounds the creative ethical task of individuals in shaping their conduct and composing their lives as open-ended projects. Drawing on the thought of Ralph Waldo Emerson, Cavell suggests that narrative cinema is ideally suited for exploring characters embarking on a quest for self-knowledge or the experience of creative self-transformation: the ethical process, as Nietzsche described, of "becoming who one is" independent of canonical moral rules or abstract theoretical reflection. What is distinctive about moral perfectionism, from a philosophical perspective, is its eschewal of universalist moral principles, a utilitarian calculus of consequences, or the cultivation of culturally valorized ethical virtues, in favor of an individualist, experimental, "existential" commitment to freedom and autonomous self-transformation. Moral perfectionism's creative response to ethics in the absence of metaphysical foundations, rationalistic calculation, or rigid moral principles makes it an ideal ethical response to skepticism on the moral-cultural plane.

So, what is moral perfectionism? According to Cavell, it is not a distinct moral theory but rather a dimension of moral thinking or "register of moral life" that can be found in a variety of philosophical texts and traditions (from Plato's *Republic*, Emerson's essays, and Nietzsche's aphorisms to Heidegger's *Being and Time* and Wittgenstein's *Philosophical Investigations*) (*CW*, 12–13). We can describe it as an "anti-foundationalist" way of conceptualizing ethical experience, one that has a practical, existential emphasis on the importance of making oneself intelligible to others, of transforming oneself throughout one's life, and of practicing "philosophy as a way of life" (13; Hadot et al. 1995, 2005). In this respect, we can find moral perfectionist thinking not only in certain philosophical texts but also in poetry, literature, drama, and, of course, in movies. Perhaps because of its broader cultural significance, however, moral perfectionism remains a neglected way of thinking ethics within academic philosophy compared with the dominant theories of morality (Kantian universalism, utilitarianism, and Aristotelian virtue ethics). Although it reaches back to traditions of ancient Greek thought, it also resonates with modern strands of romantic thought and existentialist philosophy.

Indeed, unlike ancient thought, we can define modern philosophy via a sense of disappointment with our knowledge of the world, or with the world in which we find ourselves (see also Critchley 1997). The Kantian division between our sensuous world of appearances and the supersensible world of thought is a powerful expression of this division defining modern philosophy; but so too are the Hegelian, Nietzschean, or existentialist conceptions of the self as divided against itself, searching for ways in which to create itself, reconcile with, or discover the world anew (see Pippin 1999; Taylor 1989). This sense of disappointment with our limits generates a desire to transcend them, either by transforming ourselves, or the world in which we exist, in light of higher ideals. Philosophical criticism presents a vantage point from which we can judge the present state of the world and envisage a new world in the future; or it can offer a way of evaluating our current world as preferable to future alternatives. As Cavell puts it: "The very conception of a divided self and a doubled world, providing a perspective of judgment on the world as it is, measured against the world as it may be, tends to express disappointment with the world as it is, as the scene of human activity and prospects, and perhaps to lodge the demand or desire for a reform or transfiguration of the world" (*CW*, 2). This moral-existential alienation, leading to a dialectic of disappointment with the world coupled with a desire for its transformation, is the primary motivation for the development of moral perfectionism: a "register of moral life" that precedes, intervenes in, or accompanies, the more familiar forms of moral theory (2). The moral calling of philosophy may begin with disappointment in the world, but it offers the prospect of transforming our relationship with it as well as with ourselves. This "therapeutic" dimension of modern philosophy is something Cavell finds in Wittgenstein and Heidegger, but also in Emerson and Nietzsche; thinkers who claim that philosophy is less about knowledge than about transforming our way of experiencing and being in the world. From this point of view, philosophy is about acknowledging our finitude as human beings and knowing subjects; it is about renewing our sense of being limited, mortal beings in a meaningful world, and overcoming the desire to transcend this world in favor of pure theoretical knowledge or an ideal metaphysical reality. This is Cavell's "pragmatic" version of the perfectionist path to renewing our common being-in-the-world or to creating a meaningful form of human life.

Cavell's account of moral perfectionism thus offers an alternative perspective on prevailing moral theories, one focused on achieving self-understanding and ethical self-transformation. It advocates a creative shaping of one's own existence without recourse to pregiven moral principles, social conventions, or universal duties. In this sense, it could be understood as a response to the specter of moral skepticism, cultivating a non-foundationalist way of finding meaning and value in a creative and open-ended process of self-transformation that strives to remain independent of universalist moral principles, the utilitarian calculation of consequences, or the cultivation of moral virtues. Unlike Plato's conception of perfectionism (a teleological account of striving to attain a transcendent ideal), and recalling romanticist and existentialist conceptions of ethical choice (without overdramatizing the significance of "freedom"), Cavell's nonteleological moral perfectionism involves an autonomous, practical, immanent existential quest to become what one is, to approach, as Emerson put it, one's "unattained but attainable self": "In Emerson and Thoreau's sense of human existence, there is no question of reaching a final state of the soul but only and endlessly taking the next step to what Emerson calls "an unattained but attainable self"—a self that is always and never ours—a step that turns us not from bad to good, or wrong to right, but from confusion and constriction toward self-knowledge and sociability" (*CW*, 13). For Cavell, moral perfectionism is a mode of thinking that best defines the moral-ethical significance of the two genres of Hollywood film that he studies in *Pursuits of Happiness* and *Contesting Tears*: the remarriage comedy and the melodrama of the unknown woman. These films focus on couples seeking acknowledgement and self-education as to their desire, transforming themselves in a manner that can be either comic or tragic. Such films remain related to earlier dramatic and literary traditions (Shakespearean comedy, nineteenth-century social-domestic drama) but do not fit readily in any of the three major categories of academic moral philosophy (Kantian universalism, utilitarianism, or virtue ethics). They explore the question of critical self-transformation, the characters' desire to reinvent themselves, and to explore the possibility of a transfigured world in which new ways of being with one another might be possible. In this regard, they remain closely related to Emersonian perfectionism, which does not strive for a utopian ideal, nor dismiss the existing world as inherently meaningless. Rather, in calling these films "Emersonian," Cavell suggests that they participate in the perfectionist quest for self-transformation within a world that could be itself transformed, however partially, by reinventing our relations with others within a democratic community.

Cavell explores these possibilities of transformation most comprehensively in *Cities of Words*. Based on his Harvard lecture course in moral reasoning, Cavell reveals this enduring strain of moral perfectionist thought by pairing philosophical texts by Emerson, Locke, Mill, Kant, Rawls, Nietzsche, Plato, and Aristotle with movies such as *The Philadelphia Story* (George Cukor, 1940), *Adam's Rib* (George Cukor, 1944), *Gaslight* (George Cukor, 1944), *It Happened One Night* (Frank Capra, 1934), *Stella Dallas* (King Vidor, 1937), and *The Awful Truth* (Leo McCarey, 1937). He explores how these films and texts speak to each other about the possibilities of moral perfectionism as a way of engaging in ethical reflection that is at once imaginative and dramatic, comic and tragic. These films explore ethical situations via narrative and thereby broaden our conception of moral reasoning, attuning us to more subtle and complex registers of ethical life, thus enhancing and extending the kind of moral-aesthetic experience we can have with cinema. These films are less concerned with traditional theories of morality than with how particular characters in singular situations can transform themselves through mutual acknowledgement (or show how the failure of acknowledgement can thwart such transformation). They are concerned with existential questions at the level of the ordinary, rather than the metaphysical; they explore what kind of person one is to become, rather than what the concept of a person means. As Cavell remarks:

> The issues the principal pair in these films confront each other with are formulated less well by questions concerning what they ought to do, what it would be best or right for them to do, than by the question of how they shall live their lives, what kind of persons they aspire to be. This aspect or moment of morality—in which a crisis forces an examination of one's life that calls for a transformation or reorienting of it—is the province of what I emphasize as moral perfectionism. (*CW*, 11)

As we shall see, Todd Haynes's *Carol*—focusing on a relationship crisis that will force the two women to examine their lives and how they might be transformed—will explore this province of moral perfectionism in an elegant, provocative, and critical manner.

Before turning to *Carol*, however, I wish to elaborate the philosophical and ethical dimensions of Cavell's approach to moral perfectionism. There are at least three ways in which we can relate moral perfectionism to film. The first is through cinema's egalitarian capacity to thematize and reveal the ordinary in all its rich texture of meaning. The second is through the development of narrative film and of specific genres that explore the themes of self-transformation, acknowledging others, and either reconciling with or transforming the world. The third is through film's capacity to transfigure human figures as depicted on screen, to capture and convey emotional expression and psychological complexity through gesture and performance. All three aspects are at play in the genres of remarriage comedy and the melodrama of the unknown woman. It is through these films' cinematic presentation of singular characters confronting the ordinary moral challenges of love and friendship, freedom and fulfilment, recognition and reinvention, that we can have an ethical experience of moral perfectionism.

Moral Perfectionism and Remarriage Comedy

As remarked, Cavell's two major philosophical works on film explore two related Hollywood genres, the remarriage comedy and the melodrama of the unknown woman (which Cavell is the first to identify). These genres transform the theme of marriage, either as a utopian possibility of mutual acknowledgment in the comedies, or as a block to the woman's quest for self-knowledge in the melodramas. In his earlier books, however, Cavell does not explicitly link either genre with Emersonian moral perfectionism, although Emerson's thought remains, as ever, a constant reference point. Rather, he draws attention to how such films thematize their condition as visual media, their inheritance of literary and dramatic traditions, their relationships with other films and constitution of a genre, and their reflection on morally relevant themes, including the Emersonian critique of conformity and the possibility of an egalitarian relationship between the sexes. It is only in *Cities of Words* that Cavell explicitly recasts both genres as participating in the philosophical discourse of moral perfectionism present in modern culture since Shakespeare and Milton, Ibsen and Eliot, Emerson and Nietzsche.

What are remarriage comedies? Cavell addresses these films as a particular subgenre, exemplified by a selection of "seven talkies made in Hollywood between 1934 and 1949" (*CF*, 136): *It Happened One Night* (Frank Capra, 1934), *The Awful Truth* (Leo McCarey, 1937), *Bringing Up Baby* (Howard Hawks, 1938), *His Girl Friday* (Howard Hawks, 1940), *The Philadelphia Story* (George Cukor, 1940), *The Lady Eve* (Preston Sturges, 1941), and *Adam's Rib* (George Cukor, 1944). Although they share many features with other romantic comedies, these remarriage comedies are also distantly related to Shakespearean romances like *The Winter's Tale* and *The Tempest*. Unlike classical comedy and romance, where a young couple is shown "overcoming obstacles to their love and at the end achieving marriage," remarriage comedies commence with a mature couple, getting or threatening to get their divorce, so that "the drive of the narrative is to get the original pair together *again*" (4). They are distinguished from other versions of romantic comedy (related to what Northrop Frye called New Comedy) in which a male character pursues his beloved and battles familial and social barriers to their desired marriage. Resonating with Frye's account of Old Comedy, in the remarriage comedies it is the woman who is the focus of the narrative, except that now she embarks on a "sentimental journey" to educate herself as to her desire, deciding whether the man in question is a suitable partner for her project of self-transformation. These films explore the concept of conversation, the ethical idea of marriage as a "meet and happy conversation" (as Milton put it in his tract on divorce, quoted by Cavell in *PH*, 87). They explore forms of social and personal exchange in which each partner acknowledges the other in his or her uniqueness, yet where each also provides the other with an educative perspective as to the possibilities allowing for a transformation of his or her self-identity. This raises the question of whether the relationship of equality between the sexes envisaged by the couple is realizable within the social, cultural, and ethical norms of the community in which the couple find themselves. The utopian aspect of these comedies thus lies not only in their exploration of a mutually transformative relationship between the sexes but also in imagining a form of democratic community in which self-reliance and interpersonal intimacy can be mediated with social freedom and political equality.

The remarriage motif, as Cavell remarks, is prompted by the changed situation of marriage, which is "no longer assured or legitimized by church or state or sexual compatibility or children," but rather by the "willingness for remarriage, a way of continuing to affirm the happiness of one's initial leap" (*CF*, 137). Marriage, in other words, is at once a romantic and an ethical relationship sustained by an existential will to repeat one's commitment to seek happiness through mutual acknowledgement with an equal. The focus is on not only the question of marriage but also on how the latter is linked with the self-education of the woman. Through these experiences, she learns the true nature of her desire, seeking to establish her self-identity and openness towards the future through a process of mutual acknowledgement between her and her partner. The couple's trials are carried comically thanks to virtuoso dialogue and artful performance; their mutual adventures take them from the city to the country (the Shakespearean "green world"), where the obstacles to self-realization through acknowledgment, hence to remarriage, are overcome. What the couple discover, finally, is that they are indeed "made for each other," but only after having committed themselves, through "happy and meet conversation," to educating themselves, and thus transforming and reinventing themselves, in felicitous partnership with one another.

By contrast, melodramas of the unknown woman, such as *Letter from an Unknown Woman* (Max Ophüls, 1948), *Gaslight* (George Cukor, 1944), *Now Voyager* (Irving Rapper, 1942), and *Stella Dallas* (King Vidor, 1937), appear to negate key elements of the remarriage comedy, notably the institution of marriage itself. Within these films, the idea of marriage as a route to self-creation is "transcended and perhaps reconceived" (*CW*, 6). Indeed, the route to self-creation is not through marriage but involves, rather, a "metamorphosis": a radical, "melodramatic" change in the identity of the woman that takes place independently of any conversation or marital commerce with the man, and which draws its nourishment from the otherwise marginalized "world of women" (6). It is the woman's education towards self-reliance, and her subsequent rejection of marriage, that stands in sharpest contrast with the remarriage comedy. Nonetheless, both genres share an underlying commitment to (Emersonian) moral perfectionism, namely, by "working out the problematic of self-reliance and conformity, or of hope and despair," in relation to the task of individual self-transformation (*CT*, 9).

Cavell insists, moreover, that we can accommodate the contrasts between the comedies and the melodramas within the moral perfectionist frame, the former by offering an idealized egalitarian version of marriage, the latter by questioning traditional conceptions of marriage in relation to the task of achieving independence beyond socially allotted roles. The remarriage comedies "envisage a relation of equality between human beings," which Emerson described as "a relation of rightful attraction, of expressiveness, and of joy"; the melodramas of the unknown woman, by contrast, envision "the phase of the problematic of self-reliance that demands this expressiveness and joy first in relation to oneself" (*CT*, 9). The latter involves a kind of excessive or "melodramatic" doubt, or passage through skepticism, that leads the woman beyond skeptical despair and towards a fragile recovery of herself and the world. Both subgenres allegorize these aspects of skepticism and its overcoming in relation to the problem of marriage. Both traverse the possibility of skeptical doubt over our relationship to the world, our capacity for self-knowledge, our ability to know and understand one another, through comic and tragic explorations of romantic relationships, understood as expressions of the potential for acknowledgment within the everyday and the domestic. These are some of the reasons behind Cavell's otherwise surprising claim that, contrary to appearances, skepticism, understood here as "the threat to the ordinary," should show up in fiction's favorite threats to forms of marriage, namely "in forms of melodrama and of tragedy" (10).

As critics have remarked, this emphasis on marriage as a means of overcoming (moral/social) skepticism is one of the more questionable aspects of Cavell's reading of the melodramas and romances, particularly with regard to the question of gender relations (see Sinnerbrink 2016, 123–25; Willett 2008; Williams 1984). Indeed, I would modify Cavell's claim and assert that, if melodrama is the negation of remarriage comedy, then within melodrama the moral perfectionist path is blocked or thwarted (the possibility of finding and following such an ethical path towards independence is put into question). The woman's quest for self-transformation is compromised within this world, which itself becomes the object of a critical reflection; the constraints and conflicts to which she is subject, moreover, generate the hyperbolic emotionalism and aesthetic excess for which the genre is famous.

Romantic Love and Moral Imperfectionism: *Carol* as Moral Melodrama

One way to explore this claim further, and to suggest how a revised moral perfectionism might work, is to offer a Cavellian perspective on a contemporary "melodrama of the unknown woman." *Carol* (Todd Haynes, 2015) is a critically acclaimed romance and melodrama based on Patricia Highsmith's novel *The Price of Salt* (published in 1952 under a pseudonym and republished in 1990 under Highsmith's name with the title *Carol*). The screenplay was written by Phyllis Nagy (who had been friends with Highsmith during the latter's life) and adapts the novel brilliantly for the screen. Cate Blanchett and Rooney Mara star as the romantic couple: Carol Aird (Blanchett), a glamorous society woman and mother undergoing a difficult divorce, and Therese Belivet (Mara), a younger woman working part-time in the toy department of Frankendale's (a department store based on Bloomingdale's) while pursuing photography. As a lesbian romance combining elements of the maternal melodrama, the film shifts focus from the perspective of the naive Therese towards that of the sophisticated Carol, while exploring different facets of their relationship. Both women, however, are shown in their shared vulnerability, subtly articulated passion, and suppressed desire, trying to find ways to express their love within a world that refuses to recognize or legitimate it. The film's elegant visual style—its evocative use of color, décor, costume, music, and setting—provide aesthetic means to express the emotional dynamics of a relationship that defies traditional prohibitions on permissible paths to perfectionist self-transformation through romantic love for, and between, women.

Set in New York City in 1952 and 1953 but also venturing further afield into the American Midwest (Ohio), the film explores not only the life-transforming experience of falling in love but also the challenges of same-sex love in a world where it remains suppressed and stigmatized. The film features many elements that we can identify with Cavell's moral perfectionism, notably the quest for the characters to transform themselves, to choose how they want to live and what kind of people they aspire to be, as a romantic couple struggling to have their love relationship acknowledged within the conservative constraints of the 1950s. Chiming with Cavell's observations of the genre, both women undergo a "metamorphosis": a radical, "melo-dramatic" change in identity that takes place independently of any conversation or marital commerce with a male character, and which is centered on the otherwise marginalized "world of women" (*CW*, 6). As a melodramatic romance with a lesbian perspective,[2] it offers a way of exploring what we might call "moral imperfectionism:" the difficulties involved in pursuing a moral perfectionist path of self-transformation within a socially constrained, morally prejudicial, imperfect social and cultural world that denies recognition of their freedom, equality, and individuality.[3]

Cavell's account of the melodrama of the unknown woman acknowledges that it offers something akin to the "negative" version of moral perfectionism (in the sense of an opposing version but also evoking the idea of a photographic negative). A woman who is both unknown (to herself) and to us (as various aspects of her character or motivation remain concealed) undergoes a transformative experience in which she begins to explore who she is, and has to choose what kind of life she will lead within the demands and constraints of her allotted gender role. This means, typically, either rejecting the path of marriage, questioning her traditional feminine role as mother, or choosing to venture on a new way of life on her own terms, outside of marriage or the world of men, following a more authentic and independent but uncertain and unacknowledged path. Unlike remarriage comedies, in which the woman needs to choose which partner will help educate her as to her desire, in the melodrama of the unknown woman she attempts to find or forge a new but difficult path that might allow her to reconcile motherhood with independence, romantic relationships with family or career, personal authenticity with social acknowledgment. The women in these melodramas experiment with the possibilities available within their world to transform or transcend conventional gender roles and social obligations, striving within their situation to become, quoting Stella Dallas, "something else besides a mother." Although Cavell identifies this genre or subgenre within classic Hollywood melodramas of the 1930s and 1940s, it remains a feature of melodramas that other critics and theorists have explored in relation to more recent European and American cinema, with a flourishing of new films appearing in recent years (see Rushton 2010, 2014; Staat 2016, 2019).

Many of these elements are present in *Carol*, which focuses on the passionate but thwarted romantic relationship between a wealthy and experienced New York woman trying to leave her marriage and an inexperienced young sales assistant-cum-photographer making her way in the world. The film presents its story initially from the perspective of Therese—as in Highsmith's novel—but gradually shifts towards Carol's perspective, whose difficult battle with her possessive, patriarchal husband, Harge (Kyle Chandler), over the custody of their daughter, Rinny (Kk Heim), threatens to destroy the women's relationship and casts Carol in an increasingly vulnerable role. We witness the subtle signs of desire shaping their first meeting—a chance encounter at a department store toy counter, Carol asking Therese for advice on what to buy her young daughter for Christmas, leaving her leather gloves on the counter "by accident"—followed by the blossoming of their passionate relationship until its destruction thanks to Carol's jealous husband. If this had been a more conventional melodrama of the unknown woman, the story would likely have followed Carol's trajectory, her failed attempts to find happiness in some alternative kind of life, having sacrificed her daughter and, most likely, her hopes of happiness for a tragically impossible love.

Instead, the film tracks the couple's flight into the country and the exposure of Carol and Therese's furtive love affair, which Harge and his lawyers use to discredit Carol as a mother and demonize her as a sexual being. Her admirable refusal to submit to Harge's attempts at moral blackmail and social disenfranchisement—the attempts to quash her quest for recognition as a woman on her own terms—reveal the strength of her moral character, her commitment to maintaining personal authenticity despite the threats of social stigma, institutional harassment, and heterosexist oppression. Although it tracks elements of the melodrama of the unknown woman, the film refuses to show Carol renouncing romance or her hopes for happiness in favor of family, convention, social status, or personal advantage. Indeed, it exposes the prejudices at the heart of the institutions of marriage and the family and emphasizes the values of social recognition, moral equality, and personal authenticity. In this sense, the film combines elements of the remarriage motif with elements of the moral melo-drama.[4] Therese has to decide whether to see Carol again after the seeming demise of their relationship, whether to recommit to their suppressed love and to live openly together as a couple—the film thus ending with an open moment of possible reconciliation and fragile sense of shared futurity.

As a lesbian love story, however, *Carol* deftly combines these elements with romance, the experience of love with its anxieties, ecstasies, and obsessions, exploring how romantic love between two women might be possible within a prejudicial world.[5] As remarked, Therese is an ingénue, still unformed, finding her way in life, attracted to, but not quite comprehending, the magnetic allure of the more experienced, worldly Carol. Both women undergo a shared experience of love that is profound and transformative, and both come to understand themselves and the possibility of a shared life together that will require invention and independence. The differences in age, social experience, class background, and sexual identity—Carol, as becomes clear, has already had a relationship with a woman, which only primes Harge's jealousy and vindictiveness—provide conventional obstacles that are also enabling features of their unconventional relationship. Carol's distant worldliness and experience, however, come undone thanks to Therese's youth and inexperience; Carol experiences the vulnerability of being in love beyond sexual passion while Therese matures into herself as a consequence of exploring this unfamiliar desire.

Coming under increasing pressure from Carol's husband during their fractious divorce proceedings, the women take flight from the dark and murky environs of New York. The film mutates for a time into a road movie as they travel across the Midwest—in a manner recalling Kubrick's version of *Lolita* (1962)—seeking anonymity from the gaze of others, desiring to consummate their love, all while evading Harge's attempts to track Carol and prevent her from having custody of their child. In an isolated motel, just before New Year's Eve, they meet a travelling salesman (one of Harge's private investigators), who seems innocuous but who deceives them and manages to plant a microphone to record their lovemaking as evidence of infidelity—which as a moral failing is here compounded by being evidence of a lesbian love affair. The quest to pursue a private romance beyond the prejudicial scrutiny of the public gaze proves impossible. The transgressive character of their relationship—intimately rendered with both passion and discretion—powerfully exposes the moral, social, and ideological prejudices shaping and governing the cultural space of romantic love and the public institutions of marriage and the family. In doing so, the film marks and exposes the limits of what a moral perfectionist framework assumes: a democratic space of freedom and equality in community, recognizing individuals' rights to pursue their conception of happiness, to explore and express their identities in a self-chosen manner, to become who they are despite social convention, moral prejudices, or institutional constraints.

The failure of Carol and Therese's relationship is not due to their age difference, social class, or failure to communicate. It is due to the sexist norms, patriarchal institutions, and homophobic prejudices that found and shape their social reality and possibilities of romantic intimacy. Their shared quest for moral perfectionist self-transformation through romantic love is dependent upon a social reality and ideological context that does not readily figure within Cavell's account of the conditions of personal self-transformation and existential freedom within either remarriage comedy or melodrama of the unknown woman. Their love affair challenges the moral prejudices and social conventions of the 1950s concerning heterosexuality and homosexuality but also age, class, parenthood, and social experience. This transgressive character of their romantic relationship makes it more than a tale of thwarted love, rendering their love both transformative and tragic, passionate and political. Their experiences of love and loss stress the possibility of moral perfectionist self-transformation through romantic love while acknowledging the impossibility of doing so independently of social context or ideological-political constraints. Indeed, the prejudices afflicting homosexual couples profoundly constrain the very possibility of moral perfectionist self-transformation through romantic love and/ or the questioning or rejection of marriage—the mainstay of Cavell's model of moral perfectionism in popular narrative film. Carol does not settle for "the moon" (furtive friendship or frustrated desire) but publicly commits to shoot for "the stars" (recognition of the legitimacy of her relationship with Therese and right to autonomous self-identity via lesbian love), a bold stance that gives the lie to the heterosexist assumptions and patriarchal prejudices afflicting both Hollywood film and contemporary social reality.

For this reason, their relationship seems more importantly centered on the question of desire and recognition of sexual identity than on the possibility of friendship between women and the ethical obligations that this might entail. Wim Staat's reading of *Carol*, for example, stresses the development of friendship as an ethical relationship between equals as a central ethical feature of the film.[6] For Staat, Carol's retreat from Therese when their affair is exposed—both to deal with the impact of this revelation on her custody battle with Harge and to reevaluate how she might reestablish her sense of personal and sexual identity—shows where she fails in her obligations to Therese as a friend.[7] My sense of the film rather, is that their friendship is conditional upon the possibility of both personal intimacy and public acknowledgement of their love, both romantic and sexual, and that failing to achieve acknowledgment of either the personal or the public dimensions of this love will make the possibility of their relationship surviving—even as friendship—very remote. Once again, the film shows how the conditions of moral perfectionist self-transformation are conditional upon appropriate conditions of social recognition and cultural-political freedom.

Carol also raises another important issue that has dogged Cavell's accounts of the more traditional (heterosexual) melodramas and remarriage comedies: the asymmetry between the woman's moral perfectionist quest or transformative ethical trajectory and the man's relatively unchanging status and experience (see Sinnerbrink 2016, 123–25). As a lesbian romance, there are elements of the melodrama of the unknown woman in both protagonists: both Therese and Carol are presented as, and remain to an extent, unknown women, who clearly undergo a profound shift or transformation of perspective thanks to their relationship. Both women are caught between worlds: Therese between the worlds of photography, journalism, and the student bohemian crowd and Carol's world of social privilege and bourgeois propriety; and Carol between the worlds of motherhood, married respectability, and the possibility of an alternative world that neither she nor Therese can yet name or describe. Therese's world offers the possibility of a career in photography, being part of the (male) world of journalism, but also relationships with women that may have to remain clandestine and fleeting (the young woman who appears interested in her at a friend's party towards the end of the film). Carol renounces the lie of claiming that her homosexual affair was a psychological aberration due to mental distress brought about by her husband's harsh conduct. Instead, she claims in a moving speech before the divorce lawyers that she freely chose this affair and that she would rather give up custody of her daughter (while insisting on visiting rights) than continue to live a lie that "goes against my grain."

There are no clear alternatives, however, available for either woman to find genuine acknowledgement. Their shared love must remain concealed and ambiguous, furtive and discreet, while also claiming subtle forms of social visibility and moral acknowledgement.[8] This has prompted some critics to note parallels between the protagonists of Carol and other characters in Cavell's readings of the melodrama of the unknown woman. Staat, for example, claims that Charlotte's splendid isolation in *Now, Voyager* serves as a model for Highsmith/Haynes's Carol. She, like Charlotte, appears independent but also isolated at the end of the film, thanks to the oppressive constraints facing the lesbian lovers:

> In *Carol*, both lesbian protagonists suffer the consequences of their socially unacceptable relationship. Although there is a connection with the lack of acknowledgement suffered in *Letter from an Unknown Woman*, the individuality of Charlotte in *Now, Voyager* is a more appropriate context for the independence of protagonists in *Carol*. Untouchable Charlotte sometimes seems to have inspired Carol, and possibly Therese as well. However, as a couple in Carol, they appear to be less lonely than Charlotte in *Now, Voyager*: they embrace their togetherness as if they indeed were the heroines of a remarriage comedy. (Staat 2019, 522)

The observation of a link to the remarriage theme here is apt and illuminating, but I would suggest that *Carol* does not decide the question of whether Carol and Therese recouple or remain independent as starkly as would be suggested by the parallel with independent Charlotte from *Now, Voyager*. Remaining faithful to Cavell's account of the melodrama of the unknown woman—whose protagonists, thwarted in love and failing to achieve independence through romantic acknowledgment, eschew the path of marriage or even romantic involvement—can blind us to the ambiguous possibility of a transformative relationship that Carol and Therese might envisage in the future. *Carol* does not decide the issue but leaves open the possibility of such a reinvention of romantic love—hinting at their possible reunion—even in a world that strives to thwart, stigmatize, or suppress their love.

At the same time, Therese and Carol have the possibility of inventing a new path, of finding a way of life that would allow them to live their love and transform each other within a world that remains marked by ideological, moral, and social constraints. Their relationship offers a more genuinely mutual exchange than many of the traditional heterosexual melodramas Cavell reflects upon; it suggests a genuinely transformative relationship in a reciprocal sense, educating both women in different ways to enable them to become who they are, despite the prejudices they face and the uncertain acknowledgement they seek. As remarked, their relationship also has elements of the remarriage theme: Therese must choose again, in her own way, whether to recommit to her relationship with Carol, this time more autonomously, with the benefit of experience. She knows that it may mean abandoning her place within her current social milieu and embarking on an uncertain life together, the two women having to find or invent ways to live and express their love in a world that will continue to stymie or thwart it.

The film's rich visual style expresses beautifully these psychological tensions, emotional demands, and moral ambiguities. Cinematographer Ed Lachman shot the film on retro Super 16mm film stock in order to capture the grainier and muted style of 1940s and early 1950s street and documentary photography (by Saul Leiter, Ruth Orkin, Helen Lovitt, Esther Bubley, and Vivian Maier) that served as visual models for the world of the film.[9] The careful attention to colors, muted and harmonious—greens, browns, and pinks, with occasional splashes of red—set against an urban milieu that is elegant and restrained but also gritty and subdued, serves as an expressive medium directing the viewer visually as well as emotionally. So too with the music, composed by Carter Burwell, which combines period melancholy love songs with beautifully scored, mood-setting sequences. Both characters use music to express mood and feeling in ways they could not otherwise verbally articulate (the importance of the record player, record store, and radio playing in key scenes are cases in point). The film itself does the same with the musical score, however, creating moods that both reveal the subjectivity of the characters and attune us to the social world of early 1950s New York. Costuming is another key element complementing both the individual expression of character—Therese's woolen pom-pom beret, her fashion transition from student ingénue to independent young urban photographer; Carol's opulent furs, elegant frocks, arresting hair, and striking jewelry, revealing aspects of her surface persona and of her hidden depths—and the expressive composition of an ambiguous social milieu.

The film's expressive visual style has often been noted and praised (Metz 2016). There are numerous shots incorporating various forms of framing and reflection (using car windows, mirrors, glass doors, window frames, and interior/exterior thresholds). There are shots using abstraction as well as a partial obscuring of vision (close shots within a car on a rainy night, of hands, faces, and arresting objects within a carefully controlled frame). There are also shots that foreclose background in favor of focused intimacy (the withholding of establishing shots or wider framings and use of shallow focus to emphasize textures, fabrics, jewelry, clothing, and makeup, as well as Blanchett's and Mara's facial expressiveness). All these stylistic choices contribute to showing the ambiguous inner emotional states of the characters as well as the complex interplay between image and world, interior and exterior, social self-presentation and sensuous inner feeling that define the film's mood and perspective. The expressive and intimate visual style of the film, moreover, helps convey the ambiguous imbrication of image and desire, complicating the characters' maneuvering of the difficult dialectic between "illicit" forms of desire and deadening social convention.

Dialogue in the film remains muted and understated, punctuated by pauses and silences, but also filled with subtle facial expressions, significant gestures, and telling glances. When Carol and Therese sit down for cocktails and lunch in a discreetly lit restaurant booth, ostensibly so that Carol can thank Therese for returning her leather gloves, the scene focuses closely on their face-to-face encounter in the expressively lit, evocative restaurant setting. The dialogue is both formal and intimate; each phrase Carol utters having to be at once conventional and suggestive. As their meals arrive, Carol asks what Therese does on Sundays, to which she replies, "Nothing," asking Carol the same question in turn, to which Carol gives the same reply, with a certain emphatic note inflecting her otherwise languid, sophisticated diction. After a pause, Carol invites Therese to visit her on Sunday, barely able to glance at Therese directly, combining a casual politeness with anxious vulnerability. The shift from Carol's haughty elegance to a state now more intimate and vulnerable, and from Therese's doe-eyed innocence to her subtle frankness in accepting Carol's offer without hesitation, is conveyed through mood and gesture, glances and intonation, rather than dialogue or exposition. Carol glances briefly up at Therese, who is now smiling openly, Carol adopting her feline suggestive smile in return, gazing briefly in admiration and perplexity at Therese. "What a strange girl you are." "Why?" Therese asks innocently. "Flung out of space," Carol remarks, almost whispering to herself.

This kind of subtle but suggestive exchange, communicating at the level of expression, gesture, and affect rather than explicit dialogue or action, is emblematic of their relationship. The careful framing, attention to visual detail, and aesthetic mood evoking longing as well as fascination, anxiety as well as desire, is a remarkable achievement of the film. Style and substance perfectly complement one another, combining artfully to express the moral perfectionist desire to transform oneself in partnership with an Other, where this transformative ethic of open-ended becoming is complicated by the ambiguity of romantic love and the social constraints of the characters' world. Like so many melodramas, visual style and aesthetic excess stand in for, or supplement and intensify, what cannot be openly communicated or explicitly articulated. Drawing on cinematic masters such as Sirk but adding the restraint of tragic romance (as in Lean's *Brief Encounter*, an explicit reference point for Haynes[10]), *Carol* shows how the moral perfectionist quest, within the context of a lesbian romance, necessarily encounters the prejudices and prohibitions of a straight world that cannot openly acknowledge alternative forms of love and desire.

Carol shows us both the possibilities and limits of the melodrama of the unknown woman multiplying the ethical dimensions of the romantic relationship. By following the mutual transformation of two women in love, rather than the asymmetrical trajectory of the woman and relative stasis of the man in traditional melodramas, *Carol* highlights the struggle for acknowledgment that the couple will experience together within a socially imperfect world. The ethics of moral perfectionism at one level, defines the lovers' quest, their shared experiment to find out who they are and what they might become together, while also stressing the failure of this path to allow these women to pursue their love without fear of exposure, censure, or sacrifice. To its credit, *Carol* eschews the conventional path of ultimately punishing its queer characters for their transgressive desire, opting for a more affirmative yet ambiguous denouement that suggests how the transformative experience of romantic love between women may yet make possible the invention of new ways of living. It also avoids the temptation of presenting an overly optimistic or contemporary celebration of the emancipatory potential of unconventional romantic passion. It does so, moreover, while acknowledging the uncertainty and difficulty of achieving this within a world that continues to constrain or limit the possibilities of moral perfectionism for individuals who do not conform to social and cultural norms of identity, sexuality, or desire.

Recalling Cavell's classic melodramas of the unknown woman, *Carol* both explores and extends the dialectic between acknowledgment and rejection, individual self-realization and the satisfaction of desire, the quest to become who one is in a world bent on denying that quest. Carol and Therese embark on a reciprocal form of self-transformation, a moral perfectionist rejection of the world of marriage and men, struggling to invent a new mode of existence and form of community for themselves, while contending with the unavoidable prejudice they will face in living a queer life together. We might describe *Carol*, in short, as a *self-critical* melodrama of the unknown woman, one that, by transposing Cavell's model to a same-sex romance, reveals both the possibilities and the constraints, the promises and disappointments, of moral perfectionism in an imperfect world.

Notes

1. A point noted in Rodowick (n.d.).

2. See McKee 2018; James 2018; Smith 2018; Staat 2019; White 2015; and Wallace 2022.

3. Staat refers to Haynes's *Carol* along with *Far From Heaven* (2003) and *Mildred Pierce* (2011) as "melodramas of the unacknowledged women" (2019, 530).

4. Staat also notes the "remarriage" aspect to *Carol*, noting that these films do not focus on the romantic lives of the protagonists but rather on the extent to which they are or are not successful in integrating their personal life into public life (2019, 531–32).

5. Haynes asked Blanchett and Mara to read Roland Barthes's *A Lover's Discourse* in order to prepare for their roles as Carol and Therese. White (2015) discusses the significance of Barthes's text for the ways in which the film explores their love relationship.

6. Staat refers to Cavell's discussion of Aristotle on friendship in this context, noting the "responsibilities of friendship" evident in the film, and the manner in which remarriage comedies emphasize how "a mature couple transcends romance and develops friendship so that it can be, as Aristotle would have it, both cooperative and antagonistic" (2019, 534). As I remark below, *Carol* seems more concerned with same-sex romantic love and its vicissitudes in a prejudicial world than on friendship as a moral relationship.

7. Cf. "When Carol leaves Therese behind, Carol's letter read in voiceover explaining her hasty departure is the betrayal of what Therese and Carol seemingly developed: their friendship" (Staat 2019, 534).

8. Therese's own ambivalence about how her relationship with Carol may or may not fit within the subcultural New York lesbian community is signaled in the record store scene where two older lesbians, in mannish dress, stare pointedly at Therese, who seems unsure how to respond to their gaze. That she and Carol do not fit into this subcultural world, let alone the straight world, only adds to the tragic pressure on their perfectionist romance.

9. See the illuminating interview with Haynes about the making of the film (Davis, 2015). Rob White notes that the director of photography, Ed Lachman, described the realist style deployed in scenes depicting Carol and Therese's liaison aimed to evoke a sense of them being under surveillance (quoted in Staat 2019, 531).

10. The film's circular structure—commencing with a restaurant scene in which their relationship hangs in the balance, recounting the story of their relationship and how they reached that point, and reprising the same scene having traversed the story and realized the pathos and gravity of their exchange—recalls *Brief Encounter* (David Lean, 1945) in structure, mood, and style. *Carol*, however, also departs from the film in leaving open the possibility of Carol and Therese renewing their romance on a more equal and hopeful basis.

Works Cited

Critchley, Simon. 1997. *Very Little . . . Almost Nothing: Death, Philosophy, Literature*, Revised edition. Routledge.

Davis, Nick. 2015. "The Object of Desire." *Film Comment* 51 (6): 31–35. https://www.filmcomment.com/article/todd-haynes-carol-interview/.

Hadot, Pierre, J. Aaron Simmons, and Mason Marshall. 2005. "There Are Nowadays Professors of Philosophy, but not Philosophers." *The Journal of Speculative Philosophy* 19 (3): 229–37. https://doi.org/10.1353/jsp.2005.0021.

Hadot, Pierre, J. Aaron Simmons, and Mason Marshall. 1995. *Philosophy as a Way of Life: Spiritual Exercises from Socrates to Foucault*. Edited by Arnold Davidson. Translated by Michael Chase. Basil Blackwell.

James, Jenny M. 2018. "Maternal Failure, Queer Futures: Reading *The Price of Salt* (1952) and *Carol* (2015) Against Their Grain." *GLQ: A Journal of Lesbian and Gay Studies* 24 (2–3): 291–314. https://doi.org/10.1215/10642684-4324825.

McKee, Alison L. 2018. "*The Price of Salt, Carol*, and Queer Narrative Desire(s)." In *Patricia Highsmith on Screen*, edited by Wieland Schwanenbeck and Douglas McFarland. Palgrave Macmillan.

Metz, Walter. 2016. "Far From Toy Trains." *Film Criticism* 40 (3): 1–4. https://doi.org/10.3998/fc.13761232.0040.303.

Pippin, Robert B. 1999. *Modernism as a Philosophical Problem: On the Dissatisfactions of European Higher Culture*. Second edition. Blackwell.

Rodowick, D.N. n.d. "Ethics in Film Philosophy (Cavell, Deleuze, Levinas)." *Academia.edu*. https://www.academia.edu/36412056/Ethics_in_film_philosophy_Cavell_Deleuze_Levinas_/.

Rushton, Richard. 2010. "Acknowledgment and Unknown Women: The Films of Catherine Breillat." *Journal for Cultural Research* 14 (1): 85–101. https://doi.org/10.1080/14797580903363124.

Rushton, Richard. 2014. "Cavell and the Politics of Cinema: On *Marie Antoinette*." *Film-Philosophy* 18 (1): 110–27. https://doi.org/10.3366/film.2014.0008.

Sinnerbrink, Robert. 2016. *Cinematic Ethics: Exploring Ethical Experience through Film*. Routledge.

Smith, Victoria L. 2018. "The Heterotopias of Todd Haynes: Creating Space for Same Sex Desire in *Carol*." *Film Criticism* 42 (1): 1–15. https://doi.org/10.3998/fc.13761232.0042.102.

Staat, Wim. 2016. "Christian Petzold's Melodramas: From Unknown Woman to Reciprocal Unknownness in *Phoenix, Wolfsburg*, and *Barbara*." *Studies in European Cinema* 13 (3): 185–99. https://doi.org/10.1080/17411548.2016.1222739.

Staat, Wim. 2019. "Todd Haynes's Melodramas of the Unknown Woman: *Far From Heaven, Mildred Pierce*, and *Carol*, and Stanley Cavell's Film Ethics." *Quarterly Review of Film and Video* 36 (6): 520–58. https://doi.org/10.1080/10509208.2019.1593018.

Taylor, Charles. 1989. *Sources of the Self: The Making of Modern Identity.* Cambridge University Press.

Wallace, Lee. 2022. "Stanley Cavell and the Queer Thought of Movies." *Screen* 63 (1): 115–22. https://doi.org/10.1093/screen/hjac010.

White, Patricia. 2015. "Sketchy Lesbians: *Carol* as History and Fantasy." *Film Quarterly* 69 (2): 8–18. https://doi.org/10.1525/fq.2015.69.2.8.

Willett, Cynthia. 2008. *Irony in the Age of Empire: Comic Perspectives on Democracy and Freedom.* Indiana University Press.

Williams, Linda. 1984. "'Something Else Besides a Mother': *Stella Dallas* and the Maternal Melodrama." *Cinema Journal* 24 (1): 2–27. https://doi.org/10.2307/1225306.

11

The Same Only a Little Different

A Star is Born is Reborn (Again)

WILLIAM ROTHMAN

Genres and Remakes

EXCEPT FOR THE BARBRA STREISAND/Kris Kristofferson version (Frank Pierson, 1976), which I find (despite an uncannily well-cast Kristofferson) excruciating and will largely ignore in what follows, all four of the incarnations of *A Star is Born*—five, if one counts *What Price Hollywood?* (George Cukor, 1932)—are all well-made films that reward looking at through a Cavellian prism.

If Stanley Cavell hadn't written so brilliantly about the concept of genre, the present volume wouldn't exist, of course. But Cavell never directly addressed the concept of the "remake." Except for Gus van Sant's *Psycho* (1998), remakes don't try to be carbon copies of their originals. And the two *Psychos* demonstrate that even when a remake duplicates every incident, every line of dialogue and even every shot of the original, the result is two different films. A film and its remake(s), like a couple's first and second marriages in a remarriage comedy, are always "the same, only a little different," as Jerry (Cary Grant) puts it in *The Awful Truth* (Leo McCarey, 1937).

Indeed, it's not always obvious whether to count one film a remake of another. Whether the 1937 *A Star is Born* is a remake of *What Price Hollywood?*, for example, was a contentious issue when the film was made. Executives at RKO (the studio that had produced *What Price Hollywood?*) considered suing Selznick International, the company that produced the 1937 *A Star is Born*, for plagiarism—ironically, David O. Selznick had been head of production at RKO and is credited as the producer of *What Price Hollywood?*—but ultimately decided against it. Be that as it may, whether a film is or is not a remake is a question to be settled by lawyers. Whether a film is or is not a comedy of remarriage is a question that can only be settled by an act of criticism.

In *Pursuits of Happiness*, Cavell suggests that members of a genre can be seen to have every feature in common. In the introduction he wrote after completing the body of the book, he registers dissatisfaction with this formulation, noting that what counts as a feature is itself a question for criticism. After all, a film that appears simply to lack a particular feature can compensate in one way or another for this apparent lack. In his introduction, Cavell suggests that a better way to think of what the members of a genre have in common is that they all illustrate the same myth. They can be seen to tell the same story, each in its own way, so that the myth the story illustrates is reinterpreted, revised, by each member.

In "The Fact of Television," published a year after *Pursuits of Happiness*, Cavell distinguishes between this conception of genre, which he calls "genre-as-medium" with what he calls "genre-as-cycle" (*CF*, 64). In the latter, there is, in effect, a formula that generates the members. In a genre like the comedy of remarriage or the melodrama of the unknown woman, the members generate the formula (if we think of its myth as a kind of formula). Is this an apt characterization as well of the relationship of a film and its remakes? A clear answer to this question will not be forthcoming in this essay. It will emerge in what follows that the several versions of *A Star is Born* do, and do not, tell the same story, illustrate the same myth.

Pursuits of Happiness argues that the remarriage comedy genre emerged fully formed in *It Happened One Night* (Frank Capra, 1934), its earliest member. If subsequent remarriage comedies tell the same story, illustrate the same myth, why don't we consider later remarriage comedies to be remakes of *It Happened One Night*? Is it because remakes are closer to their originals and to each other than are the members of a genre? If Cavell is right, all comedies of remarriage can be seen to tell the same story, illustrate the same myth—but no one before him had seen this, and it took writing *Pursuits of Happiness* for Cavell to see it. By contrast, we might think that it's *obvious* that a film and its remake(s) tell the same story, illustrate the same myth. But whether this is true of the versions of *A Star is Born* is a question whose answer is not obvious. This, too, is a question for criticism.

Not every remake does tell the same story, illustrate the same myth, as the original. For example, *His Girl Friday* (Howard Hawks, 1940) is regarded as a remake of *The Front Page* (Lewis Milestone, 1931). It incorporates so much of the earlier film that the studio was legally obligated to acknowledge in the opening credits that its screenplay was "from" the earlier film and the original Ben Hecht/Charles MacArthur play. The transformation of *The Front Page* into *His Girl Friday* was effected, in part, by combining two characters into one—making Hildy Johnson, editor Walter Burns's ace reporter, not a man, as in the original, but a woman—indeed, Walter's former (and future) wife. That little difference makes all the difference, launching the film into the orbit of the remarriage comedy. *His Girl Friday* is a remarriage comedy; *The Front Page* is not. Indeed, *The Front Page* doesn't even exemplify any genre, comparable to the melodrama of the unknown woman, that Cavell would have taken to be adjacent to the comedy of remarriage—that is, negating one or more of its defining features, hence telling a different story, but illustrating a myth underwritten by the same moral outlook that underwrites the comedy of remarriage myth.

As I've argued at length in *The "I" of the Camera* (1988 and 2004), *Tuitions and Intuitions: Essays at the Intersection of Film Theory and Philosophy* (2019), and *The Holiday in His Eye: Stanley Cavell's Vision of Film and Philosophy* (2021), in the years between the release of *It Happened One Night* in 1934 and America's entrance into the Second World War, films of all the leading Hollywood genres told stories, illustrated myths, that for all their differences were expressions of what in *Cities of Words* Cavell calls "Emersonian perfectionism," the moral outlook that was ascendant in Hollywood, as it was in America, in the New Deal era. *His Girl Friday* can be seen to exemplify Emersonian perfectionism. I cannot see *The Front Page* that way.

What Price Hollywood?

As I've said, the 1937 *A Star is Born* is sometimes considered a remake of *What Price Hollywood?*. But here, too, there are differences that make all the difference. For one: Max Carey (Lowell Sherman), the man who "discovers" Mary (Constance Bennet) and presides over her creation as a movie star, is a director, not an actor. This effectively eliminates the element of professional jealousy highlighted in the 1937 *A Star is Born* and the 1954 and 1976 remakes.

More crucially, Max and Mary aren't lovers. Sexual jealousy plays no more of a role than professional jealousy in leading Max to take his own life (as the man does in all incarnations of *A Star is Born*). Mary is grateful to Max and loves him as a friend, but she's not in love with him. Don't ask me why, but she falls in love with and marries Lonny Borden (Neil Hamilton), a snobby polo-playing socialite who tries, *à la* Stephen Dallas, to teach his wife to be more refined in her tastes and behavior so that she can fit in without embarrassing him in his social circle.

When Max, on a bender, drops out of sight for four days, Mary searches everywhere for him. She explains to Lonny, who has grown increasingly fed up with the demands of her stardom and her loyalty to Max, that she can't let down a friend. Lonny whines that she's letting him down. And at this inopportune moment, a very drunk Max appears at their bedroom window. I'm reminded of the way, in *Stella Dallas* (King Vidor, 1937), an equally blotto Ed Mund, carrying a turkey, arrives at Stella's door at the worst possible moment. For Lonny, as for Stephen Dallas, this is the last straw. He tells Mary that he's leaving her, saying, "We don't live in the same world." "That's right," she retorts, speaking words that Stella Dallas ought to have spoken. "In the world I live in, people are human beings, not stuffed shirts." "You live in a world where people are cheap and vulgar without knowing it. If you weren't cheap and vulgar yourself, you couldn't stand it." "If that's the way you feel, get out. Get out!" I like to think that 1932 audiences felt like cheering.

When Mary shows Saxe (Gregory Ratoff), the studio head with a comical (Yiddish?) accent and a heart of gold a telegram from Lonny saying that he had divorced her (in the 1954 remake, too, the studio head is a sympathetic figure—a flattering image of producer Selznick?—a true friend to both Vicki [Janet Gaynor] and to Norman

[Fredric March]) Saxe replies, "He never appreciated you. You'll be happy." "Why shouldn't I be happy," she sobs, "I'm going to have a baby in September."

A year later, Saxe, visiting Mary at her home, comments that he'd read in the gossip columns that Lonny will soon be playing polo in the mountains. "I betcha he would be tickled to death to have you back. Why don't you?" She says, "Stop writing scenarios." (I assume that Saxe's changed attitude toward Lonny is to be understood as motivated by some mixture of sincere concern for Mary's well-being and the desirability for him, as studio head, to squelch the gossip about her relationship with Max that threatens the popularity of the beloved star known as "America's pal.")

When the phone rings and Mary learns that Max was in jail for passing a bad check, she wants to rush off to help him, provoking Saxe to say—again motivated by a mixture of sincere concern and his desire to protect the studio's bottom line—"What foolishness are you going to do now?" "Nothing I wouldn't do for you or any friend who is in trouble." "Mary, you can't help anybody who has lost his self-respect." But Mary refuses to give up on Max. She pays off the man Max gave the bum check to and he refrains from pressing charges. After Max is released, Mary takes him home with her. She tries to cheer him up. "You know what? You're going to stop drinking. You're going back to work." But he says that he has stopped kidding himself; it's too late. "You mustn't be unhappy over a man who doesn't exist anymore . . . I'm dead inside." She insists, "You'll come back." He replies—this is one of the film's greatest lines—"From where I am, they don't come back." He adds—this is something that couldn't be said with sincerity by the man in the 1937 *A Star is Born* or any of its remakes—that he is happy she is now "top of the heap." And as she's leaving the bedroom to let him sleep, Max calls out. "Mary!" "Yes, darling?" "I just wanted to hear you speak again, that's all"—a line that was to be echoed, with variations, in the 1937 *A Star is Born* and all its remakes. Once alone, Max finds a pistol. Staring at his face in a mirror, what he sees confirms the judgment he has already passed on himself, and he shoots himself in the heart—a scene that will be echoed, down to the mirror, in the suicide of the John Barrymore character in *Dinner at Eight*, directed by Cukor a year after *What Price Hollywood?*; even Barrymore didn't play the scene more convincingly than Lowell Sherman. It is essential to all versions of *A Star is Born* that the man's suicide be a romantic gesture—the ultimate act of self-sacrifice performed for the sake of the woman he loves and who loves him, but around whose neck he has become an albatross. Max's suicide, though, is not a romantic gesture; it's an act of abject despair.

Although it's only as a friend that Mary opens her home to Max, the gossip columnists, always hungry for the salacious, treat this once-great director's death in a bedroom of "America's pal" as a scandal. Not only does Max kill himself to keep himself from dragging Mary down with him, as the man does in all versions of *A Star is Born*, his suicide, as a cynical reporter predicts, threatens to "hog the front pages" long enough to "wash her up in pictures."

Mary receives a note—from a reporter, I take it—that reads, "Is it true that Lonny Borden is on his way here to get possession of his son?" Fearing that Lonny will claim that she is an unfit mother and take the boy away from her, she hides out in a French farmhouse—shades of *Blonde Venus* (Josef von Sternberg, 1932), which was released six months after *What Price Hollywood?*. A nurse rushes in to report that Jackie has been kidnapped. Mary assumes, as we do, that what she feared has happened. A moment later, however, Lonny shows up with Jackie in his arms and explains that he took his son because it was the only way he could get to see him. And he brings a message from Saxe offering Mary a starring role in a film perfect for her comeback. Evidently the recipient of a successful character transplant, Lonny declares his undying love and asks Mary to forgive him and to take him back—a denouement that will also be echoed in *Blonde Venus*, albeit with a touch of Von Sternberg's signature irony.

Unlike any of the versions of *A Star is Born*, *What Price Hollywood?* ends with the woman keeping both the man she loves and her stardom—with the bonus that she also keeps the son the women in the later films don't have. I'd like to think that this conventional happy ending didn't make 1932 audiences happy. It certainly doesn't make me happy. Surely, it didn't make George Cukor happy. (A year later, Cukor directed *Little Women* [1933], based on Louisa May Alcott's eminently Emersonian novel, which earns its happy ending.)

That *What Price Hollywood?* concludes with the prosect of the couple's remarriage might seem to align the film with the remarriage comedy genre. But unlike, say, Dexter (Cary Grant) in Cukor's *The Philadelphia Story* (1940), Lonny hasn't earned the right to claim, or reclaim, the woman he says he loves. It is Max, not Lonny, who plays the role in the woman's education—her creation, as *Pursuits of Happiness* also calls it—that Dexter plays in *The Philadelphia Story*, and, for that matter, that Doctor Jaquith (Claude Rains) plays in *Now, Voyager* (Irving Rapper, 1943). Lonny doesn't undertake to help Mary walk in the direction of the unattained but attainable self, to paraphrase Emerson's great essay "Experience" ([1844] 2000). In an anti-Emersonian spirit, what Lonny wants to teach Mary—*à la* Stephen Dallas, as I said—is to conform to "respectable" society.

As my references to *Stella Dallas*, *Blonde Venus* and *Now, Voyager* suggest, *What Price Hollywood?* has—up to a point—an intimate kinship with the melodrama of the unknown woman, as Cavell named the genre, adjacent to the comedy of remarriage, that he studied in *Contesting Tears*. Indeed, I would go so far as to say that *What Price Hollywood?* would count as an unknown woman melodrama—its story would illustrate the same myth as *Stella Dallas*, *Now, Voyager*, *Gaslight* (George Cukor, 1944), and *Letter from an Unknown Woman* (Max Ophüls, 1948)—if it had been given its rightful ending: an ending in which Mary is resolved to go on in her quest for selfhood—an ending like that of Stella Dallas, *Gaslight*, or *Now, Voyager*, in other words. As it stands, the ending of *What Price Hollywood?* not only disqualifies it from membership in the unknown woman genre, it precludes the film from exemplifying the Emersonian perfectionist outlook that was ascendant in American movies later in the 1930s and exemplified by the 1937 *A Star is Born*, made the same year *as Stella Dallas* and *The Awful Truth*.

The transformation of *What Price Hollywood?* into *A Star is Born*, like the transformation of *The Front Page* into *His Girl Friday*, is in part effected by fusing two characters into one—Max (Mary's "discoverer/creator") and Lonny (the man she loves, marries, and chooses to remarry). In both cases, this change helps bring the film into alignment with Emersonian perfectionism. But the fact that in all incarnations of *A Star is Born* the woman stands by her man—the man she loves, who is also the man who presided over her "creation"—negates the feature of the melodrama of the unknown woman—a feature *What Price Hollywood?* negates only by its ending—that the woman breaks off her relationship with a man who's an obstacle to her quest for selfhood. And, of course, the suicide of the woman's "creator" negates the feature of the comedy of remarriage that the man and woman commit themselves to walking, together, in the direction of the unattained yet attainable self.

A Star is Born: 1937, 1954, and 1976

Do the 1937 *A Star is Born* and its remakes exemplify a genre adjacent to the genres Cavell wrote books about? With the making of *It Happened One Night*, a genre was born; subsequent members can be seen to tell the same story, illustrate the same myth, but, as I've said, they aren't considered remakes of *It Happened One Night*. However, I can't think of any films—I can't even imagine such a film—that I would take to be a member of the same genre as the 1937 *A Star is Born* that I wouldn't consider to be a remake of that film. I conclude from this that the 1937 *A Star is Born* cannot be said to have given birth to a genre. Did it at least give birth to a myth? Can the remakes of *A Star is Born*, like the members of a genre, be seen to tell the same story, illustrate the same myth, each in its own way, so that this myth is reinterpreted, revised, by each remake?

Like the films Cavell writes about in *Pursuits of Happiness*, *A Star is Born*, in all its incarnations, involves a woman's creation, achieved with the help of a man and requiring of the woman a metamorphosis tantamount to death and rebirth. This is their most evident affinity with the comedy of remarriage and that genre's Emersonian perfectionist outlook. In the 1937 original, the most explicit assertion of the film's Emersonian bona fides is the figure of Lettie Blodgett (Mary Robson), the grandmother of Vicki Lester, née Esther Blodgett (Janet Gaynor)—a character unparalleled in the remakes. No later version of *A Star is Born*—or *What Price Hollywood?*—opens the way the 1937 does, with a scene of Esther at home in a farmhouse in rural North Dakota before she goes out to Hollywood to pursue her dream of becoming a movie star. At the opening of *What Price Hollywood?*, Mary is a waitress at Hollywood's iconic Brown Derby restaurant. We learn nothing about her hometown, her family background, or how long she has been in Hollywood. The implication is that the past of a would-be star no more matters than if she were in the French Foreign Legion—or in what the Marlene Dietrich character in *Morocco* (Josef von Sternberg, 1930) calls the "Foreign Legion of women." Mary is one of that army of young women in Hollywood—Lonny disdainfully calls them "Hollywood blondes"—who all share the same dream.

In the 1954 *A Star is Born*, too—the same is the case in the 1976 version—we learn nothing about Esther's (Judy Garland) past. Unlike Mary, though, both Esthers have lives as singers that are not driven by a dream of becoming a star, whether in movies or in the music world. On the question of Esther's dreams, the 1976 film is mum. In the 1954 version, it is explicit that Esther Blodgett believes that she's satisfied with the modicum of success she has already achieved. But Norman (James Mason) helps her see something in herself that no one else had ever seen before, a wish to become "something bigger," as she puts it, than she ever dared to dream she could be. "And I'm not going to turn back now. Ever." Insofar as it is only in the course of the film that she discovers what her real dream is, the 1954 Esther may seem more like the heroine of a remarriage comedy than her counterpart in the 1937 *A Star is Born*. In the beginning of *It Happened One Night*, for example, Ellie (Claudette Colbert) believes she knows what she wants: to reach New York and be reunited with the man to whom she is legally married. Only her adventures on the road with Peter (Clark Gable) enable her to discover, with his help, her heart's true desire.

However, in their endings, the 1937 film keeps faith with Emersonian perfectionism, whereas the 1954 remake pulls back from it, disavowing the perfectionist outlook with which it appeared to align itself. (The 1976 version never even hints at such an alignment.) In the 1954 film, Norman's suicide leaves Esther/Vicki so overwhelmed by grief (and, no doubt, by a sense of being somehow to blame) that, like Greta Garbo at the height of her fame, she feels that she cannot go on as a Hollywood star. In both the 1937 and 1954 films (but not in the clueless 1976 version) there is a crucial scene in which a conversation moves Esther/Vicki to recognize that it would be wrong to walk away from her stardom. In the 1937 *A Star is Born*, it is a conversation with Lettie, who has flown in from North Dakota because she senses that her granddaughter is in trouble, that makes Esther/Vicki change her mind as she is about to leave Hollywood. Lettie reminds her of their earlier conversation, when Esther had declared her intention to go out and "live a real life," to "be someone," and Lettie had said, "You're the only one who counts," and told her that what matters most is striving to make her dreams come true. She reminds her granddaughter that she had warned her that, "For every dream of yours you make come true, you'll pay the price in heartbreak." This is the only un-Emersonian part of Lettie's teaching. It would be consistent with Emersonian perfectionism if she had said that striving to realize our dreams is a worthy aspiration even if it leads to heartbreak. At least, it would mean, to paraphrase that Emersonian sage Bob Dylan, that one was busy living, not busy dying.

With Norman's help, Esther realizes her dream of becoming a movie star, and Hollywood exacts its price. But her stardom is the one achievement in her life she can be proud of. If she were to walk away from Hollywood now, it would be as if she had never existed. It is her selfhood that is at stake. When at the end of the film she says, "I am Mrs. Norman Maine," she is publicly affirming her love for Norman, but she is not effacing her own self, subordinating her own self to his. She is keeping faith with her commitment to walk in the direction of the unattained but attainable self, as her grandmother had inspired her to do by her word and her example. She is declaring her existence, performing her *cogito ergo sum*, as Cavell liked to put it.

In the 1954 remake, it is a relatively minor character, Danny Maguire (Tommy Noonan), an assistant to the studio head, who speaks the words that move Esther/Vicki to change her mind, to overcome the temptation to break her vow to never turn back. He tells her that her stardom is the only thing in Norman's life that he never stopped being proud of. If she abandoned Hollywood now, it would be as if Norman never existed. Danny is saying, in other words, that she owes it to Norman, not to herself, to keep faith with her vow to never turn back. At the end of the film, she speaks the very words—"I am Mrs. Norman Maine"—Esther/Vicki speaks in the 1937 film, but I hear them differently. Unlike her earlier counterpart, she is not declaring her existence, performing her *cogito*. She is affirming Norman's existence, not her own, as if his selfhood, not hers, is the only thing that really counts.

To the end of his long career, George Cukor, a key figure in the ascendancy of Emersonian perfectionism in Hollywood movies of the 1930s, did his best to direct films that kept faith in his own Emersonian perfectionist outlook. But in 1954 and 1976 Hollywood—and America—Emersonian perfectionism was anything but ascendant. Even though remakes—often musical remakes—of films made in the brief period Emersonian perfectionism was ascendant were a staple of Hollywood production in the late 1940s and early 1950s, almost all were, from a Cavellian standpoint, glaringly inferior to their originals. *In the Good Old Summertime* (Robert Z. Leonard, 1949), a musical remake of Ernst Lubitsch's great—and entirely Emersonian—*The Shop Around the Corner* (1940), is a case in point. So is *High Society* (Charles Walters, 1956), a mundane remake—even with Grace Kelly and a turn by Louis Armstrong—of *The Philadelphia Story*.

The 1954 *A Star is Born* was an exception. I wouldn't say that it's a better film than the 1937 *A Star is Born* or, for that matter, the 2018 film—that it is better than the 1976 version isn't saying much—but it has great strengths; among them, Cukor's direction of both the musical numbers and the dramatic scenes; a totally convincing performance by James Mason, a great actor; and, above all, a transcendent Judy Garland at the heart of the film. But it also has weaknesses. Some can be attributed to the problems that plagued the production and led to delays, cost overruns, and a fine cut whose length so alarmed the studio bigwigs that it was released in a truncated—Cukor called it "butchered"—version.

Sadly, Garland herself, the film's greatest strength, is also a weakness. I'm not faulting her performance; Garland's Esther/Vicki has intelligence, passion and sincerity and is incomparable in the song and dance numbers. It's entirely believable that a character played by James Mason would find Esther intriguing when, early in the film, she cleverly finds a way to keep him from humiliating himself even more than he already has with his drunken outburst in a crowded theater. Esther/Vicki, as incarnated by Judy Garland, sees through Norman's belligerent behavior and comes away from their first encounter with the impression—surely shared by no one else who witnessed Norman's drunken shenanigans—that he was "nice." Norman goes out of his way to track her down to a small club, where the musicians she sings with go after-hours to make music for the sheer love of it. Garland's rendition of "The Man Who Got Away"—a beautiful torch song written for the film by Harold Arlen and Ira Gershwin—is so heartfelt, so haunting, that it's no wonder Norman falls in love with her then and there. Who wouldn't? She sings like Judy Garland! If I were a record producer, I would sign this woman up on the spot. But if I were a veteran Hollywood pro like Norman, I wouldn't see her as having what it takes to be a movie star, even in the early 1950s, that heyday of musicals. She's simply too old, her face too weathered, for her ascent to stardom to be believable. In 1954, to be sure, Judy Garland still was a bankable movie star, but when the public first fell in love with her, she was the adorable child Cukor first directed when he was involved in the early stages of the production of *The Wizard of Oz* (Victor Fleming, 1939). As Norman—and Cukor—would have known all too well, it would be impossible for Esther—this Judy Garland—to conquer Hollywood.

The film posits Vicki's meteoric rise to the heights of stardom and Norman's precipitous fall, but doesn't allow us to see even a single moment from any of their films. Musical numbers that we are meant to take as representative of the onscreen Vicki are staged as theatrical performances, not envisioned as movie sequences. The 1954 *A Star is Born* gives us no way of judging for ourselves whether Vicki Lester films are frivolous, as Esther's aunt in the 1937 film believes all movies to be, or have meaning and artistic value, like the Cukor film itself. What is at stake in this question is whether Esther Blodgett's "creation" as the movie star Vicki Lester constitutes a metamorphosis, tantamount to death and rebirth, comparable to that of the heroine of a remarriage comedy—the kind of metamorphosis envisioned by Emersonian perfectionism. The film's ending, which disavows what is Emersonian in the film, suggests that it is not.

Does Esther's transformation into Vicki Lester in the 1937 *A Star is Born* constitute such a metamorphosis? Is her dream of becoming a movie star comparable to the dream her grandmother risked everything, and paid a steep price, to realize? Only if Hollywood movies aren't frivolous, as Esther's aunt believes, but are participating in the utopian enterprise of making a "new country," as Lettie put it. If Cavell is right, that is precisely the aspiration of the leading classical movie genres in the period in which Emersonian perfectionism was ascendant in Hollywood. When Laura Augusta Gaino became the movie star Janet Gaynor—offscreen as well as onscreen?—she didn't become another person; she became more fully the person she was, the person she was capable of being. The same can be said about Janet Gaynor's incarnation of Esther/Vicki—and about the heroines of comedies of remarriage. There's the magic of film for you!

Fast-Forward to 2018

In the 1937, 1954, and 1976 versions of *A Star is Born*, the man is a generally sympathetic figure, but like the man in a comedy of remarriage, he's not without what in *Contesting Tears* Cavell calls a "taint of villainy" (*CT* 124). Both Normans—the same is true of John Howard (Kris Kristofferson) in the 1976 version, whose middle name is "Norman"—behave badly when intoxicated—not as badly as their namesake Norman Bates, to be sure, but at times their actions are almost unforgivable. They become belligerent, hostile, and violent. And we take their capacity for violence to be internal to their nature, a character trait which shows its face only when alcohol frees them from their inhibitions.

These men bear a measure of guilt. Not so Jackson Maine (Bradley Cooper) in the 2018 *A Star is Born*. Early in their relationship, it is Ally (Lady Gaga), not Jack, who punches out a man in a bar who speaks disrespectfully to him. The only punch Jack throws in the film is at his brother Bobby (Sam Elliott), when a long-standing conflict between them—having to do with their father, lionized by Jack but blamed by Bobby for his younger brother's addiction—comes to a head. And they ultimately reconcile. It is characteristic of recent films that the screenwriters feel the need to give backstories to characters, hence psychological explanations, however unconvincing, that aren't really needed for dramatic purposes. Sam Elliott, he of the velvet foghorn of a voice and granite face as cratered as the surface of the moon, is a welcome presence in the film. But I find the storyline about the longstanding conflict between the brothers on the whole to be a distraction. I feel the same about Ally's backstory revolving around her father's thwarted dream of stardom in the music world, even though, he keeps repeating, he had more talent than Tony Bennett. Dramatically, Jack's addiction is no more in need of a psychological explanation—and, indeed, no more explainable—than Iago's pathological jealousy in Shakespeare's *Othello*.

Even when Jack spoils Ally's moment of glory—another obligatory scene in all versions of *A Star is Born*—by joining her onstage, uninvited, as she's accepting a Grammy award, he is so intoxicated that he humiliates himself by farting loudly and pissing in his pants. But jealousy at his wife's success is no part of his motivation, the way it is in the equivalent scenes in the 1937 film and the 1954 and 1976 remakes. Jack is not resentful of Ally for her success. His grievance is against a music business so corrupt that it is rewarding Ally for performances that he sincerely believes—we do, too—are denials, not true expressions, of her authentic artistic voice.

In the 1937 and 1954 versions of *A Star is Born*—not in the 1976 film—Norman tries his best to stop drinking but backslides. In both films, he checks himself into a sanitarium, as Jack does, in the hope of curing his alcoholism. In the 1937 film, though, Norman has a disastrous run-in in a bar with Matt Libby (Lionel Stander), a studio press agent who has always disliked him. Libby taunts him for being such a failure that he's a parasite living off his wife's money and goads him into starting a fight that Norman inevitably loses. He's so rattled that, in a moment of weakness, he begins drinking again, which ultimately leads to his suicide.

The 1954 remake has a parallel scene. Again, a studio press agent who dislikes Norman—also named Matt Libby (but far more vividly played by Jack Carson), taunts the fallen star, who has made a sincere effort to stop drinking, and provokes him into a fight. Again, Norman loses, and then follows his ginger ale with a double bourbon chaser, again with calamitous consequences. In the 2018 film, the fateful encounter that leads to Jack's suicide—obligatory in all versions of *A Star is Born*—isn't with a press agent; it's with Rez Gavron (played by Rafi Gavron, presumably no relation), the hotshot record producer who has Ally under contract and who thus holds a position analogous to that of the studio head in the Hollywood-based films. This film doesn't tell a story about the movie business, though; it's the music business—a business the film depicts as so corrupted by commercialism that it seduces authentic artists into compromising their integrity. To be sure, the film capitalizes on the celebrity of Lady Gaga, a pop music megastar, but it is not a product of the business it critiques. The 1937 *A Star is Born* and its 1954 remake are Hollywood stories. And, of course, they are also products of Hollywood.

In both those versions of *A Star is Born*, the studio head is a sympathetic character. The implication is that it's not the studios that are blameworthy; it's the film industry's publicity machine, personified by unsympathetic figure of the press agent. In neither of these films—nor in *What Price Hollywood?*, in which gossip columnists and reporters, not press agents, are the culprits—is there a whiff of criticism of Hollywood movies themselves. (In the 1954 film, the personnel of the makeup department who feel the need to "fix" everything "wrong" with Vicki's face are treated as comically inept and ineffectual, not as self-serving or malicious.)

In the opening scene of the 1937 *A Star is Born*, Esther has just come home after watching a movie—starring Norman Maine, naturally—with her little brother. Esther's Aunt Mattie, who has lived with the family after the death of Esther's mother, dismisses her niece as "a silly little girl whose head has been turned by the movies." To Mattie, movies are frivolous and a waste of time, and she's disdainful of Esther's dream of going to Hollywood to become a movie star. Esther's father is noncommittal. This is not a comedy of remarriage in which the woman's father takes an active part in helping her in her pursuit of happiness. In this film, the mother is dead—a link with comedies of remarriage, in which the woman's mother doesn't play an active role, if she appears at all. But in a comedy of remarriage, there's no woman like Lettie, Esther's grandmother—a link with a melodrama of the unknown woman like *Stella Dallas* or *Gaslight* in which the heroine, in the absence of a men willing or able to help her, finds solace and support from what in *Contesting Tears* Cavell calls "the world of women" (*CT*, 7).

In the early scene that forms a bookend with her intervention at the end of the film, Lettie applauds her granddaughter for wanting to go out and make something of herself, for wanting to have what Esther—all but channeling Emerson—calls a "real life," wanting to "be somebody." And Lettie cites her own life story as an edifying example. She and her late husband traveled by prairie schooner all the way to North Dakota because they wished so passionately to make their dream come true. They wanted, as Lettie puts it, "to make a new country." For Emerson, realizing our personal dreams and making a new country are two sides of the same perfectionist aspiration.

As Cavell reads them, comedies of remarriage—and, by extension, films of all the leading classical Hollywood genres—are not frivolous. They call upon us to strive to make our dreams come true, to bring the world we converse with in the city and in the farm closer to the world we think, to paraphrase Emerson, and thereby to participate in the nation's utopian project of making "a new country," the more perfect union that was—we hope it still is—America's promise. By nominating Lettie to speak for the film, the 1937 *A Star is Born* is declaring its commitment to this aspiration. There's no need for us to watch scenes from Vicki Lester movies to know that *this* film sides with Lettie, not Esther's aunt, on the question of the value of movies. On this crucial issue, however, and even with George Cukor at the helm, the 1954 remake abstains. In the case of the 1937 *A Star is Born*, there's no need to look any further than the film itself to know what a Vicki Lester film is like; to know what Vicki Lester is like onscreen, one need look no further than Janet Gaynor, who incarnates her. Made when Emersonian perfectionism was ascendant in Hollywood as it was in America, the 1937 *A Star is Born* is representative of Hollywood movies of its time. The 1954 remake, made when Emersonian perfectionism was largely repressed and the movie audience was fragmented, has no such standing. No film is representative of Hollywood movies of that time.

In 2018, with Donald Trump at the nation's helm, Emersonian perfectionism was even more repressed in America and in Hollywood—can we still think of the film industry as "Hollywood"?—than in 1954, the year of the Army/McCarthy hearings, or 1976, in the aftermath of Watergate, before Jimmy Carter was elected president. Unlike Vicki Lester and Norman Maine, Ally and Jack are singer/songwriters, not movie stars, and we do get to see them plying their trade. And there's no doubt as to which side the film is on in the struggle between Jack and Rez over Ally's soul—a struggle in which Rez wins the battles but loses the war, although it is, for Jack, a pyrrhic victory.

Jack's suicide throws Ally into a funk, but there's no indication that it provokes her to decide to forsake her stardom, as do the two Esther/Vicki's until their minds are changed. And yet, how can Ally possibly go onstage again, given how consumed she is with grief and a sense of guilt? The film's counterpart to Esther/Vicki's conversation with her grandmother in the 1937 *A Star is Born* and the conversation with Danny in the 1954 remake is Ally's last conversation with Bobby, Jack's older brother. The cragginess of Sam Elliott's face is highlighted by Bradley Cooper's shrewd directorial decision to film the scene as an alternation of extreme closeups (see Figure 11.1).

Thoughtfully, Bobby muses, "Some kid started singing one of Jack's songs in a bar I was in the other night. They're playing his songs everywhere. At first, I got angry. I don't know why. I guess I felt like, how could people think they knew him, who he really was?" In this film, uniquely among versions of *A Star is Born*, keeping the memory of her "creator" alive is not a cross the woman has to bear, much less bear alone. People everywhere are now singing Jack's songs and, by implication, will keep on singing them—and it's not Ally's doing. It angered Bobby that it took Jack's death to make people remember

Figure 11.1. Bobby (Sam Elliott) framed in closeup in *A Star is Born* (Bradley Cooper, 2018). Digital frame enlargement.

Figure 11.2. Ally (Lady Gaga) framed in extreme closeup in *A Star is Born* (Bradley Cooper, 2018). Digital frame enlargement.

his songs, as if his suicide was their fault for failing to know him as he really was. But then, as Bobby puts it, "something changed." He realized that the fact that his songs will live on means that Jack's life was not—pardon Bobby's French—"all for fucking nothing." Bobby finds this thought is soothing, but it doesn't make it any less sad that Jack killed himself believing his life was "all for fucking nothing."

Ally responds to Bobby's words by sobbing, "The last day he was alive. . . ." We know—Bobby doesn't—what happened that day that is haunting her. She had told Jack that she was canceling her planned European tour to spend the summer with him, which was the truth, and that Rez, who had arranged the tour, was happy about this, which was a lie—a white lie, but a lie, nonetheless. And Jack knew it was a lie. Indeed, he knew it was a white lie because he knew how much Ally loved him. Rez had visited Jack that day and told him in no uncertain terms that he had to end his relationship with Ally; otherwise, he would drag her down, destroy her career, ruin her life. Rez added, maliciously, that sooner or later Ally would find a man who was worthy of her, and that when that happened, he didn't want Jack to be anywhere near her (see Figure 11.2).

In saying all this, Rez wasn't acting as a disinterested party; for his own self-serving reasons, he wanted Ally to continue making records for his label. He knew that Ally loved Jack too much to ever abandon him. And that unless he could talk Jack into taking himself out of Ally's life, she would rather give up her stardom than turn her back on him. Rez knew this because in forgoing the lucrative European tour so she could spend the summer with Jack, she had already made her choice—not only for Jack's sake but also her own. Would the price of choosing Jack over Rez be that her life would be ruined? Rather, it would give her a chance to restore her integrity as an artist—and save her soul. Sadly, though, Jack couldn't see this. He believed that the only way he could avoid dragging her down with him was by taking himself out of her life. And that the only way he could take himself out of her life was by committing suicide.

As if sensing that Ally is feeling that she is to blame for Jack's suicide, Bobby looks into her eyes with a steely gaze and says, with great solemnity, "Listen to me. It isn't your fault. It just isn't. You know whose fault it was? Jack's." Taken aback, Ally, who had turned away from Bobby, now meets his gaze. "No one else. Not you. Not me . . ."—his relationship with his brother had been a fraught one—". . . no one but Jack." But Ally quietly says, as much to herself as to him, "I keep going over it"—Bobby has no way of knowing, as we do, what "it" is—"in my head."

Bobby doesn't respond directly to Ally's words, but instead proffers a kind of parable. "Jack talked about how music is essentially twelve notes within any octave. Twelve notes and the octave repeats. It's the same story told over and over forever"—as if all music is, like this film, nothing but a remake. "All the artists can offer the world is how they see those twelve notes. That's it . . ." A bit of sophistry, in my book, but these words sound profound and poetic when spoken in Sam Elliott's sonorous voice, with Bobby's gravitas and Ally's rapt attention underscored by the intimate closeups of their faces. (I say this is sophistry because no matter how they are "seen," the twelve notes in every octave, are not all there is to music, any more than the words characters speak, no matter how they "see" them, are all there is to speech in movies. On and off the movie screen, the poetry of speech—the capacity of ordinary language to acknowledge what words cannot say—is a function, as Cavell puts it, of "the fact that just that creature, in just those surroundings, is saying just that, just now" [*WV*, 150].)

In an inspired directorial gesture, there is a cut from Bobby's somber face, contemplating the mysteries of art and death, to a quite beautiful shot of Lady Gaga, in profile, the bright lights behind her like so many memorial candles, seeming to be listening to Bobby, in a sound overlap, as, audibly holding back tears, he speaks the words, "He loved how you see them. He just kept saying, 'I love how she sees them, Bobby.'"

By this point, two additional cuts have revealed to us that Ally is walking out onto the stage of a packed concert hall, where she speaks this film's version of the obligatory declaration: "Hello, I am Ally Maine" (see Figures 11.3 and 11.4).

Figure 11.3. Ally (Lady Gaga) with "candles" in *A Star is Born* (Bradley Cooper, 2018). Digital frame enlargement.

Figure 11.4. Ally (Lady Gaga) onstage in *A Star is Born* (Bradley Cooper, 2018). Digital frame enlargement.

This isn't the last thing Ally says in the film, however. Speaking words that her predecessors could have spoken with sincerity, she adds, "Thank you for being here tonight to honor my husband." Her final words are: "He wrote a song for me." Then she launches into the song, which she sings, pointedly, the way Jack wanted her always to sing, from the heart and without all the claptrap—the dancing girls, flamboyant dyed hair, and outlandish costumes—that Rez had foisted on her in carrying out his plan to make her a superstar.

Earlier, I suggested that the fact that in the 1954 remake Esther discovers her heart's desire in the course of the narrative makes her closer, in this respect, to the heroines of comedies of remarriage than her counterpart in the 1937 film, who knows what she wants from the outset. Ally is closer still, however, to a remarriage comedy heroine like Tracy (Katharine Hepburn) in *The Philadelphia Story*, who in the end opens her eyes, with Dexter's help, to the awful truth that what she thought she wanted—marriage to George Kittredge (John Howard)—is not what she really wanted. It is obvious to us that George is as unworthy of her as Lonny is of Mary in *What Price Hollywood?* If only Tracy had recognized this from the outset! Marriage to George is a dream Tracy has a moral obligation not to make come true if she is to become the kind of woman, the kind of person Dexter sees her as capable of being—the kind of person she really wishes to be, although it isn't until the end of the film that she acknowledges this.

Ally similarly realizes that to become—or, rather, become again—the kind of person, the kind of artist, she really wishes to be—the kind of artist Jack helped her to make of herself—she must undo the changes Rez had manipulated her into adopting, to Jack's disapproval—and ours. The transformation Rez foists on Ally to enhance the commercial value of her "brand" ironically—or perhaps not so ironically—parallels Stefani Joanne Angelina Germanotta's transformation into the pop music megastar Lady Gaga. In Lady Gaga's case, though, this metamorphosis wasn't foisted on her by a venal record producer pandering to the debased tastes of the pop music audience—this is the film's idea, not mine, although I am all too aware of the element of truth in this judgment. Ms. Germanotta transformed herself into Lady Gaga, just as that Bristol bloke Archie Leach transformed himself into Cary Grant. Jean Rouch would have said that Lady Gaga is a fictional part of this woman's self that is the most real part of herself. In the face of the camera—again, the magic of film—Lady Gaga is Stefani Joanne Angelina Germanotta; Stefani Joanne Angelina Germanotta is Lady Gaga, just as at the end of *Vertigo* (Alfred Hitchcock, 1958) Judy is Madeleine, Madeleine is Judy, and both are Kim (née Marilyn Pauline) Novak.

In declaring that Stefani Joanne Angelina Germanotta and Lady Gaga are positively the same dame, to channel Muggsy (William Demarest) in *The Lady Eve* (Preston Sturges, 1941), is this film—is film—imposing on this woman a further metamorphosis, the way Rez, personifying the music business, foisted on Ally the transformation into a Lady Gaga-like pop star? I prefer to think that the film, from its star's perspective, is at one level an allegory about her own creation. I prefer to think, in other words, that in playing Ally—or incarnating her, as Cavell would say—this woman who gave herself the name "Lady Gaga"—"Stefani Joanne Angelina Germanotta" doesn't exactly trip off the tongue—is walking in the direction of the unattained but attainable self, to invoke Emerson yet again.

However, unlike Ally, who comes to repudiate the Lady Gaga-like pop star who was Rez's creation, the real Lady Gaga is her own creation. Lady Gaga is Joanne Angelina Germanotta; the Lady Gaga-like pop star Rez makes of Ally is no part of who she really is. (At least, that's what the ending of the film asks us to believe.) In incarnating

Ally, this woman is not repudiating her "Lady Gaga" persona; she is declaring that Lady Gaga is not all she can be. If Lady Gaga were the most real part of her identity, she could not have sung—or even wanted to sing—those musically inventive and profoundly moving duets with the aged and ailing Tony Bennett—still a far greater singer, surely, than Ally's father ever was. Nor could she have delivered that stirring and eloquent rendition of "The Star-Spangled Banner" at Joe Biden's inauguration. In taking on the role of Ally, the woman we know as "Lady Gaga," like Ally herself when she casts off her Lady Gaga-like pop star persona at the end of the film, was, in the spirit of Emersonian perfectionism, moving on.

A Very Deep "Shallow"

Revealing herself to the camera, revealed by the camera, Lady Gaga was created anew on the screen. And it's not hard to pinpoint the passage of the film in which, I can't resist saying, a movie star is born. It's in the passage in which, onscreen, Ally is created anew, reborn as an artist. The passage I have in mind is her performance of "Shallow," the Oscar-winning song she wrote with—and sings with—Bradley Cooper. This brilliant sequence is the emotional high point of the film—and its purest expression of Emersonian perfectionism. It is worth a close look.

The passage begins with Ally arriving at the packed auditorium where Jack has already started singing. She works her way through the crowd to join the people backstage. Relieved that Ally has made it, Jack says, to the audience, "There's a friend of mine who came a long way to be here, and she wrote a great song and I'd just like her to sing it on stage." Switching mid-sentence to French, as is his wont, he adds, "I think it's very fucking beautiful." He hands his guitar to a musician in the band and, turning his back to the audience, walks over to Ally and shocks her by saying, "Listen, we're going to sing that song, right?"

Hoping that he's joking, Ally says (also in French; almost everyone in the film is bilingual), "Jack, don't fuck around." Hugging her, he says, "All you gotta do is trust me" (a line the film borrows from the 1976 version). Adding "I'm going to sing it either way, so . . ." he heads back to the stage, refraining from trying to force her hand. (I think of Dexter in *The Philadelphia Story* when Connor [James Stewart] proposes to Tracy, knowing he must let her make the decision herself.)

With the band starting up, Jack slings his guitar back over his shoulder, and there is a cut to a shot, bathed in red from the colorful, shifting, almost psychedelic lights that are de rigueur for such a concert, of Ally backstage, the camera moving in to isolate her. She throws up her hands in exasperation as her loyal friend Ramon (Anthony Ramos), standing next to her, urges her to go up there and make something of herself, live a real life, to paraphrase Lettie in the 1937 *A Star is Born*. Cut to a low angle shot of Jack, from the audience's point of view, not Ally's. He looks decidedly, well, trustworthy as he plays the opening notes of "Shallow" on the guitar. (It's always Cooper's own voice, but never his guitar, on the soundtrack.)

There is a cut to backstage, the red light shifting to blue. Ally's face has the same look of wonder that is on all the faces that share the frame with her. At this moment, Ally is just an audience member who finds Jack's playing "fucking beautiful," as we must if the passage is to work its magic on us. And we must believe, as I do, that in the shots of Ally we are seeing her—"her" being at once this character and the woman we know as "Lady Gaga"—as she really is or, rather, as she is transfigured by the magic of film as she is revealed by the camera, reveals herself to the camera.

The camera movies in on Ally, her face still expressing only wonder. But when Jack sings the song's first words—"Tell me something, girl . . ."—we can discern a trace of a secret smile on Ally's lips as she realizes, I take it, that Jack has changed the lyrics of the song—a song she wrote about him that begins "Tell me something, boy"—and is singing about her, singing to her, to reiterate his invitation to join him in singing the song.

There is a cut back to Jack, viewed now from Ally's point of view, not that of the audience he is facing, and thus with his back to the camera, as if to register her dawning realization that if she doesn't act now, doesn't accept Jack's invitation here and now, she will lose him forever.

In the middle of the song's next line, "Are you happy in this modern world?," there is a cut to a closeup of Jack, almost in profile, that detaches our view from Ally's literal point of view but evokes such a sense of intimacy that it nonetheless feels inflected by her subjectivity. As Jack sings "Or do you need more? Is there something else you're searching for?," the camera's slight movement makes the luminous colors of the background continually shift, adding to the shot's sheer beauty. Of course, this is the "more" Ally needs, what she's been searching for—"this" being Jack, but also the joy of singing her songs to a loving audience. She will lose both if she doesn't join him now on stage.

On the line "I'm falling," Jack's declaration of love, there is a cut to Ally, with the others backstage, the frame bathed in red light. Her eyes widen. Emerson could have been describing Ally at this moment when he wrote, "The eye obeys exactly the action of the mind. When a thought strikes us, the eyes fix, and remain gazing at a distance" ([1860] 1983, 1037). Ally bows her head and covers her eyes with her hands, as if to ward off the frightening thought that has struck her (see Figure 11.5).

She shakes her head "No"—"No, this can't really be happening" and "No, I will not, cannot do this." But as Jack sings "In all the good times I find myself a-longing for change . . ." Ally raises her head, lowers her hands from her eyes, puts them together as if in prayer, and breathes in deeply. On the word "change," the frame's red turns to blue and Ally looks around her, drops her hands, looks down, looks up, and then, after Jack sings "And in the bad times I fear myself,"

Figure 11.5. Ally (Lady Gaga) covering her eyes in *A Star is Born* (Bradley Cooper, 2018). Digital frame enlargement.

she makes the decision (in part motivated, perhaps, by a sense, which will prove prescient, that Jack has good reason to fear himself).

Ally starts walking toward the camera, briskly and with determination, but with her eyes barely open, as if afraid of waking up from this dream, and her lips moving almost imperceptibly as she silently mouths the words she wrote, the words Jack is singing.

Without a cut, the camera moves with Ally, holding her in closeup, the light shifting from blue to natural to red and finally back to blue as she walks up to the microphone. As the music falls silent, having arrived at a natural pause, we view Ally for a moment in profile, at the right edge of the widescreen frame, alone with the microphone (see Figure 11.6).

Ally begins to sing. "Tell me something, boy . . ." As the audience cheers, the camera's continuing movement brings Jack into the frame. The shot is held just long enough for us to recognize that he had been watching Ally intently but is now so confident that his gamble will pay off that he feels that it's all right for him to turn back to face the audience.

Finally, there is a cut from this shot, surely the film's most expressive and technically impressive, to a frontal closeup of Ally, the blue bathing the frame again changing to red.

Figure 11.6. Ally (Lady Gaga) and microphone in *A Star is Born* (Bradley Cooper, 2018). Digital frame enlargement.

Ally's singing of the next words is musically impeccable, as always with Lady Gaga, but she looks concerned, as if she's worried that she will be a disappointment to the audience—and to Jack, who has faith in her.

> Aren't you tired of trying to fill that void?
> Or do you need more?
> Ain't it hard keeping it so hardcore?
> I'm falling.

As she is singing the words "I'm falling," she looks offscreen, perhaps at Jack. In the beautiful shot that follows, Jack turns away from Ally to say something to the guitarist behind him. From the nod of Jack's head, we know that he knows that Ally is a hit. As he walks, smiling, he silently mouths the words being sung, as Ally had done: "In all the good times I find myself longing . . ."

Cut back to Ally. Jack is now at ease, as we are, but she still looks worried. ". . . for change. And in the bad times I fear myself." And then, suddenly, the miracle happens—the change they both were longing for. With the words "I'm off the deep end," Ally lets loose, as only Lady Gaga can, in a way Jack had never heard her do before, with those pipes that most singers only dream of. She doesn't just belt it out *à la* Ethel Merman. The sound of her voice is "fucking beautiful." (I still remember my high school French.) It's the thrilling sound of a woman "jumping off the deep end," passionately declaring her existence, performing her *cogito*, to invoke Cavell. (The 1976 *A Star is Born* has a comparable scene in which John invites a resistant Esther to join him on stage. But in that scene Esther doesn't undergo a metamorphosis comparable to Ally's, because we—and John—had already heard her pull out all the stops when she sang "Evergreen" to him. Nor did she undergo a metamorphosis tantamount to death and rebirth in that earlier scene. Indeed, unlike the heroines of all other versions of *A Star is Born*, Streisand's Esther, onscreen, never really changes at all.)

On the words "Watch as I dive in . . . ," a brief shot of an exultant Jack crossing the frame is inserted—it's on the screen for at most half a second; not long enough, it seems to me, to have its full impact—before there's a cut back to Ally. When Ally sings, "I'll never meet the ground," her voice soars into the heavens. As she sings these words, she momentarily covers her eyes with her hands again. This time, she isn't warding off a thought that frightens her. It's as if she's saying to herself, "Yes, it is really happening. And yes, I am doing this." And it's in that thrilling voice, the voice of the new Ally, that she sings,

> Crash through the surface, where they can't hurt us
> We're far from the shallow now.

The metaphor has gotten a bit murky and it's not obvious where that whiff of paranoia is coming from, but those are quibbles. What matters is her shift from "I" to "we," all but compelling that Jack to turn her solo into a duet. And so he does—first in a backlit shot that feels like a continuation of the brief shot of Jack, retroactively revealing that in the earlier shot he was already anticipating this invitation, moving into position to sing with her.

Allie's offscreen voice blends with Jack's as he sings, "In the sha-ha, sha-ha-llow. . . ." Then there are cuts back and forth between them, as they sing, together,

> In the sha-ha-sha-la-la-la-llow
> In the sha-ha, sha-ha-llow

Another quibble: since what their words are saying is that they're now far from the shallow, the word "in" doesn't literally make sense. But who cares? That doesn't detract from the emotional impact when, after one more "We're far from the shallow now," Jack moves toward Ally, she moves toward him, and he pulls her to his microphone before stepping back with an exuberant smile to invite Ally now to sing the next lines solo. As she reaches to the microphone to adjust it, Jack's movement and the simultaneous movement of the camera make Ally momentarily eclipse him in the frame (see Figure 11.7).

From the line "I'm off the deep end" to this moment, Lady Gaga had seemed to be singing full throttle. But now that she trusts that she has Jack's approval, not to mention his love, she steps on the accelerator pedal and shifts to an astonishing, turbocharged upper register. Jack looks on with amazement and satisfaction as Ally sings out, "Oh, ha-ah-ah Ah, ha-ah-ah, oh, ah, Ha-ah-ah-ah," before reprising

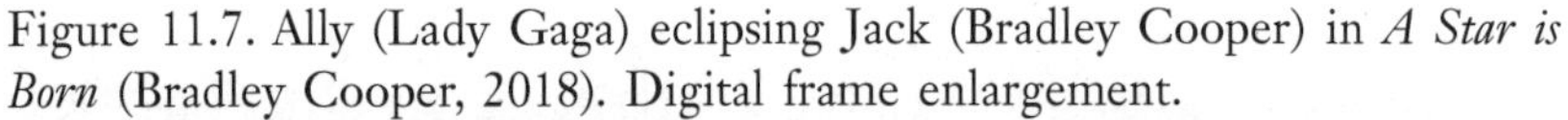

Figure 11.7. Ally (Lady Gaga) eclipsing Jack (Bradley Cooper) in *A Star is Born* (Bradley Cooper, 2018). Digital frame enlargement.

the first words she sang, still in that turbocharged voice, "I'm off the deep end, watch as I dive in, I'll never meet the ground."

As if in acknowledgment of the enormity of this moment, there is a cut to an extreme long shot of Ally singing, with Jack accompanying her on the guitar, ". . . crash through the surface, where they can't hurt us . . ." In this shot, Ally and Jack are tiny figures in the lower right of the frame, illuminated by spotlights whose rays shine down on them from the upper left, with the wildly applauding audience in the darkness filling the background. (Surely, cinematographer Matthew Libatique, whose work is so brilliant throughout the film, consciously modeled this shot—it will be echoed by a shot of Ally onstage in the film's last sequence—on the celebrated shot of Bob Dylan that climaxes the Albert Hall concert in *Don't Look Back* [D. A. Pennebaker, 1967]) (see Figures 11.8, 11.9, and 11.10.)

There is a cut back to an intimate closeup of Ally. As she sings, "We're far from the shallow now," her voice, which had been soaring in the stratosphere, calmly begins to descend, as if confident of a soft landing. When she yet again raises her hands to her face, she covers her mouth, not her eyes. I take it that she is in awe of the sublimity of the sounds that had just come from within her. It is at this moment, as the blue light yet again turns to red, that Jack's face

Figure 11.8. Spotlight on Ally (Lady Gaga) and Jack (Bradley Cooper) in *A Star is Born* (Bradley Cooper, 2018). Digital frame enlargement.

Figure 11.9. Spotlight on Ally (Lady Gaga) at memorial concert in *A Star is Born* (Bradley Cooper, 2018). Digital frame enlargement.

enters this intimate frame. He is looking right at Ally but she is not yet meeting his gaze as, in Beatles fashion, they sing, together, into the same microphone, "In the sha-ha, sha-ha-llow."

There's a cut to a longer, reverse angle shot of Ally and Jack, the frame bathed in blue, except for the blinding white of the spotlight

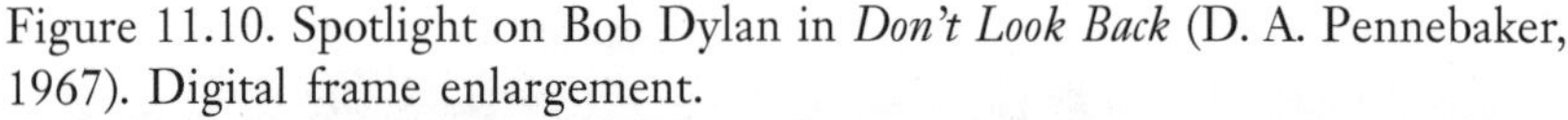

Figure 11.10. Spotlight on Bob Dylan in *Don't Look Back* (D. A. Pennebaker, 1967). Digital frame enlargement.

behind them, which almost silhouettes them. He is leaning toward her, so their faces are only inches apart. (There's a slight continuity error here: the microphone, still framed between their faces, is now in the background behind them, but is clearly further away from them than in the previous shot. Also, at head of this shot, Jack and Ally are looking into each other's eyes, whereas in the tail of the previous shot, he is looking right at her, but she hasn't yet met his gaze. These errors, too, don't detract from the emotional impact of the moment.)

Within this frame, Ally and Jack sing, jubilantly, the last words of the song:

> In the sha-ha-sha-la-la-la-llow
> In the sha-ha, sha-ha-llow
> We're far from the shallow now.

On the word "now," Jack backs away from Ally and almost exits the frame. There's a continuity cut to a surprisingly composed two shot with Ally facing away from the camera, so we mostly see her hair and a bit of one shoulder, looking at Jack, as we are, as he plays an emphatic final guitar chord. The triumphant look on his face is directed at Ally, as if to say, "There! I told you that you could trust me."

Ally turns to face the wildly cheering audience, her movement and the camera's momentarily isolating her in the frame. She looks disbelieving, but only for an instant, before Jack leans his head into "her" frame. Her face lights up with joy as he says, "You were fucking good," shouting in French into her ear so she can hear him over the din.

Pulling Back

At the end of the film, Ally casts off the Lady Gaga-like pop star persona that Rez foisted on her in his successful efforts to make her a pop music megastar, and sings the film's last song—a song Jack wrote for her, as she tells the audience. She sings it from the heart, as I said, the way he had wanted her always to sing. So far so good. Too bad that the song itself, "Wish I Could Have Said Goodbye," is inadequate for the occasion. It's unfortunate, but forgivable, that the song isn't the equal of "Shallow" musically. It's far better, though, and far better sung, than "With One More Look at You," the seemingly interminable song Streisand sings, in full histrionic mode, as the finale of the 1976 version. (The best thing about that song is its title, which alludes to the line obligatory in all incarnations of *A Star is Born*.)

I have no problem with the opening words of Ally's final song:

Wish I could, I could've said goodbye
I would've said what I wanted to
Maybe even cried for you
If I knew it would be the last time
I would've broke my heart in two
Tryin' to save a part of you.

From this point on, though, I find the lyrics to be problematic in two ways. For one, it's ambiguous whether what Ally means in saying that Jack wrote the song for her is that he wrote it for her to sing, or that he wrote it about her. If the former, then it's unbecoming, presumptuous, for him to put the words into her mouth that, having loved Jack, she'll never love again, never want to love again. And if the latter, it's indecent for her to sing in public, to an audience, what is in effect a letter to her declaring his undying love for her. Furthermore, from an Emersonian—or Cavellian—standpoint, the song expresses a decidedly un-Emersonian—indeed, anti-Emersonian—sentiment that finds its purest expression in the words—I hear these words, as she sings them, as proud declarations, as *vows*: "My world keeps turnin' and turnin' and I'm not movin' on," and "Won't let another day begin, won't let the sunlight in, oh, I'll never love again." (The words Streisand sings at the end of the 1976 film express the equally un-Emersonian sentiment that one more look at her dead husband would be sufficient—and *necessary*—for her to "let the sun shine through," to "leave a troubled past" and "start anew.")

If Ally had instead sung a reprise of "Shallow," the film's ending, like the ending of the 1937 *A Star is Born*, would have reaffirmed the Emersonian perfectionism exemplified by the passage we've just looked at, rather than pulling back from that philosophical and moral perspective, as did the 1954 version. Perhaps that is too much to expect from any film made in these troubled times.

Works Cited

Emerson, Ralph Waldo. (1844) 1983. "Experience." In *Ralph Waldo Emerson: Essays and Lectures*, edited by Joel Porte. Library of America.

Emerson, Ralph Waldo. (1860) 1983. "Behavior." In *Ralph Waldo Emerson: Essays and Lectures*, edited by Joel Porte. Library of America.

Rothman, William. 2004. *The "I" of the Camera: Essays in Film History, Criticism and Aesthetics*. Second edition. Cambridge University Press.

Rothman, William. 2019. *Tuitions and Intuitions: Essays at the Intersection of Film Criticism and Philosophy*. State University of New York Press.

Rothman, William. 2021. *The Holiday in His Eye: Stanley Cavell's Vision of Film and Philosophy*. State University of New York Press.

12

An End of Wandering

Coming to Believe in *Palm Springs*

STEVEN G. AFFELDT

"But if the LORD brings about something unheard-of, so that the ground opens its mouth and swallows them up with all that belongs to them, and they go down alive into Sheol, you shall know that these men have spurned the LORD." Scarcely had [Moses] finished speaking these words when the ground under them burst asunder, and the earth opened up its mouth and swallowed them up with their households. . . . They went down alive into Sheol, with all that belonged to them; the earth closed over them and they vanished from the midst of the congregation. All Israel around them fled at their shrieks, for they said, "The earth might swallow us!"

—Numbers, 16: 31–34[1]

~

Alive in Sheol

As the soundtrack plays Demis Roussos's "Forever and Ever," we see a lone goat standing in a barren desert landscape.[2] It is a timeless image and we could as well be outside contemporary Palm Springs as on the edge of the Israelite encampment in the wilderness of ancient Sinai. The goat looks toward a group of rocky hills in the near distance as a low rumble and the sound of tumbling stones rises and overtakes Roussos's crooning. The goat shows puzzlement as the screen fills with the quaking earth and a fissure appears, moving quickly toward us and glowing hot as it opens until the screen fills with a burst of light. Cut to a closeup of Nyles's eye opening as a disembodied female voice whispers, "Wake up." The cut suggests we have witnessed part of Nyles's dream—as though he is reliving his first experience of entering the time loop that, we will soon learn, structures *Palm Springs* (Max Barbakow, 2020; screenplay by Andy Siara and Max Barbakow). What is certain, though, is that this opening sequence represents our movement into the world of the film and declares that we too have been swallowed by the earth.

My epigraph is from an episode in the Torah recounting God's punishment of three men who led a failed rebellion against Moses and, in rebelling, "spurned the Lord." But this spectacularly cinematic punishment literalizes and makes immediately visible a collective punishment God had already decreed on all but a select few of the exodus generation. Because they have doubted God's promise and so also "spurned the Lord," they will not "see the land that [God] promised on oath to their fathers" (Numbers 14:23). Instead, they must wander for forty years until their "carcasses shall drop in this wilderness" and they too are, less cinematically, swallowed by the earth (Numbers 14: 31–35).

I propose that we read *Palm Springs* against the background of this stage in the biblical narrative of the people of Israel—the period of their wandering, unable to claim the promised land. The film incorporates a hodgepodge of biblical images and allusions: a group of (largely secular) Jewish families are gathered in a desert to participate in the creation of a people (that is, to celebrate a wedding); a sexual encounter between Abraham and Sarah plays a pivotal role; three rebellious members of the group are swallowed by the earth, resulting in them, and the rest of the group, being forced to wander endlessly through the wilderness of the same day; and we have already met a scapegoat who figures in a ritual of atonement.[3] My proposal, though, does not require that the makers of *Palm Springs* self-consciously drew on the stage of the biblical narrative with which I have linked it. It is motivated by two thoughts. First, that this stage in the biblical narrative can be read as highlighting a juncture in the life of individuals and the societies they form—a juncture that may arise at various times and in response to a range of individual and social conditions—at which belief in any promise of happiness is strained and falters. And second, that *Palm Springs* contributes to the ongoing narrative of remarriage comedy by exploring a juncture of just this kind—depicting its causes, effects, and eventual overcoming.[4]

To explain briefly: Cavell's readings of the films he takes as defining the genre of remarriage comedy show them elaborating a shared narrative of the re-creation of the human and, with that, of human society.[5] The modes of conversation of the principal pair embody their aspiration for transformation from confusion and constraint to greater intelligibility and freedom, and their willingness for (re)marriage affirms their relationship as the vehicle for this transformation while also figuring their consent to their society—imperfect as that society inevitably is. At the same time, the happiness and mutuality the pair achieve rebuke their society as it stands and call for its transformation by projecting an image of a more attractive, as yet unattained but attainable, state of society (to invoke a phrase from Emerson important to Cavell; see Emerson [1990b, 9]).

In the world of *Palm Springs*, these aspirations and affirmations are, initially, all but unimaginable. Instead, the experience of dissatisfaction with oneself and one's society that Cavell argues is an essential impetus for change threatens to become all-consuming.[6] As a result, in contrast to the pairs in classical remarriage comedy who presume their right to pursue happiness but face internal and external obstacles to doing so, the principal pair in *Palm Springs*, Nyles (Andy Samberg) and Sarah (Cristin Milioti), will not claim their right to pursue happiness or work toward achieving it because they cannot believe in any promise of happiness or their worthiness for it. In terms of the biblical narrative, if we think of claiming the right to pursue happiness as entering and settling the promised land, then Nyles and Sarah—like the generation of rebellious Israelites who spurned the Lord—cannot believe in any promised land or their fitness to enter it. Instead, they regard themselves as condemned to endless wandering through the same day, without even the hope of dying and letting their carcasses drop in the wilderness. However, as in the biblical narrative, in *Palm Springs* the period of wandering is ultimately reconceived. Rather than a punishment for lack of belief, wandering becomes a time of education and *coming to believe*.[7] For Nyles and Sarah, though, there is no powerful God whose guiding presence ensures their wandering serves higher educational aims. If they are to come to believe, they will have to provide one another the transformative education they require.

As for us, our stakes in viewing are suggested by an early scene between Nyles and a man we will come to know as Roy (J. K. Simmons). Ending a night of cocaine-fueled existential yearning, Nyles draws Roy toward a glowing cave that, we learn, is the entrance to the time loop and mumbles that it is where he will find his answers or, as he mumblingly repeats himself, where he will find his ancestors. Roy remarks that those are pretty different matters, but follows all the same. For us, though, the film suggests that if our belief in the promise of happiness has flagged and we too are caught in a desert of wandering, finding our answers *is* finding our ancestors; that is, finding those who can provide a kind of rebirth by eliciting or inspiring our belief. Whether we find these ancestors in *Palm Springs* will depend on how we regard what Nyles and Sarah achieve—and on the fate of the goat who welcomed us.

A Bottomless Pit of Sorrow

Early in his life in the time loop, Nyles stands with Roy at the wedding reception bar and, as they watch the presentation of the newlyweds for their first dance, Roy remarks: "Confucius said marriage is a bottomless pit of sorry that makes you forget who you are." When Nyles objects "He did not," Roy continues, "But there is a bottom, my friend. And it is a fucking dark place."

It is their sharing this attitude toward marriage and the broader society it emblematizes that initially connects Nyles and Sarah. As they see it, the outwardly splendid wedding is actually a spectacle of narcissistic excess and hollow ideals. They are not simply wrong. Beautiful people at a tastefully lavish resort get drunk, snort cocaine, urinate in bushes, and steal away for various sexual escapades. And the hollowness of ideals is epitomized in Misty (Meredith Hagner), a bridesmaid and Nyles's girlfriend, toasting the couple by reading definitions of "love" and "commitment" found on Google. Nyles and Sarah cannot imagine real happiness within such a society and share a bemused disdain for those who can. In this, they reflect that stage of perfectionist transformation marked by judgment and dissatisfaction. Indeed, Nyles's juvenile dress and behavior (for example, wearing his bathing suit and cracking open a beer during the wedding ceremony) strike at least some blow for truth by refusing to conform to empty appearances.[8]

However, beyond their chagrin at society, Nyles and Sarah harbor a generalized suspicion of happiness and those who seem to enjoy it due to their own anxieties and self-condemnations. Nyles cannot allow himself to believe in happiness and his name registers his self-protective nihilism. Happiness would require committing to some particular ends and exposing himself to the risk of failing in his pursuit of them. However, his transparently insubstantial relationship with the much younger Misty shows that Nyles resists commitments. As "Misty's boyfriend," he clings to the open-ended possibilities of youth and refuses the embrace of commitments involved in growing up. However, when the time loop grants his wish to evade growing up, he is unable to find any real satisfaction—as demonstrated in the extraordinary scene of failed intercourse and subsequent masturbation that first introduces us to Nyles (and Misty). As for Sarah, like her biblical namesake she could only laugh at the idea that she would fulfill a promise by producing a reborn people (Genesis 18:12–15). Her knowing refusal to believe in the possibility of happiness is shaped by her conviction that she is unworthy to pursue it. She sees herself as spiritually barren and has come to treat as definitive her family's view that she is "a liability who fucks around and drinks too much." Even more than her failed marriage, which we only learn of later, this sense of herself is focused in her sleeping with her sister's fiancé, Abe/Abraham (Tyler Hoechlin), the night before the wedding. For Sarah, this not only confirms her unworthiness for happiness but shows that she is a destroyer of happiness for others. If our pair are to lead each other toward believing in happiness and claiming the right to pursue it, they will not (directly) contest their chagrin at society but will help each other find ways beyond these debilitating pathologies.

While sharing Roy's dark views thematically links our pair, he also more directly connects them. The film's first section closes with Nyles and Sarah perched awkwardly against a rock in the desert, clumsily trying to hook up. Standing to remove his bathing suit, Nyles is suddenly struck by an arrow that, we soon learn, has been shot by Roy. This is another of Roy's recurrent efforts to punish Nyles for drawing him into the time loop, but it casts him as an unwitting Cupid. His arrow interrupts the hookup (as Nyles flees, Roy gives chase, and a terrified Sarah repeatedly screams "What the fuck is happening?!") while also binding our pair together.[9] Concerned, Sarah follows Nyles into the cave—against his emphatic urging—where she too is swallowed by the earth and trapped in the time loop.

Yoked by their common fate, the two are now effectively isolated together since trying to explain their situation marks them as mad. (Upon first waking in the time loop, disoriented and frightened, Sarah asks her parents, "This is really happening, right? . . . This day already happened," but her father is blankly confused while her stepmother accusingly asks, "Are you on drugs again?") For better or for worse, they are now in one another's care and bound to wander together.

Let's Waste Some Time

The opening scenes of the film's second section show us that we are in a time loop (largely through tracking Sarah's own discovery) and elucidate its nature (it is always the wedding day, the day can unfold differently, but after dying or falling asleep it begins again just as before). They also insist on the fact of film and some of its distinctive powers; here, film's unique power to exactly repeat footage reveals the partiality of our experience by allowing us to experience the same events differently on the basis of new information and altered perspectives. But the main work of this section is showing how the pair spend time together and what they begin learning about themselves and each other. Following Sarah's failed attempt to "earn her way out" of the time loop with a "real act of selflessness like the bone-marrow shit that Tala does," Nyles takes her to what he calls his safehouse (the home, with pool, of a family who are away).[10] Floating in the pool, Sarah raises a beer and offers, "Let's waste some time," as a montage of fun-filled days begins. However, the two main things they do—play and talk—are hardly a waste of time.

They play with the joyful abandon that comes of freedom from time, consequences, and mortality. We see them shooting rifles, floating in the safehouse pool, practicing a dance and then bursting into a dive bar and performing it before the nonplussed regulars, stealing a plane and crashing in flames when the fuel runs out, and amusing themselves with various pranks and antics at the wedding party—all intercut with shots of either Nyles or Sarah waking with happy expectancy for the day ahead. These days of play reveal, to us and them, how thoroughly they enjoy one another's company. They also create a shared "childhood" past and so satisfy the generic requirement of remarriage comedy that the principal pair share a kind of kinship or natural relationship that both grounds the eventual marriage and must be broken for that marriage to overcome incestuousness and be happy.[11]

The freedom of this play has therapeutic power. If consciousness of mortality can put paralyzing pressure on our choices, these scenes invite us to laugh at death (as when Sarah, singing joyously, tumbles from the sunroof of the moving car) and to see our being fated to make choices that create our fate as comic. This is an important lesson for Nyles. However, our laughter is edged with unease, since laughing at mortality may also serve the kind of wish we see in Nyles to imagine that our lives stretch out endlessly so we can, at any given time, evade the burden of choice. Living that fantasy, though, yields merely a succession of aimless and disconnected days; a life of wandering. As Nyles and Sarah will learn, happiness demands investments of care (and so exposure to unhappiness). But their lives at this point are predicated on not caring.

This, in fact, is an important topic of their talk.

It is partly definitive of remarriage comedy that the conversation of the principal pair centers on questions of human purpose, meaning, and happiness, and in *Palm Springs* the structure of time as endless repetition of the same day makes such conversation all but unavoidable.[12] Driving across the open expanse of desert following Sarah's realization that she is, indeed, trapped in a time loop, the pair's first real conversation involves Nyles offering Sarah an education in how to live in such a condition. Speaking from experience and exhausted resignation, he recommends a smiling nihilism: "[T]he only way to really live in this is to embrace the fact that nothing matters." To Sarah's challenge—"Well then what's the point of living?"—he adds a dash of popular stoicism: "We kind of have no choice but to live, so I think your best bet is just to learn to suffer existence."

Sarah will, soon enough, try to adopt Nyles's posture. But she never fully succeeds. Indeed, although she will ultimately find an element of wisdom in this view, the education she provides Nyles includes helping him move beyond it. At this point, however, her response is denial. Steering into the path of an oncoming fuel truck, she resolutely mumbles "No. No. I'm getting out of this." This elicits another effort at instruction from Nyles. Unfastening his seatbelt and resting his head on the dashboard to promote a quick death in the crash, he tells Sarah, "We can't die, but pain is very real. There's nothing worse than dying slowly in the ICU."

Our pair also talk about what their relationship will be. Here Sarah is more ready to embrace Nyles's avoidance of attachment and, in particular, they agree that their relationship will not include sex. When Sarah asks, Nyles recounts his sexual adventures in the time loop and, in response to her direct question, "Have we ever hooked up?" he lies: "No. At least I don't think so." He then lies again when she expresses incredulity, "We've *never* had sex?" Sarah is asking about her desirability (to Nyles), but she rebuffs his reciprocating invitation to relate her own sex life: "Nice try. I'm not going to sleep with you. I might have the other night. I would have. Not now, though." And Nyles agrees: "We're seeing each other all the time, let's just keep it simple. Don't overcomplicate it."

This agreement points to a tension between sexual intimacy and companionship that, in remarriage comedy, is tied to the pair having shared a kind of childhood. However, at the immediate narrative level, it expresses the pair's recognition that sexual intimacy will bring emotional entanglements they hope to avoid—Nyles because he fears attachment and Sarah because she sees herself as unworthy and a destroyer of emotional attachments. Given their clear pleasure in one another, their agreement becomes increasingly strained. This is palpable at the surprise birthday party Sarah throws for Nyles at the dive bar—complete with party hats for the regulars, confetti, and a banner reading "Happy Millionth Birthday Dipshit." But the agreement collapses on their magical night of camping.

Pretending Not to Care/Who Cares

Sitting beside a small fire in the empty desert night, the two are talking about what is involved in knowing another and whether a person's past matters. Appealing to his half-eaten chocolate bar, Nyles explains that he has no interest in the "who, what, why" of Sarah's past: "The next bite is all that matters." Sarah, however, shares the experience of her failed marriage to counter that "to really know someone deeper [their past] does matter." Nyles is completely unresponsive and when Sarah asks about his past claims that, after being in the time loop so long, he "honestly can't remember." Sarah regards Nyles with a blend of bafflement, incredulity, and pity while he, obviously uncomfortable, avoids her gaze and tries to shift the conversation—"These are fantastic mushrooms."

Sarah initially allows Nyles's evasion—"Too bad we're doing it in such a shithole though. I'm not a fan of this magical desert." But when Nyles responds "Well, then, I just feel sorry for you," she sees an opportunity to extract some acknowledgement of emotional investment. "Oh, wow. Look, if you feel sorry for me that must mean that you care about me, Nyles." Fumbling, Nyles protests: "When I say that I feel sorry . . . it's the same way I could say that I feel sorry that, you know, I finished one beer and now I have to open a new one." And, opening a new beer, he continues: "You know, now I'm not sorry anymore. It's just a fleeting feeling. It drifts away, just like they all do." The dismay and pity Sarah has shown throughout this scene reach a new pitch as she presses: "What do you mean, 'It just drifts away, like they all do?' Like what has 'drifted away?'" Nyles's face reveals forlorn vacancy as he sadly chuckles to himself and then quietly replies, "Everything." And then, after a pause, he raises his beer and offers "Anyway, cheers." When Sarah, in turn, offers "To pretending not to care," Nyles's mood lightens a bit—"I like that." Sarah answers "I know you do."

This may be the most intimate exchange we are given, and the scene's intimacy is heightened by the juxtaposition of long shots showing the two sitting close beside the small fire against the expanse of desert night and closeup shots framing their exceptionally, but differently, expressive faces.[13] However, the intimacy only underscores the painful gulf between them—marked by Sarah's looking directly at Nyles while he consistently looks away. Sarah's sincerity and vulnerability are paired with Nyles's evasions and mock-philosophical profundities upon a chocolate bar. The deeper gulf, though, is that Sarah reveals an inner life while Nyles seems all but entirely devoid of interiority. His fear of committing himself to anything has made his (inner) life a barren desert in which nothing can take root and grow. Instead, he wanders and everything drifts away. However, the quiet anguish of his confession that everything drifts away shows that he retains some appreciation for the value of commitments of care.

In this context, Sarah's toast—"To pretending not to care"—functions therapeutically by inviting Nyles to understand himself as pretending and so not entirely devoid of care. And as he begins to echo Sarah's toast, the magical desert and Sarah's therapeutic intervention conspire to produce a breakthrough for Nyles and for the pair. Raising his beer, Nyles begins "To pretending . . ." but stops and, looking into the distance with stunned amazement, continues, "That's new." With Sarah, the camera follows his gaze and reveals a trio of distant dinosaurs moving slowly across the desert.

The appearance of these dinosaurs registers the wonderous or miraculous (Sarah's automatic response is a quasi-reverential, "Oh my God!") and so recalls the signs and wonders through which the wandering Israelites came to believe in the reality of God's promise. It attests that, even in a parched and barren world, (our) possibilities are not exhausted. There is more to ourselves and our world than we know, and so there is an opening to what Nyles calls something "new." Their appearance also suggests that, even in the face of catastrophe (a meteor strike that decimated the dinosaurs or having sex with your sister's fiancé), life can persist. And, to go no further, their appearance suggests an archaic age, prior to the advent of humans, and projects our pair as a new Adam and Eve who may originate a new or transformed humanity.

When Sarah, awestruck, takes Nyles's hand and asks, "Are they real?" he, equally awestruck, responds, "Who cares." This is not a further refusal of emotional investment. Rather, it expresses a determined setting aside of the myriad questions and doubts that can surround any emotional investment and a resolution to invest without first calculating costs. Nyles yields to his experience of being awed. This does not deny any role for reflective consideration, but makes such consideration subsequent to the investment and concerned with remaining faithful to it and reaping its returns.

Neither Nyles nor Sarah has yet fully grasped the lesson in caring and not caring conveyed in this sequence. However, while it germinates within each of them, their shared experience of this wonder begins to transfigure them and their relationship. Sarah spontaneously moves to take Nyles's hand—a gestural equivalent of his "Who cares"—and they decide to "get it over with" and have sex; acknowledging that they are, now, undeniably invested in one another. But the film now challenges our readiness to invest in them. Breaking away from the group of dinosaurs, the camera turns its gaze on our radiant and awestruck pair, sitting side-by-side, holding hands, and watching the wonder before them. It is as if they are at the movies, awed by the vision projected on the screen. The shot is held for several seconds, inviting us to recognize that, in the desert in which we now wander, Nyles and Sarah are the wonder and daring us to ask, "Are they real?"

I'm Getting Out of This Day

We can consider the night Nyles and Sarah spend in the desert a wedding night and their having sex the ceremony. They excluded sex in order to avoid the emotional entanglements it would bring. Now, however, they recognize that they *are* emotionally entangled and their decision to have sex acknowledges and celebrates that fact—that is, functions as a wedding ceremony—and so also increases their entanglement. "Let's get it over with" are hardly words of romance, but their feelings are clear as Nyles, only now, meets Sarah's gaze and as she stays awake to tenderly consider his sleeping face.

Given the structure of remarriage comedy, if they are now understood as married we will not be surprised to find them immediately at odds and, in effect, finding cause to divorce. As Cavell has argued, the pair's rupture is necessary for our conviction in the happiness of their eventual remarriage since it removes the incestuous taint of their shared "childhood" and allows them to *choose* their marriage by reaffirming it in remarriage. But the specifics of the rupture also serve their education.

Driving along the now familiar stretch of two-lane road (Sarah, as usual, at the wheel), the step they took in having sex has impacted them quite differently. Nyles can hardly contain his delight—"Gotta say, it kind of felt a little different this morning. Like, kinda good"—while

Sarah is occupied with her own thoughts and stares straight ahead with a look of wide-eyed terror. She brushes aside Nyles's remark about their night—"Yeah, it was fun"—and then gives voice to what she has been thinking: "I can't keep waking up in here."

Nyles misses the weight of Sarah's words—"Yeah, the waking up is always weird." What he does not know, and we have just learned, is that Sarah wakes each morning in Abe's bed; repeatedly confronted with the act that crystalizes her sense of herself as unworthy of happiness and a destroyer of happiness. Like Nyles, she woke happy. We see her head on a pillow with a bright smile and light in her eyes. But Abe's emerging from the shower and remarking "Um, you should probably get out of here before anybody sees you" impales her on her horror at herself. Consequently, just when Nyles's feelings for Sarah are drawing him away from nihilism, Sarah is struggling to embrace it. This clash of positions shapes the ensuing sequence.

Trying to break through Sarah's preoccupation, Nyles asks if she wants to talk about the "fact that we had sex last night." But Sarah rebuffs the invitation: "What's there to talk about? It's all meaningless, right?"—which prompts Nyles to acknowledge, in an important advance, that he hopes "it isn't *all* meaningless." But the direction of their conversation changes when a state trooper appears. Sarah effectively forces the trooper, who Nyles correctly suspects is Roy, to pull them over and then rushes from the car pleading for help—"He's trying to kill me!" But when trooper-Roy leaves his car and walks toward Nyles, cocking the rifle he has trained on him, Sarah enters the patrol car and rams it into Roy, crushing his legs, before chirping at Nyles over the car's PA system: "You called for backup?" When actual backup arrives moments later, Sarah taunts that trooper—"Suck my dick officer bitch! Are you gonna fucking tase me, fuckface? . . . Come on, just do it!"—and then ducks out of the way, resulting in *Nyles* being tased. He writhes on the ground next to Roy, who mumbles an important question about Sarah through his own pain: "Who the fuck was that?"

As Nyles and Sarah sit handcuffed at the side of the road, a fight escalates with each hurling awful truths at the other. The fight will end in "divorce," but their development toward remarriage turns on their each coming to terms with these truths—those they have heard *and* those they have uttered.

When Sarah echoes Nyles's nihilism to dismiss his outrage at her behavior—"It doesn't matter. Nothing matters, right? Those are your words"—he responds: "No, pain matters. What we do to other people matters! Being a source of terror is not fun, okay. It's not fulfilling. I know this from experience. It doesn't matter that everything resets and people don't remember. *We* remember. We have to deal with the things that we do." This fully meant rebuttal shows Nyles's growing recognition of the existential inadequacy of his nihilism. The problem, as he will later realize, is that Sarah knows this truth about pain and memory all too well. She cannot escape the memory of her night with Abe or her sense of herself as a terror. Her desperate effort to embrace nihilism is her clearly ineffective attempt to relieve this pain.

Here, though, she deflects. Taking up the object of Nyles's rebuke—the pain she has caused Roy—she responds "Oh my God. Cry me a river, Nyles. You were never going to deal with him. I actually did you a favor. So, fuck you." This too is a truth (and, as Nyles will later learn from Roy, Sarah *has* done him a favor). Some problems must be confronted and, as Sarah shows, doing so may require causing pain. Nyles cannot yet receive this truth but instead declares, not without grounds, that Sarah is acting like a child—a rebuke that implicitly acknowledges the childishness of his own nihilistic stance.

Matters might have ended there and the two may have found a way back to their status quo. However, when Nyles adds that Sarah's childishness is "how you got stuck in this shit to begin with," the fight takes a dramatic new turn. Incensed, Sarah glares at Nyles and spits her words with the clarity of white-hot rage: "I followed you into that cave because I liked you and someone was trying to hurt you. Because I give a shit, which is something that you clearly know nothing about. If I had known that I was going to be stuck with a pretentious sad-boy for the rest of eternity, I would have stayed so far away from you and I sure as hell would never have fucked you." In declaring her kindness and concern, this speech is crucial in voicing a counter to Sarah's worst view of herself—and they will both come to incorporate this truth. At this moment, though, it is too much for Nyles who returns, "Oh please, we've fucked like a thousand times." When Sarah freezes—"What? What did you say?"—Nyles immediately regrets voicing this truth and confesses, "I lied, okay. We did hook up before. A lot. All I had to do was bail you out with that ridiculous speech at the wedding."

Because he does not know about Sarah's night with Abe, Nyles cannot realize how deep his truth has cut. It confirms exactly the view of herself that Sarah is desperately trying to escape—that she is "a liability who fucks around and drinks too much." It is hardly surprising, then, that his efforts to explain his lie and how "it's different now" are to no avail. It is not his lie that has frozen Sarah but the view of herself she sees confirmed in his truth.

Having listened to Nyles's confessions and explanations with a look of blank dejection, Sarah once again resolves, "I'm getting out of this day." She stands and, as Nyles pleads that he is sorry, steps into the path of the same speeding fuel truck she had smashed her car into when she first resolved to escape the day. This time, though, things will be different.

We All Have an Irvine

Apart now, we follow the separate trajectories of our pair through an untold number of days. Nyles searches for Sarah with growing desperation, makes a discovery, and is exposed to a powerfully seductive temptation. Sarah now conceives that escaping the time loop requires scientific knowledge rather than selfless action and devotes herself to theoretical physics. In each case, the time apart allows for integrating insights we have seen dawning and consolidating lessons of their time together.

We have seen Nyles beginning to breach his self-protective nihilism and now he moves beyond it. His mounting desperation at Sarah's absence begins to teach him that he loves her and his forlorn declarations of that love, in being acknowledgments to himself and others, enhance the lesson. But his pain, and the fact that it does not "drift away," is his most compelling teacher. It shows Nyles that he has invested himself in Sarah, that he has allowed himself to care and his feelings to take root even though doing so causes pain. But his pain also teaches that, in allowing himself to love, he has undergone a fundamental change in existential situation; his being has expanded and his well-being is now tied to Sarah's.[14] For Nyles, then, as for many unhappy lovers, it is through separation that he learns he is not a solitary being.

Also during these days apart, Nyles literally collapses into the discovery of Sarah's sleeping with Abe. Drunk in a room where Abe had slept the previous night, Nyles falls into a pillow and immediately revives as he recognizes the smell of Sarah's hair mist. Instantly, his understanding of Sarah is radically changed and he now realizes the truth in her insistence that really knowing someone requires knowing their past. Nyles's immediate response to this discovery is compassion for Sarah—"No wonder she hates herself"—and this testifies to his suitability as a partner. He is able to see, and so can help Sarah see, a better self beyond even serious failings. In an outrage that underlines his commitment to Sarah and also, likely wrongly, absolves her of any culpability, Nyles attacks Abe—"Abraham, you slick fuck"—and rebukes the crowd of family and friends gathered at the wedding dinner: "And you know what, fuck all of you. Sarah is a good person, but for some reason she's never been good enough for any of you."

The important advances Nyles has made will, however, be threatened by fantasies arising from a visit to Roy's home in Irvine. Deep in pain and despair, and illustrating Nietzsche's thought that regarding our pain as punishment for guilt makes it meaningful and hence bearable, Nyles yells from the sidewalk: "Roy! I'm turning myself in. Torture me. I don't care." But the Roy he finds is not the inventive sadist we have seen but a quiet suburban family man preparing marinade for tuna steaks. The "favor" Sarah performed has taught Roy that "being a source of terror is not fulfilling." Now, although he feels the pain of possibilities foreclosed by the time loop, Roy has come to celebrate the beauty in his life. "This was always a good day," he tells Nyles. "My wife in the prime of her womanhood. . . . Libby's gonna do a family portrait later this afternoon where we're all animals. I'm a cuddly grizzly bear. I mean, it doesn't get any better than that." Speaking from this perspective, Roy counsels Nyles: "You gotta find your Irvine." And to Nyles's dejected "I don't have an Irvine," he counters, "We all have an Irvine."

There is wisdom in Roy's position and we might almost regard him as an Emersonian sage commending the romance of the ordinary. However, in turning aside potentially fruitful experiences of dissatisfaction, his position is perilous in inviting us to accept, even delight in, lives that are unacceptable. When Nyles tries to embrace Roy's view, Sarah shows him its dangers. Indeed, Nyles's eventual refusal of its seductions begins his final steps out of the desert of wandering.

It is time to pick up Sarah's thread.

A Box of Energy

Nyles was right about Sarah's self-hatred, but this time her resolution to "get out of this day" is about moving into her future not about escaping her past. Although she does not embrace his view that nothing means anything, Nyles has helped Sarah see that nothing means *everything* and so helped her overcome the self-condemning conviction that she is defined by the worst moments of her past. Their days of play have also shown Sarah her power to experimentally and creatively shape her character, as well as her ability to take pleasure in the process. And, of course, she has learned from the vision of the dinosaurs that life continues beyond catastrophes and that wonders are possible. In stepping into the path of the speeding fuel truck, then, Sarah is resolved to become the self she has begun discovering with Nyles. She cannot be clear about, or confident in, this dawning self. However, freed from her belief that she is unworthy of happiness, Sarah now prepares to pursue it.

Waking, she confronts Abe while he showers: "That was awful and crazy and should never have happened and we both deserve every single fucking terrible thing that is coming toward us because we are very shitty people. But I am done being shitty." And then, turning her back on Abe and her self-condemnation, she turns toward the sole activity that now absorbs her—discovering how to escape the time loop. We see her wake each day with determination in her eyes, leave the resort, and spend her days in a diner reading physics textbooks, attending online classes, and Skyping with experts. The only variations place her at the cave taking measurements and conducting experiments—including leading the goat we met at the start, now saddled with C4, into the cave and rushing out to detonate the explosives. These scenes play two crucial roles.

First, they highlight the role of the woman in this pair and this film. Importantly, scenes of Sarah developing expertise in theoretical physics do not play as comic (as they would with Nyles) or as implausibly stretching her character. We believe in Sarah's intelligence, resolution, and inventiveness and our pleasure in these scenes lies in watching her own conviction grow—capped by her radiant smile as stars of insight form a halo around her head. Further, although our pair's education is more mutual than in classical remarriage comedy, these scenes show that, in key respects, Sarah takes the lead. She enters the world of knowledge controlled by men (all of the professors and experts she learns from are men), translates (male) theoretical knowl-edge into the domain of practical action, and brings her liberating (or perhaps deadly) knowledge to Nyles.

Second, the physics lesson Sarah gives Nyles when she returns to wake him one last time allegorizes central elements of the film's vision of self-overcoming and transformational change. "[W]e are trapped in a box of energy," she explains. "We get out of it by escap-ing the box in the 3.2 seconds it takes to travel through the loop itself. [That is,] we blow up ourselves and the cave in that window." For our pair, their most immediate box of energy consists of the anxieties and self-condemnations preventing them from believing in happiness or their worthiness to pursue it. These have trapped them in endless wandering and their mutual education is releasing their grip. But the broader truth expressed in Sarah's lesson is that the shapes of all of our lives are created and sustained by daily reinscriptions of investments of energy (care, value, significance). These patterns of investment—boxes of energy—open possibilities but can also be destructive due to what they foreclose. Further, even when generally beneficial, they can become fixed and entrap us (like a good day in Irvine). Self-overcoming and the prospect of change is a matter of escaping these boxes and requires breaking the cycle of daily, repetitive reinscriptions of our familiar investments. It requires stopping, within the time of travel through the circuit of our days, to identify, examine, and alter our investments. As figured here, exploding ourselves and the box opens a space of freedom by granting "an observer access to the indeterministic universe on the other side of the Cauchy horizon."[15]

Hearing Sarah's lesson, Nyles resists. Although he denies it, he is held by the fears and uncertainties attending any significant change. Following Sarah's assurance that detonating the C4 will "propel us out" of the energy box, Nyles asks, "To where?" He is asking both "Will we survive the change?" (achieve the difference we seek while also remaining recognizably the same) and "Will we be better off?" But the deeper source of Nyles's resistance is that he seems to have found his Irvine. With Sarah's return (and apparent acceptance of his apology "for not telling you about our past" and willingness to "just start over"), Nyles hopes the investment in love which brought him so much pain is paying off at last. He tells Sarah "I *want* to stay, <u>with you</u>. Look, I love you, okay." He hopes to ensure their continuing life together within the security of the time loop. Outside, he says, is "a world of death and poverty, debilitating emotional distress. At least here we get to be together." This, however, expresses (an adolescent) romantic fantasy that, in their Irvine, he and Sarah can create a private promised land of happiness.

Sarah rejects this. When, learning that Nyles discovered her hookup with Abe, Sarah tells him, "I can't keep waking up in there," she is undoubtedly expressing lingering pain from that wound. But that is not why she rejects Nyles's fantasy. His idea of a private realm of happiness, she says, is meaningless. "You have lost your mind. This isn't real, Nyles. Everything that we are doing here is fucking meaningless." Nyles's response—"So what?"—is not a return to his earlier nihilism; he wants his love and their relationship to be real and meaningful. But he seems to imagine that the two of them suffice to imbue their words and actions with that reality and meaning. Sarah knows better. In challenging Nyles's declaration of love—"How can you even know that? I am literally the only other person stuck in here with you"—she is not doubting his sincerity. She is denying the declaration's meaningfulness in their situation. Sarah *has* come to believe in the possibility of happiness with Nyles and, indeed, her invitation to him to join her life could almost be read as a marriage proposal: "I need my life back. And I am asking you if you want to leave this place and come with me." However, she insists that the reality and meaningfulness of any life they may build together will demand not only their subjection to human conditions of temporality, consequences, and mortality but also their being in community with others; their lives intelligible, at least in principle, to others.

Still within the grip of his fantasy, Nyles responds to Sarah's invitation: "And I am saying, no. But I'm also asking you to stay." Sarah has advanced too far to be drawn by this appeal. She stands before Nyles for several long seconds, presenting herself to him, hoping her resolve will awaken his. Then, giving him a long embrace, she says simply, "Goodbye, Nyles," before leaving the room and closing the door. She is not turning back. The only question is whether he will find a way to follow.

Believing in the Promise/Embracing the Pursuit

When we next see our pair together, they will stand outside the cave where the earth swallowed them and they began their days of wandering. They will reenter together to face either death or the always uncertain pursuit of happiness. (As Sarah tells Nyles during her physics lesson, when they detonate the C4, "There's really no way to be sure [what will happen]. That's why it's a theory.") Before turning to their words and actions there, we need to consider how they each arrive.

Leaving Nyles, Sarah knows she will end her day at the cave so the evening at the wedding is a kind of leave-taking—she may, as she tells Nyles, "end up dead under a pile of rocks." More importantly, though, it is a new beginning. Her new conviction in her worthiness for happiness and her readiness to risk all pursuing it transform her relations with her family and the broader society of the wedding party. She exudes a confident lightness of spirit, takes pleasure in being with others, and contributes to the festivities; offering a toast that wins the glad approval of her family by declaring her appreciation of, and need for, Tala (Camila Mendes). Praising Tala's selflessness and hopefulness, Sarah tells how, when she was twelve, "terrified of the world" and suffering "awful nightmares," the five-year-old Tala had comforted her. She concludes: "Big sisters are supposed to teach baby sisters, but I will today, and forever and ever ever, be learning from you"—learning, whatever else, a kind of selflessness and the ability to offer comfort and inspire hope. But Sarah also declares herself a guardian of Tala and Abe's marriage through a public warning to Abe. In words freighted with meaning only she and Abe will know, she punches a pointing finger at him as she slowly and emphatically commands: "Don't fuck this up."

As for Nyles, immediately following Sarah's exit, he gives reason for hope in breaking up with Misty—"We should break up. . . . You don't like me." And yet, we next find him at the dive bar, lamenting "I've felt everything I'll ever feel, so I'll never feel ever again." Darla (Dale Dickey), a middle-aged regular familiar to us, gives him a crucial lesson. Hearing Nyles confess "I thought I knew how to live. But I didn't. Or I don't," she responds: "Honey, take a look around. Whatever you're after, it ain't here."

Darla's words interrupt Nyles's repetition of the same circuit of lament he traveled when Sarah left him the first time. He stops, breaks the circuit, and reflects. In an extraordinary short sequence we are taken into Nyles's reflection. We hear Leonard Cohen singing words of overcoming fear and refusing to surrender from "The

Partisan"—an anthem of the French Resistance during WWII. With this, we see Sarah facing us at the millionth birthday party. That party showed Sarah fighting to break the undifferentiated repetition of their time and begin a new year. Now, smiling as brightly colored confetti slowly falls over and around her, she is an image of the triumphant victor. The words of the Resistance anthem combined with this image are presented as both causing and expressing Nyles's realization that happiness will not simply be found—in the bar, the time loop, or anywhere else. It must be worked for, perhaps fought for, and any chance of victory will demand that he overcome his fear, refuse to surrender, and grow up.

Emerging from his reflection, Nyles declares "Oh my God. I'm an idiot!" and when the bartender, Ted (Martin Kildare), assures Darla, "The kid's just mopping," he steps into his new readiness to fight for happiness. Downing his shot of whiskey and shattering his glass on the floor, Nyles exclaims "I'm a fucking *adult*, Ted with the pickup truck!" as he begins a brawl to surreptitiously grab Ted's keys. Thrown from the bar, he steals Ted's truck and races toward the cave. He reaches it just as Sarah, wearing her bridesmaid dress and explosive vest of C4, has concluded a final moment of reflection and, with a deep breath, is beginning to head in.

The last-second arrival of a man who, only now, says the words that win the woman is a staple of romantic comedy—speaking to the belated insight of (the) men, the forbearance of (the) women, and how easily the chance of love may be missed. *Palm Springs* adopts this convention but allows Sarah to importantly subvert it. Unlike after the physics lesson, our pair's conversation at the cave is not about whether Nyles will join Sarah's effort to escape. They have each come to believe in the promise of happiness and their worthiness to pursue it. The question is whether they will pursue it *together*; that is, whether they will have a relationship outside the time loop. Sarah pushes their exchange past the expected, emotionally charged "Yes" to a serious, yet comic, consideration of the character of any such relationship.

Stumbling in breathless, yelling "Sarah! Sarah, wait! Wait!," Nyles begins to deliver the kind of rom-com lines we might expect: "From the first time that I saw you . . ." But Sarah immediately interrupts: "No. Stop it Nyles. I don't want another one of your speeches." She knows Nyles hides behind words, but now she sees, more specifically, that he is unwittingly casting the two of them in familiar rom-com roles. Accepting those roles will block, or warp, their own words and experience and *this* is what Sarah stops.[16] The familiar roles and hand-me-down tropes we easily adopt, as social creatures who absorb our ways of being and speaking from others, can become another imprisoning box of energy. Sarah's interruption of Nyles's incipient speechmaking demands a mode of conversation that resists this conformity. She wants conversation that incorporates the exploratory spontaneity of their earlier play but that will also enable and enrich their own authentic experience. The "grammatical nightmare," as Sarah calls it, that Nyles produces when allowed "one sentence" is hardly an ideal of spontaneous and authentic speech. It is a halting string of blurted phrases, continually tipping toward expected rom-com tropes. However, Sarah's interventions and corrections show that their quest for authentic expression will be engaged together.

Ending his single sentence, Nyles declares: "I'd rather die with you than live in this world without you. Emphatic period!" Sarah's long pause giving way to a slight smile shows that she appreciates and accepts Nyles's declaration—while also recognizing that he has again grabbed a typical sentimental trope. However, by directing her initial response not to the sentiment declared but to the punctuation—"an emphatic period is just an exclamation point"—Sarah gently lets some air out of Nyles's rhetorical bubble—"I didn't want to seem desperate," he replies—and opens space for a crucial exchange.

SARAH: What if we get sick of each other?

NYLES: We're already sick of each other. It's the best.

SARAH [after pausing to weigh Nyles's words]: I can survive just fine without you, you know. But there's, there's a chance that this life can be a little less mundane with you in it.

NYLES: Yeah. Less mundane. That's a super low bar. That's a great place to start.

This is not embracing lowered expectations or celebrating the sad truth that many relationships amount to enduring a partner one is sick of. It is most directly a counter to an idealized vision of marriage suggested by the picture-perfect wedding of Tala and Abe. But the exchange is also a more general repudiation of disabling forms of idealism that are a standing threat of perfectionism. The chagrin that inspires perfectionist transformation can also lead to the projection of an ideal state of self and society that provokes despair as everyone and everything invariably falls short.[17] Indeed, we can now see, in retrospect, that it was as disappointed idealists that Nyles and Sarah formed their wholesale repudiation of society and their condemnation of themselves. Here, they refuse the siren song of such idealism but still affirm ideals and aspirations. Sarah's "a bit less mundane" speaks clearly of escaping the humdrum and routine and it also suggests incorporating a register of the spiritual or extramundane. We might think of this as a perspective, discovered in the vision of the dinosaurs, that opens the pair to the reality of possibilities beyond what they so far know of themselves and their world and so encourages continued becoming.

While not wedding vows in any traditional sense, the words of this exchange suffice for our pair as expressing their commitment to moving forward together. Considering Nyles's response to her "low bar" declaration of sentiment, Sarah smiles, nods her head, and says simply "Okay." Nyles too nods and returns "Okay." With that, Sarah's expression becomes determined: "Come on," she declares, "Let's see if we blow up and die."

Walking into the cave, hand-in-hand, teasing about what to do on their first date, the soundtrack plays Kate Bush's "Cloudbusting"—another anthem, now about the power of believing "something good is gonna happen." They stop and, as on the magical night in the desert, we see them framed in close-up, looking directly toward us, again staring wide-eyed, this time at the cave's glowing and pulsing core. The shot is held while we absorb this vision of their apprehensive anticipation and resolve. Sarah turns toward Nyles and delivers what, for all she knows, may be her last words: "In case I don't see you again, I love you too." They embrace, kissing. We rotate around them and in the glow of the cave it is as though they are framed against the rising or setting sun, marking a change of day. The focus expands to show Sarah clutching the C4 detonator at her breast, thumb over the button. Their kiss continues as she presses down. The button lights, we hear an electronic beep followed by an explosion, and we are propelled through nebulae and interstellar space, past stars and a supernova, all intercut with flashes of Nyles and Sarah; laughing beneath a resort window as a sexual prank they have staged unfolds, bursting into the dive bar to perform their dance, Sarah steering the car into the grill of the fuel truck, Nyles doing a cannonball, their kiss as they "get it over with," and their clasped hands as they stare in wonder at the vision of the dinosaurs. Their hands are replaced by a sphere at the center of an explosion that projects a ray of light across the screen. The light spreads, the screen goes white, and, with a final explosive sound, black.

Wanderers, Scapegoats, Dinosaurs

Following several seconds of total blackness, we see a blazing midday sun (the maker of days), then a drink caddy with five beers floating in shimmering blue water, and finally Nyles and Sarah, wearing bathing suits and sunglasses, side by side on slice-of-pizza-floats in what we only now recognize as the safehouse pool. We do not immediately know whether they have escaped the time loop or whether, having failed, they are again taking refuge.

At the narrative level, the question is soon answered by Nyles remarking that he should pick up his dog from neighbors and by the sudden appearance of the family who own the house and the man's angry shout, "What the fuck are you doing in our pool?!" At the thematic level, the question is not so easily resolved. Nyles and Sarah have decisively committed to their pursuit of happiness. Even before Sarah pressed the detonator button, they committed when they said "Okay." However, as Sarah showed in rejecting Nyles's fantasy of a private Irvine of happiness, the reality and meaning of their pursuit require that it be conducted in community with others. Their being at the safehouse rather than the wedding and the angry shout of the homeowner show that this community will not be found within their given society. They must create the others who find them intelligible, must found the people with whom they can undertake to enter and settle any promised land of happiness. This means their fate is in our hands—as ours is in theirs.

This was to be expected. The perfectionist aspirations of classical remarriage comedies involve not only depicting the transformation of their principal pairs but also, through that depiction, working to inspire our own. Further, it is only our transformation that ratifies that of the principal pair as we become the community that affirms their intelligibility. In *Palm Springs*, the film's effort to affect a transformation in the viewer and so found a new or reborn people that can affirm the intelligibility of Nyles and Sarah is embodied in three elements. I will close by briefly considering each.

While depicting characters trapped in a box of energy that creates a time loop, *Palm Springs* also declares itself to be that very box. As we saw at the outset, we enter the world of the film being swallowed by the earth and then, along with its characters, are subjected to repeatedly reliving the same day.[18] But *Palm Springs* equally shows itself to be the force that can release us from our various imprisoning boxes of energy by providing a form of therapy for (some of) the pathologies that impede our ability to believe in, and pursue, the promise of happiness. These two self-understandings of the film are connected in its construing us, the viewers, as wanderers. It condemns us to wander with Nyles and Sarah (hence our being trapped), but that wandering, for us as well as them, provides transformative education (hence the possibility of our being released). In wandering with Nyles and Sarah, *Palm Springs* allows us to learn about them—primarily by observing what they teach each other. However, it also invites us to learn about ourselves by relating our lives to theirs. In our wandering we are able to determine the extent to which Nyles and Sarah are representative of us; that is, the extent to which we share (forms of) their chagrin and despair, their anxieties and self-condemnations, their idealism, and the like. And we are equally able to determine the extent to which they are exemplars for us; that is, the extent to which are we attracted by their newfound belief in the promise of happiness and are inspired to end our wandering and join them in the modes of conversation and relationship through which they are beginning to pursue it. Here we approach the second way in which *Palm Springs* works to transform us and found a people; its use of the figure of the scapegoat.

The scapegoat, of course, derives from a ritual of atonement—cleansing, purification, and renewal—practiced by the ancient Israelites with whom we began. As described in Leviticus, the high priest "shall lay both his hands upon the head of the live goat and confess over it all the iniquities and transgressions of the Israelites . . . putting them on the head of the goat." The people are then purified and renewed through removing this goat from their midst: "Thus the goat shall carry on it all their iniquities to an inaccessible region; and the goat shall be set free in the wilderness [through a "designated man]" (Leviticus 16:21–22). The use of scapegoat imagery in *Palm Springs* is plain enough; the opening shot of a goat free in the wilderness begins to suggest the idea and Sarah's use of that same goat in preparing for her own release and new beginning confirms it. She places her burdens (figured in the C4) on it, sends it to an inaccessible region by detonating it as it passes through the time loop ("I don't know where she is," she tells Nyles, "but she's not here anymore"), and only then returns to Nyles renewed and ready to move forward. Most crucially, though, in having Nyles and Sarah recapitulate what we have seen with the goat—entering the cave laden with C4 that is then detonated—the film declares that they function, for us, as both scapegoat and "designated man." When, in wandering with Nyles and Sarah, we recognize them as representative of forms of our own "iniquities and transgressions," they serve as scapegoats in that we place these burdens on their heads. These iniquities and transgressions are removed in our learning from Nyles and Sarah how they help each other overcome them. This illustrative overcoming of the obstacles blocking their pursuit of happiness is how they function as designated man, but their doing so is figured in the climactic and culminating act of entering the cave and detonating the C4 and themselves. The final scene of Nyles and Sarah in a pool is the crowning touch to the scapegoat imagery; for Leviticus tells us that, after setting the scape-goat free, the designated man "shall wash his clothes and bathe his body in water" and "after that he may reenter the camp" (Leviticus, 16:26). Floating in the pool, our pair are bathing themselves in water in preparation for beginning to create a new or transfigured camp.

If, as scapegoats, Nyles and Sarah have begun preparing us to join them by releasing us from (some of) the obstacles standing in our way, it remains a question whether the modes of conversation and relationship through which they are beginning to pursue happiness attract us and draw us to emulate them. This is the question posed by the film's final image.[19]

Nyles and Sarah continue floating in the pool, chuckling about the sudden appearance of the outraged homeowners. The soundtrack plays Hall & Oates's "When the Morning Comes" as the camera pulls up and away, allowing us an aerial view of the pool with Nyles and Sarah on their pizza-floats and the family standing in a cluster on the deck. Then, rising higher and panning out ahead, it reveals a barren desert landscape with no signs of human life or habitation. Moving over the open desert, the camera tilts up, looks toward the horizon, and there, in the far distance, stand dinosaurs. The image is held for several seconds, granting us time to register the presence of the dinosaurs, and then, as we begin moving slowly toward them, the screen goes black and the credits roll.

Since these are presumably the same dinosaurs Nyles and Sarah saw on their magical night, one function of their concluding appearance is to ask whether we share the vision and sense of wonder they experienced. However, on that night the camera turned from the dinosaurs and directed our gaze toward Nyles and Sarah to suggest that, for us, they are the wonder. This concluding image recalls that earlier gesture and so employs the dinosaurs as a figure for Nyles and Sarah. It was their awe inspiring vision of the wonder of the dinosaurs that moved Nyles and Sarah to acknowledge and embrace their investment in one another. Now, with this closing image, the film asks whether we have found in them the answers or ancestors we seek; whether they have provided us a rebirth by inspiring a new or renewed belief in the promise of happiness and whether we are prepared to join them in pursuing it. We know no more than they do about how that pursuit will unfold and whether it will succeed. They are just beginning to make their way in the barren desert of the promised land they have entered. It remains to be settled and cultivated. The question is whether we have found them a wonder, whether our vision of them has elicited our awe, and, if so, whether we are prepared to entrust ourselves to that sense of wonder and awe.[20]

When we first see Nyles and Sarah after the explosion, released from the anxieties and self-condemnations that prevented their believing in the promise of happiness and cleansing themselves in the safehouse pool before setting out on its pursuit, Sarah reaches across to Nyles, lays her hand on his leg and asks what we can hear as the film's final question for us: "So, now what do we do?" It is a question each of us will have to answer for ourselves.[21]

Notes

1. Biblical quotations are from JPS (1985).

2. The film's soundtrack is extraordinary and would repay more attention than my few mentions will give.

3. The structure of the time loop appears to be this: the day repeats for everyone, but only those who have been swallowed by the earth experience this fact.

4. When released in June of 2020, early in the lockdowns enacted in response to the Covid-19 global pandemic, critics often suggested its appeal lay in its resonance with the mood of that time—feeling trapped, enduring confinement with some and unable to interact with others, barred from normal life, and all with no idea how and when the situation would change. My own sense is that its appeal is rooted in speaking to a deeper malaise; to doubts about both the possibility of happiness and our right to it—as though we are all deservedly cursed.

5. In elaborating this shared narrative, Cavell argues, they continue the philosophical thought of what he calls Emersonian or Moral Perfectionism. See especially *Cities of Words*.

6. For his discussion of the experience of dissatisfaction, see *CW*, 2.

7. In the biblical narrative, this re-conception occurs in Deuteronomy. For a useful consideration of this issue, see Kugler 2019.

8. Here Nyles is aligned with the boy in "Self-Reliance" who would "disdain as much as a lord to do or say aught to conciliate one" and whose "nonchalance" Emerson says is the "healthy attitude of human nature" (Emerson 1990c, 31).

9. Sarah's screams also speak for us. At this point, we know no more than she about what is happening and Roy's arrow pierces any expectations we may have begun forming about the nature of this film.

10. Sarah seems to have arrived at the idea of escaping the day through selflessness from *Groundhog Day* (Harold Ramis, 1993)—a film that, while never mentioned, is clearly in the background of *Palm Springs* and is here gently mocked.

11. On this point, see *PH*, 103.

12. Endless repetitive time plays the role of wealth in classical remarriage comedy, affording the pair the "leisure to talk about human happiness, hence the time to deprive themselves of it unnecessarily" (*PH*, 5).

13. It is impossible to miss the extraordinary expressiveness of Cristin Milioti and, especially, her capacity for allowing distinct and often conflicting thoughts and emotions to register on her face and in her eyes. However, Andy Samburg is in some ways equally astonishing. Here, though, his gift

lodges in his capacity for psychic blankness. His face in this scene reveals a human being searching for, and failing to discover, an inner life.

14. Nyles later, uncharitably, describes this as his being codependent. He cares for *Sarah* and not simply, as in codependence, about how she makes him feel about himself.

15. The ideas and images introduced here seem to be drawn from actual physics (see Sanders [2018]), but they also echo Emerson's thinking in "Circles" (1990d). He emphasizes that "it is the inert effort of each thought, having formed itself into a circular wave of circumstance, . . . to heap itself on that ridge, and solidify and hem in the life" (1990d, 174) and that moving beyond these circles can feel like blowing ourselves up—"All that we reckoned settled shakes and rattles" (178).

16. The ways in which *Palm Springs* reflects on acting, authenticity, the demands of genre, and its relation to romantic comedy, simply touched here, is a fascinating dimension of the film that I cannot develop.

17. Nietzsche describes this as being crushed by the "intoxicating vision" of a quasi-Platonic ideal that leaves us "subject to an even deeper dissatisfaction" (1983, 156).

18. Our being in the box of energy explains why we are never shown what the characters see inside the cave and why they never speak of it. We do not need to be shown or told because we are seeing what they see; the various iterations of the same day that constitute *Palm Springs*—with the difference, and in accord with the multiverse physics Sarah relies on in planning her escape, that they presumably see the days simultaneously while we see them serially.

19. I am discounting a short sequence cut into the credits that returns to the wedding reception and shows Roy discovering that Sarah's plan of escape has apparently worked and that, therefore, he can escape as well. Although such a scene might have been used to suggest that Roy will be the first member of the people Nyles and Sarah seek to create, the film has not provided grounds for such an understanding. Instead, the sequence is tacked on and serves merely to tie up a loose end.

20. This question about our relation to Nyles and Sarah is the same question we face in reading a film (or any work of art): do we trust our necessarily limited initial experience sufficiently to follow it and to invest ourselves in the work of developing a reading; for it is only in the work of reading that we will discover whether our investment was well-placed.

21. Bill Day and Bill Rothman not only provided wonderful comments and suggestions on drafts of this chapter, their encouragement of my reading provided invaluable assurance that I was not simply being carried away by the delight I experienced in *Palm Springs*. I am more than grateful.

Works Cited

JPS (The Jewish Publication Society). 1985. *Tanakh: A New Translation of the Holy Scriptures According to the Traditional Hebrew Text*. The Jewish Publication Society.

Emerson, Ralph Waldo. 1990a. *Essays: First and Second Series*. New York: Vintage Books/The Library of America.

Emerson, Ralph Waldo. 1990b. "History." In Emerson, *Essays*.

Emerson, Ralph Waldo. 1990c. "Self-Reliance." In Emerson, *Essays*.

Emerson, Ralph Waldo. 1990d. "Circles." In Emerson, *Essays*.

Kugler, Gili. 2019. "Did the Exodus Generation Die in the Wilderness or Enter Canaan?" *TheTorah.com*. https://thetorah.com/article/did-the-exodus-generation-die-in-the-wilderness-or-enter-canaan/.

Nietzsche, Friedrich. 1983. "Schopenhauer as Educator." In *Untimely Meditations*. Translated by R. J. Hollingdale. Cambridge University Press.

Sanders, Robert. 2018. "Some Black Holes Erase Your Past." *Berkeley News*, February 20, 2018. https://news.berkeley.edu/2018/02/20/some-black-holes-erase-your-past/.

13

The Comedy of Remarriage in the Age of Lean-In Feminism

Sofia Coppola's *On the Rocks*

FIONA HANDYSIDE

IN MARCH 2022, JANE CAMPION won the Best Director Oscar for her film *The Power of the Dog* (2021). The first question she was posed at the backstage press conference asked her to comment on her win as only the third female director to win an Oscar in this category (preceded by Chloe Zhao for *Nomadland* in 2021 and Kathryn Bigelow for *The Hurt Locker* in 2009). Campion responds that "I am very proud to have won tonight for my film and for my crew and for my cast, but also just to be another woman, who is going to be followed by a fourth, fifth, sixth, seventh, eighth . . . I am very excited by the fact this is moving fast now" (Campion 2022). Campion's comments indicate the rapidly shifting landscape for female directors in the wake of concerted feminist activism in the film industry. This activism targets sexual abuse and harassment as well as lack of transparency and accountability for how films earn nominations and prizes

321

at award ceremonies and on the film festival circuit. In the decade since the Cannes film festival did not feature a single film directed by a woman in its main competition in 2012, female directors have made common cause with other women in the industry, comprising writers, producers, actors, cinematographers, talent agents, editors, distributors, and sales agents in pushing for gender equity. The pressure group 5050 in 2020 shows how institutions of power in creative fields may affect women's access to the highest honors and levels of success. Cannes and the Oscars both represent gatekeeping forces that may appear to operate as a meritocracy but call out for social and institutional critique. In this context, Campion's Oscar win does mark a watershed of sorts: one in which, as she explains, women gaining prestigious directing awards may no longer be a historic exception but part of a wider social change that broadens opportunities for women in film. The last decade has been one in which the film industry and its practices have been the object of sustained feminist critique. This marks an emergence into the more visible and glamorous end of the film business of a feminist discourse that privileges female voices and attempts to fashion a structural realignment of how female labor is recognized in the creation of female images.

This irruption of feminist analysis of female creative labor in the film industry is part of what Diane Negra and Hannah Hamad astutely diagnose as a changing attitude towards feminism in politics and culture (Negra and Hamad 2020). The postfeminist consensus of the 1990s and early 2000s dismissed feminism as old-fashioned and irrelevant while simultaneously embracing aspects of it as a hegemonic common sense. In contrast, the increased disparities of wealth rendered strikingly visible by the 2008 financial crash and the aftermath of austerity coupled with the affective intensities of social media and its community-building potential have paved the way for proliferating new popular and celebrity-endorsed feminisms to compete with and complement residual postfeminist ideas of empowerment and agency via femininity, consumerism, and choice. No longer a derided philosophy, feminism has a new visibility and luminosity, promoted by a plutocratic elite such as high-profile female businesswomen (Ivanka Trump, Sheryl Sandberg) and film and music celebrities (Emma Watson, Beyoncé Knowles Carter). Feminism has been swallowed up into digital capitalism, enabling privileged women to stake their claim and while doing so providing the digital platforms with rich datasets. While digital media might appear to offer a new kind of political public sphere, it does so through a way that generates capital for fabulously wealthy private tech companies in which feminism becomes one more niche marketing device cleaving to neoliberal individualism and global capitalism. There's an uneasy tension in the promotion of female directors winning Oscars and the sense that feminism itself has become repurposed as a way for a few women to privilege from elite structures rather than tackling the systemic institutional problems of the film and media worlds. This question over whether the digital world's promotion of glossy diversity offers women greater recognition of their subjectivity than the more openly patronizing charm of earlier generations is one posed by *On the Rocks* (Sofia Coppola, 2020), if we read it in the light of Stanley Cavell's insights that romantic genres work through trouble in the social and sexual realm. Through a light and sparkling tone, Coppola nevertheless "looks sharply and critically at the conveniences of wealth and the prerogatives of privilege" (Brody 2020). How far should a woman "lean in" to get a slice of this particular pie?

Stanley Cavell's landmark studies of mid-twentieth-century Hollywood may at first seem removed from this renewed emphasis on feminism and questions of feminist activism in film, especially its synergy with social media and digital network culture. Yet of course, as scholars of Cavell are very aware, the question of female experience is central to much of his work on film, not least because he believes film to show a much greater interest in female subjects than male subjects. Film is, Cavell believes, "about the creation of woman, about her demand for an education, for a voice in her history" (quoted in Wheatley 2021, 175). Cavell turned particularly to two genres he defined—the comedy of remarriage and the melodrama of the unknown woman—arguing that they provide data on "the inner agenda of a culture" (*PH*, 17). The cultural shift that these films illuminate is how men and women's relations change in wake of the granting of universal suffrage, that is to say woman becoming representable as a subject in the public sphere. Ben Little and Alison Winch convincingly argue that the 2007–8 financial crash has given way to the rise of digital capitalism which brings together tech companies and financial institutions to strengthen the reach and power of each leading to a "full-spectrum social, cultural, economic and political shift that is transforming our world" that revisits questions of the battle of the sexes (Little and Winch 2021, 4). This shift has been refracted through a series of films that recall the screwball comedies of the 1940s that provided Cavell with his initial corpus. A flurry of recent scholarship confirms the ongoing existence of the remarriage comedy in contemporary cinema and its openness to reading through a Cavellian lens. David LaRocca acknowledges what might seem like "a compulsive testing of traits" (2021c, 274) from Cavell's two favored genres as critics explore films by directors such as Noah Baumbach, Greta Gerwig, the Coen brothers, and Richard Linklater using a "compare-and-contrast methodology" (LaRocca 2021c, 275). While of course there remains the anxiety that all that is accomplished is "accretive canon formation" (LaRocca 2021c, 275), might the persistence of this genre not also indicate the persistence of its ability to work through the impact of feminist discourse and recalibrated gender roles of how men and women relate to each other?

In this chapter, I demonstrate how *On the Rocks* offers a critique of digital capitalism and how it has made a certain kind of invisible and unmoored—and thus all the more invasive—patriarchal power omnipresent in our everyday lives. I am using the term digital capitalism here in the sense developed in the work of David Harvey, in which

> What was initially conceived as a liberatory regime of collaborative production of an open access commons has been transformed into a regime of hyper-exploitation upon which capital freely feeds. The unrestrained pillage by big capital (like Amazon and Google) of the free goods produced by a self-skilled labour force has become a major feature of our times. This carries over into the so-called cultural industries . . . It is also interesting that some of the most vigorous sectors of development in our times—like Google and Facebook and the rest of the digital labour sector—have grown very fast on the back of free labour . . . Factory labour still dominates in some parts of the world (for example, East Asia) but in North America and Europe it is much diminished and replaced by various other labour systems (digital labour and the like). (quoted in Fuchs and Chandler 2019, 13–14)

For Cavell, the power of the comedy of remarriage is in how it yokes together trouble in the sexual and the social realm through the threat of divorce. Here, divorce's possibility is raised because a busy husband, working for an unnamed digital tech company, fails to recognize his wife when they are in bed together after he returns from a business trip. Recognition and acknowledgement are the basis for human connection for Cavell; Coppola's film astutely links the husband's absorption into the world of the digital to the precarious relation the film describes—life "on the rocks." As Kate Rennebohm and Catherine Wheatley explain, the "moral panics about truth and falsehood in the digital era" constitute a climate of uncertainty (2022, 96). Such uncertainty invites an appreciation of Cavell's philosophy at this particular historical juncture and its relevance to how the expansion of Big Data (that is, data too voluminous and acquired too quickly to be processed by humans) into the nooks and crannies of our everyday lives changes how we come to know the world and how we may seek to improve it.

The tech start-up that Dean (Marlon Wayans) is establishing kicks off Laura's (Rashida Jones) doubt about her marriage. This doubt is further fueled when he has a party to celebrate its growing number of users and shares on its web page. This forms the background to *On the Rocks'* implicit study of the rise of digital media and algorithmic Big Data. It is important here to understand that Big Data is crucial to the creation of digital content for companies such as Facebook and its users who share over 5 billion posts and upload more than 300 million images per minute. More than 500,000 comments are posted per minute. Facebook's 2016 advertising profits of US$ 10.2 billion were generated by targeting users based on the analysis of Big Data generated through users' activities and content (Fuchs and Chandler 2019, 4–5). Cavell stresses how our quest for knowledge is a philosophical problem as we rub up against the unknownness of other minds and other lives. The digital undermines our connection to the reality of the world while giving the impression we can know others more completely (and that some may amply profit from that knowledge). First, it unmoors the indexical relationship of the image to its referent, creating codes and images out of bits of infinitely manipulable data. Second, it corrals together like-minded communities into self-referential bubbles via algorithms, so that differences of perspective and opinion become unknown. Indeed, it is revealing that the term "gaslighting" has recently become widely used to explain contemporary phenomenon of feeling like one lives in a faked reality, often due to the manipulation of social media. Oxford University Press listed the term in its Word of the Year 2018 shortlist, commenting on its sudden explosion in use (and the possible dilution this might cause in its precise psychological application) (Oxford Languages 2018). *Gaslight* (George Cukor, 1944) is one of Cavell's key texts in his discussion of the unknown woman melodrama, suggesting Paula's madness, to which she has been reduced by her husband, is now a far more widespread social condition. Can contemporary women find their voice in the maze of the digital realm without succumbing to Paula's fate?

On the Rocks also thematizes aspects of Coppola's public persona, specifically her relationship with her father, to raise questions of how a daughter is to assert the singularity of her voice. This is a connection which takes us back to the Oscars ceremony where my chapter started, and the continuous suspicion that Coppola in particular has attracted that she is not worthy of awards in her own right. Possibly more than any other female filmmaker of similar critical and commercial success, Coppola's work is shadowed with negative associations of nepotism and money. Through hybridizing a comedy of remarriage with a father-daughter caper, Coppola's film revisits Cavell's concerns with female voice from a perspective informed by audience knowledge of her own authorship's complex relationship to daughterhood, feminist politics, and questions of self-knowledge and education in the contemporary mediascape. In her recent study of female authorship in contemporary Hollywood, Mary Harrod argues that the heightened genericity such self-awareness and hybridization points towards can realize a feminist potential, especially when combined with autofiction. This is because they create the image of an individualized female author who is "an expert in the communicative art of genre" and thus offer us a dynamic and provocative mixing of the personal and the public, echoing again Cavell's insight that films raise intimate and political questions together (Harrod 2021, 165). By making this film one which asks to what extent the daughter should trust her father's way of seeing the world, Coppola poses the Cavellian question of a woman's education in a context which is also informed by her auteur persona and the travails she has had imposing her worth as a film director who is also the daughter of a famous film director.

This film, Coppola's seventh feature film, tells the story of an upper middle-class Manhattan dwelling writer, Laura. Laura is married to Dean and they have two young daughters, Maya (Liyanna Muscat) and Theo (Alexandra and Anna Reimer). When Dean returns from one of his frequent business trips, he climbs into bed and begins kissing Laura passionately. When she calls his name, he stops, looks confused, and turns away, falling asleep. This causes Laura to suspect that he may be having an affair with a colleague. She confides her misgivings to her father, Felix (Bill Murray), a wealthy art dealer. Felix, himself a roué who divorced Laura's mother years before, is convinced that Dean is having an affair. He persuades Laura to spy on Dean. Because her father is a philanderer investigating another potential philanderer, Laura wonders if Felix's "flawed rapscallion way" of seeing men and women is accurate, or does he "see what he wants to see?" (Gleiberman 2020). Meanwhile Felix also attempts to compensate Laura for her lack of romantic and sexual connection with Dean. He takes her out to sophisticated bars and gifts her a vintage watch for her birthday. He takes her to a party and they slip out together to admire a Monet painting, *Waterlilies*. Laura and Felix forge a connection which allows her to express her deep sadness. As she sits at the glorious Bemelmans Bar in the Carlyle Hotel with its famous whimsical murals of Central Park, drinking martinis with her dad, a single tear drops into her cocktail glass, caught in a slow-motion closeup. The film contrasts these affirmative conversations and significant gifts between father and daughter to the overcrowded noisy restaurants and mundane domestic appliances that Dean offers. The film culminates with Felix and Laura travelling to Mexico, where Dean is on yet another business trip. Laura expects to surprise Dean in bed with his colleague Fiona (Jessica Henwick); instead she discovers he has flown home early in an attempt to surprise her. They discuss their insecurities and doubts with each other and reconcile. The film works through a woman's identity crisis through the techniques Cavell favors of domestic settings, witty conversations, and plot resolution through an escapade to a golden world (here Mexico).

The basic outline of the narrative offered here indicates already how the film may be considered a variation of the comedy of remarriage, as it raises the threat of divorce only finally to reject it. Coppola's discussion of the creative processes that inform the film further indicate to us how closely it hews to Cavell's structuring concerns and his conviction that this genre has an ability to help us think about our relationships and the world that contains them. Explaining that she had first registered the title seven years earlier, Coppola comments that it's her most dialogue-heavy feature and that her writing method differed from her earlier pattern.

> I wanted to do a buddy story about a father-daughter relationship that explored that generational divide because I haven't seen that story. It was my way of exploring the identity crisis of a woman in different phases of her life but also the sort of clashing relationships between men and women . . . I've always been drawn to finding a way to express emotion through visuals and atmosphere. I was talking to Buck Henry about this idea early on, and he said, "Why don't you write some dialogue?" I thought I'd try writing something dialogue-driven that was almost like a play for me. *On the Rocks* started with just Felix and Laura sitting in different restaurants and bars having conversations. It was fun to try something I hadn't done before and focus on the dialogue, with the story evolving from there. (Bell 2020)

This hybridization of a comedy of remarriage with a father-daughter comedy caper appealed to Coppola as way to address serious themes in a lighthearted mode. She explains her rationale as "I wanted to do like a father-daughter buddy movie with martinis discussing life and relationships. And I was missing that kind of smart, sophisticated comedy that I grew up with and trying to embrace something a little sillier than my usual realm of what I know how to do. It's sort of out of my comfort zone" (Olsen 2020).

Coppola's summing up of her film here points to its imbrication of the silly and the serious, another aspect that can be further illuminated through reference to Cavell. As LaRocca points out, it was in the madcap, zany, screwball comedies that Cavell found philosophy (LaRocca 2021b, 21). Comedies are vectors for giving significance to the medium of film, showing the intelligence of an art whose ontology brings it close to the everyday. He drew attention to the need to pay attention to the very syllables of the dialogue and their imbrication into sequential moving images, arguing that here significance be discovered. It brings interest to the everyday matter of our lives—dialogue as the very stuff of our relations and our connections. LaRocca concludes that "deliberating on what is serious and what is silly in our lives (the two often uncannily overlapping or trading places); in this lucky labor, arbitrating what matters—becoming perspicuous about the meaning of our ordinary experience—may deliver unanticipated results, among them that what appear to be trivialities and ephemera can take on substantive, transformative import" (2021b, 21). It is this rich seam of the silly-serious that *On the Rocks* combines.

The film's punning title alone confirms its joint interest in intertwined stories of a marriage in trouble (a marriage "on the rocks") and a sparkling sophisticated bar room culture (where cocktails are drunk "on the rocks"). The cocktail drinking lends itself to the discussion and evaluation of marriage (both Laura's own marriage and the institution per se) but also a kind of lighthearted tomfoolery and witty exchange. As Wheatley notes, Cavell was drawn to the films of the Marx Brothers because their "pun-crammed air" alerts us to "how language can be slippery and multivalent, subject to twists of intention and interpretation" (Wheatley 2019, 48). *On the Rocks'* title indicates that it is asking us to view its world through a doubled perspective which captures neatly the contrasts the film offers between Laura's quotidian routine of child-rearing and (attempting) work and the impact of the domestic routine on her marriage and Felix's brash and cosmopolitan world of travel, sex, risk, and seduction. Laura has to choose between *faith* in her marriage—the fact she can never truly know her husband's full intentions—and the *certainty* of her father's concepts of beauty. To place the dilemma in a more Cavellian tone, the film illustrates her time of indecision between the ordinary of a domesticated life in marriage, and the isolation of a search for certain knowledge which can be provided only by glittering art and not by messy humans. This means, however, that Laura is also being asked to place her faith in a marriage whose economic basis is sustained through digital capitalism, providing a new twist to the Cavellian female dilemma. With the film's release in September 2020 during the Covid-19 pandemic, the urbane world of chic, upscale New York bars and restaurants and spontaneous jaunts to Mexico the film shows operated like a document of a lost culture to an audience mainly confined to watching the film at home via Apple TV's streaming service.[1] This added a further uncanny layer to the film's knowing invocation of films such as *The Thin Man* (W. S. Van Dyke, 1934), Blake Edwards movies, and screwball comedy as the film itself became something akin to "a period movie" (Hattersley 2020). The film's capturing of a prepandemic New York City that feels lost to audiences watching it less than a year after recording renders more palpable the situation Cavell outlines for us generally about our uncertainty about the existence of the world. The world recorded in Coppola's film is a world we both know and do not know, enhancing Cavell's insight into "our precarious position in relation to the world" and illuminating his discussion of faith and certainty even in its mode of distribution, itself an outcome of the impact of digital technology on the media industry (Klevan 2000, 12).

My alignment of the film's explicit attention to female becoming to a new postrecessionary feminist luminosity may at first seem in contradiction to its depiction of a world of significant material comfort. Sam Adams comments that Coppola "seems to pack every frame with artefacts of contemporary urban extravagance, sometimes so many at a time it can be difficult to take them all in" (Adams 2020). Echoing the typical paradox that enjoys Coppola's spectacle of wealth while condemning it as shallow and narcissistic, he goes on to say "we've highlighted some of the most pronounced, most bougiest signifiers for your delectation and/or condemnation" (Adams 2020). These include (in order of ascending value): Vanessa's (Jenny Slate) limited edition designer Rodarte sweatshirt, valued at about $250; Laura's vintage Chanel handbag, valued at about $6,000, which she pairs with a $30 dollar The Strand Bookstore canvas tote bag; the Cartier watch Felix buys; the office where Laura procrastinates writing her next novel, that the article locates at 81 Wooster street, where a second floor apartment costs approximately $6.1 million; and the Monet hanging in an acquaintance's home whose value is somewhere upwards of $100 million. Here again it is worth recalling Cavell's original corpus in *Pursuits of Happiness*. These films were often referred to as "fairy tales for the Depression" (a description Cavell expresses some reservations about) and "took settings of immense luxury and . . . depicted people whose actions often concerned the disposition of fantastic sums of money" (*PH*, 2). Cavell argues that a certain level of comfort is essential to these films' examination of what happiness is and what a happy marriage might look like, since, as Wheatley explains, "these concerns are, in and of themselves, luxuries of a sort" (2019, 110). It is significant that Laura's sadness and exhaustion comes from a combination of concerns about the state of her marriage, learning more about her parents' failed marriage, and the monotony of her routine looking after two small children. This enables Coppola to focus on the emotional labor Laura performs in managing the life of her household, a topic the films Cavell discusses avoid as children are absent. Coppola's focus on a middle-aged woman (the birthday Laura is celebrating is her thirty-ninth, placing her on the cusp of ageing toward invisibility) relocates Cavell's concerns with how a woman is to understand her role and herself outside of her functions as daughter, wife, or mother. It does this especially through an investigation of the attractions and deceits of male charm.

Bill Murray and Charming/Toxic Masculinity

The question of the specificity of female voice, and how we may come to hear it, is illuminating to consider in relation to the entirety of Sofia Coppola's filmography. As the daughter of renowned Hollywood film director Francis Ford Coppola, Sofia Coppola has had to assert her legitimacy and difference in the face of his reputation. She did so above all through voice, recounting how her father visited her on the set of her first film, *The Virgin Suicides* (1999). He told her she should say "Action" louder, from her diaphragm. Recounting the anecdote, Coppola laughs and explains, "I'm not going to say it wasn't intimidating, but when you direct is the only time you get to have the world exactly how you want it. My movies are very close to what I set out to do. And I'm super opinionated about what I do and don't like." She pauses, and then adds, "I may say it differently, but I still get what I want" (Hirschberg 2003).

Coppola's difference is expressed as both a personal, biographical difference—the contrast to her father's voice—and as an institutional, professional difference—her films bear an auteurist signature. Her films that place a father-daughter relation on screen articulate the ambivalence of a daughter loving a father who treats women as sex objects, and do so through an attention to problems of communication. In *Somewhere* (2010), Johnny's (Stephen Dorff) final farewell message to Cleo (Elle Fanning)—an apology that he hasn't been a more active father—is drowned under the noise of whirring helicopter blades. In *On the Rocks*, Felix tells Laura that he can't hear women's voices because of their pitch—to which she incredulously responds, "You can't go deaf just to women." Laura has also lost her ability to whistle since she had children, and Felix exhorts her to practice. The father wants the daughter to find her sense of self, her voice, and her difference, even while he views the world through a prism of self-serving sexism. Coppola encourages us to read the father-daughter relation on screen through the lens of her own relationship with her father. She explains the initial spark for the film came from a "really vivid memory from my twenties going out with my dad having martinis. I was caught up on some guy. I thought he liked me, but he disappeared and I was so confused . . . [My dad] was like, "Let me tell you what's really going on and what he's thinking" . . . Not that he's a playboy . . . but [it was] from a man's point of view. It's so fascinating for a man to have a grown daughter that's dealing with relationships and to have these different perspectives" (Nolfi 2020).

Bill Murray takes the role of Felix. Murray has functioned as a muse for Coppola since he played the role of Bob Harris in *Lost in Translation* (2004); he also starred in her 2015 Netflix special *A Very Murray Christmas*. While *Lost in Translation* was awarded three Golden Globes and an Oscar, one of its most important legacies was the revival of Murray's career. Alongside *Rushmore* (Wes Anderson, 1998), *Lost in Translation* recalibrated Murray's star persona and associated him with an indie or Indiewood cinematic sensibility. His career was rooted in countercultural dissent and misrule, with his breakthrough coming in 1977 as one of the *Saturday Night Live* team. Along with comedians John Belushi, Don Aykroyd, and Harold Ramis, Murray performed improvised skits and scripted satire. The character he played in *Lost in Translation* shared Murray's *SNL* deadpan delivery and wry sardonic wit, but with an undertow of greater sincerity, melancholia, and yearning. This is especially noticeable later in the film as Bob gets closer to Charlotte (Scarlett Johansson) and they discuss deep personal issues: her uncertainty about what to do with her life, about which he offers advice; his relationship with his wife and children. The sincerity of his feelings for Charlotte is especially underlined by his performance of Roxy Music's *More Than This* during a karaoke session he enjoys with Charlotte and some of her friends. As Geoff King remarks, the performance is entirely directed to a fictional audience, filmed at a ninety-degree angle. Its sincerity is all the more striking as one of Murray's most famous roles on *Saturday Night Live* was as the smoothly insincere Nick the Lounge Singer (a character which was part of the inspiration behind his performance in *A Very*

Murray Christmas) (King 2010, 109). The lengths Coppola went to secure Murray's involvement in *Lost in Translation* have now become part of the myth of this film. The script was written from the start with Murray in mind and Coppola insisted in interviews that she planned to make the film only if she could persuade Murray to take the role. A lengthy period of wooing followed, some five months, and Coppola only secured a verbal rather than a written agreement before production began.

The character of Felix provided an opportunity for Coppola to work with Murray again, and many of the reviews concentrate on this aspect of the film and Murray's "easy charm."[2] Bob and Felix share Murray's hangdog vulnerability, awkward gait, wry detachment, and bursts of zany energy. The question of how possible it is to reform the cynical, charming playboy hovers over both films. Bob is an action-hero movie star who comes to learn the value of commitment and connection; Felix is a misogynist whose offensiveness is made tolerable by the charm he exudes and the excitement he creates. The sentimental education in *Lost in Translation* is a two-way process where Bob comes to realize, as Paul Julian Smith aptly puts it, "that a hard-won middle-aged marriage is worth more than a fling with a girl half his age" (quoted in McCabe 2009, 169). Bob can manage to both reassure Charlotte that she will emerge from the disappointment of her first marriage and retain his commitment to his wife despite the intimacy he shares with Charlotte. He learns to recognize the worth of marriage as the hero of a comedy of remarriage does—as a continued commitment to the ordinary and the daily. "There is no happy ending; there is only the beginning of a new day" as Wheatley neatly summarizes the logic for us (Wheatley 2019, 119). It is imperative then that *Lost in Translation* finishes with Bob leaving Japan and returning to his usual domestic setting. This is because reconciliation is easy away from the irritations of the daily grind, but it is this a marriage needs to reckon with.

We see this logic at work in *On the Rocks*. For all it shows us an enticing New York furnished by Felix's wealth, it is the golden world of Mexico that carves out a special place where Laura and Felix can listen to each other in healthy, affirmative ways. They share a difficult dinner where they discuss the unhappiness his infidelity caused to Laura's mother and Laura. For a moment, Felix stops his self-justifying rhetoric, explaining that when he and Laura's mother were first married, she "shone all her light" on him. Once they had children, she shifted that attention to them, and Felix began his affair with Holly. Laura responds with disgust and characterizes his behavior as childish, exclaiming "It's exhausting trying to love you enough!" The conversation then takes an unusual turn. Felix shares with Laura his sadness concerning Holly, telling Laura that she died recently. He then shares his happy memories of Holly, saying that she was funny, intelligent, and a good artist. When Laura asks if "it was worth it," Felix replies that it was "heartbreaking for everybody." This is a moment of profound recognition of both Laura and Holly as people, rather than as providers of "light" to shine on Felix. Felix holds back tears and turns to look at the ocean. Tragically, this moment of acknowledgment and recognition cannot be sustained within the logic of Felix's worldview. It is in the aftermath of this conversation that they discover Dean has already left Mexico to return to Laura in New York. Laura is distressed because she might have allowed Felix's jaundiced view of marriage to threaten her family and she accuses him with the question, "Can't you let anyone be happy?" The implied conclusion is that because of Felix's inability to commit to the daily routine of marriage but rather to continue to glide by on a superficial flirtatious charm he harms those he loves and deprives himself of meaningful connections. We see his ability to charm young children, waitresses, ballet dancers, hotel porters, and even police officers. What we don't see is the ability to acknowledge something beyond this and exist with adult people in the testing environment of everyday stresses and pressures of the wider world—family, work, society. In this light, Felix's retort to Laura after that question—"What happened to you? You used to be fun" shows everything that is toxic about this view of the world. Felix equates fun with novelty whereas the comedy of remarriage insists on the need to find pleasure within repetition and routine. His moment of recognition of the pain his behavior causes Laura is only too short-lived.

Blended Families on the Rocks

Coppola's film also acknowledges the toxicity of Felix's charm in other ways. It is noticeable that Laura is played by biracial Rashida Jones. Jones is the first prominent actor of color to be admitted into

Coppola's rarefied world, frequently criticized for its investments in melancholic whiteness as expression of feminine essence (Marsten 2018). Jones's presence inflects Coppola's study of a daughter finding her voice against a charming but overpowering patriarch with racial as well as gender difference. This plays out most clearly when Felix charms his way out of a speeding ticket. His biracial daughter, married to a Black man, tells him "It must be very nice to be you" as the police help him jump-start his car so he can be on his way. Jones discusses that moment in the film with *The Hollywood Reporter*, explaining,

> It is every level of privilege: older white man privilege, money privilege, charm privilege. All these things that are coming to this moment to conspire to really understand that character [Felix] and also her [Laura's] relationship with that character. We talked about, like, "What does she say? She has to say something. You don't have a Black family at home and see that moment happen and think, "Oh that was fun." You think, "If my family was in this car, that would go down in a completely different way." (O'Connell 2021)

Laura's difference from her father is racial as well as gendered, and the blended family that Coppola creates onscreen echoes Jones's own family heritage. The daughter of a Black father, Quincy Jones, and a white Jewish mother, Peggy Lipton, she is light-skinned with hazel eyes and wavy rather than curly hair. She has played characters who are explicitly white or of an ambiguous ethnicity, such as Karen Filipelli, an Italian-American woman, in *The Office* (2006–2009; 2011) and Ann Perkins in *Parks and Recreation* (2009–2015). In a 2005 interview with *Glamour* magazine headlined "Are You White or Are You Black?" Jones discusses her racial identity along with her sister Kadida and her parents. As children, they attended a majority white school in Los Angeles. Kadida stood out with her dark skin and curly hair, whereas Rashida blended in. When Kadida says that Rashida passed for white, Rashida responds that she had no control over her genetic inheritance, and that she never claimed whiteness. She explains that her ethnic ambiguity meant she felt she floated between different racial groups and identified more strongly with her Jewish ancestry than Kadida. Navigating Blackness as a white-passing person is a source of both privilege and pain for Rashida. She explains, "I feel guilty knowing that because of the way our genes tumbled out, Kadida had to go through pain I didn't have to endure"; Kadida later responds, "Rashida has it harder than I do. She gets rejection from both parties." (Weller 2005). In *On the Rocks*, Laura has a white father and a Black mother, and marries a smart, good-looking Black man. Coppola's city is notably diverse, full of different races and nationalities, but the one character who glides through it all, accessing all areas, is her white, art dealer father, Felix, able to flit between different locations with ease. The suspicion of infidelity that hovers over her husband is marked too by other tensions—despite his wealth and success, he cannot secure the access to the nostalgic old-time white New York of Bogart and Bacall that Laura's dad can, and they leave a noisy, overcrowded restaurant dejected and hassled. This is the first feature film in which Jones has played a character whose family background is the same as her own. She comments to the *LA Times* that:

> I wanted it to feel like my family and also I'm aware of the fact that representation is important. That's not something that's lost on me. At the beginning of my career, I didn't have a lot of say as to how I was portrayed, what my family looked like. And it was important to me to have a Black family. We had a lot of discussions about what that meant . . . We wanted to build a real family and a real relationship that felt like it could exist right now in a way that felt complex and complicated, but you know that they love each other. And that, to me, is part of filling in the spectrum of representation. It doesn't always have to look exactly the same to be Black on-screen. (Olsen 2020)

Cavell argues that the great question for both the comedy of remarriage and the melodrama of the unknown woman is the fitness of the man to undertake her education. The rivalry between Felix and Dean to fulfil this role in Laura's life is informed by a racial edge, as Dean cannot access all of Felix's unthinking charm and ease.

Felix's conception of beauty comes from a world that predates mechanical reproduction, let alone the dizzying virtuality of the digital. The Monet that he admires hanging in the corridor at the private party moves him not because he is trying to work out how to acquire it (he is attending the party to try and sell a Hockney) but because of its aura. He admires its shimmering depiction of ephemeral flowers; it prompts memories of the first time he saw a Monet at the Tuileries and driving to Giverny with Laura's mother. As Felix and Laura look at the painting, the background drone of the party conversation fades and is replaced by quasi-celestial electronic music that comes up high in the sound mix. The painting is signaled to us as sublime through this device. When Laura walks away from the camera, it stays staring at the painting, as if the viewer should also be entranced. The film here shares Felix's perspective rather than Dean's, valuing the unique and the bespoke over the ubiquitous and the democratic. The substantive import of *On the Rocks* lies in its rubbing up of Felix's universalizing conceptions of beauty as classical, white, privileged and corralled into enchanted spaces against Dean's racially coded urban, cosmopolitan cool, in which as many likes as possible are key to success. The film advances a critique of the digital and its ability to hollow out and misrecognize the world; the extent to which it critiques the embeddedness of the beautiful objects it enjoys in value systems that are redolent with racist and sexist worldviews remains an open question.

This leaves it all the more interesting to consider an exchange about hair between Felix, his granddaughters, and Laura. We see a lot of Laura's love and care for her daughters through her attention to their hair, watching her braiding their hair as part of their morning and evening routines. In an utterly beguiling moment, we see Felix and his granddaughters watching *Breaking Bad* (2008–2013) together (an incident that occurred with Coppola's own daughters and her father when he was babysitting) (Olsen 2020). Maya says that they have learned "that girls should grow their hair long and pretty, how boys like it!" Laura retorts "You can have your hair short or however you want!" Maya snaps back "Long and pretty!" and Felix tells her never to grow up. Felix's offhand linking of long hair to prettiness and sexual attractiveness ("how boys like it") belongs to the beauty ideals of white, European cultures. Popular contemporary cultural texts such as the Disney Princess franchise promote free-flowing long locks as the hair ideal for girls. Black hair, haunted by the specter of racial difference, can never be considered as neutral organic matter. The natural 'napped' characteristics of some Black hair are reclaimed by Black Pride and civil rights movements diametrically opposed to the straight blonde-hair ideals of white beauty cultures and the wigs, weaves, and extensions Black girls and women have deployed arguably to conform to such ideals (Lester 1999). Maya and Theo both have bouncy, textured curly hair. In the scene with Felix where they watch *Breaking Bad*, Maya's hair is sleekly pulled into a bun as she has been at ballet class and Theo's is in two thick fluffy bunches.[3] Neither girls could naturally wear their hair long and straight. Felix's comment, delivered lightheartedly, reflects his worldview that the most beautiful objects are those that reflect European heritage and ideals; he says this with no thought for how this might impact his granddaughters' sense of self.

Digital Patriarchs: Everywhere and Nowhere

In Cavell's 2005 letter to *Film Comment* on *Mr. and Mrs. Smith* (Doug Liman, 2005) he discusses "the present world's inhospitability to the comedy of remarriage in its active negating of the worlds of words and work" (*CF*, 432). Such inhospitability is acknowledged through Coppola's decision to split Laura's becoming between the worlds of her father (art, film, civilization, privilege, sexism, racism) and her husband (tech, digital, cool, progression, business, busyness, lostness). This is a comedy of remarriage in which it is Laura's father who has the leisure and thus the luxury to reach for recognition (however short-lived). Dean, her husband, is too busy with his job. Significantly, we never learn exactly what the business Dean works for does. Laura attends a party to celebrate the website hitting 500,000 active users, suggesting it is closely aligned to data capitalism that extracts profit from understanding people as specks of human capital, tracking them through their online lives and extracting and profiteering from information about their race, gender, and class. While *On the Rocks* shows a greater diversity and awareness of the politics of racial representation than any of Coppola's earlier work, especially as Jones's comments cited above indicate, this is immediately tempered by its setting in a world in which diversity is valued as a way of extending market share rather than militating for social justice. The film thus illuminates a struggle between Dean and Felix for the education of Laura. Felix is able to use his considerable privileges of charm, wealth, and whiteness to access spaces that remain closed off to Dean. Felix and Laura meet in secluded, quiet bars that allow for conversation, mainly in which Felix offers questionable riffs on evolutionary theory to justify his attraction to nubile young women, but which also permit moments of connection, recognition, and acknowledgement, such as a story about changing Laura's diaper when she was a baby, or the death of his second wife. Dean and Laura eat in overcrowded, noisy restaurants in which they can barely hear each other. Despite his considerable professional success, Dean cannot access the old New York and its provision of civilized space in which to converse; Felix's power to do this belongs to an outmoded culture, summed up both by his vintage car and his discussion of Humphrey Bogart and Lauren Bacall when he takes Laura for a drink at Bar 21.

Laura's anxiety about how to maintain her romantic and sexual connection with her husband, continue her own career as a novelist, and care for her daughters permeates the film. Coppola establishes the disconnect between the promise of the wedding ceremony and Laura's daily life with two contrasting shots. At Laura and Dean's wedding reception, the two slip away for time on their own. The camera points to the floor: it tracks to reveal the shoes and clothes they have removed, finishing on Laura's wedding dress. This is a pre-credits sequence. Following the title card, the camera mirrors the previous tracking shot, but to nonromantic effect. In a near-identical movement, the camera follows Laura's bare feet, showing a floor littered with children's clothes, toys, and food. Laura stoops to pick up the toys but leaves the food. These mirrored tracking shots exemplify the ongoing feminist debate over how to combine maternity and career. The evidence from the film is that Laura is trying to follow the advice of the tech gurus who also set up the kind of companies that demand the kind of busy absorption that pulls her husband Dean away from the home. Sheryl Sandberg's book, *Lean In: Women, Work, and the Will to Lead* (2013; cowritten with Nell Scovell), advocates a philosophy she names "lean-in feminism." This book features prominently on Laura's bookcase in the office where she tries—but fails—to express herself and write her next novel. Sandberg advises that women build resilience and find ways to prosper within current structures rather than advocating for revolutionary feminist change. It is no coincidence that Sandberg was the COO of Facebook, one of the five biggest and richest companies in the world (the others being Apple, Amazon, Microsoft and Alphabet-Google). In other words, Sandberg's book is Laura's problem while it masquerades as Laura's solution. Her husband is so absent as he has been absorbed into the alternative family of the digital tech companies that have risen to such prominence in the aftermath of the financial crash. His justification for going to Mexico when Laura points out that she does not get to escape the responsibilities of family life so easily is that "the whole team's going!"

Laura's kitchen door bears stickers for the "democratic social-ist" Democrat presidential nominee Bernie Sanders and Democrat voting rights activist Stacey Abrams. While this support might seem in contradiction to her embrace of Sandberg's book, such a combi-nation of progressive politics and pragmatic feminism in service of maintaining profit lines above other concerns is typical of the digital tech companies. They largely supported Sanders's bid rather than eventual Democrat nominee Hillary Clinton or Republican candidate and eventual winner Donald Trump. Despite this, on Trump's election he convened a power-meeting of many of the CEOs of these com-panies, at which Sandberg represented Facebook (one of only four women present, of whom another was Ivanka Trump. Twenty-one men attended) (Little and Winch 2021, 2–4). The everyday life where Cavell finds the philosophical truth of our need for recognition and acknowledgment is surveilled for economic exploitation. The logical outcome of lean-in feminism and its advice to women, that the answer to patriarchal oppression is to earn large sums of money working in digital tech companies so they become ever more powerful, is the total corporate penetration of the intimate sanctum of domestic life. What characterizes the digital and its constant collection of data via users, celebrated by Dean and his coworkers at the party where Laura feels so isolated, is the seizing of our "spaces of subjectivity" without us even realizing (Fuchs and Chandler 2019, 12). How are even economically comfortable men and women such as Laura and Dean meant to equitably share the work of raising a family when digital culture makes us available for work twenty-four hours a day and bonded to our colleagues as "a team"? These companies mold a new kind of patriarchal power that embraces a "geek" masculinity that *seems* more intersectional and socially aware but throws all the emotional labor of resilience and household management back onto women. A core quality of the network of "tech bros" according to Little and Winch is nevertheless that women have a subaltern role. Sandberg exemplifies how woman are encouraged to participate in and benefit from an elite patriarchal structure, striking bargains to find a place in its hierarchies. Her work argues that the problem is not the system, but that women lack the confidence to "lean-in" to the male-dominated workplace. She masquerades as a progressive thinker while advocating that the solution is for women to manage the balance between the private household and the corporate workspace as *the* way to achieve happiness. Part of the resilience the woman develops in this process comes from sharing, connecting extensively. As Little and Winch point out, this version of feminism conveniently also enables Facebook to monetize the data her female subject provides (Little and Winch 2021, 169).

It is no coincidence in this perspective that Laura's husband works for a digital tech company, allowing us to read Coppola's film as data from a society that demands extensive emotional labor from women as the price to manage their happiness and advocates resilience strategies rather than significant change. Dean says that he was working so hard to impress Laura and make the company successful, but there's no sense that he will (or can) fundamentally change. Laura finishes the film choosing the new Cartier watch her husband has bought her over the vintage watch gifted to her by her dad. She chooses the promise of a fresh start via a present that depends on Dean continuing to earn his generous salary working at his tech company over the gift from her dad, whose value derived from its uniqueness and the memories it evoked, linking it back to the aura generated by the Monet painting. The film ends then in a double bind. The sophisticated bars Felix and Laura retreat to are visions of cozy entitlement, where waiters and porters are ready to be charmed by even the slightest bit of attention and whose own sense of regret (from being a ballet dancer trained at the Bolshoi to serving cocktails?) would not even register. Yet it is in these beautiful bars, waited on by quasi-invisible staff shoring up old hierarchies of wealth and class, that Laura can actually carve out an intimate space to really be recognized and acknowledged by her dad (rather than sharing her story onto some anonymous digital platform ready to be monetized as Sandberg promotes). The film finishes then perhaps not so much on the rocks as in another uncomfortable place. Laura is caught between the rock of Dean's incorporation into a world that values people only as nuggets of profitable data and demands complete loyalty of its workers as the price for the generous salary; and the hard place of her dad's old-school charm that depends on a universalizing concept of beauty and truth impervious to the racist and sexist structures that enable its continuation. Computer algorithms cannot understand love, ethics, morals, solidarity, care; the distinctly human qualities that Laura aims to nurture within her marriage for her to become truly known.

Notes

1. The film was the first fictional feature film to be distributed under the terms of a new agreement between the indie film and television company A24 and Apple TV. The film had a limited theatrical release before being streamed on Apple TV. As Ryan Briggs comments, the industrial relationship confirmed the synergy between the two brands as concentrated on the prestige end of the media content market. By extension it confirms Coppola's own auteur brand as cool, hip, and media savvy (Briggs 2021, 101).

2. Alongside Gleiberman 2020 and Brody 2020, see also for example: Smith 2020 and Thompson 2021.

3. It is possible to achieve a sleek bun on natural Black hair and it seems that this is what Laura has done here. Even this style can be damaging for Black hair though—see Brown Girls Do Ballet (2021).

Works Cited

Adams, Sam. 2020. "What Is the Bougiest Status Symbol in Sofia Coppola's New Movie?" *Slate*, October 23, 2020. https://slate.com/culture/2020/10/sofia-coppola-on-the-rocks-movie-bougie-accessories.html/.

Bell, Keaton. 2020. "Sofia Coppola on Dressing Her Characters, Working With Her Husband, and Why We Need a Love Letter to New York Right Now." *Vogue*, October 31, 2020. https://www.vogue.com/article/sofia-coppola-on-the-rocks-interview/.

Briggs, Ryan. 2021. "'A Singular Fusion of Taste and Edge': A24 and the Indie Sector in the 2010s." PhD diss., University of Texas at Austin.

Brody, Richard. 2020. "*On the Rocks*, Reviewed: Sofia Coppola's Self-Questioning Film About a Father's Destructive Dazzle." *New Yorker*, October 22, 2020. https://www.newyorker.com/culture/the-front-row/on-the-rocks-reviewed-sofia-coppolas-self-questioning-film-of-a-fathers-destructive-dazzle/.

Brown Girls Do Ballet. 2021. "Ballet Bun Alternatives for Natural Hair." February 4, 2021. https://www.browngirlsdoballet.com/blog/2021/2/4/9xorlo4mx79e9ppstjvkgrzx1kvxap/.

Campion, Jane. 2022. "Jane Campion Best Director for *The Power of the Dog* Full Backstage Speech." *Variety*. https://www.youtube.com/watch?v=NH2gS5IWD_0/.

Fuchs, Christian, and David Chandler. 2019. "Introduction." In *Digital Objects, Digital Subjects: Interdisciplinary Perspectives on Capitalism, Labour and Politics in the Age of Big Data*, edited by Christian Fuchs and David Chandler. University of Westminster Press. https://doi.org/10.16997/book29.

Gleiberman, Owen. 2020. "*On the Rocks* Review: Bill Murray, His Scampishness Undimmed, Reunites with *Lost in Translation* Director Sofia Coppola." *Variety*, September 22, 2020. https://variety.com/2020/film/reviews/on-the-rocks-bill-murray-rashida-jones-sofia-coppola-1234777605/.

Harrod, Mary. 2021. *Heightened Genre and Women's Filmmaking in Hollywood: The Rise of the Cine-fille*. Palgrave. https://doi.org/10.1007/978-3-030-70994-5.

Hattersley, Giles. 2020. "We Didn't Know We Were Making a Period Movie: Behind the Scenes of *On the Rocks* with Sofia Coppola." *Vogue*, October 11, 2020. https://www.vogue.co.uk/arts-and-lifestyle/article/sofia-coppola-on-the-rocks-interview/.

Hirschberg, Lynn. 2003. "The Coppola Smart Mob." *New York Times Magazine*, August 31, 2003. https://www.nytimes.com/2003/08/31/magazine/the-coppola-smart-mob.html/.

King, Geoff. 2010. *Lost in Translation*. Edinburgh University Press.

Klevan, Andrew. 2000. *Disclosure of the Everyday: Undramatic Achievement in Narrative* Film. Flicks Books.

LaRocca, David, ed. 2021a. *Movies with Stanley Cavell in Mind*. New York: Bloomsbury Academic.

LaRocca, David. 2021b. "Introduction: The Seriousness of Film Sustained." In LaRocca, *Movies with Stanley Cavell in Mind*.

LaRocca, David. 2021c. "Contemplating the Sounds of Contemplative Cinema: Stanley Cavell and Kelly Reichardt." In LaRocca, *Movies with Stanley Cavell in Mind*.

Lester, Neal A. 1999. "Roots That Go Beyond Big Hair and a Bad Hair Day: Nappy Hair Pieces." *Children's Literature in Education* 30 (3): 181–83. https://doi.org/10.1023/A:1022481118075.

Little, Ben, and Alison Winch. 2021. *The New Patriarchs of Digital Capitalism: Celebrity Tech Founders and Networks of Power*. Routledge.

Marsten, Kendra. 2018. *Postfeminist Whiteness: Problematising Melancholic Burden in Contemporary Hollywood*. Edinburgh University Press.

McCabe, Janet. 2009. "Lost in Transition: Problems of Modern (Heterosexual) Romance and the Catatonic Male Hero in the Post-Feminist Age." In *Falling in Love Again: Romantic Comedy in Contemporary Cinema*, edited by Stacey Abbott and Deborah Jermyn. I. B. Tauris.

Negra, Diane, and Hannah Hamad. 2020. "The New Plutocratic (Post)Feminism." In *The New Feminist Literary Studies*, edited by

Jennifer Cooke. Cambridge University Press. https://doi.org/10.1017/9781108599504.007.

Nolfi, Joey. 2020. "Sofia Coppola Says Dad's Spirit Lives in Bill Murray's *On the Rocks* Character." *EW*, October 22, 2020. https://ew.com/movies/sofia-coppola-francis-ford-coppola-inspired-on-the-rocks/.

O'Connell, Mikey. 2021. "*On the Rocks*: Sofia Coppola and Rashida Jones Talk About Their Long History and Bill Murray's Stunt Driving." *Hollywood Reporter*, February 1, 2021. https://www.hollywoodreporter.com/movies/movie-news/on-the-rocks-sofia-coppola-and-rashida-jones-talk-about-their-long-history-and-bill-murrays-stunt-driving-4120731/.

Olsen, Mark. "How Sofia Coppola and Rashida Jones Put Their Own Family Lives into *On the Rocks*." *LA Times*, September 23, 2020. https://www.latimes.com/entertainment-arts/movies/story/2020-09-23/sofia-coppola-rashida-jones-on-the-rocks/.

Oxford Languages. 2018. "Word of the Year 2018 Shortlist." https://languages.oup.com/word-of-the-year/2018-shortlist/.

Rennebohm, Kate, and Catherine Wheatley. 2022. "Projecting Cavell: New Contexts, New Questions." *Screen* 63 (1): 92–99. https://doi.org/10.1093/screen/hjac002.

Sandberg, Sheryl, 2015. *Lean In: Women, Work, and the Will to* Lead. W. H. Allen.

Smith, Orla. 2020. "*On the Rocks* is a Retrograde Disappointment from Sofia Coppola." *Seventh Row*, October 22, 2020. https://seventh-row.com/2020/10/22/on-the-rocks-review/.

Thompson, Anne. 2021. "Sofia Coppola Speaks for Bill Murray and Defines His Elusive Charm in *On the Rocks*." *IndieWire*, May 1, 2021. https://www.indiewire.com/awards/industry/bill-murray-movie-on-the-rocks-sofia-coppola-1234619973/.

Weller, Sheila. 2005. "Are You White or Are You Black?" *Glamour*, October 2005.

Wheatley, Catherine. 2019. *Stanley Cavell and Film: Scepticism and Self-Reliance at the Cinema*. Bloomsbury Academic.

Wheatley, Catherine. 2021. "Passionate Utterances: Cavell, Film, and The Female Voice." In LaRocca, *Movies with Stanley Cavell in Mind*.

14

The Proving Window

Inversion, Perfectionism, and the Unknown Woman in Christopher Nolan's *Tenet*

Stephen Mulhall

IT IS HARDLY SURPRISING THAT the initial reception of *Tenet* (Christopher Nolan, 2020)—already muffled and distorted in various ways by the Covid-19 pandemic—would be dominated by the most obvious features and consequences of its defining idea: the technology of entropy inversion, which allows objects and people to move backwards through time. The most immediate effect of Christopher Nolan's realization of this idea is a new, exhilarating, and compellingly pure form of cinematic pleasure: directly apprehending bullets travelling back into guns, and fights and car chases involving the inter-action of normal and inverted people and vehicles, and indirectly marveling at how little CGI was involved in achieving these sequences. The next most immediate effect was, however, less pleasurable. Most viewers were willing, on the basis of their experience of earlier Nolan films, to assume that the plot he constructed to contain and exploit his idea would be rigorously faithful to its internal logic; and Nolan is very careful to introduce the full range of inversion technology and its ramifying implications gradually. First there is a single inverted gun, then the turnstile technology that effects inversion realized first on the scale of a single man, then one large enough for cars, then one capable of inverting an army, and finally the sought-after algorithm's ability to invert the world. Even so, when watching the film for the first time, it was extremely challenging to see how the (local and general) course of events cohered with the rules of this idea. More bluntly, it was difficult simply to grasp what was going on, and became increasingly difficult as more of the inversion technology's powers were disclosed. As a result, much of the critical discussion of the film has focused on evaluating whether, and if so how, Nolan actually succeeded in cleaving to his rules for inversion in each set piece. Much of the initial audience reaction suggested that worrying about this aspect of the film had got in the way of the suspension of disbelief that Nolan achieved so effortlessly even in such conceptually complex films as *Memento* (2000) and *Inception* (2010).

In this chapter, I intend to follow the advice the Protagonist (John David Washington) receives from Barbara (Clémence Poésy) when he is first introduced to the Tenet research program on inverted munitions: "Don't try to understand it. *Feel* it." I propose to try to understand the film by concentrating on what the theory and practice of inversion technology allow Nolan to achieve emotionally and imaginatively—on the mythology of inversion rather than its logic. Instead of obsessing over whether inverting entropy would or wouldn't allow an inverted person to drive a noninverted car, or render the simultaneous implementation of two opposed temporal pincer movements feasible, I want to ask what a narrative dependent on such a patent impossibility might nevertheless be in a position to tell us about matters of real and perennial human significance—what themes and questions it allows the filmmaker to articulate and reflect upon that he would not otherwise be in a position to project and screen, including questions about the conditions for the possibility of his doing this at all, and about the likely responses to it (questions about the nature of the medium of cinema). And in doing so, I will in part be assuming that these themes and questions constitute extensions or elaborations of those with which his previous films are preoccupied—matters that (as I have argued extensively elsewhere) bear upon some themes and questions in Stanley Cavell's body of work on film.[1]

The Protagonist's Antagonist

We can usefully begin with the Protagonist, and approach the way inversion technology weaves itself into his mission by considering the miraculous fight scene in the Oslo freeport facility. This phase of the mission involves the Protagonist and Neil (Robert Pattinson) breaking into the facility in order to steal a forged painting that Sator (Kenneth Branagh) is using to maintain control over his wife, Kat (Elizabeth Debicki); she is willing to betray her husband if they can render his blackmail strategy impotent. But before they can locate the painting, they find one of Sator's turnstiles, from which we see two men emerge simultaneously on either side of the glass window that divides the space: Neil chases one and the Protagonist grapples with the other, who turns out to be inverted, and we are thereby granted a vision of an impossible struggle in which each perceives the other as fighting backwards. At the end of the fight, the Protagonist's inverted opponent escapes—although only because Neil (returning from his chase empty-handed) prevents the Protagonist from shooting him. But the two Tenet operatives have no time left to look for the painting, so their plan has been derailed—apparently by a very peculiar contingency.

It doesn't take long for the film to make it clear that the two men who leapt from the turnstile were in fact one: what we saw, by virtue of what is later called the "proving window," was one man entering the turnstile, being inverted, and exiting. But it takes much longer for us to appreciate that this man is in fact the Protagonist. Having inverted himself in the Tallinn turnstile after the failure of the "plutonium" heist that follows his failure to steal the painting, he has travelled backward through time to in order to save Kat from the consequences of being shot by an inverted bullet—the only possible treatment is inversion, and the only turnstile he knows of that will be available for her reversion from that inversion is in Oslo. In other words, the Protagonist's antagonist was himself.

Mythologically speaking, this tells us that the Protagonist's story is one of internal conflict, that this point in his narrative is one at which that conflict becomes particularly pronounced, and that how one adjudicates that conflict depends on which side of the Protagonist one sides with. The noninverted Protagonist is at this point attempting to find a way of using Kat to gain access to Sator: her abject condition is of interest to him only insofar as it helps him to attain his mission objective, and when he is prevented from seizing the tool that will allow him to extort her aid, he simply lies to her about his failure, and thereby encourages her to act on a mistaken assumption of renewed freedom that only further humiliates her in Sator's eyes (when he reveals that he still has the painting).

But the inverted Protagonist is on a mission to save Kat's life even though it risks derailing his campaign against Sator. From his perspective, the fight he goes through in Oslo is part of an attempt to rectify the moral degradation of his earlier approach to Kat, and to life. Our second pass as viewers through the Oslo sequence reveals to us that the noninverted Protagonist was fighting against his better nature, his unattained but attainable self. Even as he executes this phase of his cynically consequentialist strategy, something he doesn't recognize within himself—something that presents itself as threatening to upend his world—resists his current belief that the stakes of his mission justify pretty much any kind of mistreatment of others, making it legitimate for him to regard them solely as either obstacles or resources. And once that repressed aspect of himself has made its mark on him, obscurely and bewilderingly but undeniably, it initiates a shift or rebalancing of his sense of who he is, and allows him to find another way of interpreting (and so a way of reclaiming ownership of) his earlier trajectory through the world.

For by inverting himself in Tallinn, the Protagonist transfigures what he had earlier regarded as a dazzling coup baulked by an arbitrary obstacle into a life-affirming self-sacrifice. The noninverted Protagonist's unsuccessful attempt to treat Kat as a mere means is at one and the same time his inverted counterpart's successful attempt to acknowledge her as an end in herself. From one point of view, this manipulative act was always already an act of altruism; from another point of view, it only becomes an act of altruism if the Protagonist comes to want it to be so, and to act on that desire. In other words, it becomes an act of altruism only if the Protagonist becomes altruistic; but in so transforming or inverting himself, he becomes what he always already was. This is Nolan's way of employing inversion technology to project and screen—to interpret cinematically—perfectionism's conception of our unattained selves as neighboring our attained ones, only a shift of perspective away, but one whose attainment requires us to become our own antagonists.

Unknownness as a Defense, as a Weapon

This interest in a perfectionist conception of selfhood is not just consonant with Nolan's more general perfectionism as a director; it is one of the central points of connection between his and Cavell's thinking, and—like Cavell—it is one that he further links with the issue of skepticism (and in particular the way external world skepticism and other minds skepticism mirror one another), and so with the interrelated genres of remarriage comedy and the melodrama of the unknown woman. *Inception* is perhaps the exemplary instance of Nolan's receptive interrogation of these Cavellian themes, and briefly recapitulating its creative revisions of those themes will help to understand the ways in which *Tenet* constitutes a further step on that philosophical path.

Inception's nested dreamworlds are presented not only as the site of larcenous attempts to implant and extract ideas that problematize our assumption that our minds are our own but also as the backdrop to the life and death of a marriage in the grip of skeptical doubt. It shows Cobb (Leonardo DiCaprio) and Mal (Marion Cotillard) awakening from a shared dream in which they grew old together, to find that their marriage no longer enables the fulfilment of reciprocal desire. Mal's loss of faith finds expression in a skeptical paroxysm: she turns their previously "meet and happy" (Milton, qtd. in *PH*, 87) conversations into a mutually uncomprehending argument about the reality of their present world, in the course of which her judgement of it as inherently uninhabitable by her—epitomized in her doubt that her children are hers—transcends her husband's capacity to refute it. Her passion to reach a genuinely real reality is such that she is willing to abandon her children and force her husband to choose between suicide, incarceration, and exile in order to attain it; she wants Cobb to choose death (and so real life) with her over life with their children (but without her). This is the fanaticism of love: Cobb can truly be hers only if nothing and no one else stands between them—only if they are everything to each other, exemplary of the world as such in a world that is utterly subject to their essentially single will. In comparison to this, the real world of independent others (including the autonomous offspring of their love) becomes as toys; she chooses to die to a world that has gone dead for her, and in a manner calculated to make chaos come again for her family.

Cobb's and Mal's relationship thus draws faithfully upon the founding myths of remarriage comedy and their companion melodramas. For their story pivots around the point at which the two people's prior willingness endlessly to remarry one another (in effect renewing their vows every time they return from dream to reality) runs out, in which their meet and happy conversation is negated by skeptical irony and mutual victimization, and the root motive for their subjecting themselves to the accelerating threat of divorce (one person's passionate refusal to accept the other's independence, or the independent reality of the world they inhabit, or the internal relation between the two as that finds expression in the natural consequence of their sexual satisfaction) is apparently death-dealing.

Inception thereby addresses a question that the generic adjacency of the comedies and the melodramas invite us to pose: what happens to the spouse who appears immune to, or at least capable of, resisting or overcoming skepticism when the spouse who succumbs to it has definitively removed herself from the scene? In the comedies, the irruption of skeptical anxiety can be overcome in light of the couple's continuing willingness to remain available to educate one another. In the melodramas, when the unacknowledged woman divorces herself from the villainously inadequate man (even removes herself from the scene altogether, as Lisa does in *Letter from an Unknown Woman* [Max Ophüls, 1948]), she reveals their relationship as never having been (or even having had the potential to be) mutually satisfying, hence not something that could be recovered or redeemed. The issue Cobb faces is how to accept the incomprehensible and unalterable transformation of his marriage from a state in which it realized the best aspirations of the comedies to a state in which it realized the worst fears of the melodramas.

This creative revision of the founding myths of these genres also negates a fatefully central clause of Cavell's skeptical myth as it finds expression in the Shakespearean source of its cinematic incarnations, *The Winter's Tale*—the one which states that insofar as skepticism finds expression as a doubt as to whether your children are yours, it is not a feminine business. For *Inception* positively underlines the fact that Mal is someone whose skepticism finds expression in that form, and thereby dictates the basic shape of events in her world: the fate of her children is the fundamental issue for its protagonist, and its resolution provides the climax of the film. Mal is what it would look like if Hermione doubted whether her children were hers.

Cavell's consequent conception of skepticism as a gendered business canvasses two possible ways of distinguishing its feminine from its masculine inflections—by reference to the object of the doubt, and by reference to its prevailing passion. The object of Mal's doubt is definitely masculine (the children as opposed to their father, and as subject to the telling of specific differences), but her passion—being an exemplary instance of obsessive or fanatical love, a drive towards an unconditioned form of its fulfilment that amounts to a refusal of finitude (as manifest in her devotion to the Limbo version of her marriage)—is equally definitely feminine. And yet Cavell also ends his discussion of the fanaticism of love understood as the refusal of finitude with the (far from transparent) declaration that "this . . . is what permits me to describe Leontes as a portrait of the sceptic as fanatic" (*DK*, 17). Perhaps, then, we should regard Mal as a projection of the actual Leontes rather than of an imaginary Hermione—as the cinematic realization of a Cavellian interpretation of Leontes's skepticism as combining masculine hyperbolic doubt with feminine hyperbolic love, declaring each inflection of skepticism as internally related to the other (and so available either as proxy or disguise for the other), as the feminine is to and for the masculine.

A further complication arises from the film's way of envisioning other minds skepticism as an issue of plagiarism. For although it is Mal who becomes possessed by the skeptical idea and destroys her husband and children as a consequence, she brings it back with her into the real world because her husband devoted all of his energies in Limbo to the task of implanting it in her (achieving its inception by locating and manipulating the telltale cone totem which she had consigned to irrelevance out of love, so that it might once again activate her desire to reinhabit the everyday reality of their marriage and family life). Mal's subjection to skepticism, and her family's subsequent subjection to it, is thus ultimately the responsibility of her husband: the idea is his, although she gives it expression and application. In other words, Mal's fate is to live her husband's skepticism, and his simultaneous persecution by the monstrous hostility of his projections of Mal whenever he subsequently enters a dreamworld amounts to a further acknowledgement of his own guilt about the consequences of that originally sinful act of inception.

So understood, Cobb resembles the villainous males of the melodramas—perhaps most closely Paula's husband, Gregory Anton (Charles Boyer), in *Gaslight* (George Cukor, 1944), whose attempts to locate a hoard of jewels leads him to implant ideas in Paula's mind which loosen her grip on reality, deprive her of words for the world of her experience, and threaten to destroy the psyche they inhabit. Nolan's film presents a comparable image of marriage as vampirism, of cursed or curdled intimacy as a matter of one life's sapping of another, driven by the man's wanting to know what the woman knows, or more precisely by his picturing the woman's unknownness as a matter of her knowing something that he does not, something she prevents him from knowing by withholding it, locating it somewhere inaccessibly private. Hence the man devotes himself to gaining control over it, whether by penetrating that privacy or by ensuring that whatever it contains never finds expression—both approaches being routes for mastering the woman's voice, more precisely for depriving her of a voice of her own.[2] But this obsessive desire to open or close the woman's private chamber or closet is in fact a projection: it pictures her individual reality as posing a problem of knowledge rather than of acknowledgement, and it externalizes a secret about himself that he cannot not know but that he nevertheless refuses to acknowledge—Cavell calls it the feminine register or tone of his own (human) voice, a register that the man thinks of as essentially private in order (according to circumstances) either to account for his failure to use it, or to deny that it finds expression despite himself in everything he says.

Cobb's act of inception against his wife involves him in penetrating and manipulating the contents of just such a private space; he does so in order that she do what he wishes without doing it because she wants to do it, so that from that point on her life and her voice are no longer her own; and even after her real voice is silenced, she endlessly reappears within him as a persecutory self-projection, more specifically as someone who knows everything he does (from whom nothing can be hidden) and whose implacable hostility must therefore give expression to a feminine aspect of himself that he experiences as essentially beyond his control, and as having lethally violent designs on his subjectivity.

In the end, however, to demonize Cobb would be no more accurate to the film's perception of things than to demonize Mal—who first creates both the private safe and its contents, which Cobb violates only in response to her hyperbolic attempt to make their relationship infinite and all-consuming. Ultimately, however, attempts to assign responsibility for the corruption of their marriage fail to appreciate the most significant thing about it—the fact that the boundary between Mal and Cobb is one that neither finds it possible to draw, or to acknowledge. Just as their creations in Limbo are essentially joint affairs, so neither seems in a position confidently to claim any idea about themselves or their world as theirs as opposed to their partner's. Ownership of the skeptical idea is not ultimately settleable between them, because neither Mal nor Cobb has succeeded in acknowledging the separateness of each other's minds, and so their individual agency and independent reality.

The Cavellian reference point here is his reading of *Macbeth*, according to which the Macbeth marriage is one in which each reads the other's mind so readily and exhaustively—each constantly articulating what the other has it in mind to say, or not saying what the other will not say, each imagining the other to have conceived of the idea on which he or she is acting, hence thinking of himself or herself as the embodiment or externalization of that other's thoughts—that they seem to be trapped or imprisoned in one another's minds, quite as if the idea that there are two such minds at issue remains unacknowledged or unrealized (and of course, in a way that raises questions about their children). Nolan likewise presents Cobb's inability to mourn as a matter of his mind's being ineradicably inhabited by Mal, and identifies his redemption as requiring a willingness to acknowledge that the Mal he encounters in his nested dreamworlds all the way down to Limbo is not Mal herself—not the real, independent person whose separateness is definitively established by the fact that her death does not cause or constitute his. Only when Cobb acknowledges himself as alive can he free himself from the limbo of his current existence, and confront the existing consequences of his love for his dead wife.

Understood in the terms I've just laid out, then, *Inception* shows how, for Nolan, the collapsing boundaries between the pair in a marriage rendered vampiric by skepticism mirror the way the boundaries between the neighboring genres of remarriage comedy and melodramas of the unknown woman might similarly break down, and thereby motivate an investigation into the consequent transpositions and inversions of Cavell's original assignments of skeptical and antiskeptical traits between the men and women of both genres. And one illuminating way into *Tenet* is to appreciate the extent to which—despite the film's commitment to tracking the Protagonist's perspective on its events—its primary dramatic context is in fact the death-in-life of the marriage between Sator and Kat, and its primary concern is consequently to track that relationship's specific transfigurations of Cavellian skeptical tropes, both gendered and generic.

Kat—Katherine Barton—is the eldest niece of Sir Frederick Barton (Michael Caine), and so a means by which Sator can penetrate the British establishment and its security services in the furtherance of the goals of his patrons from the future. Initially happy, she quickly realizes that she is simply one more beautiful object in Sator's collection; and when (in the course of her work at Shipley's, an auction house specializing in fine art) she authenticates a fake Rubens that is bought by her husband before the error is spotted, he interprets her action as a betrayal and uses it to blackmail her—threatening her with prison unless she accepts his complete control over her and her relationship with their son Max (Laurie Shepherd). So when the Protagonist offers to steal the Rubens from Oslo Freeport in return for her help in infiltrating Sator's operation, Kat leaps at it. But the Protagonist fails and then lies to her about his failure, giving her false hope that Sator takes pleasure in destroying; having redoubled her humiliation, the Protagonist then thwarts her attempt to kill Sator during a catamaran race, and—by requesting her involvement in the Tallinn theft—ensures that she is available to be punched, kicked, and then shot with an inverted bullet, whose devastating impact is akin to a lethal dose of radiation poisoning.

So far, then, we have a peculiarly bleak melodrama of a woman for whom the villainy of her husband is matched only by the villainy of the man who presents himself as her longed-for means of escape from that cursed marriage: neither evince the slightest concern for her or her son, the slightest inclination to overcome her unknownness by acknowledgement. It's as if the detective in *Gaslight* was revealed as only another Gregory to Paula, another man whose real attention lies elsewhere (an interpretation of Joseph Cotton's character that is not entirely ungrounded, if one considers the extent to which his interest in Paula is driven by his earlier childhood fixation with her aunt). And the Protagonist never shakes off this taint of villainy, even after his choice to privilege his unattained self in Tallinn, and thereby to alter Kat's fate; it is this—and not some failure of chemistry between the actors or failure of storytelling by the director—that accounts for the fact that *Tenet* refuses to satisfy its viewers' expectation that the Protagonist will constitute Kat's erotic salvation. But matters are in truth rather more complex than this initial impression of Kat's absolute victimhood would suggest.

First, although Kat wants to believe that her authentication of the Rubens was a mistake on her part, she also admits that during the authentication process she may have got rather too close to the forger (Tomas Arepo), so she cannot honestly say that it was simply a professional failure, and hence that Sator is simply wrong to view it as a betrayal. Kat thus resembles Will Dormer (Al Pacino) in Nolan's *Insomnia*, in that she is in this crucial respect an enigma to herself. It's not that either she did or she didn't mean to misidentify Arepo's painting, but she isn't certain which: it's that there is no truth of the matter—the real meaning of what she did, and to that extent of who she is (fallible expert or unfaithful spouse), is essentially indeterminate, unknowable because there is nothing to know. In which case, Sator's error is not being overly confident that he knows what this woman is trying and failing to conceal from him; it's more that he errs in thinking there is something here to know—some specific fact about Kat's motives and character, some particular secret in the closet of her consciousness. In fact, with respect to her faithfulness as a wife, this woman is unknown because she is unknowable, even to herself; and as such, she is bound to constitute a particularly painful pebble in Sator's shoe, because his access to our descendants' knowledge and inversion technology allows him to manipulate our present and anticipate our future so extensively (as when he renders the Protagonist's raid in Oslo pointless, or when he deploys a temporal pincer movement during the Tallinn heist) that he appears effectively omniscient and omnipotent with respect to achieving the outcomes he desires regardless of what happens to happen in the world. Little wonder that he reacts so brutally to any suggestion of unknownness in the world of his marriage, preferring to disdain Kat as transparently unfaithful rather than admit that her fidelity exceeds his cognitive grasp.

The second complication is that Kat's response to her husband's brutality is hardly lacking in brutality itself. She hurls him from the catamaran with the words "Burn in hell, Andrei," and ultimately she proves willing to shoot him even before she knows that the Protagonist's efforts have neutralized his dead man's switch, which amounts to risking the annihilation of the world (including herself and her son) in order to ensure that Sator dies knowing his plan has failed. And the film makes it clear that the taproot of this vengeful fury is not simply Sator's cold malevolence towards her; it is the fact that when (on the holiday in Vietnam) he offers her a divorce on condition that she leave Max with him, Sator sees in her eyes that for an instant she was tempted to accept. On this ground, Kat would give a great deal to have remained unknown—because here there was something about her to know, and Sator's coming to know it makes it impossible for her to deny it to herself, let alone to him. Unknownness here becomes a condition she yearns for, rather than a coercive imposition; to keep it within the closet of her consciousness would allow her to avoid acknowledging it to herself, let alone to Sator.

This sense of debilitating exposure explains why she is willing to return to the yacht (and the afternoon) on which that fateful moment of self-revelation took place—the moment to which Sator plans to return and activate the algorithm's world-inverting power because it was the last golden moment at which she tried to recover her initial love for him. It's not because she is truly committed to her official role as a backstop should the Protagonist's temporal pincer strategy at Stalsk-12 fail; it's because she wants to weave into the fabric of that horrifying afternoon a compensatory or counter-revelation of herself as master rather than victim, as the one whose scarring by her husband has made her stronger rather than weaker, someone who responds not by offering a placatory mimesis of love but an aria of death-dealing revenge.

Should we, then, regard the point at which the film's inversion technology is made known to Kat—during her inverted trip from Tallinn to Oslo—as the moment at which, due to the Protagonist's willingness to overcome his own initial villainousness, she acquires the possibility of escaping her husband's control and recovering herself and her son from their shared condition of lacking a voice in their own histories (Max is strikingly mute throughout the film)?

Tenet's presentation of this scene certainly allows for such a reading. For when she is initially recounting it to the Protagonist before the events at Oslo, she mentions returning to the yacht with her son after having rejected her husband's offer and seeing another woman dive off its top deck into the water. Kat the narrator assumes this woman is another of Sator's mistresses, and describes her as an enviable image of the freedom she yearns for; but it turns out that it is Kat herself, as she makes another pass through the scene after recovering from her wound. One might see this as an exemplary image of perfectionist self-overcoming, in part because the film doesn't tell us that the scene could have had two different outcomes between which Kat chooses (and then regrets her choice); it rather makes clear that it is only by accepting and undergoing the full pain of the consequences resulting from the choice she did make that she arrives at the possibility of attaining her freedom. The Kat whose dive from the yacht encapsulates her freedom is and could only be the Kat who hesitated over and then refused Sator's offer: the diving woman is not the person Kat might have become had she chosen otherwise, but rather the person she does become only because she chose to reject her freedom on the terms in which Sator presented it—it is the self she attains only because she rendered it attainable by refusing (however hesitantly) to attain it then and there, when it could only have been a freedom that was not authentically hers, but rather one made in her husband's demeaning image (of her as defined by her hesitation rather than its overcoming).

On the other hand, the woman who dives off the yacht has just murdered her husband; and she has chosen to do so in violation of her backstop role, in a way which risks world-annihilating inversion, essentially because she cannot bear her husband to die in the mistaken belief that his plans have succeeded, and more specifically in the mistaken belief that the woman with whom he is spending his final golden moment is the one who earlier left the boat with her spirit broken, rather than the one he thinks is dead, but who has been resurrected by inversion and is hell-bent on ending his life. In short, Kat acts prematurely because she requires her husband's acknowledgement of her self-overcoming, as if she still attributes authority to his gaze—the gaze which exposed her self-condemning hesitation earlier that afternoon. She needs him to hear that she has recovered her voice, and to know that she is ending the shared world of their marriage, even if her absolute repudiation of it risks becoming a repudiation of the world as such—as if her final judgement on her marriage amounted to the Last Judgment. In this respect she mirrors Sator's solipsistic willingness to make the end of the world of his experience coincide with the end of the world.

In his phone conversation with the Protagonist just before his murder, Sator claims that his solipsism is rooted in his lack of belief in the distinctness of the world from his experience of it; but this invocation of epistemology is a cover for an essentially emotional logic—the logic disclosed when Kat asks why he won't give her a divorce. He replies, Leontes-like, that if he can't have her no one can; and the film implies that the fanatical jealousy with which he maintains the world of his marriage merely reflects his attitude towards the world as such: if he can't have it, no one can. The deity after whom Sator fashions himself is thus not just omniscient and omnipotent, but possessive: he is a jealous God. So could fashioning herself after Sator really amount to Kat's achievement of freedom—from him, from her marriage, and from the person that marriage had reduced her to? It seems rather that it is only by taking on her husband's jealous rage that she finds the strength to escape him, and the world that rage informs; it's as if Kat can recover her own voice only by internalizing one villainous inflection of the masculine register of the human voice.

Whether she can then dispense with that register is something that the film leaves open, by concluding its narrative immediately after the Protagonist saves her from Priya's (Dimple Kapadia) desire to destroy anything and anyone who might reveal the truth about the algorithm's fate to the future. We might draw an optimistic conclusion from the fact that Kat in effect saves herself by accepting the Protagonist's offer to leave him a message should she feel unsafe—that is, by accepting that there is at least one man whose responsiveness to her voice might prove life-giving. Or we might feel that the matter could only be definitively settled by seeing and hearing the voice her son acquires by virtue of her single parenting; but here Nolan maintains his silence by maintaining Max's silence—instead offering us Neil's voice, over an image of Kat and Max walking hand-in-hand away from the camera, talking of the bomb that doesn't go off as the one with the real power to change the world.

Is Max the unexploded bomb? If so, is that because Kat will fail to overcome the masculine register of voice and experience that his father has already implanted in him? Or is it because he represents the future generation whose confrontation with a climate catastrophe created by their ancestors is precisely what led to the desperately vengeful deployment of inversion technology to make a future out of the past for those whose (grand)parents have deprived them of the kind of future their predecessors took for granted? Just before Kat kills him, Sator looks out at the setting sun and remarks that tomorrow it will rise in that exact spot, and all because he has told it to. This certainly underlines his kinship with the wife in the Grimm Brothers' fairy tale "The Fisherman and His Wife" ([1812] 2007), who comes to resent the sun's and the moon's rising and falling independently of her will; but it does so by turning or transfiguring a perfectionist trope beloved of Emerson and Thoreau, and of Nietzsche, who variously tell us that the sun is but a morning star, and that the overman (the man of self-overcoming) belongs to tomorrow and the day after tomorrow. If Sator has his way with the world, the new morning, like tomorrow, lies behind us; but if we refuse to allow the possibility of a future generation's having a future, where else can they look for the time in which to aspire to, let alone to realize, their unattained but attainable selves?

Impossible Perspectives and Inordinate Meaning

Kat is not the only person who is present in more than one place on the day on which the film's narrative begins and ends. Sator is on the yacht and in Kyiv stealing a component of the algorithm from the CIA team at the opera house; the Protagonist is at the opera house and in the battle at Stalsk-12; and Neil is at the opera house (rescuing the Protagonist with an inverted round) and at several different locations around Stalsk-12 during the climactic temporal pincer movement (having to invert and revert multiple times in order to do so). In this respect, the film as a whole exemplifies the recuperative or redemptive inversion structure of the temporal pincer movements that are enacted at various points and at both individual and collective scales throughout its individual episodes: one might say that it takes the whole of *Tenet* to properly fill out the picture of the particular day that it so partially presents in its opening scene.

The events at Stalsk-12—in which inverted and noninverted individuals on both sides confront each other in a disorienting array of interlocking combinations—loom large in the film's second pass through that day; and as result, they offer a large-scale reprise of the Protagonist's fight with himself in Oslo that invites us to view Stalsk-12 as a mythological representation of our struggle with ourselves over the climate catastrophe we are already preparing for our future selves. Most immediately, the struggle is between the Tenet operatives and Sator's gang—a conflict that the Protagonist characterizes as one between our generation looking out for our survival and a traitor bringing death to his own generation because his own life has run out. In this respect, the film plainly invites us to identify with the Tenet operatives, and since their success spells defeat for our descendants' attempt to provide themselves with a future, one might think that this amounts to Nolan's endorsing the general principle that one should privilege the present generation over future generations. Such a conclusion could only reinforce concerns that critics have already voiced over *Interstellar* (2014), which has been interpreted as assuming that our planet is beyond redemption, fit only to be abandoned.

However, endorsing such an inference depends on overlooking two crucial points. First, Sator was produced by our past, and more specifically by our willingness to gamble the future of our planet for the sake of proliferating nuclear weapons kept under control only by the insane doctrine of mutually assured destruction. He discovers the first cache of money and weapons from the future only because he grew up in a secret city devoted entirely to the production of those weapons, and he acquired the plutonium that fueled his criminal career and caused his lethal cancer because he was exploited to clear it up from accident sites. In other words, in struggling against Sator, Tenet is struggling against the outcome of a previous, radically life-threatening choice made by an earlier generation: the betrayers of the present generation are the product of a previous generation's utter lack of concern for their descendants, so to oppose their betrayal is to reject the idea of repeating the same mistake—it is to turn away from one aspect of our attained state as a species.

The second crucial point is that to oppose a future generation's plan to invert the world is not to oppose their right to have a voice in their own history, which is after all the story these characters (and their viewers) are currently writing. Sator's sponsors are only driven to view the deployment of the algorithm as their sole way of saving themselves because we are not, here and now, bringing about an unattained but attainable state of ourselves that will ensure—step by attainable step—that they will not have to look to the past for a viable future. To work to defeat Sator is not, then, to endorse denying our descendants a future: it is to reject the attachment to our current and long-established state of solipsistic self-privileging in the name of a future that will include a future for our descendants, and so avert any desire on their part to use time as a weapon.

But Stalsk-12 is not the only location in which this film's presentation of that fateful day has mythological implications; its second pass also permits us to reconsider the significance of the opening events at the opera house. On our first pass, of course, those events contain only one, brief and puzzling trace of inversion technology—the inverted bullet that Neil uses to save the Protagonist's life during an extended firefight in the auditorium. But that event also provides an anticipatory trace of one of the most fundamental mythological implications of inversion. One might think of this as an effect of the sequence's palimpsestic structure: an orchestral musical performance before a large audience is interrupted by a terrorist incursion that prompts a brutal antiterrorist operation by Ukrainian police. This will be used as cover both by Sator's team (to kidnap a CIA agent in the audience who has secured one component of the algorithm) and by a CIA team including the Protagonist (to either rescue or kill that agent before he and his package are seized). Even though the Protagonist switches the agent's exit route, and later swallows what he believes to be a suicide pill rather than talk to Sator's thugs, he doesn't prevent their boss from acquiring the component.

So begins the apparently ceaseless narrative procession of the Protagonist's best efforts to thwart Sator being themselves thwarted by the latter's future-bequeathed knowledge of their nature and location (at least until the former's change of heart, and the film's consequent narrative inversion, at Tallinn). The Protagonist's improvised switch of exit route also provides a first intimation of how that thwarting might itself be thwarted—by showing how dividing or concealing knowledge is the only way of preventing hostile forces in the future from acquiring and communicating it to their collaborator in the present. As Priya puts it, "Ignorance is our ammunition." Of equal importance, however, is the fact that this chaotic interaction of large groups of people simultaneously attempting to carry out very differently motivated plans of action also engenders an overwhelming sense of a place bulging at the seams with characters jostling for the sheer physical space needed to achieve any of their purposes (something the film's concluding focus on two other sites of simultaneous conflict that day—in Vietnam and at Stalsk-12—only amplifies).

On one level, this opening that is also a conclusion thereby gives us a flavor of the way in which the deployment of inversion technology by a future generation fleeing their own impossible future might interweave backward-streaming objects and people into our forward-streaming ones so excessively that our world becomes a plenum, simply ceasing to function as a viable scene for agency (as the interwoven-fingers gesture of the "Tenet" team immobilizes both hands). On another level, it gives us a sense of the difficulties and opportunities that the narrative device of inversion technology creates for the filmmaker deploying it. On the one hand, he has to anticipate the inverted narrative strands that will later weave themselves through any given scene as initially presented, and so must know from the outset which spaces to hold open at which points. On the other hand, if he succeeds in doing so, he will have ensured that every substantial scene in the film is imbued with an unprecedentedly complete or total field of meaning—for in principle, any detail, however minor or sheerly contingent it may appear on our first pass, can be revealed on our second pass to be not only nonaccidental but pivotally significant. If one defines a perfect work of art as one every element of which is meant by its maker, and so possesses a sufficient reason for its existence in relation to every other meaningful element, then the temporal pincer movements that make up the basic formal structure of *Tenet*'s central scenes and of the film they constitute impose a demand of what one might call inordinate meaningfulness on their maker, and on their viewers.

Otherwise put, the creator of *Tenet* wants its audience to relate to it as if viewing each scene through both sides of a proving window (of the kind that separates the two sides of the turnstiles in Oslo and in Tallinn). The first pass we make through such a scene results in a perspective upon it that must be supplemented by the complementary perspective that results from our second pass through it. It's as if the scene itself could be taken in as a whole only by someone capable of occupying both perspectives at once, standing on both sides of the proving window at the same time. But this is impossible: it is not possible for any of the characters in the film (since even when they see themselves on the other side of the window, they don't see what they're seeing from that other side); and it is not possible for viewers of the screen on which those proving windows are projected (since although the film can offer them two passes through a scene, it can't offer them two passes through the scene at the same time). No wonder we feel that grasping this film is beyond us.

But that feeling should be questioned; or more precisely, we should distinguish between the idea of completely grasping something so inordinately meaningful, and the idea that however complete our present grasp of something may appear to be, it can always be improved upon. Then the "proving window" fantasy of being fully present in more than one place at the same time can be turned to account as a regulative rather than a constitutive ideal (as Kant might put it). It is a regulative ideal for anyone attempting to live a life in accordance with perfectionist tenets, insofar as we take it as an encouragement to regard our present perspective (on the world of our experience, and so on ourselves) as provisional, partial, always capable of being enriched by attaining a further, unattained but attainable perspective. And it is a regulative ideal for any critic of film, insofar as we take it as an encouragement to regard our present account of a particular film as similarly provisional and partial, and so maintain our willingness to be prompted to take another pass through a scene that we think we know, but know that we cannot regard as absolutely exhausted—essentially beyond illumination from another unattained but attainable critical perspective. If this means assuming that, however many passes we take through one of this film's scenes, Nolan will remain one pass ahead of us, then the question of whether he merits such inordinate praise can only be answered by finding and following out each new critical path as it discloses itself, or finding instead that our previous critical path so far appears to be the last. Both possibilities hold open the only kind of future that criticism, and perfectionist self-criticism, have to offer.

Notes

1. This material is gathered in the first part of "Essay Three: Knowing, Framing, and Enframing" in my *The Ascetic Ideal* (2021).

2. Cavell's most extended discussion of this theme occurs in "Postscript: To Whom It May Concern" (*CT*, 175–90).

Works Cited

Grimm, Jacob, and Wilhelm Grimm. (1812) 2007. "The Fisherman and His Wife." In *Grimm's Fairy Tales*, edited and translated by Jack Zipes. Vintage.
Mulhall, Stephen. 2021. "Essay Three: Knowing, Framing, and Enframing." In *The Ascetic Ideal: Genealogies of Life-Denial in Religion, Morality, Art, Science, and Philosophy*. Oxford University Press.

Contributors

Steven G. Affeldt (BA, University of California, Berkeley; PhD, Harvard University) is Associate McDevitt Chair in Religious Philosophy and Faculty Director of the Manresa Program at Le Moyne College. Informed by the teaching and writing of Stanley Cavell, his work elaborates ways in which philosophical practices and philosophical texts may be redemptive—possessed of the power to inspire, inform, and effect liberating transformations of both individuals and societies. He has published influential work on Rousseau, Wittgenstein, and Cavell and is currently composing a collection of essays on Emerson, Wittgenstein, and Cavell under the title *At the Feet of The Familiar*.

Rex Butler is Professor of Art History in the Faculty of Art Design and Architecture at Monash University. He has written extensively on Cavell, including *Stanley Cavell and the Arts: Philosophy and Popular Culture* (2020) and "A Divided Self and a Doubled World: On Stanley Cavell's Perfectionism" (2021). He once interviewed Cavell on *The Pursuits of Happiness* as "An 'Exchange' with Stanley Cavell" (2001).

William Day is Professor of Philosophy at Le Moyne College. He is contributing coeditor, with Victor J. Krebs, of *Seeing Wittgenstein Anew* (2010) and has published numerous articles and book chapters on Wittgenstein, Cavell, and topics in aesthetics. These include readings of post-1940s films in light of Cavell's study of remarriage comedies (*Moonstruck, Eternal Sunshine of the Spotless Mind*), unknown woman melodramas (*Woman at War*), and the paradox of time in our experience of film (*Cave of Forgotten Dreams*). He has also written several pieces addressing Cavell's thought directly, most recently "Impressions of Meaning in Cavell's Life out of Music" (2024).

Paul Deb is a Research Associate (previously Stipendiary Lecturer) in Philosophy of New College, Oxford. A former Commonwealth Scholar and British Academy award holder, he has also taught at the University of Cambridge, and the University of East Anglia. His main research interests are in the work of Stanley Cavell, existentialism, and the philosophies of film and literature. He has published papers in *Film-Philosophy*, *Philosophy East and West*, and the *Journal of Comparative Literature and Aesthetics*; and contributed chapters to the collections *Literature, Voice, Meaning: Philosophical Aspects* (2025) and *Life Writing, Representation and Identity: Global Perspectives* (2024).

Richard Eldridge is Charles and Harriett Cox McDowell Professor Emeritus of Philosophy at Swarthmore College and a Lecturer in Philosophy at University of Tennessee, Knoxville. He has published widely in the Aesthetics, German Idealism, and the philosophy of language, especially Wittgenstein and Cavell. His most recent books are *Werner Herzog: Filmmaker and Philosopher* (2019) and *Images of History: Kant, Benjamin, Freedom, and the Human Subject* (2016). He is the general series editor of *Oxford Studies in Philosophy and Literature* and the volume editor of *Stanley Cavell* (2003) and *The Oxford Handbook of Philosophy and Literature* (2009).

Fiona Handyside is Associate Professor in Film Studies in the Department of Communications, Drama and Film at the University of Exeter, UK. She is the author of *Cinema at the Shore: The Beach in French Film* (2014, reissued 2023), *Sofia Coppola: A Cinema of Girlhood* (2017) and *Girls' Hairstories: Resilience and Sparkle in Contemporary Screen Cultures* (2025). She is also the coeditor of *International Cinema and The Girl* (2016) and has written extensively on the filmmaker Éric Rohmer.

David LaRocca is the author or contributing editor of twenty books, including Stanley Cavell's *Emerson's Transcendental Etudes* (2003), *The Thought of Stanley Cavell and Cinema* (2020), *Movies with Stanley Cavell in Mind* (2023), *Television with Stanley Cavell in Mind* (2021; with Sandra Laugier), *Music with Stanley Cavell in Mind* (2024), and *Inheriting Stanley Cavell* (2020). Author of *Emerson's English Traits and the Natural*

History of Metaphor (2013), he served as Harvard University's Sinclair Kennedy Fellow in the United Kingdom and, like Cavell before him, was honored with the Distinguished Achievement Award from the Ralph Waldo Emerson Society.

Sandra Laugier is Professor of Philosophy at Université Paris 1 Panthéon Sorbonne, Paris, France, Deputy Director of the Institut des sciences juridique et philosophique de la Sorbonne (UMR 8103, CNRS Paris 1). She has published extensively on ordinary language philosophy (Wittgenstein, Austin, Cavell); moral philosophy and the ethics of care; democracy and civil disobedience, and gender studies. Her two most recent books are *TV-Philosophy: How TV Series Change our Thinking* (2023) and *TV-Philosophy in Action: The Ethics and Politics of TV* (2023). She is the translator of most of Stanley Cavell's work in French, and is an advisor for the publication of Cavell's *Nachlass*.

Stephen Mulhall is a Professor of Philosophy, and the Russell H. Carpenter Tutor and Fellow in Philosophy, at New College, University of Oxford. His main research interests include Wittgenstein, Heidegger and Nietzsche; the philosophy of religion; and the relationship between philosophy and the arts (especially film and literature). His most recent book is *In Other Words: Transpositions of Philosophy in J. M. Coetzee's "Jesus" Trilogy* (2022).

Murray Pomerance is an independent scholar and Adjunct Professor in the School of Media and Communication at RMIT University, Melbourne. He is the author of *The Hitchcock Quartet* (*An Eye for Hitchcock*, *A Dream of Hitchcock*, *A Voyage with Hitchcock*, and *A Silence from Hitchcock*) as well as numerous books including, most recently, *Edge of the Screen* (2024), *Uncanny Cinema: Agonies of the Viewing Experience* (2022), and *Color It True* (2021). His book *Light Thoughts* is forthcoming. He edits the "Horizons of Cinema" series at SUNY Press and the "Techniques of the Moving Image" series at Rutgers University Press.

William Rothman is Professor Emeritus of Cinematic Arts at the University of Miami School of Communication. A student of Stanley Cavell, he received his PhD in philosophy from Harvard University, where he taught for many years. His many books include *Hitchcock:*

The Murderous Gaze (1982; 2nd edition, SUNY Press, 2012); *The "I" of the Camera: Essays in Film Criticism, History, and Aesthetics* (1988; 2nd edition, 2004); *Documentary Film Classics* (1997); *Reading Cavell's* The World Viewed (2000; with Marian Keane); *Must We Kill the Thing We Love? Emersonian Perfectionism and the Films of Alfred Hitchcock* (2014); and *Tuitions and Intuitions: Essays at the Intersection of Film Criticism and Philosophy* (SUNY Press, 2019). He is the editor of *Cavell on Film* (Suny Press, 2005; 2nd edition, 2025).

Robert Sinnerbrink is Professor of Philosophy at Macquarie University, Sydney. He is the author of *New Philosophies of Film (Second Edition): An Introduction to Cinema as a Way of Thinking* (2022), *Terrence Malick: Filmmaker and Philosopher* (2019), *Cinematic Ethics: Exploring Ethical Experience through Film* (2016), and *New Philosophies of Film: Thinking Images* (2011). He is also the editor of *Emotion, Ethics, and Cinematic Experience: New Phenomenological and Cognitivist Perspectives* (2021) and a coeditor (with Lucy Bolton and David Martin-Jones) of *Contemporary Screen Ethics: Absences, Identities, Belonging, Looking Anew* (2023). He is also a member of the editorial boards of the journals *Film-Philosophy*, *Film and Philosophy*, and *Projections: The Journal of Movies and Mind*.

Daniel Varndell is a senior lecturer in English Literature at the University of Winchester. He has published widely on literature and film, including two monographs, *Hollywood Remakes: Deleuze and the Grandfather Paradox* (2014), and *Torturous Etiquettes: Film Performance and Social Form* (SUNY Press, 2023).

Catherine Wheatley is Professor of Film and Visual Culture at King's College London. She has published widely on questions pertaining to film, ethics and aesthetics, and is the author of four monographs, including *Stanley Cavell and Film: Scepticism and Self-Reliance at the Cinema* (2019). Catherine also writes regularly for *Sight & Sound* magazine, and is a convenor of the BFI's Philosophical Screens series.

Index